For all who have taken up or ever will take up the call to serve
in the United States Armed Forces.

WRITTEN UNDER FIRE

Baltimore Sun Correspondents' Dispatches From Normandy to the German Surrender

Published by Lightning Source Inc.,
1246 Heil Quaker Boulevard
La Vergne, TN 37086

Library of Congress Control Number: 2014932731
ISBN-13: 978-1-893116-27-6

COVER: June 1944 — WOUNDED — A wounded soldier of the 29th Division is helped to the
rear during the Normandy offensive. Photo by Holbrook Bradley. BEL-309-BS

TITLE PAGE: GERMANS DUG THIS TRENCH — Men of B Company, 175th Infantry, on the
alert in a slit trench on high ground above Julich. The position was taken from the Germans, and
now provides these Yank riflemen with protection as they scan the country ahead for targets.
Photo by Holbrook Bradley. BKI-465-BS

CONTENTS PAGE: Detail from page 185: Yankee Division Infantry on march toward Wiltz
River in pursuit of retreating Germans after the Battle of Ardennes. Photo by Lee McCardell.
ADX-422-BS.

CONTENTS

FOREWORD

By Dan Rodricks ı The Baltimore Sun

In 1984, for the 40th anniversary of D-Day, my editors assigned me to write stories about the Allied invasion and the role that Marylanders had played in the liberation of France. In preparation for a June trip to Normandy, I spent hours interviewing Baltimore-area veterans of the 29th Infantry Division and even more hours in the Sun library, reading most of the dispatches you'll find in this collection, stories by men who had become newspaper legends as war correspondents — Lee McCardell, Holbrook Bradley, and Mark Watson among them.

I had expected stories written in the kind of formal, wire-service style found back in the day throughout the gray pages of the Sun and The Evening Sun, with perhaps an occasional human-interest feature along the way.

Instead, I found a rich, free-form prose that rises at times to what those of us in the trade like to call literature-on-the-run. Narrative voices are clear and distinct. Many of the stories read like personal journal entries, with grunt-level descriptions of the scenes of combat (as graphic as military censors would allow).

Throughout, there were numerous references to the Marylanders at war. In fact, it appears to have been a hallmark of the Sun's reporting — the listing by name (and sometimes home address) of soldiers with whom the correspondents had come into contact during their travels with the 29th. World War II was the biggest story of the 20th Century, but the Sun regularly reminded readers that their friends and neighbors were doing the fighting and dying.

Bradley's reports, in particular, pushed the local angle, with his editors tallying and publishing the number of names in each story.

Another thing that struck me as astonishing: the amount of space the Sunpapers — until the 1990s, the collective name for the morning, evening and Sunday publications — devoted to war coverage. The correspondents, particularly McCardell and Bradley, were allowed to write at impressive length, and they took full advantage of the opportunity.

Judging from the stories, editors back in Baltimore either had little control of their correspondents or full confidence in them, giving them great freedom to roam with the 29th and other Army units as the Allies fought German forces in the summer of 1944 and through to the German surrender in 1945. Clearly, there was editorial respect for each reporter's writing style and for a story well-told.

That's why these reports from the Sun are so special — vivid first-hand accounts, exclusively the Sun's and not aggregate reports from reporting pools or wire services. While the dispatches were often delayed in transmission, the Sun's men were either on the front lines or one step back.

McCardell flew over Omaha Beach during the D-Day invasion; by war's end, he was filing stories from a concentration camp in Bavaria. His account of the mass funeral for Jews at Neunburg is ingeniously conveyed, contained anger informing his reporter's voice. In defiance of his editor and a Navy captain, Bradley climbed down ropes off a ship in the English Channel to arrive at Omaha Beach a day after the initial Allied attack. His descriptions of D-Day's aftermath and the Army's push through the sniper-infested farmland of Normandy are lengthy, extravagantly detailed and fraught with tension. Bradley was wounded by a mortar fragment and out of action for a few weeks, but in August 1944 he returned to covering the 29th as it pressed into Brittany. Fluent in German, he served as a translator during the enemy's surrender after the Battle of Brest.

I also note a short dispatch by Bradley at a place called La Cambe. By the time he arrived at that French village, in late June, burials were under way for Americans killed on D-Day and in the days following the massive invasion.

By the time I arrived at La Cambe, 40 years after Bradley, the American dead had all been disinterred; their remains had either been repatriated or buried in the U.S. cemetery at Coleville-sur-Mer, overlooking Omaha Beach. What remained was a beautifully maintained cemetery of German war dead, more than 20,000 of them. At the center of the cemetery was a great dome of earth, covered with grass — a mass grave ringed in granite and inscribed with the words: "God Has The Last Word."

That same day, in a hamlet close to Omaha Beach, I came across some American men, all in their 60s or 70s. They were veterans about to re-dedicate a memorial to their comrade engineers who had been killed coming ashore on D-Day. The memorial was on the farm where the company of engineers, having suffered significant casualties, camped after the invasion.

To my surprise and delight, the man leading the group was from Catonsville, and the new iron plaque he planned to rivet to the stone memorial had been cast in a foundry in Baltimore. I had my local angle on a D-Day story. I think Holbrook Bradley, Lee McCardell and many other honorable Sun ancestors would have been pleased.

CHAPTER 1

MARYLAND MEN IN ENGLAND

THE EVENING SUN, SUNDAY, OCTOBER 18, 1942

Departure of Maryland's First Contingent For War Overseas Described

Shortly before departing overseas with the first contingent of Maryland, Virginia and Pennsylvania troops, Mr. McCardell wrote the following article, describing the preparations for embarkation and the feelings of the men as they set out. It has been approved for publication by the War Department in Washington.

Troops In High Spirits At Embarkation Point

Baltimore Soldiers Bid Home Town Good-By As Train Halts Briefly At Camden Station

By Lee McCardell [Sunpapers War Correspondent]

This story, written on a late September afternoon, in an army barracks near an eastern port of embarkation, violated all the fundamental principles of good journalism. To conform, as it properly should conform, with wartime constrictions of army censorship, it must avoid the specific mention of certain names, dates and places.

It is being written for release, by the War Department, many days hence when the task force with which it deals will have crossed the Atlantic Ocean to a destination now unknown to the soldiers of that force.

Through an open window of this barracks — for the afternoon, though overcast, is warm enough for the windows to be open — comes the peculiar and unmistakable grind of army trucks. The trucks, loaded with task force baggage, are rolling down a road, past the barracks, to steamship piers some miles away.

Many Marylanders In Line

Across the road, opposite the barracks, a long queue of soldiers, many Marylanders, Virginians and Pennsylvanians among them, stands patiently in line at the door of an army post dispensary, awaiting final inoculations against typhoid, tetanus, typhus. The officer in command of this dispensary, one of several within an area assigned the task force, is Col. William H. Triplett, of Baltimore.

This story is being written hastily with a portable typewriter balanced on the edge of an army cot. On the next cot sits Private John Hamburger, of Philadelphia, a member of a task force headquarters company.

With a small paint brush and an old mess cup filled with white paint, Private Hamburger is painting out the names of certain military units stenciled upon officers' foot lockers and bedding rolls, substituting for those names a code symbol which means nothing to the reader.

Now Known By Code Symbol

All units of this task force suddenly have lost their former designations. Each is now known by a code symbol. The units will travel across the ocean and go into combat under these code symbols. Not until the war is over, or until official communiqués see it fit to identify them, will they be mentioned again by name. Even if identified in official communiqués, they will never be associated by name with the name of a place.

That is one of the rules of military censorship. Its purpose is plain: to withhold all such information from the enemy.

Tomorrow the first combat team of this task force to go overseas will board ship. With that force will go some of the Marylanders, Virginians and Pennsylvanians now waiting at the army dispensary across the road for their final shots.

Off At Last, Silently, Secretly

The order for which many of them have waited since last December 7 finally has come.

They are off to the wars, silently, secretly.

When army maneuvers came to an end last summer, many of the soldiers in this task force were ordered to an army training camp several hundred miles from here. They anticipated a long period of further training — and waiting — in the United States. When bets were made as to the length of the time they would remain in the country, the odds were on the month of December. Many a soldier envisioned a Christmas leave at home.

Leaves, Furloughs Canceled

Three weeks ago they were alerted. That is, they were warned that a movement was imminent. All leaves and furloughs were canceled. All railroad trains serving the camp area virtually became troop trains as soldiers who had been on leave hurried back to their units.

There was no immediate restriction upon camp mail, no interruption of normal telephone and telegraph communication. And the alert brought the descent of hundreds of soldiers' wives and sweethearts upon the camp.

From the number of blankets, the type of clothing and other new equipment issued to him, each soldier drew his own conclusions. Some figured they were going to Alaska. Others said Australia. Others said Iceland . . . Brazil . . . Russia . . . Gradually their excitement subsided. They went on the rifle range. In the evening, at post exchanges and officers' clubs, dopesters figured that it would require a minimum of at least ten days to two weeks to complete preparations for any general movement.

But a staging order, directing the troops to proceed to a port of embarkation, came more quickly than generally expected. It arrived about 10 o'clock one night. From headquarters to company kitchens the entire camp, which had settled down for the night in comparative darkness, blazed suddenly with light, stirred with noisy activity.

All outgoing mail was frozen in the camp's military Post Office. All public telephones were cut out of service temporarily. Camp telegraph facilities, under army control, were restricted to official messages.

Long before morning the baggage and passenger cars for the first troop train had been backed into the railroad yards of the camp area. Barracks bags were being packed into box cars. Soldiers were rolling their equipment up loading inclines onto flat cars.

Designations Blotted Out

The original alert had been followed by an order to remove all regimental and divisional insignia from uniforms. Now paint brushes and buckets were brought out. All unit designations and insignia on field desks, packing cases, and personal equipment were blotted out. (The ones that Private Hamburger is painting out now are a few that were overlooked then.)

Within less than four days the entire command had moved on toward the port of embarkation by special railroad train. Some of the troops traveled in Pullmans. Some traveled in ancient wooden day coaches with rattan seats.

The railroads, which did a rather magnificent job, used any and every available type of passenger cars they could assemble. Hooked to the rear of each troop train was a caboose for the train crew. A brigadier-general, George M. Alexander, of Lynchburg, Va., rode in one caboose. He found it more comfortable than the ancient day coach in which he had been assigned a seat.

One Stops At Camden Yards

One of the last of these trains passed through Baltimore on a mid-September Sunday afternoon. It stopped for a moment on the lower level at Camden Station while an electric locomotive was coupled in front of the steam engine to take the train through the long Howard street tunnel.

The station platform was empty, guarded by railroad police. Military police, traveling aboard the train, forbade any of the soldiers to leave their cars.

Good-By To Baltimore

Field kitchens had been set up in blind baggage cars on each train to feed the troops while en route to their final staging area, the camp in which this story is being written. The side doors of at least one baggage car were open and crowded with soldiers as this train stopped in Camden Station.

Among those soldiers was Private Wolf Holzman, of Baltimore.

"The old town looks mighty good," he said.

Corporal Charlie Rohlfing, another Baltimore soldier, leaned out of the open window of a Pullman car.

"Good old Camden Station," said Charlie. "I'd give the $30 I won in that crap game yesterday for thirty minutes here."

Sergt. Stanchfield Payne, also of Baltimore stood at the half-open door of a Pullman vestibule.

"Why can't we catch a boat here?" he asked.

Officers On Rear Platform

On the rear platform of the last car, taking a last look at old familiar scenes, was a little group of Maryland officers: Lieut. Col. Carey Jarman, Major William J. Witte, Capt. Benjamin F. Cassell, Capt. Richard Curzon Hoffman 3d, Capt. Robert L. Slingluff, Jr., Lieut. Thomas Van A. Dukehart.

Their train did not even pause at Mount Royal Station, as deserted as Camden's lower level. It rolled right on through . . . through the Belt Line tunnels . . . past Clifton Park . . . over Belair road just as a blue-uniformed boys' drum corps was marching under the railroad bridge . . . past Bugle Field whose stands were crowded with amateur baseball fans that sunny Sunday afternoon.

It was after midnight when the last of the troop trains pulled into the staging area. But many a soldier got no sleep that night. They were ordered to check their equipment at once. At dawn the lights were still burning in headquarters buildings, barracks, supply houses.

That morning the soldiers got their first good look at the staging area, a brand-new camp of camouflaged barracks whose color scheme is a drunkard's nightmare — and a bombardier's despair.

Cooks and mess sergeants learned, with considerable satisfaction, that all meals here would be served in large regimental cafeterias maintained by the camp's regular complement of troops, although KP details would continue.

High Speed And High Spirits

Since then things have been moving at high speed. New and special equipment, both arms and clothing, have been issued to the troops of this task force with a promptness and dispatch that knocks supply officers dizzy. The work goes on day and night. There is no bedtime here.

And the soldiers, eager to get on with the job before them, are in high spirits. You hear them singing now when they march — singing as they never sang before. They drill, they race over obstacle courses with a new enthusiasm . . .

Meanwhile, Private Hamburger has finished his painting. The footlockers and the bedding rolls of this particular barracks are being carried out to be loaded onto army trucks that will take them on to the docks. Passenger lists have been completed and approved. Some of the troops already are aboard their transport.

Last-Minute Pictures

In these last few minutes a long series of pictures flash through the mind of every man in the task force. Pictures of homes . . . and faces . . . and farewells.

Pictures of a crack streamline train, crowded with soldiers and racing back to camp when the alert canceled all leaves . . . the club car filled with soldiers and solders' wives . . . a soldier standing in the aisle, leading the whole car in song . . . Old familiar songs, like "When Irish Eyes Are Smiling". . . and newer sentimental songs, like "You Are My Sunshine". . .

Pictures of the enforced gayety of last dances in camp service clubs . . . Groups of soldiers in camp post exchanges, calmly but grimly discussing their last chances against an enemy . . . Last meals in camp mess halls, with a scattering of wives and small children at the tables . . . Closed gates at camp reservations, and a middle-aged mother explaining to an MP: "I've come all the way from Pittsburgh to see my son. And now they say he's gone. Where has he gone? Why can't you tell me?" . . .

Memory's Panorama

Soldiers climbing aboard troop trains, sternly forbidding puzzled pet stray dogs to follow them . . . Home towns and country sweeping past troop-train windows . . . A captain, nodding toward a tumble-down shanty by the tracks and murmuring: "I used to wonder how people could live in such a house. But after all, it's home." . . .

A lieutenant calmly remarking: "I was to have been married today . . . She got to camp before we left. She brought her wedding dress with her. But we talked it over and decided . . . it would be better for both of us to wait. . . . "

Personal Censorship

You, too, reading this report will have your private pictures if you have a soldier or a sailor overseas. If you saw him or talked to him just before he sailed, if you saw or talked to somebody else who saw him, you may know many details that are not mentioned in this story.

For his own safety and the safety of those who will follow him across the sea, it's best to keep those details to yourself. All such personal censorship, voluntarily enforced, may speed his journey home one of these days. It will not delay him.

"We're Coming Over"

JOURNEY'S START — Rested after extensive maneuvers in the South, Maryland soldiers entrain in Florida on the first leg of a long journey by land and sea, their destination — England. Faces tanned by tropical sun, they wear lightweight uniforms as they walk to waiting trains that will take them to embarkation point. AGP-716-BS

FOND FAREWELLS — Florida's sunshine reflects the expressions of these troops as they bid farewell to friends. AGP-672-BS. At left, Corporal Arthur B. Hartman, a Virginian, has a last minute shake with "Lighthouse" company mascot picked up during Carolina maneuvers. AGP-714-BS

"LOOK SHARP, SOLDIER" — Another squad crunches railroad siding gravel as the march to the cars continues at the Florida camp. Soldiers toting full pack and rifles entrain with a smile as officers supervise the big job of assigning Maryland fighting men to their proper trains. AGP-748-BS

ALL ABOARD — The train is loaded and wheels roll. These men get their last glimpse of Florida scene as Sergt. Paul A. Meluh, of Baltimore, waves goodbye. AGP-715-BS

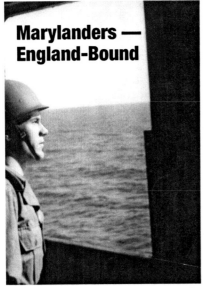

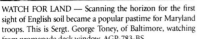
Marylanders — England-Bound

WATCH FOR LAND — Scanning the horizon for the first sight of English soil became a popular pastime for Maryland troops. This is Sergt. George Toney, of Baltimore, watching from promenade deck window. AGP-783-BS

LEE McCARDELL — Sunpapers Correspondent with Maryland troops in England, snapped these pictures of shipboard life during the trip overseas. Cameraman McCardell caught this scene as troops enjoyed a siesta in the sun following the noonday meal. All the soldiers but a few, from all appearances, have their eyes closed. AGP-769-BS

SOLDIERS AT SEA — In surroundings far different from the dust and smoke of maneuvers completed just before they embarked for Britain, Maryland's soldiers had plenty of time for relaxation. Here are some of the men at ease on the long promenade deck while others exercise and view endless stretches of ocean. AGP-815-BS

FAMILY PORTRAIT — Father and son, intent on fighting for the common cause, are with Maryland's troops. At left is Sergt. Leonard M. Mutter, at right his son, Corporal Leonard Mutter, Jr. They are artillerymen from Portsmouth, Va., and are in the same outfit. AGP-782-BS

THE DAILY MASS — Spiritual life of the men aboard ship goes on as usual. Catholic Chaplain Father Griffey gives Holy Communion to soldiers assembled on blacked-out promenade deck for the daily mass. AGP-786-BS

SOLID COMFORT — Activity in some other part of the ship occupies the attention of some soldiers in this photo as the man in foreground enjoys an afternoon nap. Ship's dog sits quietly at soldier's feet. AGP-768-BS

Safe Arrival – Maryland Men Reach England

FALLEN LEAVES — A mishap punctuates the arrival of Baltimore's Lieutenant Colonel Chris Claypoole (left). Leaf insignia fell from his shoulder, is pinned on by Lieutenant John King. AGP-772-BS

HELLO, ENGLAND! — Lee McCardell, Sunpapers Correspondent, was among the first ashore as ships bearing Maryland troops reached England. He snapped these photos of soldiers disembarking. Man looking through left porthole is Sergeant Michael Halick, of Bayonne, New Jersey. AGP-817-BS

ALL ASHORE — Another view of Maryland troops stepping on English soil. Toting gear and rifles and wearing helmets, the men file down a gangplank from a lighter at British port of debarkation in the rain. Note British officer at right of photo. AGP-740-BS

FERRY SERVICE — Here are some fully equipped soldiers photographed aboard a British lighter after leaving the troop transport. Troops are lined up on the deck waiting to be ferried ashore. Typically wet English weather attended the debarkation work. AGP-706-BS

STEPPING LIVELY — Walking single file, men carry their gear from ship to lighter under supervision of English officer (back to camera). U. S. officer (right) looks on. AGP-776-BS

TO THE TRAINS — Ashore on the quay of a British port, the march begins to a railroad station, where troop trains wait for trip inland. AGP-739-BS

British Bivouac — Maryland Troops

BALTIMOREANS are among these Maryland troops photographed by Sunpapers Correspondent Lee McCardell as they reached quarters in England. Men are shown boarding buses for last leg of journey. HAG-323-BS. In photo at left Lieut. Guy Graffen receives orders from Captain Roger Whiteford, Baltimorean. AGP-707-BS

SMILES — AND FOOD — Cheerful over the prospect of their first meal in new billets, troops in fatigue uniforms line up with mess kits. AGP-732-BS

CHOW IN A BLACKOUT — Staff Sergeant Sidney Gumenick (left) and Private George Ackerman, both of Baltimore, enjoy their chow in a blacked-out British mess hall. AGP-712-BS

AFTER MESS — Come dishwashing chores. Every man washes his own eating gear in boiling-water compartments of a British army kitchen unit. AGP-713-BS

Maryland Men On The Firing Line In England

TRIGGER FINGERS ITCHING — Typical of a day's training for Maryland fighting men in England, the artillerymen in these photos by Sunpapers Correspondent Lee McCardell are pictured on a rifle range. First comes a "dry run." Kneeling troopers aim their rifles and click triggers of empty magazines to get the "feel." AGP-700-BS

GO TO IT BOYS is what Private Fred Whaley (right) might be saying to Sergt. Richard Herklotz, Baltimore (left), and Corporal Orville Barber, Cumberland (center), as clips of cartridges are passed out for serious shooting on the English range. HAG-366-BS

ALL CLEAR? — Battery officers (left to right): Capt. Clinton Thurston, Norfolk; Lieut. Louis Shuford; Fredericksburg, Va., and medical officer Capt. Aaron Caplan, Ellwood City, Pa. (right), wait at field telephone held by Corporal John L. Bauman, of Baltimore, for word from target crew that all is clear for real shooting to start. AGP-726-BS

DRAWING A BEAD, Private James Springman, of Washington (foreground), prepares to shoot as an unidentified corporal watches. Note gun strap slung under left arm of Private Springman to steady his rifle. AGP-725-BS

EYE TROUBLE — It isn't serious, but Private William Eidys, of Wisconsin, had some trouble in keeping his left eye closed while aiming his rifle, so Private Frank L. Virotto, of Philadelphia, ties a bandage over the troublesome optic just to make sure. HAG-369-BS

GUN CHATTER — Here is a scene typical of the day's work. Men take regular turns at firing, kneeling as well as standing on firing mats. HAG-367-BS

IT'S EASIER for Corporal Nick Gregorio, of Pittsburgh, to do his shooting with a bandage over a left eye that just won't stay shut. Here is a head-on view of rifleman. HAG-365-BS

AUDIENCE — An informal audience of soldiers watches as a rifleman takes position before the row of targets for his "crack" at the shooting. HAG-368-BS

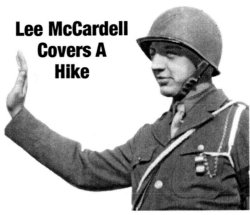

Lee McCardell Covers A Hike

THE WEEKLY WORKOUT — Gasoline and tire rationing pose no problems to Maryland troops undergoing training in England. By way of "keeping 'em tough," weekly hikers through the English countryside are routine as ordered by the commanding general. When staff officers of a force including Marylanders, assembled in front of barracks for weekly hike, Lee McCardell, Sunpapers Correspondent with the troops, snapped this pictorial story of the men on the march near training center. BBU-662-BS

"SUN SQUARE" COP — Swinging through training center area, nicknamed "Sun Square," troops get right of way from Private Earl Myers, 721 North Streeper street, the military police on duty. Myers raises arm in traditional "cop" style. AGP-681-BS

HERE WE GO AGAIN — It's easy going down hill. Captain Porter (first man, right column), leads the march as Maryland's fighting men resume trek through a town. AGP-731-BS

FIRST REST — Major Robert Archer, Jr., of Bel Air (left) and Capt. James Porter, of Baltimore, seek support of a friendly tree during first rest period. AGP-682-BS

WOODLAND VISA — Here are some of the officers of the force as they paused for a rest on a wooded slope. The men smoke and chat before a blaze of burning leaves in the background. AGP-679-BS

TIRED AND WEARY — Major Graham Dougherty, of Berryville, Va., scrapes mud from shoes after return. AGP-676-BS

VITAMINS PLUS — American Red Cross officer Kirkland (left), gets a smile from Capt. Edward Casey, of Washington, with chocolate. AGP-678-BS

HOLD EVERYTHING! — Back in "Sun Square," Private Earl Myers halts a jeep driven by Sergt. James Rhodes, of Queenstown, Md., to pass Private John Buchanan, 2423 Llewellyn avenue, Baltimore. AGP-680-BS

PLAYTIME FOR FIGHTERS — Rigorous though training routine may be, Maryland troops in England include regular softball, volley-ball, soccer and touch football competition as part of their recreation. When a field day was staged to determine championships among the soldier athletes, Lee McCardell, Sunpapers Correspondent, turned sports reporter and snapped this pictorial story of the activities. Here, an artillery band lends color. Sergt. Anthony Terpko, of Jeannette, Pa., toots the trombone. HAG-334-BS

On The Sidelines With Lee McCardell

YEAH, MARYLAND — The volley-ball championship was at stake when this spirited action between men from Hyattsville, Md., and an infantry company from Virginia was in progress. The Marylanders won. ABS-813-BS

IN THE BLEACHERS — The peanuts, popcorn, hot dogs and pop were missing, but this large gathering of soldier spectators appears intensely interested in the panorama of athletic competition under way. BBF-789-BS

TOUCH AND GO — This might have been an informal game of touch football on the campus of any Maryland school. Maryland men were on both teams that played a scoreless tie in the first game. Later it was settled, 12-6. HAG-341-BS

ACTION, PLUS — Here is another scene from the championship volley-ball game. Soldier spectators exhibited great interest in the swift action. Note large crowd at left of photo watching the teams in action. HAG-338-BS

SOCCER SCUFFLE — This is a close play at goal during the force championship soccer game between anti-tank company commanded by Capt. Albert Warfield, of Baltimore, and quartermaster team. The Baltimoreans won. HAG-340-BS

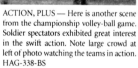

SOFTBALL HERO — Sergt. Leon Derda, of Baltimore, proved to be the all-round hero of the softball championships. He pitched for his team and won his own game and championship by blasting out three hits. HAG-364-BS

FORWARD PASS — The man with ball (partly screened at left) didn't forget how to toss a forward pass in this exciting bit of touch football action. HAG-339-BS

Lee McCardell
Watches The War Games

A "FOREST" THAT WALKS — Military leaders supervising the intensive training program for Maryland troops now stationed in England place great stress on the art of camouflage. The pictures on this page, made by Sunpapers Correspondent Lee McCardell, who is with the troops, tell the story of the work keeping the troops busy. This photo shows an infantry company, helmets and uniforms bedecked with tree cuttings, ready to start out on a camouflage maneuver in the troop training area. HAG-342-BS

HEAD DRESS — What the well-camouflaged foot soldier will wear in action in this war is displayed in a photo of Sergt. William H. Childress, Lynchburg, Virginia. HAG-346-BS

THE REAL McCOY — The men handling this machine gun are firing live ammunition over the heads of advancing Maryland infantrymen. Left to right, Sergt. J. A. Eller, of Ronda, N. C.; Corporal Miles Seagraves, of Bel Air, Md., and Private John Bonanni, of Jessup, Pa. HAG-344-BS

TRIAL AND ERROR — Following maneuvers against actual machine gun fire, Sergt. William Barbee, of Washington, delivers a critique to a group of Maryland infantrymen who were among the troops participating in the field problem. HAG-345-BS

POINTED PICTURE — Corporal Harry Hendricks, of Dundalk (center), appraises the technique of Corporal Eugene Gehley, York, Pa. (blindfolded), in getting through barbed wire. Private Americo Liberatore watches. HAG-343-BS

TOUGHENING UP exercises provide fun and prove beneficial. Corporal Ebber Green, of Baltimore, plays hurdle for other infantrymen during exercise period. HAG-348-BS

ALLEZ OOP! — Emulating gymnasts, this group of Maryland soldiers show aptitude for building human pyramids, a regular part of physical exercise program. HAG-316-BS

OVER THE HURDLES — Infantrymen in training must develop skill handling bayonet on combat reaction course. This is Private George Schneider, of Baltimore. HAG-347-BS

With Maryland Engineers In England
Photos By Lee McCardell, Sunpapers Staff Correspondent

FLAMES OF WAR — When a detachment of army combat engineers, including Marylanders, staged a demonstration of tactics recently, Maj. Gen. Leonard T. Gerow (right), on tour of English bases, was among observers. AGP-746-BS. Above, flame throwers attack an enemy "pillbox." BBF-802-BS

THE COLONEL TALKS — Lieut. Col. John T. O'Neill (left), of College Park, Md., commanding an engineer battalion, explains orders to Lieut. Leonard Lepicier. BBF-854-BS

ATTACK! — Here is a platoon of Lieut. Col. John T. O'Neill's combat engineers advancing under cover of a "captured" anti-tank ditch to assault an "enemy" strong point during the demonstration. ABF-334-BS

BALTIMOREANS AT WORK — Corporal Jack Levering (left) and Sergt. Daniel H. Murray, both of Baltimore, members of battalion headquarters, read the orders. BBF-823-BS

CLEARING THE WAY — This realistic photo was made as engineers in foreground detonated demolition charge to blast an opening in barbed wire of "enemy" entanglements for subsequent attack by advancing infantrymen. AGP-757-BS

"ZERO" HOUR — Sergts. Fred Zimmer (left) and George N. Anderson, Jr., both of Baltimore, await in protection of ditch for orders that will send them "over the top." ABF-441-BS

THE TANKS COME THROUGH — after engineers have cleared a path through enemy lines with heavy demolition charges. Note mine exploding. ABF-336-BS

CHAPTER 2

THE GREATEST AMPHIBIOUS EXPEDITION IN HISTORY

THE EVENING SUN, MONDAY, JUNE 6, 1944

M'Cardell — In Air

By Lee McCardell [Sunpapers War Correspondent]

London, June 6 — Marauders of the Ninth Air Force led one Allied air attack early today when our armies began landing on the northern coast of France.

The Marauders swept in over the Channel at daylight to bomb and strafe one long stretch of sandy beach, while warships were bombarding the shore from the sea and landing craft were speeding in to put the first tanks ashore.

With three other American correspondents I flew over the beach with the first group of bombers making the attack. We had taken off before dawn. It was about breakfast time when the returning formation landed at its base. An army car brought us direct to London, arriving here a few minutes after Supreme Headquarters of the Allied Expeditionary Force had released the first invasion communiqué.

Attack At Dawn

The Marauders made the attack at dawn — at what is known as "first bombing light." They roared in at a much lower altitude than that from which they usually bomb. From the windows of the pilot's compartment and the waist gun windows the crew and the correspondents who flew with them looked down on the curtain-raiser of the battle for western Europe.

At briefing at their base a few hours earlier the Marauder men had been told they would spearhead the air attack. Fighter cover of thousands of Allied fighter planes had preceded us.

Nazi Batteries Blaze

We saw one of our aircraft shot down in flames over the target. We saw but one enemy aircraft during our mission. German anti-aircraft batteries blazed away at our formation while we were on the bombing run, but we saw no enemy troops in the dawn's early light.

The guns of our warships lying off the coast were blazing. Their shells were bursting in a belt a mile or more deep along the shoreline, .50 caliber machine-gun bullets, the blinding twinkle of Marauder bomb bursts and the muzzle bursts of enemy flak batteries provided the sort of vast fireworks display that all of us knew we probably would see but once in a lifetime.

Smoke And Flash

We heard nothing but the roar of our planes' motors and the rattle of their machine guns. All the rest was merely smoke and flash. Our formation turned out of its bombing run at a speed in excess of 200 miles per hour as it streaked for home.

On our way in we passed over great fleets of landing craft and other vessels, all headed toward the beach where our target lay. In the wide sweep we executed to come out and the course we took on our return we saw no more, but we had seen enough for a first chapter of the story.

Enthusiasm Tremendous

The bomber group which made the attack is commanded by Col. Reginald F. C. Vance, London-born naturalized American whose family home is at Fredericksburg, Va., and who was General MacArthur's air liaison officer at Corregidor. The formation was led by Colonel Vance's air executive officer, Lieut. Col. Bob Willy, of Cleveland, Ohio, piloting a Marauder named "Cleveland Cyclone" and bearing a huge ace of spades insignia on the nose of its silver fuselage.

Correspondents Get Break

Four American correspondents who enjoyed the unique privilege — purely by accident — of being the first to cross the enemy coastline on D-day and return in time to tell their story before the news was on either radio or in first afternoon editions of London newspapers, were Si Peterman, of the Philadelphia Inquirer; Donald MacKenzie, of the New York Daily News; Howell Dodd, of the Associated Press and myself.

We had been assigned to cover the air phase of the invasion from the American bomber base commanded by Colonel Vance, whose Marauder group is known as "Silver Streaks."

Col. Willy Reveals Plan

At 10.30 last night strong forces of military police were posted around the entire airfield. No one was permitted to enter or leave the base. All telephone communication was cut off. Colonel Willy, dropping in unexpectedly on four correspondents who were writing letters and chewing the rag, announced:

"Gentlemen, I am authorized to inform you that the Allies will make a bid for a beachhead on continental Europe early tomorrow morning. I need not tell you that you will not be permitted to leave this post until further notice. Briefing at 2 o'clock tomorrow morning. If you wish to visit your quarters before then I would advise you to do so now. You will proceed directly from the briefing room to the ships in which you will fly."

All afternoon the ground crewmen of Marauders at the base have been painting around the bombers lined up on hard stands just off the perimeter of the track.

Poker Games Abandoned

A few late poker games were still under way in the lounge of the officers' club. Colonel Willy, on his way to his own quarters for a few hours' rest, walked through the lounge and said quietly:

"Gentlemen, if you want any sleep tonight I would turn in now. You may have an early mission in the morning."

The poker games broke up immediately without a single word of comment. Players drifted off to their Nissen huts in silence and went to bed. Nobody slept very long. Reveille was at 12.30 A. M. this morning. Breakfast was at 1 o'clock.

Briefing Room Described

When we reached the blacked-out Nissen hut in which bomber crews are briefed for missions there was a double guard of military police at every door. A staff sergeant at the entrance to the briefing room checked off our names on a long typewritten list of those who were to fly. We found every seat on the hard wooden backless benches in the briefing room occupied. Aisles and footways at the rear of the room were filled with other airmen standing.

The roller screen on which maps and aerial photographs of bomb targets are projected for briefing had been lowered to conceal the huge map of Europe on which the impending mission is always outlined by thumb-tacked lines of black string marking, the course into the target, the bomb run and the return course to home base.

Colonel Willy Explains

The room was hushed as Colonel Willy, a dark, broad-shouldered man of 28 who once played end on the Miami (Ohio) University football team, appeared before the screen with a wooden pointer. He said:

"As some of you may have guessed by now, the Allies will make a bid for a beachhead this morning."

Then he rolled up the screen and the entire company seated in the room rose as one man to get a closer look at the thumb-tacked lines of black string on the big large-scale map. Briefly Colonel Willy explained the purpose of the mission and the course the bombers would take.

Airmen instructed

When the group's flak officer who took over from Colonel Willy told the airmen "you shouldn't get too much flak where you're going," and then proceeded to tell them what measures they should take to avoid enemy anti-aircraft fire, the flyers laughed aloud.

They also laughed — this time with delight — when Colonel Vance told them how many Allied fighters would provide top cover for their mission. The number he gave sounded almost incredible.

The tall, lean, British-born commanding officer, who looks and talks more like a native Texan, then read his men three letters, one from General Eisenhower, one from Air Chief Marshall Sir Trafford Leigh-Mallory and the third from Brig. Gen. Sam Anderson, commanding general of their own Ninth Air Force Bomber Command.

Col. Vance Confident

"Good luck and good hunting," was the conclusion of General Anderson's letter to his airmen.

"You're going down the straight-away now," were Colonel Vance's parting words to the men of his Marauder group, "and I know doggone well it's gonna work. Good luck."

From the briefing room the flyers went to their crew room to put on Mae West parachute packs, flak suits and flying helmets, Military police were still posted all around the building. Flyers had been cautioned not to mention a word about their targets until they were aboard their ships.

McCardell In "Bunny's Honey"

From the crewrooms the Marauder men were taken by army truck directly to the hard stands on which their ships were waiting, bombed, fueled, pre-flighted and ready to go. It was still dark.

I had been assigned to fly in a Marauder named "Bunny's Honey." The ship was to be piloted by Capt. Elgin R. (Shorts) Bowers, of Lockhard, Texas, with Lieut. Richard I. Hagen, of Beaver, Pa., as copilot.

Other members of the crew were: Lieut. N. A. Davenport, navigator, of Salida, Col.; Lieut. (Honest) John A. Bangert, bombardier, of the Bronx; Sergt. William J. Wright, waist gunner and radio operator, of Suffolk, Va.; Sergt. Elza F. ("Ace") Drummond, turret gunner and engineer, of Cleveland, Ohio, and Sergt. James N. Williams of Rye, N. Y., tail gunner.

Some Carried Pistols

I noticed that several of them carried army automatics, a rather unusual procedure for bomber crews. This was the first mission they had ever made over enemy territory where they thought they might have a chance of shooting their way back into their own lines if forced down.

We had a rather long wait out there in the dark on the hard stand. It wasn't time yet to start the engines.

Knowing that the nose of the ship would be rather crowded with her four flying officers, I elected to ride in the waist after solemnly promising Sergeant Wright that I wouldn't prematurely pop my parachute, as I had done two days before in a trial run to get myself conditioned for the real thing.

We walked over to a nearby Nissen hut used by airfield's ack-ack men as a mess and felt our way around in the dark for a water can for a last drink.

Off On Schedule

We were off on the dot of our schedule at 4.12 A. M. Majestically the Marauders of our formation climbed to the level of the full moon. Even on the ground, the Marauder is a graceful ship, poised as if air-borne and eager for flight even when at rest upon its tricycle landing gear. In flight and in formation with its new black-and-white striped insignia, it has an exquisite mothlike quality.

I wasn't particularly happy back there in that waist, even though I did admire the view of our formation in full flight. It wasn't flying in any beauty contest this morning. Once over the Channel, where Sergeant Wright unbuttoned the waist windows and test fired the guns, we lost interest entirely in appearances.

Speed Was Terrific

We left the English coast shortly before 6 o'clock. Captain Bowers poured on the coal and the whole formation tore over the sea at what seemed a terrific speed. I had brought along a pair of field glasses, but at the rate we were travelling it was impossible to focus them correctly even on the surface of the sea.

A number of landing craft on certain portions of the Channel over which we flew looked as if a regatta might be in progress. These thinned out as we approached the French coast and war vessels, bombarding the shore line, were more in evidence off the actual beachhead.

Bunny's Honey In Lead

Bunny's Honey led the high flight of the first box in the bomber formation. As ships lined up for their bombing run the formations following the first box were stepped down, closer to the beach, and many bombs were dropped from an altitude which normally would have been considered suicidal for bombers coming in over the Nazi coast defenses.

The formation whipped down the sandy beachline at what seemed an ever-increasing speed. The bomb-bay doors were open and bombs away almost before we realized it, leaving a trail of exploding bomb flashes and plumes of black smoke behind it. The Germans opened up with both light and heavy flak. The light of early dawn was a crisscross of red tracers because the Marauder gunners were returning the fire from remotely controlled nose guns bracketed on the fuselage as well as from the top and tail turrets.

The first landing craft to touch the beach were coming in under the cover of a white smoke screen.

Picture Not Lively

On the whole, the beachhead did not present a particularly lively picture at that early hour. The operation was still largely in the stage of naval gunfire and bomber preparation. We saw no troops of either army. Warships and dive bombers were still pounding the coastal belt when the Marauders turned away from the target.

The French highways appeared deserted. No locomotives steamed along the railway line that the Marauders crossed. Towns looked empty. Except for small, cultivated strips of farmland peculiar to the French countryside, rural France didn't look much different from rural England from the air.

All Marylanders Safe

We don't know how effective the first Marauder bombing was. It looked pretty good to us, but we haven't seen strike photographs of the results. We do know, however, that the Silver Streak group chosen to lead off the day's missions of medium bombardment force was picked for the job because it has established an excellent record for that type of attack.

We also didn't know what the group's losses might have been until we landed. Then we checked over the list of Maryland area men on the mission and found that all of them at least had returned safely.

From McCardell to Bradley

THE EVENING SUN, MONDAY, JUNE 12, 1944

This is the first dispatch received from Holbrook Bradley, Sunpapers' war correspondent, who accompanied the 29th Division in the Normandy landing. For some reason, as yet unexplained, Mr. Bradley's dispatches have been delayed in transmission.

Bradley Views Opening Attack

By Holbrook Bradley [Sunpapers War Correspondent]

With the 29th Division in France [Delayed] – American assault forces stormed ashore on the French channel coast today (June 6) in the opening phases of the Allied invasion of the continent. Early reports from this beach indicate heavy opposition to the landing by enemy artillery fire. There have been no estimates of the strength ashore or the casualties sustained.

From the bridge of the LST, which carries support troops, including many Maryland men, we are watching the progress of the greatest amphibious expedition undertaken in history. Anchored two miles from ashore, our landing craft rolls on the channel swell, surrounded by hundreds of other vessels guarded by racing patrols, destroyers, minesweepers and other naval craft.

Smoke Covers Sand

As we watch the shore line through binoculars we can see the effects of enemy shell-fire as columns of smoke arise from our vehicles that have just been hit. It is difficult to determine the disposition of troops which were landed earlier today for heavy smoke of battle covers the sand.

We have heard that most of the men have made high ground immediately behind the shore and hope the report is true, for the stretch between looks like an unhealthy spot.

Seaward and upchannel are heavy concentrations of troopships and other larger craft, which are unloading or waiting to unload support troops, cargoes and materials for battle while naval vessels circle in constant patrol.

Smoke Rises Behind Beach

On both sides of us heavy battleships and cruisers are letting loose with salvo after salvo as they direct fire on invisible targets ashore. Only towering columns of smoke miles behind the beach indicate the effectiveness of this floating artillery.

Inshore gray-hulled destroyers range along the beach, firing in quick, short blasts at nearer targets guarding LCIs, LCTs and LCVRs, which are facing back and forth across stretches of shallower water. Overhead skies are dominated by Allied Lightnings, Thunderbolts, Mustangs, Spits and heavier bombers. So far the Luftwaffe hasn't put in an appearance.

We knew when we loaded aboard our LSTs, LCIs and LCTs last week that we were at last on the eve of the operation all of us have been waiting for since reaching England. All the troops involved had been briefed as to the location of our assault, which was but a phase in the combined American, British and Canadian operation. What we didn't know was the time — D-day and H-hour.

Looked Like Real Thing

When we pulled out it looked like the real thing. But disappointment came soon, for at 8.30 o'clock the same morning our convoy, some LSTs, LCTs and escort vessels, turned back on its course and headed for anchorage. Rumors again flew: We were merely on a dry run; we were trying to confuse the enemy; the weather wasn't right for landing paratroopers and air-borne troops.

Whatever the reason, we sat on mooring all day as a southwest storm blew up, bringing low clouds, drizzle and generally nasty weather. Perhaps prognosticators were right this time. Then, shortly before sunset, the clouds suddenly broke and we saw blue sky to the west; over the harbor two rainbows broke the mist in radiant color. That night we sailed again.

The first men on deck next morning found we were well along the coast in convoy with LCTs and support naval escort vessels. The size of the Allied undertaking began to dawn on us as heavier naval craft picked us up from astern, then passed on ahead to their rendezvous.

No Feeling Of Uneasiness

Battleships, both American and British, then heavy and light cruisers and finally a large number of destroyers and smaller craft steamed between us and the shore then disappeared ahead.

Late yesterday afternoon Capt. Otto H. Graas, Baltimore commander of headquarters troops aboard our vessel, read General Eisenhower's message to his troops and lead men. D-day had been set for June 6, H-hour for 4 A. M. Once the men knew the details of the work ahead, they settled down to routine shipboard life — lining up for chow or washing mess kits, sleeping on deck or watching the passing shore line or Channel activity. There was no feeling of uneasiness or apprehension regarding the forthcoming operation.

Below decks, officers and men who were lucky enough to have bunks caught up on the sleep lost during the past months or indulged in sessions of poker or blackjack for spearhead francs. The only real excitement came during the night when general quarters blared over the ship's Klaxon-bell system, calling the crew to gun and boat stations. The army personnel that did stumble from their bunks stopped momentarily, then wondered where to go next, and finally turned in again.

Planes Pass Overhead

Early this morning we reached our rendezvous point. From all quarters came convoys, similar to ours, convoys of LSTs,

LCIs, LCTs and their escorts. Scanning the horizon we could see patrol vessels of all types and kinds wherever we looked. Overhead passed flights of our fighters and bombers, heading in for the French coast and back for refueling and reloading.

We had no contact with enemy planes or surface craft, something even the most experienced personnel aboard couldn't understand.

As the convoy turned into the beach, radio reports came in telling of Eisenhower's opening announcement, then giving details of a report picked up from a German newscast. We knew our own and British paratroopers had landed early that morning, that Allied assault forces had stormed their way ashore on several beachheads. We also learned H-hour had been advanced to 6.30 A. M. putting our own schedule up to 4 P. M.

No Action So Far

Although we were in the fighting zone we still had no real feeling of combat. So far there had been no action, not even a scare from an enemy plane or E-boat. Even when the lookout on the bridge sang out that the French coast was in sight, officers sitting in the sun on the bridge jokingly remarked that we might be on a pleasure cruise to the continent. A few minutes later the sound of distant heavy gunfire brought reality to the scene. Then almost before we realized it, we were in the thick of it.

Our minesweepers had buoyed the channel the night previous and as we swept down the narrow lane at the head of the support force making up our convoy, we suddenly picked up other convoys converging toward the distant beach. The number of vessels mounted from dozens to hundreds. Escorts ran up and down the lanes, bawling at ships out of line, pointing out mines, drifting to one side or the other. Ahead we could pick up the low coastline, broken here and there by steep cliffs, covered by haze, smoke and clouds. The concussion from heavy naval and shore gunfire shook the ship now, occasionally we could see an orange-yellow blast curling up from the guns.

As our LSTs picked up speed under orders from a small craft which crossed our bow, the ship's loudspeaker announced a nondenominational service to be held on the tank deck by Chaplain Harold F. Donovan, of Baltimore. Army personnel and navy crew alike crowded among the parked vehicles to attend the service as the vessel rolled from a short Channel chop, and as gunfire boomed in the distance.

From the bridge we could pick up shore activities. The assault waves' initial progress was indicated by the huge number of vessels lined up along the beach and by the number of LCIs and LCVPs and other smaller craft left around as the tide swept out. Flashes of gunfire along the shore line showed a battle was raging. Northward toward the British line we could see a heavy cruiser or battleship slamming the full effect of her heavy fire into enemy pillboxes, forts and other strong points along the ridge. Bursts on targets indicated the efficiency of the fire.

Through the smoke and haze which hung over the battle area, occasional sharp flare-ups of light told us vehicles or munition supply dumps were under enemy mortar or artillery fire. As we watched a column of high smoke, we saw one beachhead LCI receive a direct hit, then go skyward as flames reached the fuel and magazine. Angry blasts from the heavy guns of the battleships to westward of us showed answer as dirty clouds of smoke broke above the trees on the hills behind the beachhead. Floating artillery was aimed to rout enemy positions.

To the north a column of smoke rising from a group of buildings on the beach indicated the Nazis were abandoning their position. At the other extremity, a tremendous smoke ring curled toward the sky as German shells lobbed into the area on which were parked a group of our vehicles.

Overhead P-38s, Forts, Bostons and other planes streaked across the battle area unopposed, unloading on enemy costal and rear positions, keeping close watch over the ships and the shore. Troops abroad, who now stared in the direction of the battle as if at a baseball game at home, turned momentarily to look skyward, then said "Thank God for these boys today." The absence of the *Luftwaffe* was concrete evidence of what they felt.

Wounded Come Aboard

Tonight as we sit off the beach we know this is at its grimmest. Above the echo of gunfire ashore and from nearby craft we can hear the steady thump of metal against metal as our small LCVPs return from their run into the beach. The first wounded from this battle are coming aboard. Troops waiting their turn to hit the beach walked the T-rail and looked down upon their buddies returning. Somehow it wasn't quite what they had expected, if they had thought about this phase much before.

Dozens of soldiers lay on stretchers or leaned against the side of the boat. Salt spray soaked through their battle-stained uniforms, some bearing patches which indicated that they belonged to our outfit. White-faced, with strained expression, they sat motionless, saying nothing, apparently not even noticing where they were or where they were going. One lay on a stretcher in the corner covered with a blanket, apparently dead.

Men Are Eager To Go In

Aboard ship, the wardroom has been rigged for operations, below decks space set up for a little hospital. Casualty aide men and hospital corpsmen carry stretcher cases up passageways to the doctors and their assistants. Some are wounded seriously, some will die. But many others have received only slight wounds which will keep them out of combat momentarily but from which they will recover rapidly.

Our men are still eager to go in. They have been brought up with a smart blow and know they're in the real thing at last. This is what all of us have been waiting for.

THE BALTIMORE SUN, WEDNESDAY, JUNE 14, 1944

The following cable dispatch from Holbrook Bradley, who is with the 29th Division, was delayed in transmission.

Bradley Describes 29th Division's Landing On Normandy Beachhead

By Holbrook Bradley [Sunpapers War Correspondent]

Allied Beachhead in France, June 7 [By Cable — Delayed]— We landed today on a war-torn stretch of the French Channel coast which only a few hours back was a raging battle area.

Although the frontal positions have advanced several miles inland, there is still a grim pall from the recent heavy fighting about the beach.

Although we arrived off the beachhead at midafternoon of D-day, conditions ashore prevented our landing with other elements of our division, and it wasn't until yesterday noon that our commander was given orders to proceed to within a mile of the sands preparatory to unloading.

Nazi Shell Landing Craft

A heavy rhino barge, operated by navy Seabees, pulled alongside to unload vehicles and personnel, but sharp explosions in shallow water shoreward brought a quick stop to the work. A near miss on one LST close to us told that Jerry artillery was giving the area a working over again.

Almost immediately, a patrol destroyer escort, carrying Commodore Campbell D. Edgar, the commander of Support Force B, of which we were a part, came along side to order us to stand out to sea.

In answer to the German shelling of our unloading point, a line of capital and lighter naval craft standing out in the Channel opened with a salvo of 16 and 14 inch gunfire, aimed at knocking out the Heinie batteries. A flareup of smoke and flame from one of our shore dumps indicated the Germans hit the range accurately.

Enemy Hits Indicated

Several minutes later a column of smoke spiraling skyward from a small French coastal village on a near-by hill indicated further enemy hits on our forward areas. Naval artillery fire opened again in angry reply. By nightfall the enemy batteries apparently were silenced.

During our second night off the beachhead, the *Luftwaffe*, which was still absent during daylight hours, came over for a night attack on the ship and shore installations. We were lucky again.

Our turn to run ashore came during midmorning, when Capt. Otto H. Graas and other company officers finally made arrangements with the navy to get headquarters and other priority personnel ashore in small LCVP's.

Clambering over the side of our LST, we slid down the cargo nets into the small gray craft below that bounced and banged about on the Channel swell.

Whisked Toward Beach

Crowded into the vessel, some two dozen of us were whisked in through the fleet toward the beach.

Wondering whether the sweepers and engineers had removed enemy mines and underwater obstructions, we hung on as the ship bounced over one wave, then through the next. We passed vessels showing evident signs of hits by enemy shorefire or underwater mines. Then we were on the beach.

The navy enlisted personnel in our craft rammed the light LCVP well up on the sand, but even so we found some 20 yards of waist-deep water to wade through when we dashed out of the forward ramp.

White tape set up by the first engineer group ashore indicated a path cleared through the enemy mines. To the right and left were American trucks, burned out after receiving direct shell hits. Equipment of all kinds lay scattered along the beach, clothing, vehicles, weapons and supplies.

MP's Direct Traffic

Groups of MP's stood on the cleared road to direct traffic up and down the beach. We were warned to watch for the white tape and signs indicating mines. On the ridge above us we could see our infantry crawling, rifles in hand, watching for snipers. Sporadic fire and an occasional sharp ping indicated action going on along both sides.

The first dead we saw was a navy man covered with a piece of tarpaulin, lying almost as if he were asleep.

Spreading out in a line so that casualties would be small if an enemy shell landed near us, we started up the beach toward our division command post. With us were Capt. Arnold W. Ellis, Richmond; Capt. Thomas Dukehart, Baltimore; Warrant Officer Milton Nadel, Richmond; Major John Goetz, Washington; Lieut. Paul Clapper, Cumberland, and Lieut. W. Henry Hubbard, Farmville, Va.

Scene A Desolate One

The scene through which we passed was one of the most desolate we've ever seen. The few houses along the shore were almost blown to bits, evidence of the heavy navy gunfire early on the first day. Up on the hills, German concrete emplacements were completely blasted off the ground, and mazes of barbed-wire entanglements were ripped through in huge sections.

A few hundred yards up the beach we came upon one of our burial grounds. Long rows of bodies, sewn in white cloth, lay face up to the sky. Medics and members of Graves Registration units checked the bodies to make sure of their identification.

More Dead Are Seen

A few yards farther on we came upon those dead who hadn't yet been prepared for burial. They were the boys who had hit the beach first, for the most part lads who went in before any of the installations had been cleared out.

Some never made the shore, for their white and almost waxlike bodies still had pieces of seaweed hanging from them. Somehow, although many of them were men of our outfit, they all seemed most impersonal.

We knew now why our landing had been held up, why there were still others behind our division yet to come ashore. Those first few hours on the beach must have been living hell. And we saw there had been no discrimination in the way the men fell, for the two bars of captains were among the plain uniforms of the privates.

Command Post Set Up

The objective of our first day's march was a limestone quarry off the hillside facing the Channel. There the division command post was set up. A few grimy, unshaven men, the headquarters personnel who had been ashore since the night of D-day, greeted us. Others stretched in or alongside foxholes dug in the hard ground.

Here and there pitifully small fires were used to heat the semblance of a noonday meal.

Among the Marylanders in the area were Major Sewell S. Watts, Capt. Asa B. Gardiner, Lieut. Robert Wallace and Sergt. Barry Cassell, all of Baltimore, and Majors William Bratton, of Elkton, and Lloyd B. Marr, of Silver Spring.

We learned the situation was well under control, that our regiments were well on the way to their inshore objectives. We were told also that the first two nights ashore had been hell. Enemy air and artillery fire had been coordinated on our positions with an accuracy that made the position seem uncertain, to say the least.

Today things look up.

7 A.M. THE SUN EXTRA

Registered United States Patent Office

Vol. 215—No. 18—F   PAID CIRCULATION MAY MORNING 162,501 EVENING 183,442 345,943 | SUNDAY 268,914   BALTIMORE, TUESDAY, JUNE 6, 1944   Entered as second-class matter at Baltimore Postoffice   Zone 3   24 Pages   3 Cents

ALLIES INVADING FRANCE, TROOPS LAND IN NORMANDY

BULLETINS

London, June 6 (AP)—Prime Minister Churchill told the House of Commons today that an immense Allied armada of 4,000 ships with several thousand smaller craft had carried Allied forces across the Channel for the invasion of Europe. Churchill also said that massed air-borne landings had been successfully effected behind the Germans' lines.

"The landings on the beaches are proceeding at various points at the present time," Churchill said.

"The fire of shore batteries has been largely quelled."

He said that 'obstacles which were constructed in the sea have not proved so difficult as was apprehended."

The Prime Minister said the American-British Allies are sustained by about 11,000 first-line aircraft, which can be drawn upon as needed.

"So far," he said, "the commanders who are engaged report that everything is proceeding according to plan."

"And what a plan!" he declared.

Churchill said the vast operation was "undoubtedly the most complicated and difficult which has ever occurred."

New York, June 6 (AP)—The Berlin radio broadcast a DNB dispatch today saying that one Allied cruiser and a large landing vessel carrying troops had been sunk in the area of St. Vaast La Hougue, 15 miles southeast of Cherbourg.

ALLIES PURSUE FLEEING NAZIS NORTH OF ROME

Rome, June 5 (AP)—Allied armor and motorized infantry roared through Rome today—not pausing to sight-see—crossed the Tiber, and proceeded with the task of destroying two battered German armies fleeing to the north.

Allied fighter-bombers spearheaded the pursuit, jamming the escape highways northward with burning enemy transport and killing and wounding many Germans.

The enemy was tired and disorganized by the Allied assault, which in 25 days had inflicted a major catastrophe on German forces in Italy and liberated Rome almost without damage.

Rail Yards Bombed

Joining the program of destruction, 500 American heavy bombers blasted rail yards at five points in northern Italy between Venice and Rimini along which the Germans might attempt to move reinforcements and equipment to bolster Marshal Albert Kesselring's armies.

At 10 A. M. today Lieut. Gen. Mark W. Clark, commander of the Fifth Army, entered Rome in a jeep and drove to the city hall, where he formally proclaimed the Allied occupation and praised the valor of his troops.

Addressing his corps commanders and looking out over thousands of cheering Italians, Clark declared that both the 10th and 14th German armies had been at least partially destroyed, more than 20,000 prisoners taken and untold quantities of Nazi equipment captured.

Allied Troops Praised

He lauded individually the French, British and American troops of the Fifth Army and paid tribute to the "gallant men and women who made the supreme sacrifice" that made today's occupation possible. Mussolini's famous balcony in the Palazzo Venezia, a few blocks from where Clark spoke, looked empty and deserted.

Pope Pius XII, addressing an enormous crowd including many Fifth Army soldiers in St. Peter's Square, expressed thanks to God that Rome had not been destroyed by war.

The inhabitants' reception to the troops approached hysteria as the day wore on and homemade confetti soon littered the streets. There was an almost carnival atmosphere. Little damage to the city was visible, the Nazis having limited demolitions to a few installations of no artistic or religious importance.

Much Material Taken

The speed of the enemy's flight once his lines before Rome burst was evident in the great quantities of war material left behind, stock piles sufficient to equip several divisions. An Allied spokesman expressed the official opinion that the tremendous pressure exerted by the Allies in the final phase of the battle for Rome had forced the enemy to flee beyond the capital rather than make a protracted fight for the city itself.

Just 24 hours after the first Allied troops made their way through

(Continued on Page 2, Column 8)

KING TURNS RULE OVER TO UMBERTO

Naples, June 5 (AP)—King Vittorio Emanuele III stepped aside as monarch of Italy today as he previously had said he would upon the liberation of Rome and handed to his 39-year-old son, Crown Prince Umberto, all "royal prerogatives."

Italian political pressure had been brought to bear against him since the conquest of Naples.

In a decree signed by himself and countersigned by Premier Marshal Pietro Badoglio, head of the Italian liberation government, the King named his son lieutenant general of the realm.

Still Heads House Of Savoy

The monarch, however, retained his title as head of the House of Savoy and remains as King without power.

King Vittorio Emanuele, who became ruler July 29, 1900, had announced last April 12 his "irrevoc-

(Continued on Page 2, Column 5)

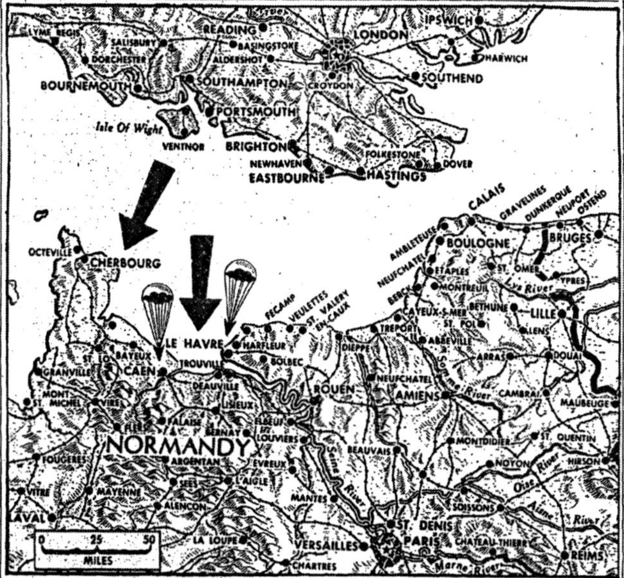

INVASION BEGINS—American, British and Canadian troops landed this morning in France. According to the Germans, landings were made all along the coast between Cherbourg and Le Havre, as indicated on the map by the arrows and parachutes.

VICTORY NOT NEAR, ROOSEVELT WARNS

"Fiercer Fighting" Before Nazi Defeat Forecast

By DEWEY L. FLEMING

Washington, June 5—President Roosevelt tonight hailed the liberation of Rome by armed forces of the United Nations, but warned against "inflated" estimates of the accomplishment.

In a radio speech heard around the world, the Executive emphasized that the Allies must endure a long period of "greater effort" and "fiercer fighting" before the Nazis are crushed; that the campaign will be "tough" and "costly"; that total victory lies "some distance ahead."

Distance Will Be Covered

But, he said:

"That distance will be covered in due time—have no fear of that."

The President's only reference to forthcoming blows at other parts of Hitler's European "fortress" was the observation:

"Our victory comes at an excellent time, while our Allied forces are poised for another strike at western Europe—and while armies of other Nazi soldiers nervously await our assault."

"One up and two to go!" was the way he referred to the capture

(Continued on Page 3, Column 2)

WAR DEPARTMENT WORKS ALL NIGHT

General Marshall In Office Almost Continuously

Washington, June 6 (AP)—Key offices of the War Department were fully manned and working feverishly when the long awaited invasion of Europe began early today.

Gen. George C. Marshall, the chief of staff, was in his office continuously since yesterday except for a brief interlude last evening when he went to the Russian Embassy to receive from Ambassador Gromyko the Order of Suvorov, First Degree—the Soviet Union's highest military decoration.

The operations section of the general staff, the Signal Corps message section and the Military Intelligence Division were islands of frantic activity in the otherwise dark vastness of the Pentagon Building, and officers and messengers scurried through the dim corridors relaying messages between them.

Assistant Arrives At 10

Secretary of War Henry L. Stimson was not in his office, but the Assistant Secretary John J. McCloy came in about 10 P. M.

The German broadcasts on the invasion began to bring news reporters and radiomen into the department in the early hours of this morning.

Maj. Gen. Alexander D. Surles, director of public relations, and his deputy, Col. Stanley J. Grogan, told the waiting reporters about 3.20 A. M., that the announcement was expected at 3.32 o'clock.

Copies Distributed

As soon as the news was flashed from General Eisenhower's headquarters duplicate copies of his first communique were distributed in the Pentagon, along with the text of the statement by the General of the Armies John J. Pershing and a background information discussing the general terms of invasion preparations.

The White House was dark, except for the usual points where guards are stationed.

Elmer Davis, director of the Office of War Information, was at his office, helping check on incoming radio reports through the night hours.

King George Speaks Tonight

New York, *Tuesday*, June 6 (AP). The London radio, in a broadcast recorded by the Federal Communications Commission, said that King George VI would deliver a special broadcast tonight at 9 P. M. London time.

Eisenhower's Order Of Day

London, June 6 (AP)—Gen. Dwight D. Eisenhower issued the following order of the day to his invasion troops today:

"Soldiers, sailors and airmen of the Allied Expeditionary Force:

"You are about to embark on a great crusade. The eyes of the world are upon you and the hopes and prayers of all liberty loving peoples go with you.

"In company with our brave allies and brothers in arms on other fronts you will bring about the destruction of the German war machine, elimination of Nazi tyranny over the oppressed peoples of Europe, and security for ourselves in a free world.

Will Not Be Easy Task

"Your task will not be an easy one. Your enemy is well trained, well equipped and battle hardened. He will fight savagely. But in this year of 1944 much has happened since the Nazi triumphs of 1940 and 1941.

"The United Nations have inflicted upon the Germans great defeats in open battle, man to man. Our air offensive has seriously reduced their strength in the air and their capacity to wage war on the ground, our home fronts have given us overwhelming superiority in weapons and munitions of war, and have placed at our disposal great reserves of trained fighting men. The tide has turned and free men of the world are marching together to victory.

"I have full confidence in your courage, devotion to duty and skill in battle. We will accept nothing less than full victory. Good luck and let us all beseech the blessing of Almighty God upon this great and noble undertaking."

American Paratroopers Land In Back Of Foe's Defenses

By HOWARD COWAN

With United States Parachute Troops, June 6 (AP)—American paratroopers—studded with battle-hardened veterans of the Sicilian and Italian campaigns—landed behind Hitler's Atlantic Wall today to plant the first blow of the long-awaited western front squarely in the enemy's vitals.

The Allies' toughest, wiriest men of war cascaded from faintly moonlit skies in an awesome operation.

By Plane And Glider

Twin-engined C-47s—sisters of America's standard airline flagships—bore the human cargo across the skies, simultaneously towing troop-laden CG4A gliders—to merge in a single sledgehammer blow paving the way for frontal assault forces.

Armed with weapons from the most primitive to the most modern, the paratroopers' mission was to disrupt and demoralize the Germans' communications inside the Nazis' own lines.

There was no immediate indication that their dynamite and flashing steel and well-aimed fire was not succeeding in the execution of plans rehearsed for months in preparation for the liberation of occupied Europe.

The steel-helmeted, ankle-booted warriors wore a red, white and blue American flag insignia on the sleeve and camouflaged green-splotched battle dress.

Series Of Feints By Allies Revealed

Supreme Headquarters, Allied Expeditionary Force, June 6 (AP)—It can now be revealed that the Allies have been conducting a series of feints in advance of the invasion today.

These feints were predicted sometime ago by Prime Minister Churchill, and were designed to lull the Germans so they would never know when the blow was coming.

Army In Rome Is Greeted By Thousands Of Flags

By PRICE DAY
[Sunpapers War Correspondent]

With the Fifth Army in Rome, June 5—Weary soldiers of the victorious Fifth Army are slogging through and around Rome toward the front, but for the people of this lovely city, today is a day of festival.

Streets which all night seemed full today flow with streams of citizens of the capital where the word "citizen" came into being.

Now and then one says: "Welcome to you, welcome," stressing the second syllable, or "Hello, boss." But for the most they don't talk or cheer.

Sound Of Clapping

Instead they clap their hands. Rome today is filled with the staccato sound of clapping.

Tens of thousands of flags fly in the brilliant sunshine. They are of almost every kind—except Nazi—and size and even shape.

Some in windows wave the British Union Jack. A great American flag is draped over the balcony near Pincia Gardens.

From the flagpole on Corso del Popolo flies another American flag. It is home-made and has only 20 stars, and the background of stars is green instead of blue, but the intention is right or at least expedient.

Somebody with an eye to profit has printed thousands of Italian green, white and red flags, seven by ten inches in size, and of the quality of small cotton flags sold in America before each Fourth of July.

Description Of Flags

These flags have the arms of the House of Savoy in the center but a huge flag flown from the front of an American engineer jeep is without this embellishment. It is a Fascist flag, but the men in the jeep, unschooled in the niceties of politics, are very proud of their prize.

Some Italian civilians are more politically minded. A few Soviet flags with hammer and sickle are along the streets. A small speeding civilian car flaunts a banner of the

(Continued on Page 2, Column 6)

AMPHIBIOUS OPERATIONS AIMED FROM CHERBOURG TO LE HAVRE, NAZIS SAY

General Montgomery In Charge Of Assault, Eisenhower's Headquarters Reports—Strong Naval And Air Support Backs Troops

London, June 6 (AP)—The German radio reported today that four British parachute divisions had landed between Le Havre and Cherbourg in France.

This was four times the size of the Nazi parachute force dropped on Crete in the Mediterranean.

By THOMAS M. O'NEILL
[Staff Correspondent of The Sun]

Allied Expeditionary Force Headquarters, England, June 6—Allied forces launched the assault on Europe today.

Air-borne troops, naval forces and infantry combined in a thrust at northern France, opening the invasion for which troops have been massing in the British Isles for months. The fighting men were Americans, Britons and Canadians. General Sir Bernard L. Montgomery was in command of the army group.

The "This Is It" Communique

A 26-word communique from the supreme headquarters of the Allied Expeditionary Force brought the announce that meant "This is it." The communique, No. 1 from the Allied camp, said:

"Under the command of General Eisenhower, Allied naval forces, supported by strong air forces, began landing Allied armies this morning on the northern coast of France."

Another announcement disclosed that the Allied troops were under the command of the Briton with the winning ways, General Montgomery, and that the American, British and Canadian troops were taking part in the assault.

Giving No Secrets To Enemy

There was no more—no suggestion as how the troops were faring, no clue to the number of separate landings, no inkling as to the numbers of the fighting men involved in the attacks by land, sea and air. All that is information the command left for the Germans to discover by themselves, the hard way.

There had been signs the long-awaited communique was about to appear. For hours aircraft had roared out to sea—fighters, bombers and transports—in clouds surpassing even the fury of the sustained bombing attack with which the air command has been softening the invasion coast and crippling German communications.

First Announced By German Radio

Then the German radio said that landings had been made, though that was no proof since the Germans have frequently made that announcement.

Both navies, British and American, sent ships to sea to protect the soldiers, to put them ashore, to blast the enemy fortifications. Some of the landing ships flew the red duster of the British merchant navy. Air and naval forces jointly scoured the waters for German craft—torpedo boats, destroyers, E-boats and U-boats.

Minesweepers went ahead of the landing craft, aware that the Germans in the many months at their disposal had done their best to make the waters impassable.

Ships Of Other Allies In Armada

Among the naval forces were ships flying the ensigns of Norway, Poland, Holland, France and Greece.

It was said at headquarters that the operation provided the first example in the centuries of northwestern Europe's warfare of "triphibious" strategy in which sea and air forces move as a unit with the armies, the ships and planes to aid the army gain a foothold, the army in turn to seize ports for the ships and airfields for the planes.

Superiority at sea had long been held by the Allies, but today's undertaking could never have started without control of the air above the Channel.

Fighting In France Heavy, Nazis Say

Supreme Headquarters, Allied Expeditionary Force, June 6 (AP)—Gen. Dwight D. Eisenhower's headquarters announced today that Allied troops began landing on the northern coast of France this morning strongly supported by naval and air forces.

The communique was read over a transatlantic hookup direct from General Eisenhower's headquarters at 3.32, E. W. T.

The Germans said the landings extended between Le Havre and Cherbourg along the south side of the bay of the Seine and along the northern Normandy coast.

Parachute troops descended in Normandy, Berlin said.

Berlin first announced the landings in a series of

(Continued on Page 2, Column 1)

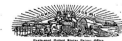

APPROACHING NORMANDY AT EARLY STAGE OF INVASION — This is how things looked off the French coast to the 29th men on June 6. Ships in this convoy are of all sizes and diverse types. Overhead float a great number of small balloons towed by the vessels to discourage enemy airmen. BKI-472-BS

THE 29th ON D-DAY PLUS TWO

DRAWING CLOSE TO THE SHORE OF FRANCE — The eyes of the 29th men on this invasion craft are on the Normandy beach which they are approaching and over which hangs a cloud of smoke created by exploding Allied projectiles. BKI-500-BS

BRADLEY'S CAMERA CROSSES FRANCE

Last week's metrogravure section carried a page of pictures of the Blue and Gray Division fighting in Germany, made recently by Holbrook Bradley, Sunpapers' war correspondent, attached to the division for many months, made the pictures on this page, which were long delayed. They are of notable events in the Maryland-Pennsylvania-Virginia unit's career — events described by Bradley and other correspondents last summer. At that time the 29th, though well trained, was unseasoned. Since then it has been tempered in many battles, in all of which it has given a good account of itself.

SUPPORT TROOPS ARE LANDED ON VIERVILLE BEACH — Picture made June 7. Four men facing camera in center of picture are, left to right: Capt. Henry Hubbard, Farmville, Va.; Lieut. Paul Clapper, Cumberland, Md.; Major Thomas Dukehart, Baltimore; Capt. Arnold Ellis, Richmond. BKI-498-BS

OUTSIDE DIVISION COMMAND POST SET UP IN QUARRY — This picture was made during the first few days after the 29th landed in Normandy and shows men going about various duties and their equipment scattered over the stony ground. BKI-501-BS

CHAPTER 3

ROUGH, TOUGH DAYS IN NORMANDY

THE BALTIMORE SUN, MONDAY, JUNE 12, 1944

Vital Role Taken By 29th As Yanks Gain In Normandy

By Mark S. Watson [Sunpapers Military Correspondent]

London, June 11 [By Cable] – Fierce fighting which has been unceasing since the Allies' first landing in Normandy now has produced several admirable gains.

One of the best continuous advances of the wide front seems to be that in the lower Aure Valley, which runs roughly from Trevieres almost due west to empty into the bay near Isigny. This is the area in which we are now permitted to say the American 29th Division is fighting.

This division originally was made up of Maryland and Virginia troops and of which perhaps still has one fourth of its personnel from these States.

Heavy Fire Met 29th

On D-day the division encountered heavy fire on the beaches until naval bombardment silenced the concealed batteries which had been causing trouble. Thereafter they moved forward and attained a road which runs roughly parallel with the shore. Then the Americans encountered a real difficulty just beyond the roads where the Germans had inundated the whole lower Aure Valley by admitting sea water through the dikes at Isigny.

Previous dispatches have announced the taking of Isigny and Trevieres, a dozen miles upstream. Now the division has succeeded in clearing the entire valley and attained firm ground to the south of that troublesome swamp.

Likewise the firm ground above the marshes between Isigny and Carentan at least has been gained by other Americans.

Allied Holdings Firmly Linked

There now is a real opportunity to maintain a substantial link of Allied holdings east and north of embattled Carentan, where the Germans are still putting up a ferocious resistance. Farther west the British armored forces have made an admirable thrust southeast of Bayeux and have taken Tilly-Sur-Seulles. But our advance in that direction still needs to reach Juvigny before we will be clear of particularly troublesome terrain.

Our pressure on the Cherbourg peninsula seems increasingly violent. Northwest of Carentan we have made our way across the little Merderet river and our fighter-bombers have been extremely active in support of the ground troops today.

These various gains are small on the map, but their importance is real. They are not high save relatively. But they are on firm ground over which men can move and over which wheeled traffic can ultimately operate.

Gains Fairly Continuous

The gains are fairly continuous over most of the 51-mile stretch which we control along the Normandy coast with fair promise of deepening our holdings very considerably at more than one point quite soon.

That little patch of firm ground at the edge of the marsh near Carentan offers special encouragement, for some of the Germans' fiercest efforts have been expended keeping the Allies away from the juncture they have been seeking for days.

Here again we must recognize the prime service of air-borne troops who seized the area around Sainte Mere Eglise on the very first day.

In today's operations, the air forces are said to have given the closest support ever extended to ground troops and one can hardly doubt this important factor in certain territorial gains which are at last achieved.

At longer range the RAF heavies did mighty blasting on the Versailles-Acheres traffic arteries.

Pleasant to record is that the British officer, who today authorized the publication of the name of the 29th Division did so in extremely laudatory terms.

"It is absolutely first class, a magnificent division," he said warmly. The division's capture of firm ground on the front sector supports that judgment.

From Watson back to Bradley

THE BALTIMORE SUN, FRIDAY, JUNE 16, 1944

Bradley Recounts Trip To Post Close To Front

By Holbrook Bradley [Sunpapers War Correspondent]

On the Allied Beachhead, France, June 8 [By Cable — Delayed] — German artillery and mortar fire let up this afternoon, so Capt. Arnold W. Ellis, Richmond engineer, suggested that we set out to find his command post which was reported three or four miles up toward the front lines.

A division guide posted at a dirt road just outside the quarry in which the headquarters setup was located, told us to follow the column of men and vehicles which was moving toward the fighting in a steady flow from the beach some hundred yards or more behind us.

Young, But Hard Fighters

As we turned up toward a small town, the scene of some bitter fighting during the first two days, we passed three or four Heinie prisoners with their hands over their heads. Military police guards told us that the prisoners' youthful appearance belied the tenacity with which they fought.

All along the road we found signs of the battle which had raged as late as this morning. Equipment of all types lay everywhere, indicating the great waste of material in actual war. Occasionally we saw men newly dead, lying as they fell, covered with a camouflage net or a raincoat, waiting for grave registration and burial parties.

Zing Of A Bullet

Soldiers crouched behind a stone wall along the road warned us to keep low as we drew abreast of them, indicating that there were still snipers active in the wooded areas to the left and right. The sharp zing of a bullet sent us into a ditch.

A group of five or six small buildings at the road intersection some hundred yards along still smoldered from the effects of the first day's Allied naval bombardment and yesterday's German counter artillery barrage.

Shooting Flares Up

In a field to the left stood two American halftracks, completely burned out. Across from us we could make out a sign reading Hotel de la Place; through a blasted wall section we could see plates and silverware strewn about and a picture of Marshal Foch hanging on the wall.

Our interest in the hotel ceased suddenly with an outbreak of small-arms fire down the road to our left. We hit the dirt again as a group of our men came flying around the corner and a volley of fire hit the roof of the hotel opposite us.

Dives For A Ditch

The military policeman on duty at the intersection dove for a ditch at the side of the road as a jeep with five men aboard came flying down the road, skidded around the corner and disappeared in the direction of the beach.

Several minutes later we decided to poke our heads out again as the fire receded into the distance.

From the military policeman we got directions to the command post we were looking for. It was down the right-hand intersection some two miles. Taking cover under the wall on our left we set out to hike it, careful to space ourselves so that an enemy burst of shell-fire would not get both of us.

Riflemen Watch Woods

Groups of our riflemen lining both sides of the road kept their eyes peeled toward the distant wooded areas for snipers, who were still working.

Evidence of the effectiveness of our naval and initial shore-artillery fire was found all along the road.

At what had once been a small French repair shop, two United States six by sixes stood completely burned out. Blackened, twisted equipment strewn about the area told the story of a hit on a supply dump.

Outside the gates of a farmhouse a little farther along we found an infantry guard with the shoulder patch of our division. Our division's forward artillery command post was in a near-by barn.

A Look At The Battle

A brigadier general and a colonel showed us the progress of the battle on the situation map. We gathered the Germans were getting full benefit of our medium and heavy weapons.

Outside in the cobblestoned courtyard a family of ducks ran around — as usual — searching for food. An old French peasant dressed in dirty blue trousers and blouse and wearing wooden shoes trudged off to round up a herd of cattle.

An old woman and a middle-aged housewife stood in the doorway watching the arrival of the Yanks with a vacant expression. In a field some cattle lay dead, their legs sticking stiffly, grotesquely skyward.

A Sniper Caught?

We learned that the engineer command post was a mile and a half father down the road and started off again, on the alert for snipers. Behind us the military police came along with a prisoner in civilian clothes. We had heard rumors that many Germans stayed behind in civilian clothes to act as snipers. We wondered if this was one of them.

Two or three GI's, crouched behind a low, grass-covered wall, shouted warning that they were in the process of flushing a sniper from a grain field. We waited a bit, then decided to take a chance and dashed ahead through an open gate.

A Yank Face Down

No shots followed our move, but we found a dead Yank lying face down in the ditch beside the road — the sniper's work.

But as if to even up the score, a dead Jerry stared up at us from another section of the same ditch. Crossing to find his rank and regiment, we were surprised to find that he appeared to be well over 50, confirming G-2 reports that the division we are fighting was one of Hitler's holding forces rather than one of his crack outfits.

Evidences of Jerry's preparations against coastal attack appeared everywhere we looked. Stone walls and buildings were pocketed with firing holes, roadsides covered with barbed wire and an occasional sign bearing a skull and crossbones warned that the area was mined. Few trenches or other fortifications were in evidence.

Many Missing

The end of the trail for this exploratory run came a few hundred yards on down the road when we found division engineer headquarters. In a grove of trees slightly in from the road, members of the staff lay on the ground or squatted about breaking out rations for a quick meal.

Unshaven, haggard, dirty and worn, they told of coming ashore early on D-day and of the heavy fighting which had just let up. Many familiar faces were missing, but the engineers had stood up under the severest test and had held their positions.

After checking the location on our map, we headed back to the division command post. Growing traffic of all types and descriptions on the roads indicated we were getting more and more unloaded at the beach and were pressing inland with dispatch. That we were still very much in the fighting was made very clear when we saw a group of engineers probing their way out through the minefield to reach a boy lying dead on a hill.

THE BALTIMORE SUN, FRIDAY, JUNE 16, 1944

Bradley tells about 29th –

Takes Trip From Front Back To Invasion Beaches

By Holbrook Bradley [Sunpapers War Correspondent]

With the 29th Division in Normandy, June 11 [By Cable — Delayed] — Those of us in the actual combat zone have little chance to keep up on the progress of the battle elsewhere or learn what is happening in the territory we have come though, so an opportunity today to run back to the beachhead was most welcome.

With Corporal Al White, of Rutherford, N. J., I headed back along the roads over which infantrymen had been fighting on a few days before. Everywhere was war's aftermath. Most of our dead had been buried but here and there we still saw Germans lying where they fell.

And then we saw something unforgettable; French peasants — in Sunday best — going to church. Our artillery thundered and the German guns thundered back, the dead lay rotting in the fields, yet the women with lace shawls and caps walked quietly to worship as they had time out of mind.

Most Churches Wrecked

Most of the churches are wrecked because Jerry has a habit of setting up strong points and snipers at such locations to obstruct our advance.

Some five or six miles down the road behind our front the driver of the weapons carrier, with whom we had grabbed a ride, told us that he had to turn off so we went on afoot. A few miles down the road we decided to have our Sunday dinner — the usual K-ration cooked over a fire in a ditch.

Our feast was interrupted by a French farmer who came tearing up on a two-wheeled cart and shouted something about two German officers in his barn. We decided to investigate and rode off down the road to the farmhouse where we took a quick look about.

Germans Had Fled

The farmer's wife greeted us profusely, told us how she and he husband had been forced to work for the German Todt organization for three years and said the two we were after had fled upon our arrival. We promised to send a search party and went back to our meal with three pounds of butter the farmer pressed into our hands.

Back on the highway we flagged a jeep. The driver turned out to be Major Harold T. Perkins, of Elkton, from one of our infantry regiments. He told us of coming through the town of Isigny (which we had taken two nights before.) Buildings were burning, he said, and snipers still about, many in civilian clothes.

Going To The Front

The magnitude of the Allied invasion preparation became evident as we drove along past column after column of infantry and steady streams of all types of military vehicles and equipment. Hundreds of army amphibious ducks were running ammunition and other supplies up to the concentration areas, then returning for another load.

Back at the crossroads, where enemy snipers had held up our advance for some time during the first and second days of the fighting military police were directing traffic over roads that we had already marked for one-way movement.

Out on the Channel we could see thousands of ships of all kinds, some just arriving, others in the process of unloading and still more on the way back for more personnel and cargo.

Fields and buildings were practically all taken over for bivouac areas. At army headquarters we found an officers' mess set up with white tablecloths and shiny china and hot water for Washington mess kits — a strange contrast to conditions up front.

Goes Hitchhiking

After lunch we started out again. We had to hitchhike to see anything and by any transportation which was at hand.

Major Don Dresden, of the Air Forces, was most cooperative. He picked us up on our way to headquarters and gave us directions when he turned off.

We got a lucky break when we picked up a ride with some messengers bound for headquarters. Rolling along narrow roads at some 50 miles per hour makes chances of getting hit by a sniper unlikely. We passed one spot which bore signs of heavy fighting.

Bodies At Crossroads

At one crossroad there were bodies of German artillerymen and infantrymen. At another we passed two Heinie artillery pieces still in the emplacements. Farther on there was a burned-out tank with its crew lying beside it, then a series of armored cars all knocked out by our guns.

We failed to establish contact with the press relations officer at headquarters, but we managed to arrange a ride back to our 29th Division command post with a messenger.

It was well past 10 o'clock at night before we finally shoved off. Lingering daylight, and later a full moon, made conditions bad for us but good for snipers. We felt fairly safe, however, with two men carrying tommy guns ahead of us and one with a Springfield rifle in the rear. Nonetheless we made as fast time as possible through the deserted, small war-torn towns along the route.

"Home" To Bed

As we pulled into the division forward command post, our heavy artillery was just opening up its nightly barrage. Overhead a few Nazi planes roared, their motors giving off a waspish rhythm, familiar to all of us by now. Guards challenged us every few feet as we stumbled across unfamiliar terrain to try to find our bedding rolls. All of us were dead tired and covered with dirt and dust.

With us in camp were: Sergt. James E. Floyd, Turpin, Va.; Capt. William H. Beehler; Privates Joseph H. Kuzyk, Neal Dubois, Robert Main, Arthur Maccis, John McWilliams, Joseph Gresco and Early Myers, and Lieut. Leslie McCorkle, all from Baltimore.

THE BALTIMORE SUN, MONDAY, JUNE 19, 1944

The Bells Tolled Too Much

By Holbrook Bradley [Sunpapers War Correspondent]

With the 29th Division in Normandy, June 17 [By Radio — Delayed] — Signal Corpsmen laying communication lines along railroad tracks today grabbed their weapons in a hurry when bells in a nearby church tower began pealing what sounded like some form of code.

Their first thought was that snipers, who have caused many behind-the-front casualties in this battle, were about to open up or to send information of our troops' movement to the Germans.

The signalmen called in a medium tank from a near-by outfit, then opened up with a few bursts from their own .50 caliber machine gun.

After a couple of rounds had been fired through the tower, five Germans suddenly appeared in the doorway of a house across the street, their hands in the air.

Then a slightly inebriated Yank engineer, clutching a bottle of French wine, poked his head from the church belfry and grumbled:

THE EVENING SUN, WEDNESDAY JUNE 21, 1944

Engineers in 29th Drop Usual Work To Fight

By Holbrook Bradley [Sunpapers War Correspondent]

Allied Front in Normandy, June 19 [Delayed] — This is a war in which anyone may be called upon to do anything.

Tonight our engineers, normally busy building bridges and roads or removing mines, are holding the line against an enemy strongpoint of unknown size, but known to be reinforced with heavy artillery, mortars and fortified gun emplacements.

As with all elements of the army, other than the medics and chaplains who are not armed under the Geneva Convention rules, the engineers are trained as soldiers. The engineers are fully acquainted with tactics and use weapons. Emphasis in training and action usually is, however, on construction, repair work or the removal of anti-personnel and anti-equipment explosives left by the enemy in the path of advancing troops.

Snipers Reported

During the progress of the battle yesterday a situation developed in which "snipers" were reported in a wooded area behind the front line at a spot between two of our advancing infantry units.

As troops on the line were busily engaged in offensive action against Nazi troops, it seemed best to dispatch the battalion engineers to mop up the few enemies evidently left behind during the previous day's action.

When the first engineer elements arrived in the area, they were greeted with a hail of small-arms and machine-gun fire; then, as they advanced farther, the enemy's 88 artillery and heavy mortars opened up to blast the roadways entering the area and to cover the surrounding terrain generally.

Force Bigger Than Believed

Information gathered by patrols and resistance encountered indicated that an enemy force of considerable size, rather than a few snipers, manned the pocketed area, generally surrounded by our troops. A call for assistance from others of our forces brought in some armored vehicles and infantry elements, including mortar sections.

MPs on duty on the road leading down to the area where the engineers still hold out today warned that enemy snipers are still active from scattered buildings and groups of trees. Vehicles still are prohibited from the area because they are easily observed by the enemy. A few rounds of artillery generally landed in the area immediately after a jeep or truck ventured in the direction of the action.

Terrain And Men Wet

A driving rain slanting down from the dull skies, reminding one of the stories of wet weather and mud encountered by our troops during the last war, had wet the terrain and men thoroughly by the time I reached the forward CP this afternoon.

Standing against the slight protection of a hedge-row were Major George Mensik, of Washington; Capt. Robert W. Steward, of Shreveport, La., and Tech. Sergt. Daniels Murray, 3205 Elgin avenue, Baltimore.

Hard To Dig In

The engineer truck loaded with packs and shovels had just pulled in alongside headquarters, with orders from the colonel commanding the outfit to dig in for the night at the present location. As usual, the men already dead tired from more than 24 hours on duty at this spot during which most had eaten only one meal — cold — found the ground full of roots and stones that make slit trenches a nightmare in this section of France. Fresh holes only a few yards out, made by the recent explosion of Heinie mortar shells, convinced most of the men to dig right away.

One look at the troop's dress, soaking wet denims or olive drab issue, is enough to convince one that this is a tough war. The men weren't complaining. They merely asked when they would be relieved, when they would get the next hot meal and a chance to get into dry clothes.

Fighting A Matter Of Course

The fact that they were engineers fighting an infantry war was accepted as being in the line of duty.

Although there had been little sign of enemy action during the last few hours, the engineers still knew that the Germans were about for every once in a while mortar lobbed onto the road with precision, signifying that they had the coordinates down with precision.

Clouds Hamper Patrols

Along the firing line set up behind the hedge-rows, GIs with rifles in hand stood peering across the fields of waving grain for signs of German infiltration. Overhead, the unusual early evening darkness, brought on by thick layers of clouds, indicated more than usual difficulties with patrol.

Among the men seen with the battalion were T/5 Francis Meyers, of Westminster; Private Maurice Singer, of Baltimore; Private Anthony Micriotti, 1006 Warden street; Pfc. Michael P. Quinn of Beckley, W. Va.; Private Melvin F. Bosetti, of Smithton, Pa.; T/5 Earl Steidler, of York, Pa.; Pfc. John J. Olenick, of Scranton; Private William L. Miller, of Philadelphia; Private Bill Marcinko, of Winburne, Pa.; Private Earnst Wiegand, of 105 North Howard street; Private Edward Aherns, of Philadelphia, and Pfc. Ray Miller, of Claremont, Va.

THE BALTIMORE SUN, THURSDAY, JUNE 22, 1944

29th Infantry Digs In As Resistance Stiffens

By Holbrook Bradley [Sunpapers War Correspondent]

With the 29th Division, Normandy, June 20 (By Radio — Delayed) — Heavy clouds and intermittent rains have slowed up Allied air activities over France today but the thundering of our heavy artillery just before dawn indicated that the ground forces were still slugging it out against a stubborn enemy in this sector.

The usual nightly barrage of our medium and heavy guns kept up during most of the hours of darkness with an occasional added flurry of smaller ack-ack guns when the Luftwaffe was overhead. Then about 5 this morning most of us wakened to deafening volleys as round after round whistled over us toward the enemy installations.

Action Flares Up Again

A few moments later we could hear renewed activity along the line held by our infantry. The chatter of machine pistols, reports of rifle fire and grenade explosions told us our boys in the slit trenches were on the move again.

At that spot an hour or so later it was reported that one unit had moved into position among the apple trees and along the narrow dirt lanes the night before under German 81-mm. mortar fire.

About a hundred yards away a doughboy lay dead under a blanket. The shells had been close.

Mud Ankle-Deep

The mud along the lanes as we picked our way forward was ankle-deep. Most of the men had dug their slit trenches back against the hedgerow so they would have overhead as well as all-around protection. Lined with straw from a near-by barn, these individual trenches made fairly snug hideouts. Most important, they were protection from mortar fire.

K rations are usual along the front — cold tinned food and crackers and coffee sometimes. Once in a while the men have a chance to build a fire that won't be observed by enemy snipers or artillerymen and then hot food can be substituted.

Low clouds and generally damp conditions gave that opportunity to Sergt. William H. Tipton, 1905 Deering avenue, today. Gathered about a blaze, started in an old frying pan filled with gasoline and dirt, he and four or five others cooked up a variety of canned vegetables and corned beef. It didn't take long for a crowd to gather around this feast.

Doughboys Dig In

At other command posts along the line infantrymen were busy digging in to hold positions taken during the past 24 hours against the now stiffening resistance. At one such spot Capt. Grant B. Hankins, 21 North Wickham road, observed that the battalion to which he was attached had run up against a strong-point backed by 81-mm. mortars and heavy German 88s.

On the right of one of the main roads leading from the beachhead was an area marked by the usual plaid pattern of grain-fields, apple orchards, all bounded by shoulder-high hedgerows. Small holes from mortar fire and larger ones from heavy artillery shells showed that the field had been under fire. A few bodies lay in the fields.

At the time of our arrival action seemed to be static. An ambulance with big red crosses emblazoned on its sides stood at the roadside, waiting. Headquarters infantrymen and another company stood guard in slit trenches and foxholes along the embankments.

In the next field two more companies were about to take off for another push down the long lane lined on either side by tall maples.

In another field some tanks were hunting the location of some enemy heavy weapon carriers. Occasionally one would swing its turret around and fire with a deafening roar. The usual answer was the rattle of Jerry machine-gun fire.

The Explosion

We moved up the line of GI's in the slit trenches and ditches looking for men from Maryland and surrounding States. After 15 days of fighting the boys looked tired but were in excellent spirits. The general query was for news of the progress of fighting in other sectors and for world news in general. Unfortunately we were as much in the dark on that subject as they.

Except for occasional rifle and machine-gun fire and the distant rumble of artillery, we had little feeling of being on the battlefront. Then things began to happen.

A blast less than forty feet away sent us flying. There was a flash, we felt the concussion of the explosion, then we were knocked down.

We Got The Hell Out

Almost as soon as it was over and we had looked ourselves over for signs of hits, cries came for medical aides from the other side of the area and from men at the head of our own column. As the litter bearers came along to pick up the half dozen or so wounded, most of us realized that we were still shaking. Then another landed near us and we got the hell out of there.

A checkup showed that most of those hit were not seriously wounded. While we waited for the medics to arrive we helped one soldier whose foot was pretty severely cut — he laughed and said that at least he would have a few days' rest now. Others were already on the way to the ambulance as we went down the line to find an officer to give us an over-all picture of the progress of battle.

Among Those Seen

Among the men seen on our trip through the division area today were:

Sergt. Edward R. Elburn, Chestertown; Sergt. Philip E. Hague, Technician (third class) Franklin G. Bigelow, and Corporal Maxwell B. Moffett, Rock Hall; Sergt. James H. Smith, Betterton; Corporal Lawrence E. Meeks, Wroten; Sergt. Sterling W. Hoover, Manchester; Sergt. Jesse L. Nussbaum, Sergt. Frank R. Leidy and Sergt. Francis Hape, all of Westminster; Private Vernon O. Marr, Catonsville, and Private Joseph M. Wise, Leonardtown.

Corporal Kenneth Q. Harsher, Sergt. Miller B. Cassell, Sergt. Mehrl Riddlemoser, Sergt. Elijah N. Hartman, Sergt. Murray A. Fauble, Private Albert Dutrow and Corporal John B. Jones, all of Frederick; Private Gerald E. Fogle, Union Bridge; Technician (fourth class) Arthur P. Stewart, Cambridge; Sergt. John E. Tarbutton, Private William S. Sparks, Sergt. William Turner and Sergt. Robert Wallace, of Centreville; Corporal Fred J. Haker, Laurel; Private James R. Robey, La Plata; Technician (fifth class) Eugene Hurley and Private Owen A. Marshall, Easton.

Sergt. Frank A. Grady, 432 Charter Oak avenue; Sergt. Francis Kinlein, 2913 Hamilton avenue; Private Marvin A. Geyer, 1505 De Soto road; Sergt. Robert L. Bruchey, 1714 Moreland avenue; Capt. Al Warfield; Lieut. Col. Louis Smith, 2508 Newland road; Corporal Lawrence Brandon, 3 St. John's road; Private George W. Heilman, 2574 Hollins streets, and Capt. James Porter, all of Baltimore.

THE EVENING SUN, TUESDAY, JUNE 27, 1944

U. S. Invasion Dead Buried In Green Normandy Field

By Holbrook Bradley [Sunpapers War Correspondent]

La Cambe, France – June 25 (By Radio – Delayed) – This small green corner of Normandy, where yesterday cattle grazed oblivious to war, has become part of America, for here are buried men who died during the first weeks of the western assault.

Those who fell on the beaches in the early light of dawn, those who lay in green fields of grain or along dusty country roads, lie here in simple graves surmounted by a white cross bearing the identification tag of each man, without distinction of race, color or creed.

Almost within sight of the sandy shore where the doughboys first charged ashore to take the heavily fortified German positions with rifles, pistols and cold steel, the plot still is within sound of the battle being waged on land. Past the entrance roll the heavy vehicles of war. Overhead fly the winged fighters and cargo planes which already are using the Allied landing strips built on French soil.

This afternoon, as every afternoon at 4 o'clock, services — Catholic, Protestant and Jewish — are being held for men who are about to be buried today. These are no elaborate ceremonies, merely with military tradition and the spirit of the men who died.

From Bradley back to McCardell

THE EVENING SUN, FRIDAY, JUNE 30, 1944

This is part of a series of dispatches from Lee McCardell on the 313th Infantry and the 79th Division in action in Normandy.

How 79th Broke Cherbourg Line

By Lee McCardell [Sunpapers War Correspondent]

Somewhere in Normandy, June 27 — So called pillboxes in the first line of German defenses which the 79th Division assaulted in the attack on Cherbourg were actually inland forts with steel and reinforced concrete walls four or five feet thick.

Built into the hills of Normandy so their parapets were level with surrounding ground, the forts were heavily armed with mortars, machine-guns, and 88mm. rifles — this last the Germans' most formidable piece of artillery.

Around the forts lay a pattern of smaller defenses, pillboxes proper, redoubts, rifle pits, sunken well-like mortar emplacements permitting 360-degree traverse, observation points and other works enabling the defenders to deliver deadly cross-fire from all directions.

Anti-Tank Ditches

Approaches were further protected by mine fields, barbed wire and anti-tank ditches at least 20 feet wide at the top and 20 feet deep.

Each strong point was connected to the other and all were linked to the mother fort by a system of deep camouflaged trenches and underground tunnels. The forts and pillboxes were fitted with periscopes. Telephones tied in all defenses.

Underground Storerooms

Entrance to these forts was from the rear, below ground level, through double doors of steel armor plate which defending garrisons clamped shut behind them. The forts were electrically lighted and automatically ventilated.

Below a casemated gallery in which the guns were located, firing through narrow slits, were two underground bomb-proof levels packed almost solidly with cases of canned food, artillery shells and belted ammunition for machine-guns.

In several instances after forts had been captured and apparently cleared of the enemy, more Germans were found hiding in these deep bomb-proof sub-basements. Sometimes the sub-basements were not discovered until our engineers had blown up captured works with dynamite.

Such was the Cherbourg Line which the 79th Division cracked. How they managed to crack it still baffles us.

Looked Impregnable

Had you seen these fortifications before the attack you would have pronounced them impregnable. Even after our infantry and tanks had overrun them they looked impregnable to us.

On the morning of Friday, June 23, we left division headquarters where we had spend the night and returned to an infantry regiment command post.

The command post consisted of a captured German Ford delivery truck and 30 foxholes, in a wet gully strewn with hay off a country lane below Hau de Haut. Neither the Old Man — the colonel — nor any of his staff were around.

Marking Map

"Where's the colonel?" we asked Major McConell, who sat on a folding camp chair drawing fresh red and green lines with grease pencils on a big position map set up like a screen before him.

"Still up front with the troops," said the major. "He has been up there all night."

"And where are the troops?"

"Right there," said the major, putting his finger on two fresh-blue brackets well beyond the first line of German defenses, abreast a strong point of the second lines less than three miles from Cherbourg.

Couldn't Believe It

We stared bug-eyed. We couldn't believe it.

"What the hell are they doing up there? Did they get away up there — what time did they break through?"

"Oh, they went through early last night," the major said.

Later the Old Man told us:

"We took the Germans completely by surprise. I honestly believe that if we had kept going and had troops to follow us up and protect our rear we could have marched right into Cherbourg that night."

Believe It Now

When he first told us this we took it with a grain of salt. We hadn't seen the 79th in action. But we believe it now.

The only trouble was that one unit was going too fast. It was at least a mile ahead of the supporting elements on either flank. It stuck out on the front like a sore thumb waiting for a German counterattack to step on it.

About an hour later Capt. John McCabe, of Toledo, Ohio, a regimental anti-tank company commander, came in.

"Well, we just retook a pillbox and did it by the book," he said. "The Old Man was right in there with us, helping with the guns. We had ourselves quite a time."

By-Passed Fort

McCabe pointed out the pillbox location on the map. It was one that troops had passed the previous night. It seemed the Germans had infiltrated back through our lines after dark, reoccupied the position and resumed fighting. Little by little we pieced together the entire story. Here it is:

The Old Man; his executive, Lieut. Col. Edwin M. Van Bibber, of Bel Air, Md., and other key officers of the regimental staff had personally led infantry assault teams across fields, fighting their way from hedgerow to hedgerow after dive bombers had made their low-level attack on the first line of German forts.

The Old Man took his infantry up so fast they by-passed the largest fort before its defenders knew what the score was.

Caught Foe In Rear

The assault teams closed in with bangalore torpedoes and flame throwers, catching the Germans in the rear and cleaning them out of the fort as either corpses or prisoners in short order.

German artillery never let up. From gun positions farther back toward Cherbourg, Jerry shelled the regimental command post in the gully, sheltered only by rows of trees, hotly during the night.

One lucky hit had landed in McCabe's motor park, blowing up a 2½ ton truck loaded with dynamite intended for demolition of captured German fortifications.

Dig In For Night

Meanwhile, the Old Man and his Joes, leaving a reduced fort in their rear, reached a road intersection on the main Valognes-Cherbourg highway, a mile or more farther forward. Here they dug in for the night under harassing fire of German snipers and artillery.

The Germans had no idea that the unit had advanced in strength so far. About midnight, Joes at the road intersection heard a German motorcycle putt-putting down the road from Cherbourg.

"Halt!" yelled an American sentry.

The astonished German officer skidded to a stop, tried to turn around in the middle of the road and go back the way he had come.

The Old Man Shoots First

Out of the shadowy roadside bushes leaped the Old Man, automatic in his hand. He called to the German to surrender. Instead, the German yanked out his Luger. But the Old Man fired first.

"I never thought the time would come when I would have to shoot people under circumstances like that," the Old Man said quietly when the dead officer and his cycle had been dragged off the road. "I just didn't have any choice in this case. It was either him or me."

And it was the first of three Germans shot down by the Old Man that day during almost hand-to-hand fighting.

Old Man Investigates

At daylight something went wrong with the field telephone wire laid between the Old Man's forward observation post and his command post at Hau de Haut. He decided that he had better go back and make contact.

Two staff officers, Maj. David A. de Armond, of Ridgewood, N. J., and Capt. Raymond Godwin, of Indianapolis, a rifle platoon and two light machine guns went with him.

Before starting back the Old Man had traded his automatic with Captain Godwin for Godwin's carbine. The Old Man figured he would have to do some more shooting and he preferred the carbine.

Three Running Fights

Godwin promptly swapped the automatic with a tanker for the tanker's tommy gun and Major de Armond also traded his automatic with another tanker for another tommy gun.

As it turned out, this exchange was a happy chance because the Old Man's party fought three running fights on the way back with Germans who either had slipped through our front lines or come out of hiding in underground tunnels to reoccupy pillboxes our troops had captured the night before.

"I'm telling you we came through there going like hell when we discovered the Germans had come back, unknown to us, and threatened to cut us off," de Armond told me later. "All along the way we were challenged by German sentries and fired at by snipers."

Fires Old Betsy

"As we were passing a fort a German officer jumped out and yelled 'surrender.' I swung old betsy (his tommy gun) around and pulled the trigger. When we finally got through we had killed four Jerries and taken one officer and nine enlisted men prisoners."

But the Germans still held the fort. They had remanned an 88-mm. gun there and showed no signs of surrendering.

The Old Man called up a platoon of tanks attached to his regiment. While waiting for them to move up, he ran into McCabe around a bend in the road just below the fort.

"How would you like to do a little shooting this morning, John?" he asked.

Then Let's Go

"Fine, colonel," said McCabe, a stocky round-faced fellow whose spectacles give his cherubic face more the expression of a school teacher than a tank destroyer.

"Then get a couple of your guns up here and let's go," said the Old Man.

Tanks rumbled up the dusty road toward the fort. Commanding the first tank in the column was Sergeant Charles Jones, of Hagerstown, Md. The tanks crossed the anti-tank ditch at a point where engineers had blown away its sharp crests.

One tank was hit by the Germans and set afire. Its crew got out safely. Another German shell knocked the track off a second tank, immobilizing it, but the other two kept going.

57's Lined Up

McCabe's anti-tank company manhandled two 57's up a narrow lane into position behind shell-scarred stumps and blasted brush, from where they could fire directly upon the recaptured fort.

The Old Man was with them, pointing out the target and directing the fire. Gunners laid it in two by two — two rounds of high-explosive, then two rounds of armored piercing shells.

"Hit 'em again!" the Old Man yelled as bursts found their target.

Sergeant Jones' tank was creeping upon the fort from the rear.

Tank Blows Door Open

When within a range of about 100 yards it nosed over a rise to bring its .75 to bear directly upon the fort's back double doors of armor plate and sent a dozen rounds of armor-piercing high-explosive shells crashing into it in rapid fire. The doors disintegrated and flew open. Three Germans ran out with their hands up.

The Old Man and his rifle platoon followed the tank into the fort to mop up.

"I swung old Betsy around, spraying the place with a long burst, caught another German running away and that was number 5 for the day," de Armond told me.

Joes Blow Up Gun

The Old Man's Joes also put the fort's last serviceable .88 out of action with an explosive charge that blossomed its slim muzzle into a black lily.

And when McCabe drove me up to the fort in his jeep an hour or two later Lieut. Robert C. Johnson, of Seattle, Wash., had planted enough dynamite and TNT around it to blow up the Baltimore Trust Building.

"The Jerries will never occupy this one again," McCabe said grimly.

First-aid men were still picking up the wounded. Ambulances were hauling them back to aid stations. German and American dead, including two aid men — all aid men deserve Silver Stars in our opinion — still lay where they had fallen.

Jeep A Casualty

At the foot of the fort's forward stoop was the charred and twisted wreckage of a burned jeep, a casualty of the previous day's fighting.

Parking his own jeep farther on, near one of the forts' sodded redoubts where he thought it would be defiladed against enemy fire, McCabe told his driver:

"And you stay right with that jeep and watch it."

He explained to me that he had two jeeps shot from under him within the last two days. Transportation was growing scarce in his anti-tank company.

Awed By Fort's Strength

We climbed over the fort. It was my first opportunity for close inspection and I was awed by its massive strength. I still don't know how those Joes reduced it, even with the help of tanks.

Yet they went through another line of similar forts the next day and took a third belt of so-called pillboxes to reach the Cherbourg waterfront two days later.

While we were stepping gingerly over wreckage and scattered German military equipment and I was trying to assemble one good bicycle — I had no transportation of my own — from the remnants of a half-dozen broken German bikes lying in the rubbish, more of our infantry moved up through the area toward the front line.

Joes Stop And Marvel

Scores of Joes stopped for a moment to look at the fort and marvel at its concrete walls and armor plate doors. They didn't know their own strength.

We went inside the fort for protection when German artillery began shelling the area. We felt as safe there as the Germans probably had.

You could have driven a two and a half ton, six by six truck through that back door — and the Germans probably had, judging from the amount of food and ammunition stored on the level where we were.

A Joe came in to get out of the shrapnel that was bursting outside.

"To whom does that burned jeep belong?" he asked.

McCabe Loses Third Jeep

"I don't know," said McCabe, thinking he was talking about the burned vehicle we had passed when driving in, "it has been there since yesterday."

A few minutes later when firing had ceased and we had gone outside again I went back to where McCabe had parked his jeep to return a monkey wrench I had borrowed to assemble my refabricated bike.

The jeep was in flames. The driver was safe, but spare gas cans and hand grenades in the back were exploding right and left. A burst of shrapnel had caught it. I called McCabe.

"Well, I'll be damned." he said when he saw it. "There goes my third one — my radio — my cigarettes and my chewing gum — my musette bag — everything!"

Declines Bike

I offered him my bike but he said no, thanks.

The demolition squad blew up the fort and its satellite pillboxes that night. When I saw McCabe next day he said:

"Let me tell you a funny thing about that fort and those pillboxes. When we blew them up last night we discovered they had a lower level of sub-basements we didn't know anything about. Two groggy Germans crawled out of a hole under one of the smaller pillboxes after we had blown its top.

"There were two other dead Germans, killed by blasts and fumes, in the same hole. They must have been down there yesterday while we were in the fort.

"We don't know how many have been under the main fort. We couldn't go down into its subterranean tunnels last night because fumes from the demolition charges are poisonous. But we think we understand now why the fort was remanned so quickly after we had taken it the first time and passed on.

"Some of the Germans who showed up there again yesterday morning undoubtedly had infiltrated back through our lines during the night.

"But it is very likely that others about whom we didn't know were hiding down there underneath. After we had passed the fort they simply came up the stairs, closed those armor plate doors and started to fight again. Can you beat it?"

THE BALTIMORE SUN, SUNDAY, JULY 2, 1944

This is part of a series of dispatches from Lee McCardell on the 313th Infantry and the 79th Division in action in Normandy.

The Long, Long Road to Cherbourg — McCardell's Trek With The 313th

The Joes Begin To Tire A Bit After Solid Week Of Attack — Nazis Irritate Old Man

By Lee McCardell [Sunpapers War Correspondent]

With the 313th Infantry in Normandy, June 27 [By Radio — Delayed] — Last Friday night the Old Man established his command post in a sandstone quarry half a mile beyond a German fort, which he and the Joes of his 313th infantry regiment had recaptured that day and which the engineers blew up that night.

The regiment was still leading the attack northward, well in advance of all the other units closing in on Cherbourg from the east and west. But the Old Man was irritated by the delay caused by the reoccupation of the fort by the Germans after his men had overrun it once.

"Held Me Up Whole Day"

"Damn it, those so and so's have held me up for a whole day," he fumed. "We ought to have been in Cherbourg tonight."

He gave orders that every German gun and fortification captured hereafter should be destroyed immediately.

"If it's a gun," he said, "all you got to do is to leave the breechblock slightly ajar, pull a pin on a hand grenade and chuck the grenade down through the muzzle. That'll finish it."

The regiment had been in the attack now for exactly one week. The Joes looked like they could stand a Saturday night bath anywhere – not necessarily at Cherbourg. Those with beards looked like burlesque tramps. All were beginning to tire a little.

"How Far?" Universal Query

Every time you got to talking to a Joe he'd ask:

"How far are we from Cherbourg now? They tell me you can see it from the next hill — is that right? How long do you think it will take us to get there?"

Many a Joe hadn't had his shoes off for a week. His feet were killing him. He would have given ten bucks for a clean pair of 10-cent socks. Aside from canned rations and hand grenades which filled all the pockets of his grimy, mud-stained fatigues, he carried only what he wore plus his canteen, a shovel, an ammunition belt, an extra bandolier, a knife, bayonet and his rifle.

Sold On His Bazooka

There were of course a few exceptions to this rule. One was Private Apodaca, 22 years old, of Los Angeles, whose armament also included a revolver he had bought in Lancashire, England, and a bazooka. Apodaca was sold on that bazooka.

"One night back at Morville a sniper with a machine pistol or rifle was firing from a house on our medics," Apodaca told me. "People around there told us there wasn't anybody in the house, but I put two rounds of old bazooka in just in case.

"Next morning we found a Jerry's legs in the ruins. The rest of him had just naturally disappeared."

Blankets Lost Or Dropped

Many soldiers had lost their blankets or had dropped them farther back to lighten their loads. During the week of steady advance and almost continuous fighting they had slept in foxholes at night with any cover they could find. That is they tried to sleep. The German artillery never allowed them too much rest even after dark. And most of the officers were very patient with the weary men.

I remember one afternoon when Maj. Gen. Ira T. Wyche, the division commander, came up to the Old Man's forward observation post. A heavy weapons platoon also was moving forward with its backbreaking load of machine guns, tripods, base plates, motor barrels and ammunition and had stopped along the road to await orders. Men sprawled in a ditch under cover of a low stone wall while German shrapnel whistled and whunched overhead.

The general stopped beside one limp soldier and asked:

"What's wrong with you?"

No Reprimand

The fagged-out Joe straightened up, anticipating a reprimand.

"Resting, sir," he said.

"That's the right thing to do," said the general kindly. "Rest while you can."

He passed on. Joe relaxed and grinned.

I dug my own foxhole that night in a corner of the quarry under the stern of a parked tank and having left my bed roll at division headquarters, several miles away, slept none too comfortably in what I wore — winter underwear, woolen uniform, woolen sweater and a wool-lined combat jacket. Late June nights in this part of Normandy would be late October or November nights in Maryland.

Earlier in the evening at dusk I had paid a visit to Sergt. Charles Jones, of Hagerstown, a tank commander, who has two brothers over here with the 29th Division.

The tankers were bivouacking in an apple orchard near the quarry. While we were talking, Jerry sneaked up a self-propelled gun and sent 25 or 30 rounds of high-velocity shells zipping down a tree-lined road beside the orchard.

Three Lengths Ahead

I beat Jones and the other members of his crew by three lengths in getting under their tank.

But the rest of the night was fairly quiet in our area. The quarry hole was deep enough to provide complete defilade against anything but a direct mortar hit.

At dawn everybody was up, the Old Man still in his coveralls with his gun on his hip. And Ed Van Bibber (Lieut. Col. Edwin M. Van Bibber, the regiment's executive officer), supervised the brewing of the morning coffee.

Every Joe in the outfit did his own cooking. The regiment had left its kitchen in England. But from a corner of a headquarters truck somebody had resurrected an old gasoline field range burner unit.

Hammer Effective

The burner was sooted up and balky and after various people had tinkered at it with tools borrowed from the regimental motor pool across the road, Colonel Van Bibber began hammering on it.

"I belong to the hammer school of thought," he said.

And presently the burner was working.

Ninth Air Force Martin Marauders and dive bombers came over soon after daylight to "soften up" the second line of German defenses around Cherbourg.

As soon as the planes had pulled out the Old Man led his command post group across the Valognes-Cherbourg road, following the tanks and assault infantry toward the strong point that was the next objective.

Supplemented Rations

Crossing a field scorched with *Nebelwerfer* (screaming meemies) fire. I noticed the Joes who had spent the night there in foxholes had supplemented their rich uncle's rations with tins of jellies and jars of butter picked up in captured German billets.

Never in the battle for Cherbourg did we encounter the slightest sign of shortage of food or good living for Hitler's army.

The line of attack lay through fields fenced with hedgerows. Colonel Van Bibber had gone ahead to keep the assault troops on their course. They captured another pillbox, another 88-mm. gun and moved in with tanks to attack another strong point which they wrecked and left in smoke and flame.

Six Wireless Towers Taken

Moving parallel to the axis of the attack, through dense thickets of wooded hills and down into the boggy bottoms of the little stream in the valley, we could watch the infantry and the tanks through field glasses. We saw them capture the great steel towers of the Cherbourg wireless station, hated by every Joe, who suspected that the tall masts had been used by German artillery observers to call down concentrations on his head.

Prisoners were coming in now in ever-increasing numbers, 15 and 20 at one time, most of them small and sorry looking men in soiled and wrinkled rat-colored uniforms.

We crossed the hard-surfaced road running east toward the village of La Glacerie where Capt. Herbert S. Brown, of Stamford, Conn., acting regimental surgeon, had become lost the day before, driving four American ambulances smack into a German position.

Jerries Waved To Him

Captain Brown, a 1936 graduate of the University of Maryland Dental School, had taken four ambulances forward to pick up wounded Joes. A wrong turning put him on the hard-surface road. Nobody stopped him. The road looked pretty good, so he just kept going.

The he noticed some enemy barbed-wire defenses which had been unbreached by our troops and realized that La Glacerie was still in German hands. Turning his ambulances around he started back, passing through a German army installation where a whole flock of Jerries, evidently anxious to call it quits, waved frantically to him from the ditch in which they had taken cover. Captain Brown had no means of bringing them in, so he waved back and came on.

Later, he told Capt. Thomas Lyons, regimental adjutant, of Cincinnati, and Lieut. James J. Baker, communications officer, of Palatka, Fla., about the Germans he had seen. Lyons and Baker were supposed to remain at the regiment's rear command post, but could not resist the temptation to take the Germans prisoner.

"We found about 60 of them around emplacements and other buildings," Lyons said. "They were in all stages — dead, wounded and alive. We brought in all those who could walk. We didn't waste too much time hanging around that place. I looked into one cave, heard a Mauser bolt click and gave it the works with my gun. Somebody, a sniper I guess, put a bullet through a tire of my jeep going along the Valognes-Cherbourg road."

That afternoon Lyons' jeep driver Private John J. Skvarka, of Joliet, Ill., disappeared. Lyons waited around 45 minutes for him to return.

"Where the hell have you been?" he asked Skvarka when the driver finally showed up again.

"Hunting Germans"

"Hunting Germans," Skvarka replied.

He had brought in two, a docile Russian and a blond, arrogant 19-year-old German Nazi.

The regiment's objective Saturday afternoon was high ground above the village of Hau Gringor, a broad flat-topped hill whose far side fell away in a steep cliff overlooking the city of Cherbourg.

Troops and tanks pressed on slowly, but deliberately, through open fields and shady lanes under the very muzzles of a German battery of seven huge 170-mm. guns strung across the southwestern crest of the hill they were attacking.

Pinned Down At Times

Two or three times enemy artillery fire pinned down that advance. Our own artillery registered direct hits on an ammunition dump in a shady lane behind a German battery. But the big German guns, jacked up on revolving bases, were so thickly camouflaged with freshly chopped-down trees that many Joes did not know the guns were there until they had passed them.

On the other hand, the German gunners had no idea that the Joes had advanced so far so quickly. The cannoneers had left their pieces for midday chow when the American infantry swept into the battery position.

A majority of the Jerries had fled, leaving buckets of hot coffee and mess cans of steaming stew behind them. Those few who did not run were either shot down or captured.

Help As Well As Hinder

The fact is that those hedgerows and tree-lined lanes, of which the Old Man had complained as interfering with his observation, were as much a help as a hindrance. If they were preventing him from seeing the Germans, they also prevented the Germans from seeing the Americans except in those areas where the lanes of fire had been cleared for the prepared German positions.

The Joes who overran the 170-mm. gun battery were astonished when they saw those huge guns. Stacked along the hedge-rows and fences behind the gun positions were thousands of rounds of ammunition. Hastily abandoned tents and dugouts of the Germans were filled with their gear and personal belongings.

The road leading out of the area was literally carpeted with discarded German haversacks, side arms, rifles and helmets.

Reports of 500 Prisoners

The Old Man sat down in an open field behind the captured battery and called his battalion commanders by radio. The battle was still in full swing a few hundred yards farther west, where the Joes were having it out with the German riflemen, and German shrapnel was coming in from other batteries nearer Cherbourg.

Colonel Van Bibber came over the fence.

"Colonel!" he shouted, "we've just taken 500 prisoners!"

"Good work," said the Old Man, and went quietly on with his radio conversation.

"Five hundred?" I repeated.

Rounded Up In Quarry

"Five hundred," insisted the exuberant regimental executive. "Got 'em all rounded up back here in the stone quarry — come along and I'll show you."

I followed him down the road, around the hill crest.

"Man, you should have been with us!" exclaimed Van Bibber. "We've had a hulluva fight. I've had more damn fun. We got some of them out of a strong point and some of the out of a tunnel back here in the cliff.

"You know these Germans are funny people. We captured a colonel and told him he'd have to surrender. He said he couldn't surrender because he was an officer, but he called over another German soldier, a noncom, and let him do it for him.

"The German colonel thought I was a full colonel commanding our regiment. He gave me a bottle of cognac after the surrender. I've got it hid down here in a ditch. I'll pick it up later and give it to the Old Man."

The road we were following came out of the trees and ran along the edge of a cliff. In a big semi-circular quarry hole at the foot of the cliff, 200 feet below the road, was a mass of German soldiers guarded by a half dozen Joes.

"There they are," said Van Bibber. "Five hundred — count 'em."

Gaze At Roofs Of Cherbourg

He had them all right. But the picture which will live longest in my mind is of the moment we debouched on that cliff and saw the line of tired Joes, strung along the road, gazing beyond the quarry hole of prisoners and the roofs of Cherbourg further on, at the broad blue expanse of English Channel stretching away to the hazy horizon. I doubt if Balboa discovering the Pacific experienced any more satisfaction than they did.

"By God!" murmured one. "Cherbourg — at last."

We took a steep path down the face of the cliff for a closer look at the prisoners. They were sitting on the ground, a group of about a dozen officers apart from the other 480 odd.

Dropped Arms And Helmets

They already had dropped their arms and helmets. Now ordered by an interpreter to empty their pockets, they stood up and good-naturedly tossed all manner of stuff into a heap in front of them — cigarettes, cigars, pocketknives, razors, razor blades, combs, brushes, hand mirrors, soap, scissors, darning eggs, knives, forks, spoons, mess kits, canteens, socks, handkerchiefs, bedroom slippers, black leather army belts, books, newspapers, snapshots and letters.

One Jerry threw a child's doll onto the pile. But the stuff you noticed most — because you could smell it all over the quarry — was at least 500 cakes of green-scented German army soap.

While this purge was under way, two Joes came into the quarry with another prisoner, a half-pint sized German, dead drunk, whom they had found asleep in a German barracks across the way. He stumbled along in a perfect daze, completely unaware of what was happening. Then a couple of his cronies in the mob of prisoners saw him.

Heinrich Is Thankful

"Heinrich," they called to him in German. "We have been captured."

Heinrich teetered and stared at them. Then his eyes lighted up. His face broke into a silly grin.

"Merci bien!" he cried and began to unload his pockets wildly, flinging pipes and tobacco tins in all directions.

By the time the prisoners had been lined up two by two and marched out of the quarry hole up the cliff path to the road on top of the hill, three women had attached themselves to the end of the column. Two were French. They had been working in the kitchen of a captured German mess and did not know what they were supposed to do.

The third was a weeping blonde, wearing heavy black leather German army boots. She trudged along beside a young German soldier who carried a small hand satchel and explained in answer to questions:

"Meine Frau."

Woman Is Freed

It was obvious she was about to become a mother. The Joes let her fall out of line and one gave her a drink from his canteen. The last we saw of her she was sitting on the roadside, still in tears. Joes were trying to find transportation for her.

The bulk of the prisoners, we were told later, had been captured by a small group of about a half dozen Joes from F and H companies, including Privates Sidney Kelly, of Mississippi; Bill Fowler, of Houston, Texas, and John Schmidt, of Clifton, N. J. Schmidt, who speaks German and who had acted as interpreter when the prisoners gave themselves up, told me:

"I went along with the German commander when he went to his quarters to get his things. There was a big silver-framed picture of Hitler hanging on the wall. I asked him if I could have it and he said 'yes.' Then he asked me what I was going to do with it. I didn't have any reason to lie about it so I told him I'd show it to the boys and then I'd break it.

"'Allow me that pleasure,' he said, and he took the picture away from me and smashed it against his desk."

THE BALTIMORE SUN, MONDAY, JULY 3, 1944

This is part of a series of articles by Mr. McCardell on the part played by the 79th Division in the fight for Cherbourg.

79th Division's Wait On Heights Overlooking Cherbourg Described

McCardell Tells How Troops Watched Shelling Of Forts While Other Units Came Up

By Lee McCardell [Sunpapers War Correspondent]

With the 79th Division, Normandy, June 27 [By Cable — Delayed] — All afternoon the "Old Man" and his regiment sat on the heights behind Cherbourg waiting for orders to take the city that lay below them. They were still leading the attack, still far ahead of all the supporting units.

To the left the 79th Division had not yet cleared their end of the high ground on which we waited. They had encountered stiff resistance at a fortress built into the end of a hill rising steeply from the narrow valley of the Divette river. The Fourth Division attacking on our right, was not yet in sight.

Small Groups Holding Out

Between the heights we had captured and the fortress a supporting force was attacking and small groups of Germans were holding out behind stone fences and hedgerows. Rifle and machine-gun fire was terrific. A few snipers were still around and at least one strongpoint on our left called for attention of the infantry assault team.

The "Old Man" sent patrols down through the village of Haute Gringor, which lay just on the other side of the quarry in which 500 prisoners were impounded. The village had been abandoned by the Germans and apparently was deserted by most of the inhabitants.

A few French who were still there greeted the Joes with wine and cognac. Patrols pushed on into the outskirts of Cherbourg picking up German stragglers.

View Of Water-Front Defenses

From a cliff above the quarry, overlooking Cherbourg, its harbor and the sea, the Joes had an unbroken view of the German water-front defenses and the last line of fortifications holding up the American advance from the east. Through field glasses they could distinctly see German artillerymen working their guns.

The Germans could also see the Joes. They probably could see our tanks lined up behind the stone wall on the cliff's edge, their 75s commanding the city. Our forward artillery observers had moved out on the cliff to direct our own artillery fire and a couple of anti-tank guns were taking potshots at anything within their range.

"It's an artilleryman's dream," said one officer. "Why, it's just like shooting ducks."

Trouble From Coast Battery

A German coastal battery on the harbor's edge gave us some trouble. Through our glasses we could see the Jerries run out of the bombproof concrete shelters and load the guns. Muzzle flashes would twinkle in the distance. A moment later shrapnel would shower the cliff.

Counter-battery fire, called for by our observers, was on the way. We could see it hit the German position. The thunder of its blast rolled back over Cherbourg against our cliff.

When the smoke thinned you could see the Germans running again, this time back to their shelters.

Straps On German Pistol

Back in the field where he was still waiting, the "Old Man" had strapped a German Luger pistol in a black German leather holster around his waist over his own automatic. Capt. Raymond Godwin, of Indianapolis, had taken the Luger from a captured German officer,

"With the compliments of the regiment" he said when he handed the gun to the "Old Man."

Joes who were not fighting drifted over to a French farmhouse where some captured German officers had been quartered. The farmer and his wife got out their best china teacups, filled big pitchers with cider and set them on the oil-clothed kitchen table for the thirsty Joes.

From kettles in another room where the German officers had mess, the Joes ladled rich German beef stew into their own meal cans — first hot meal they had had since reaching France.

Nazis Provided First Bread

Among the abandoned German vehicles standing around the farmhouse and barnyard was an army wagon filled with brown bread. The Joes also went to work on that — first bread they had eaten since the beachhead.

Other Joes went foraging around in the German barracks in the stone quarry where they found bushels of fresh onions, beans, cauliflower, jars of real butter, tins of jelly, canned tuna fish, sardines, cases of cognac, big Sweitzer cheeses and vast quantities of German sausage. They loaded this stuff into clothes baskets and carried it back to their units.

Everybody ate well that night.

"But somehow I choked on it," Technician Frank A. Majewski, of Detroit, one of the "Old Man's" radio operators told me after supper.

Remember Men Lost

We were sitting in the shelter of a hedgerow while the Jerries whipped up a sunset concentration of airbursts overhead. I had commented on the cheese, best I had tasted since the war began.

"It was good all right," said Majewski. "But I couldn't help thinking of all the boys we lost before we got it. My cold rations tasted better to me."

Fire had broken out near the Cherbourg waterfront.

Our tankmen were playing with a small captured German tank they had found, giving each other driving lessons in it around the fields where our own tanks were parked.

Still Waiting For Orders

When darkness fell, we were still on the heights waiting for orders to advance. The German prisoners were still coming in.

One group of eight gave themselves up to an unarmed medical aide man, Private Bill Green, former North Carolina Holy Roller preacher. Another group of seven surrendered to another medic, Private Raymond Richardson, of Beckley, W. Va.

Many Joes bedded down for the night in abandoned German tents and dugouts, sleeping on the straw-stuffed German bedsacks under German blankets.

Those of us with the "Old Man's" command-post group dug foxholes in the stony ditches along the hedgerows. As usual it was cold after the sun went down and being still without blankets of my own I was glad to borrow a pair of German covers from the captured barracks.

Buys Helmet Full Of Milk

It was a rough night and when I went around to the farmhouse the next morning to wash at the well and buy a helmet full of fresh milk from the farmer milking a herd of Guernsey cows in the barnyard, a gloomy group of Joes were working the ancient windlass that lifted the water bucket.

"They got our first sergeant last night" said Private Phil Reckon, of Los Angeles. "And what a great guy he was. I'm for shooting every German I see from now on. It's funny how you feel after they get a guy you really know. It changes your whole attitude."

"The so and sos!" muttered another Joe. "Why don't they give up? I have had three buddies killed now. If it's yourself it's not so bad, but when you seen your buddies killed it's different."

The trees around the farm had been ripped and slashed, their bark and limbs torn away by the night's shell-fire. The "Old Man" later told me the regiment had suffered heavier casualties while holding the heights than in the original attack to take it.

He had lost all track of time since the battle began.

"Ray, what day is this?" he asked Captain Godwin.

"The 25th," replied Godwin.

"Sunday, June 25th?"

"That's right, sir."

Five Women Among Prisoners

Captain Brown, regimental surgeon, went down into the quarry where the prisoner-of-war collection had been established and found five more women there among the newly captured Germans.

The Joes guarding them tittered when the five Fraus had to have some shrapnel splinters picked out of them.

The doctor also held a clinic for the villagers, who were beginning to crawl out of their cellars. He examined and gave advice to several expectant mothers.

Brings 80 More Captives

The second rifle platoon of G Company was taken out on patrol beyond the village by Lieut. Shirley Landon, of Spokane — the lieutenant says, "No comments of the Shirley, please," and returned with eighty more German prisoners.

"Damn them," grumbled a Joe.

"They all come in happy and laughing. What the hell do they go on fighting for?"

Lots of us wondered. They were caught. They couldn't get out.

"It's a matter of their military honor," said one of the officers.

"Why Don't They Give Up?"

"To hell with their military honor," said the Joe. "They are licked. Why don't they give up?"

The Germans had resumed the shelling. The Ninth Air Force dive bombers, circling Fort de Route, which was holding up the force on the left, draw a heavy concentration of ack-ack fire. Jerry *Nebelwerfers* also were in action, tossing their ugly balls of red fire and black smoke into the suburbs of the city reached by our patrols.

But Jerry was licked beyond a doubt. The Allied naval forces had joined the attack. Far out in the channel beyond the harbor breakwater we could see destroyers laying smoke screens to conceal the larger warships. Through the smoke screens we could see the gun flashes. The naval broadsides rained down on a half-dozen targets along the waterfront.

Joes Cheer For Gobs

The bombardment became a sort of a game with the Joes, who lined the crest of the cliff cheering for the gobs, "right in there pitching" one terrible salvo after another.

They cheered their own artillery, whose gunners, working by direct observation, raked the Jerries' shoreline batteries from end to end.

Off to our right the Fourth Division was now in sight. Through glasses we watched its infantry reduce a German strongpoint. We watched its tanks demolish one fort and creep up on another whose garrison finally assembled and marched out in formation to surrender before the final assault was launched.

General Visits Cliff

Major Gen. Ira Wyche, the division commander, came up on the cliff to see how things were going. The regiment was still waiting word to go. In lieu of anything better to do, one of its demolition squads was blowing up tunnels under the cliff from where we had taken many of our prisoners yesterday.

Sometime around noon we got news flashes over the old grapevine:

"We are going into Cherbourg tonight!"

THE BALTIMORE SUN, TUESDAY, JULY 4, 1944

This is part of a series of articles by Mr. McCardell on the part played by the 79th Division in the fight for Cherbourg.

The Old Man Leads The 313th Into Cherbourg

By Lee McCardell [Sunpapers War Correspondent]

Somewhere in Normandy, June 27 [By Cable — Delayed] — Late Sunday after, the Old Man took his 313th regiment down from the heights behind Cherbourg and struck out for the city's waterfront.

First went the infantry, then the tanks, then the anti-tank guns. The Old Man's CP (command post) group, his staff, his radio men, liaison officers and security rifle platoon moved forward with the column, sometimes leading, sometimes in the middle, never at the rear.

From time to time this mobile CP halted along the road while Old Man called his battalion commander by radio. Then he would push on again. During the street fighting and assault on the waterfront pillboxes, the next morning, he was right on the front line, conducting as well as directing the attack.

The Old Man 'One Real Guy"

Never reckless, but utterly fearless, as far as any of us could see, he set the example for every officer in the regiment. The percentage of casualties among his officers in battle was just as high as that among the men who worshipped the Old Man. They'd look at him when he passed and say:

"There goes one real guy — the best in this outfit — I mean the Old Man."

Always with him, in addition to his staff, were Lieut. Col. Robert Safford, another West Pointer, of Leominster, Mass., commanding the 310th Field Artillery, and Capt. L. A. Hedges, of Columbus, Ohio, commanding the attached tanks. Capt. John Timmons, of 810 Beaumont avenue, Baltimore, commanding the regiment cannon company, also was a member of the CP group.

The aid men had picked up the American dead along the road we took, but there had been no time gather up the German dead. At one point, where the column of German vehicles, including a rolling soup kitchen, had been either bombed or shelled, the road had vanished in a deep, muddy crater. Engineers following close behind the regiment with bulldozers, quickly built a cutoff around this block.

Hangs Out Tricolor

The column's entry into suburban Cherbourg occasioned no demonstration among the French still there. They had welcomed our patrols the day before, asking how and whether they should "*parte.*" The Joes didn't know what to tell them as they stayed where they were. One house hung out the French tricolor.

Like the Norman country folk below the city, the Cherbourgers stared at the soldiers' divisional shoulder patch, the Cross of Lorraine, which is also the insignia of the French underground.

Many were eager to trade food and wine with Joes for those patches which they pinned to their breasts. One French woman stopped Corporal Clarence Oyster, of Detroit, in the middle of the road, to pin a blue enameled gold Cross of Lorraine on his field jacket's lapel.

One Or Two Hits

From Fort Du Rout or some other gun position in its neighborhood, German *Nebelwerfer* fire and 88 shrapnel came in on the column. Once or twice the advance halted while troops sought cover. But patrols well forward had driven in snipers and were reconnoitering in the streets ahead when, a short distance from the harbor's beltline railway, we turned aside to bivouac for the night in an open field.

The Fourth Division also was moving into the city. Ebullient Van Bibber (Lieut. Col. Edwin N. Van Bibber, the regiment's executive officer) went forward to contact the Fourth and keep it out of the 79th's sector so as to avoid confusion in our covering artillery fire.

He met a force of infantry and tanks from the Fourth noisily shooting its way into the town. When the infantrymen reached the La Bretonniere, marking the boundary of the 79th Division's sector, and started crawling over the barricade, Van Bibber rushed up shouting:

"Hey! Wait a minute — that's our part of town. You're getting out of your own sector."

A Captain O'Malley, company commander, whom Van Bibber remembered from his own days in the Fourth Division, was leading the infantry.

"Look here, O'Malley," said Van Bibber, "we didn't come all the way up this lousy road just to let you in here. This is our part. You guys keep out."

A jaded Joe, who didn't seem to be enjoying himself as much as O'Malley, looked up at Van Bibber and said:

"Colonel, let me shake your hand."

"O. K." said O'Malley. "I'll see you tomorrow."

"I'll meet you right here in the morning," said Van Bibber.

All The Nazis Had There

When he got back to the Old Man's CP, Van Bibber reported:

"The Germans haven't got anything in there except some 20-millimeter rapid-fire guns, some mortars, machine guns and machine pistols."

The enemy artillery was shelling the bivouac area just then and Van Bibber added:

"Gosh! I get nervous hanging around here. Never know what's gonna happen. I'd like to get in that town. It's just like a cold shower. Peps you up. Nobody likes to be the first around a corner when they're shooting at you. I don't care for it myself. But after you get around, it isn't bad.

Never Gets A Chance To Shoot

"The trouble is I never get a chance to do any shooting," mourned Lieut. Joe Macrino, of Orrville, Ohio, engineering officer. "All I do is carry a shovel around with the Old Man and give him advice as to whether this is a bridge job or a mine job." The Old Man was dressing down another young lieutenant, a rifle platoon leader, who had been with the advance patrols since the battle began and who had commanded the group which took most of the 500 prisoners captured Saturday. Tonight, he had been up front looking over the German machine-gun positions. The Old Man was reading him a lecture for having gone too far forward.

He's The Old Man's Eyes

"You're my eyes," said the Old Man. "You're no good to me if you don't come back."

"Yes, sir, but I wanted to see" —

"You heard my orders," said the Old Man, cutting him off.

"Yes, sir," said the lieutenant, kneeling on his carbine.

"Then carry 'em out," said the Old Man, crisply.

Shortly before dark a heavy-set mustached old Frenchman wearing a ridged helmet of the last war and a Red Cross armband was brought in to the CP. He said he was a gardener living in Cherbourg and knew all German gun positions between the Americans and the waterfront. He also talked about the *"une maison blanche"* in which German troops were billeted.

He Preferred Map Fighting

Private Charles Lambert, of New York, interpreter, questioned the old man, who put on spectacles and, in the fading twilight, pointed out the enemy installations on a map. He wanted the Americans to sneak in after dark and blow up "la maison blanche avec les sales Boches." They told him he could lead the midnight patrol. He said he would rather show them the places on the map and let them do the job without him.

"To hell with that," Captain Godwin told Lambert. "We don't know anything about him or who he is. He'll go with the patrol and you'll go with him. If he's lying and anything goes wrong, you'll know how to take care of him."

"Yes, sir," said Lambert.

He knew.

Only "Real French" Left

Waiting for midnight, we sat around on the grass talking to the old Frenchman. He said a majority of the Cherbourgers had been evacuated the previous week. Those left were "Real French" who had been waiting three years for the Americans. They were not supposed to leave their homes. He had slipped away.

"Food? Very scarce for the French. An adult was allowed 250 grams of bread, 50 grams of butter, 85 grams of meat weekly. He had not tasted chocolate for three years. The Germans had seized all the better-grade wines, he said.

The midnight patrol which the old Frenchman was sweating out never got started. Fires along the waterfront were burning so fiercely they reddened the sky for miles around. The patrols might have been working by flood light for all the cover the night afforded.

Into Deserted Area Of City

We borrowed some straw from a farmer's loft, made beds in a narrow footway between a stonewalled cottage and a hedgerow, wrapped up in our Jerry blankets and turned in. Rain was falling in our faces when we awakened. It was a cold, gray, misty dawn. The column was forming up in the mud for the final advance into Cherbourg.

We moved forward into a deserted quarter of the city, evidently a section in which working people had lived. Concussion had shattered every window, every bit of glass. The telephone and electric light wires were broken tangles. But most of the buildings did not appear to have been damaged seriously by either the bombing or shell-fire.

The Germans had bricked up many windows and doors, leaving only narrow embrasures from which machine guns could sweep the street. A few small concrete pillboxes had been built into some houses along the street down which we advanced — Rue De La Bretonniere — but the defenders must have withdrawn during the night or been driven in by our patrols. We heard only a few shots fired by snipers in back alleys.

Old Man Climbs Over Gate

At the intersection of Rue De La Bretonniere and a broader main avenue, with streetcar tracks, our way was barred by a ponderous steel gate fabricated from huge I-beams. The Old Man and his riflemen climbed over. Other Joes put ropes to the gate from jeeps and swung it open.

An unearthly quiet prevailed. But at the next corner, Rue Don Pedro, Joes at the lead of the column scattered as machine gun tracers ripped into the stone wall across the line of advance. Our tanks came up, swinging their turrets broadside, and halted at the intersection to flush Rue Don Pedro with direct fire.

But the German snipers stuck to their guns. The infantry couldn't cross the street without drawing a hail of tracers.

"Bar Men Forward!"

"Come on," shouted Col. Van Bibber. "We'll have to clean 'em out — Bar Men forward — pass it back."

(Bar Men are Browning automatic riflemen.)

Joes passed word back down the column:

"Bar Men forward!"

Two Browning automatic riflemen hurried forward. One crouched by either corner at the end of the street. Tanks were pouring fire from .50-caliber bow guns down Rue Don Pedro. Bar Men opened up.

"Come on," shouted Van Bibber, waving his automatic. "Come on!"

Turned The Corner Firing

He turned the corner and started up Rue Don Pedro, firing.

"Come on!" yelled Godwin, waving his Tommy gun and leading the way up the street on the opposite sidewalk.

The Joes followed the two officers, shooting as they turned the corner. Godwin was hosing dormer windows with Tommy gun bursts. The tanks took the middle of the street. Gusts of rifle, machine gun, and Browning automatic rifle swept the facades of Rue Don Pedro, sending a cloud of bricks and roof tiles flying.

"Aid man — pass it back — aid man."

Aid Men On The Run

Aid men came running up, stooped low to miss tracers, crept around the corner to pick up the wounded. They left one Joe lying where he had fallen. They couldn't help him. He was dead.

While other patrols fanned out through parallel and intersecting streets, the Old Man led the main column down Rue De Le Bretonniere toward the waterfront. We passed blazing German storage dumps and the burned out skeleton of a French airplane factory. One Joe looked at the empty steel framework of the factory warehouse and said:

"What a shame! Think of all the chocolate bars the quartermaster could have stored in there for us — after we get this damned place cleaned out."

Where the street meets the water-front railway tracks, the column halted. A cluster of German pillboxes, just around the corner to the left, stopped its advance with 88 and machine-gun fire. A tank officer examined the pillboxes through glasses.

"Afraid we can't get our tanks up to fire on them, Colonel," he told the Old Man. "They've got us blocked."

Double steel gate-barriers had been placed across the only street approach to the pillboxes. A broad belt of ferro-concrete tank obstacles stretched from the street across the railway tracks to the harbor's edge.

Two Joes came running across the railway tracks where they had been lying behind a freight car.

Death Of The Lieutenant

"They just got the Lieutenant!" one of them sobbed.

"He was settin' there eatin' his chow," said the other.

It was the same lieutenant the Old Man had reprimanded last night for going too far forward.

A mortar shell killed him, the aid men reported, when they had carried his wounded runner on a litter. His runner couldn't talk. He had been shot through the mouth.

It was raining hard now. We backed up against the walls and buildings, pulled out our K-rations and ate breakfast. From nowhere appeared a bottle of vile French beer as a substitute for morning coffee.

A Forlorn Nazi In The Rain

On our way down the Rue de la Bretonniere, one off our patrols had swept up a moth-eaten German prisoner, the only one we had seen that morning. Nobody paid the slightest attention to him. He wasn't even under guard. He was just there. He stood in the rain, bareheaded and miserable and looking mighty hungry while he watched some Joes eat.

General Wyche drove up in a jeep. The Old Man took him around the corner and up the rising slope toward the railway tracks from where they could see the enemy pillboxes. They didn't stay there too long. The Germans were throwing in more 88's. Our tanks were still out there, trying to fire on the pillboxes.

The Jerries didn't seem to bother the tanks much. They show a preference for officers as targets.

Capture Of 500 Germans

Van Bibber came back from the Rue Don Pedro jubilant.

"Colonel, we've just captured 500 Germans," he announced. "I've got the officers up the street here waiting for you, if you want to talk to them."

Later we saw the 500 prisoners, a sorry looking lot, marching to the rear under guard. In contrast, three officers who had been captured with them were almost dapper. Washed and shaved, combed and brushed, their uniforms clean pressed and well fitted, they stood nonchalantly on the street corner as if they were enjoying a day off, while three battle-stained Joes with fixed bayonets watched them suspiciously.

"We went down that street just shooting the hell out of it," Van Bibber told me. 'Sticks and stones and bricks and slate were flying every which way. We didn't see one German till we came to a big building — city hall or something, I guess — and we started shooting hell out of it, too."

"Then the Germans began running out, holding up their hands. The came piling out of doors and windows by the hundreds."

The building which Van Bibber and his Joes had shot up was a large, modern three story concrete barracks in which the Todt Labor Organization had its Cherbourg district headquarters.

Food Liquor — "Everything"

The building also contained German army officers, officers' quarters and the officers' post exchange. One of the Old Man's staff officers drove back to the Rue de la Bretonniere in a German army car to bring the colonel a box of ersatz German chocolates.

"Sir, they got everything in that PX (post exchange)," he told the Old Man. "Food, clothes, liquor and flashlights."

The flashlights aroused my interest. Half an hour earlier I had used the last exposure of film in my Voigtlander camera to shoot tanks in action. The real battle to take the pillboxes was now warming up and I was anxious to make more pictures.

If the PX was stocked with flashlights, it might have camera film, too. I asked the staff officer if he had seen any.

"No," he said, "but they've got everything else."

The Old Man Takes A Look

"I'm going around and take a look at this place, if you'd like to go along," said the Old Man.

The German car's back seat was loaded with a disorderly jumble of German knapsacks, blankets, clothing, bayonet, rifles, mess kits, bread, sausage and cognac, as it prepared for a hasty flight. The Old Man climbed up on the engine hood and sat there in the rain while we drove around to the captured barracks.

The street in front of the barracks was ankle deep with discarded German military accouterments. Deep ill-smelling bombproof shelters on either side of the main entrance to the barracks were filled with such equipment. Parked in the central courtyard were all manner of German army vehicles, cars, trucks, trailers and motorcycles.

"Enough To Make An Army Drunk"

Never in my life have I seen as much liquor as filled shelves and bins of the German officers PX on the ground floor of one wing of the barracks — sauterne, champagne, sparkling burgundy, cognac, hundreds of cases of bottles and more in wooden barrels.

The Old Man took one look at it and called an officer.

"Get out an order immediately," he said. "No American soldier is to be sold or given any cognac until this battle is over. And put this stuff under guard. There's enough here to make an army drunk."

The barracks was complete with tailor shops, a barber shop and an infirmary. Its storerooms were packed with food, clothing and enough stationery and office supplies to last an army for ten years. On one upper floor was a large and elaborate furnished suite of rooms with a sign over the entrance:

"*Das Kasino ist Jeden Montag Geschlossen.*"

"Well, today was Monday."

Pictures And Busts Of Hitler

Every office in every room seemed to have a picture or bust of Hitler. In the barracks dining hall, a large converted auditorium, a huge bust of the Fuehrer occupied the geometrical center of the stage, screened in by dark draperies to set it off.

Everything was in the confusion you'd have expected in a state of siege, but packed-up gear indicated that the occupants had hoped to move. Van Bibber's Joes had certainly barged in a little sooner than had been expected.

One or two Germans had stood their ground to fight. Their bodies lay where they had fallen.

They must have raided that liquor-laded PX downstairs the night before. The floors and tables of every room I looked into were strewn with empty bottles. But lying on the floor of an upstairs corridor was what I wanted most to see — one dozen rolls of unexposed Voightlander film!

The Joes were still gunning in the streets for snipers. Directly behind the captured barracks our anti-tank guns, mortars and machine gunners were pouring a murderous fire into three German pillboxes which our tanks couldn't reach.

Our machine gunners were firing into slits and embrasures of pillboxes from second-story windows and roofs of houses facing the waterfront. Our mortars were set up in the streets and alleys behind the houses.

An anti-tank platoon commanded by Lieut. Richard Lawson, of Upperville, Va., who used to ride in Maryland Hunt races for John Bosley, of Baltimore, had manhandled one of its guns up the ramp leading to the waterfront and was firing point-blank at the pillboxes from just in front of their barbed-wire barriers at a range of less than 300 yards.

They silenced one pillbox, blasted a clean hole in another, whose defenders poked a small white flag out of the top. The firing ceased on the third, from which the Germans hung out a dirty white towel and a long-sleeve undershirt.

Joes Suspect A Jerry Trick

But the Jerries were slow emerging from their forts and the Joes didn't trust them.

"It's a trick," yelled one anti-tank gunner, "watch them — that's the way they killed a captain the other day."

And they were swinging their gun around, ready to reopen fire, when the Germans began streaming out of all three pillboxes.

Our artillery farther back was still firing. Orders to cease hadn't reached some batteries yet. The Germans were fearful they would be caught in some of those big bursts. When they came out of their pillboxes, they came out running, sprinting around their barbed-wire, waving bedsheets, handkerchiefs and towels in token of surrender.

The Old Man Moves In

The Old Man had moved his command post out of the rain into the office of a construction engineer's shop near the waterfront. "Emil Ludwig" was the name painted on the shop and stenciled in yellow paint on concrete mixers and other machinery which was standing idle in a lot beside the shop building.

The assistant division commander was there. And while demolition men walked back to the captured pillboxes with little groups of German prisoners to locate and blow up their mine fields, and aid men walked over the barbed wire to pick up a wounded American lieutenant lying on the German side, the Old Man filled his staff's mess cups from a bottle of captured red wine in Emil Ludwig's office.

"To Cherbourg," said the Old Man, lifting his cup.

From McCardell Back to Bradley

THE EVENING SUN, SATURDAY, JULY 1, 1944

Both Weather And Gunfire Are Hot In Normandy, Bradley Says

By Holbrook Bradley [Sunpapers War Correspondent]

With the 29th Division in Normandy, June 30 [By Radio] — Fighting along our front has been hot today — in both senses of the word.

Retreating Jerry is pulling up stiffer resistance than expected, and the late June sun makes olive drab definitely overweight.

The present advance toward St. Lo began yesterday when elements of our armor moved in to clear out Germans in a section of higher ground in front of us. The mission of the infantry was to follow up the tanks to take over the ground occupied.

Field-To-Field Fighting

In this country of small fields, and hedgerows and apple orchards, any offensive action is found to be a slow process. Tanks are severely restricted in movement by the checkerboard pattern of hedgerows, behind which German anti-tank guns can fire from well-provided cover.

And as Jerry has all the main and intersecting roads zeroed in on his artillery firing pattern, ground must be gained in literally field-to-field fighting.

Enemy tactics which have delayed infantry action now seem to be to leave a few well-armed units behind while the main body retreats to prepare defensive positions. Taking advantages of the hedgerows, wooded areas and contours of the terrain, the Germans can delay the advance of our troops.

Even sniper units, completely cut off from their organization, will go into action, usually at night, harassing American troops behind the front.

Seem to Expect Extermination

During the present phase of the fighting in Normandy it has not been at all uncommon to find a group of one or two Heinies dug in a well-protected-spot. It looks as if these groups expect extermination, for they are well supplied with arms, ammunition and essential foods and show no signs of intending to escape.

During a rather hot session of yesterday's fighting, a group of us trailing tanks with infantry found one such position where two Germans finally had been blasted out.

Even our own infantrymen admitted the enemy had guts, for he evidently had been expecting doughboys when the tanks showed up and stayed to try and stem their advance. About their blood-filled split trench were two machine guns, two rifles, submachine guns, automatic pistol, several thousand rounds of ammunition for each and two boxes of grenades.

Battle Tempo Picks Up

The pickup in the tempo of the artillery, mortar and small-arms fire along our front this morning indicated that the boys were still on the move.

The route to the unit holding the sector along the front led down a mud-filled ditch strewn with broken branches, ammunition and ration boxes and pockmarked with holes from our own and enemy mortar and artillery shells. Directly in front of us in the crackle of small-arms fire indicated that the infantry following the tanks had engaged the enemy.

Our objective was a chateau some 100 yards to the right, where the Jerries had hung on for almost two weeks, but which now is in our hands.

Into Trench In Nick Of Time

Climbing a steep bank to the left, we rolled into a slit trench as a spray of machine-gun bullets clipped the branches over our heads. Sergt. Thomas R. Farr, of Morgantown, W. Va., looked around from his rifle pointed over the lines to remark that the spot was rather warm.

A look about showed that the area had been the scene of fighting for some time. Right behind the slit trenches was a stake marking an unexploded German 88 shell. Four or five dead calves under the splinters of an apple tree indicated that all the shots hadn't been duds.

Across the field in front of us lay the bodies of one or two Germans, evidently killed during yesterday's fighting.

Back To Hedgerows In A Hurry

With the hedgerows as protective cover, we reached the outer buildings of the chateau, but a quick check failed to disclose any of our troops. A mortar burst a short distance away and the rat-tat-tat of a machine gun from the direction of the buildings sent us back a couple of hedgerows in a hurry.

It wasn't too soon, for a 60-mm. shell burst where we had just been standing and a smoke grenade followed even closer as Private Earl J. Wilson, of Cumberland, Md., called from a foxhole asking us in. The invitation was a most welcome one.

Jerry Firing By Guess

It still seemed evident that Jerry was firing where he thought our troops were, rather than on direct observation, for the mortar bursts were not consistent. Instead, they covered a wide area in a rough pattern. Luckily we suffered no casualties from the burst but, nevertheless, it made most of us uncomfortable.

A few fields over was Sergt. Thomas A. Shorter, Jr., of La Plata, Md., who extended us an invitation to lunch. K rations, no matter how often one eats it, can be the best food in the world at times. This was one of those times.

Dinner Under Difficulties

Jerry interrupted the meal once or twice with mortar and artillery bursts which sent us diving into foxholes, but we managed to finish the meal, even to after-dinner coffee, without mishap. When we were through eating, Shorter pointed to a hedgerow and noted that one of the boys was hit there last night.

Armored vehicles were rolling along to the front and we headed in the other direction some few minutes later. We still had to keep on the alert and dive into a ditch the minute shells sounded close. A burned-out American jeep on its side emphasized that Jerry still was very active. A few yards farther on the presence of a signal siren crew indicated that the battle was moving forward.

Some Men Seen At Front

A few of the men seen along the front included: Sergt. David C. Nicholson, Hyattsville; First Sergeant Paul Johnson, Cumberland; Pfc. Paul Schisler, 1800 Frankfort avenue, Baltimore; Pfc. James H. Burch, Waldorf; Private Ray Bowman, Cumberland; Staff Sergeant William Nemec, 4423 Raspe avenue, Baltimore; Pfc. Charles W. Ketterman, Rockville; Staff Sergeant Ward R. Vaughn, Baltimore; Staff Sergeant Alfred W. Ballard, Hyattsville; Sergt. Walter S. Durbin, Cumberland; Staff Sergeant Charles W. Bury, Coleman Manor, Md.; Staff Sergeant Joseph Polt, Valley George, Pa., and Pfc. Kermit Quensberry, Hillsville, Va.

THE EVENING SUN, MONDAY, JULY 3, 1944

Bradley Travels Hedgerow Route To 29th Division Front Near St. Lo

By Holbrook Bradley [Sunpapers War Correspondent]

With the 29th Division in Normandy, July 1 [By Radio] — Elements this morning are dug in along a stabilized front established yesterday after spearheading tanks pushed the Germans back along the slopes leading to St. Lo. There has been little action reported today.

Handicapped by hilly ground, broken up by dividing hedgerows, both armor and infantry found the advance to new positions slow. Adding further to the difficulties, the enemy sent over a heavy barrage of artillery and heavy mortars during the operation.

Late last night, however, advance platoons had moved into the area held by the tanks to take over the job of maintaining the positions. Forward movement, although in the face of mortar and small-arms fire, was made with few casualties. As usually seems the case, in this fighting there were few German dead about.

Evidence Of Jerry's Fire

Our main supply route to the sector of the Allied front on which we are fighting showed evidence of Jerry's fire when we drove along it last night to get first-hand pictures of the progress of the battle.

As we approached a sign warning that the road ahead was for combat vehicles only, Lieut. Tucker Irvin, of Washington, Ga., public relations officer, suggested parking our rather cumbersome command car under an apple tree and walking forward along the protecting ditches. A blasted jeep a few hundred yards further on made the suggestion seem even more reasonable.

The persistent rattle of machine-gun and mortar bursts ahead indicated that the action was far from calmed down as we climbed across hedgerow barriers, stopping to check the progress of the battle with infantrymen dug in behind each one.

Warned of SS Troops

A hundred yards down the road, a captain in an armored outfit warned us of a report that German mobile SS troops were attempting to cut into our rear and suggested we keep our eyes peeled. We thanked him, then dove over the next hedgerow to push on.

Apparently past the forward units we had been in contact with, we found ourselves crawling across a grainfield in the direction of a chateau which we knew a few days before had been a German strongpoint. As we hesitated momentarily, wondering about the advisability of going farther, a Yank with a rifle slung across his back walked unconcernedly around the corner of a building. We picked ourselves up and walked the rest of the way.

Everywhere about the building area was the evidence of the accuracy of our artillery fire. German strongpoints, trenches, shelters and gun positions that evidently had been prepared with the intent of a long stand, had received direct hits from 105 or 155-mm. shells. Buildings reinforced as headquarters, observation posts and defensive areas now were but piles of rubble and masonry.

Direct To Front

In a grove of heavy pine trees at one side of the chateau we found Lieut. Cameron Books, of Hamilton, Ohio, and his platoon digging in against a possible enemy counterattack. When we asked the direction of the front, Brooks said he had to make reconnaissance there and would lead us up.

A hilltop ahead, which had been under artillery fire for the better part of two weeks and the scene of heavy tank action for the past two days, presented a desolate picture. Tall pine trees and cedars, once part of the formal landscaping of the estate, were splintered and broken off, in some cases just at the ground. The field itself was chewed and churned up with tank tracks, pockmarked with shell holes. About the area was the smell of burned wood, acrid powder smoke, the sour smell of decaying animals.

A hundred yards or so in front of us out in "no man's land," a burning tank was outlined against the sky. A column of black smoke and flame soared upward, sounds of exploding bullets and shells came from the raging inferno inside.

GIs Digging In

All along the near side of the hedgerows, GIs were digging, scraping slit trenches in the soft earth as a measure of protection against the expected enemy artillery-and-mortar attack. To one side of us a dead Yank lay sprawled grotesquely on his back, and a mortar tripod lay where it had fallen at his feet. Someone, evidently a buddy, had pulled his helmet down over his face.

For a few moments we stood with the most advanced element of our force, talking over the situation. Down the road running parallel with the front we could see a few bombed and broken buildings, a civilian car almost entirely demolished in the road where it had been hit. The thud of mortar shells in front of and behind us showed that Jerry was still busy.

The only safe route on our left was across the main road, still reported under fire, thence up a long series of hedgerows to another section of our front. Following the lead of Lieutenant Irvin, the rest of us ran across the road, then dove into a ditch opposite, to come face to face with a Jerry, dead a week. We moved on in a hurry.

Fallen Trees Bring Halt

According to our map, the route turned left at the next intersection so we followed up a steep defile heading in the general direction we wanted to go. A few yards up a series of fallen trees caused us to halt momentarily for they looked like typical Jerry ambush installations. But after gathering ourselves together we went over the first one and from then on it was easy. All along the trench there were signs that the Germans had pulled out only a few hours before, for all about were crusts of bread, half empty bottles of wine. The meal in one mess-kit was still warm.

The nearer we got to the front, the more wary we became. Overhead we could hear the whine of our own artillery, seemingly very low. On both sides of us were the cracks of rifles and machine-gun fire. Then we broke into a clearing and found ourselves in a group of small clay-roofed stucco farm buildings. The biggest relief of our lives as we peered cautiously from cover was to see two GIs digging in.

They turned out to be Private William B. Ross, of Santa Monica, Cal., and Private Edward Popp, of Elgin, Ill. A sudden burst of shrapnel about us sent all of us diving underground, where the two doughboys were assured they didn't have to come from Maryland to get their names in the paper.

Maryland Directs Them

When the artillery let up momentarily we climbed out of the slit trenches, cut across fields to our left. Along the way we found Technical Sergt. William R. Turner, of Centreville, who told us the way back to the command post. He also gave us a warning to watch for snipers in the late twilight period. A few moments later we were at the headquarters of Lieut. Col. Arthur T. Sheppe, of Staunton, Va., who was digging in in forward positions with the rest of his men.

Among the few men seen about the area were Staff Sergeant Lester Lease, of Cumberland; Pfc. Kenneth Thorne, of Hagerstown; Pfc. Robert B. Fawley, of Poolesville; Pfc. Seth H. Charles, of Clear Spring; Pfc. August L. Brogley, of Greensboro, Md; Sergeant Paul Chaney, of Avilton, Md; Private Joseph C. Zeigler, of Lancaster, Pa.; Capt. G. B. Hankins, of 21 North Wickham road, Baltimore; Capt. Jacob L. Jones, of Cambridge; Lieut. William E. Dryden, of Crisfield; Capt. John J. Whittington, of Exmore, Va.; Private Frederick T. Whitley, of Easton; Capt. Maurice A. Tawes, of Crisfield; Pfc. Walter M. Butler, of Pocomoke City; Staff Sergeant Jesse Packard, of Princess Anne; Capt. William D. McMillian, of 12 East 33d street, Baltimore; Pfc. Gerald Biehl and Sergt. Charles Dronenburg, both of Frederick.

THE BALTIMORE SUN, TUESDAY, JULY 4, 1944

Jerry Disguised In Joe's Uniform

By Holbrook Bradley [Sunpapers War Correspondent]

With the 29th Division, Normandy, July 3 [By Radio] — American patrols on a routine mission today reported actively engaging a group of the enemy wearing parts of United States uniforms and armed with our weapons.

Sent to investigate the group reported as digging in an area about to be subjected to fire from one of our batteries, troops commanded by Major Thomas S. Dallas, of Martinsville, Va., flashed back the word that the soldiers were an unidentified unit. Check with other outfits in this area indicated that none had such a patrol out.

As the American patrol closed in to make sure of the situation, men wearing GI helmets and field jackets over their German uniforms opened fire with M-3 Tommy guns. The Americans reported back to their battalion headquarters and brought mortar shells down on the area.

THE BALTIMORE SUN, SATURDAY, JULY 8, 1944

Action on 29th's front described

Bradley Tells Of Visit To Edge Of No-Man's Land

By Holbrook Bradley [Sunpapers War Correspondent]

With the 29th Division in Normandy, July 6 [By Radio — Delayed] — Chattering machine-gun fire and the sharp crack of rifles and other small-arms from the direction of our lines this morning indicated more than normal activity in a sector where artillery recently has been taking over the show.

Infantry outfits have been active, even during lulls, with the far from easy job of holding their sections of the Allied line. Day and night, patrols find a few hot moments when they contact the enemy and outposts scattered along the front may brush with Germans on occasion, but the main chore has been one of watching and waiting for the next push.

Officers on duty in our section today pointed out an area where sporadic firing had broken out, and suggested the most favorable route to reach the battalion engaged.

Increased Resistance

Early reports from the front told only of increased enemy resistance in one sector, but gave very little detail as to what either side was attempting to accomplish.

Dust swirled up behind our jeep as we rolled down the main road, which a week or ten days ago had been a supply route for German units at the front. As an indication of our rapid progress in installing ourselves in the area, signalmen already were setting up heavy-duty telephone poles and stringing wire.

A mile and a half down the road we met a truck hauling a smashed jeep toward a rear salvage depot. A house on the corner of a road into which we turned was now merely a battered shell, the result of earlier bombardments in which our gunners had given Jerry a going-over.

Battles Sounds Increased

The sounds of battle increased as we skidded down the road, along which torn German uniforms, gas masks and other pieces of equipment lay as a sign of hasty retreat.

Amid apple trees in a field on our right we could see a few dead cows lying on their sides. A few seconds later we could smell the sickening odor of decaying flesh which all of us know only too well now.

Vehicle tracks across a field ahead showed the way to the command post we were seeking. As our jeep approached a break in a hedgerow, a guard warned us to park under cover of apple trees, for signs of movement any farther ahead were liable to bring down Jerry mortar fire. A sharp burst to our right emphasized this fact, and we were quick to dismount.

GI's Take It Easy

Men wearing OD's or with shirts stripped off sat beside slit trenches dug along hedgerows as we walked up through the apple orchard under a bright July sun. It was a welcome change from the showers of the last few weeks. The clear, hot weather gave the men a chance to air their blankets and get themselves and their equipment cleaned up.

A few who were off duty lay on the ground asleep, while our own and enemy artillery and mortar fire tore through the skies above to burst ahead or behind us.

Major Maurice G. Clift, of Cambridge, Md., battalion commander, and a group of his officers sat about a well-constructed command-post foxhole, dug in against a hedgerow a few hundred yards farther on.

Artillery Checked

Phone in hand, the commander checked with an artillery unit in the rear on the results of a recent firing mission. To our question about the activity he noted that little was doing in his battalion area at the moment.

At a company command post 50 yards over on the right flank there was some indication of artillery fire during the night before. First Sergeant Albert H. Ruth, of Elk Mills, Md., pointed to a crater beside his dugout and remarked that a Nazi 88 had landed a shell there during the night.

Pieces of a raincoat and of a rifle scattered through the trees near by told the story of a hit. Luckily, Sergeant Ruth was well down in his foxhole and escaped injury.

Another Unit Visited

After chatting a few minutes with Maryland men in the company we headed for the command post of another unit a couple of fields farther on. A platoon leader, Lieut. Brayton Canner, of Ipava, Ill., offered to show us his forward command post.

Rifle and other fire had quieted down as we pushed out through the fields waist high with grain, but artillery and mortars were still very active. Resounding explosions to the right of us came from Jerry gunners located in a tile-roofed farmhouse we could pick up through our glasses.

The sudden chattering of machine guns from a strafing Allied plane broke the comparative stillness as we watched. The route to the command post led by a series of scattered defense positions along hedgerows.

Hesitated A Moment

Once we hesitated a moment before crossing a narrow dirt road which was in our hands but was still subject to occasional artillery fire. Then we broke into another apple orchard along the side of which our men had dug in.

About the fields on either side of us were traces of some sort of construction work in which Jerry had been engaged when we pushed him out. Concrete foundations, earthen entrenchments and piles of prefabricated buildings lay about, signs of what evidently was to be a permanent military area.

The lieutenant guiding us motioned us to keep low and move fast as we crossed the opening of a hedge ahead. Across 100 yards or so of grain was another hedgerow, then a group of tall trees under which some Germans were busy digging in at that moment.

Forward Positions Reached

Keeping a good distance between us, as a precaution against sniper or mortar fire, we hurtled over the break in the hedge to land amid a shower of dirt in a protecting roadway beyond. This was our most forward position.

Fallen trees to our right marked the end of the line beyond which was Jerryland. Outpost guards along the south side of the road motioned to a gap in the hedge through which we could see the enemy lines clearly.

We were assured that if we watched long enough we would see Germans moving about, but we took the guards' word for that. A few dead Germans lying about in green shafts of grain were mute evidence of what happens when Jerry gets careless.

Artillery Post Visited

At Lieutenant Canner's suggestion, we moved on along the line to visit an artillery command post. A series of broken hedgerows and open fields leading to the enemy lines forced us to keep low and move fast. German snipers with high-powered rifles and telescope sights make any other movement inadvisable.

We were almost at the command post when we noticed the same sour odor we had run into on our way into the area. In the next moment we learned why. A dead German lieutenant — he was killed during an attack a week earlier — lay 25 or 30 yards out in no-man's land in the hot sun. There had been no chance to bury him.

The command post lay along a hedgerow ahead of us, covered with planks and piled high with dirt. Inside, Lieut. Roberti Herwitz, of Hollywood; Private James E. Vogan, of Oil City, Pa., and Corporal Charles R. Farver, of Westminster, Md., were about to start their lunch — K ration. We were asked in for a cup of lemonade, crackers and jam.

Little Action In Section

Although the rifle fire on our left was still going on as heavily as before, we were told that there had been little action in this sector since an artillery barrage the night before. Observers cautioned us, however, to talk low or Jerry would hear everything we said — at least our men had been able to hear the enemy all morning.

As everywhere along the line, the boys here do very little complaining. By now they are used to wearing the same clothes day in and day out, for weeks on end.

Seen Along The Front

Seen along the front today were the following Baltimoreans: Capt. George M. Nevius, Lieut. Dean C. Magalis, Staff Sergeant

Albert T. Simmons, Jr., Sergt. Joseph Lenoch, Sergt. Frank Grady, Sergt. Francis E. Kinlein, Pfc. Sidney Suskin, Lieut. Samuel Press, Technical Sergeant Charles Randle, Sergt. Paul H. Pierson, Sergt. John J. McKenna and Technical Sergeant William J. Dircks.

THE BALTIMORE SUN, MONDAY, JULY 10, 1944

Bradley Finds No Man's Land Unpleasant Place

By Holbrook Bradley [Sunpapers War Correspondent]

With American Forces in Normandy, July 8 [By Cable — Delayed] — No man's land is not a pleasant place to be, especially after dark.

We found this out last night while on patrol duty behind the enemy lines.

The first word concerning the night's mission came at noon yesterday when Lieut. Paul Clapper, of Cumberland, Md., said that he and his men were heading out on a reconnaissance patrol and suggested that this might be a good time for us to come along.

Gives Review Of Mission

Our assembly point was to be a near-by barn, which was located close to another company headquarters. Other members of the patrol, Corporal Kenneth Jordan, of Tenafly, N. J., and Pfc. Adan Baron, of Plains, Pa., already were making last-minute inspections of their automatic weapons when we arrived at 8 P. M. to get our instructions.

Lieutenant Clapper picked up a machine pistol and a few hand grenades and passed them out to the two enlisted men and then told us to follow him over to headquarters photo-interpretation office for a briefing.

As the four of us gathered around a group of aerial photographs of the area we were to cover, Lieut. Joe Sweeney gave a brief review of the mission. At 11.30 we were to leave the forwardmost outpost of one of our rifle companies, cut across a series of apple orchards and grain fields until we reached a point 400 or 500 yards inside the Jerry lines. Here we were to make a reconnaissance movement along a road the Germans were thought to be using to bring up supplies.

Terrain Studied

Our route, which had been marked on a map with black crayon, was roughly oval shaped and designed to bring us back to our own lines at the point at which we left them.

We were told that we should be back by 4 in the morning, but guards would wait at the outpost until 6 A. M., in case any of us got separated from the others.

Through powerful magnifying glasses each of us studied the terrain, checking hedgerows, characteristics of the fields, locations of the buildings and signs of enemy movement. The officer who was instructing us warned against any talking once we left our own lines, suggested that we avoid following hedgerows whenever possible, since Jerry likes to shoot along them whenever he hears a noise he can't immediately identify, and cautioned us to freeze in position if any signs of our approach were detected by the enemy.

Still Daylight

We were impressed with the fact that taking our time was most important.

Two jeeps waited outside headquarters to carry us as far forward as possible when we started on shortly after 9 o'clock. It was still daylight, and the absence of any clouds indicated the night would be a bright one — not too good for us; but at least it wasn't raining, as often is the case on such jobs.

Jerry gunners were sending in a few rounds of mortar when we arrived at the area of the forward battalion from which we would take our departure. A rather rough greeting sent us diving for foxholes momentarily, then the lull allowed us to push on. As we filed down the narrow gully leading forward, men were busy digging in along the banks for the terrain was still under artillery fire.

Blacken Faces, Hands

Our route led to a crossroad, then down through a group of farm buildings and on into an orchard, where a company outpost was set up.

Here Clapper checked with the company sergeant to make sure our map was correctly oriented and find out the latest information of enemy movement or activity in the area. Overhead artillery shells from both sides hurdled through the skies to land with echoing explosions at our forward or rear.

We still could see our watches at 10.30 as we made final preparations for moving out. Using a piece of burnt cork we blackened our faces and hands, then discarded our helmets, put on woolen caps and turned our field jackets inside out to avoid a glare in case the enemy threw up a flare.

Signals Agreed On

Earlier all of us had emptied our pockets of everything but identification cards in the event we were picked up.

The hands of our watches were synchronized at 11.25 when Paul came along the line with final instructions. He and Baron would go first, Jordan last, with a five-yard interval between each man.

The signal for move ahead or stop would be two short raps on the rifle or palm of the hand. There was to be no firing unless we were surrounded and we would return immediately no matter where we were if a prisoner were taken. Then we were off.

There was still a good deal of light ahead of us to the west as we crossed the 50 yards of field crouching low. We knew that was a good thing, for anyone in our path would be silhouetted against a skyline while we would benefit with concealment against the dark background. One thing all of us noticed was the single star low on the horizon in the direction for which we were bound.

Evidences Of Jerry

Paul and the man following dropped to the ground in midfield, stopped to listen five or ten minutes, then began a slow crawl forward on their bellies. We followed close, watching for a twig or branch in our way that might break and give away our movement. The only sound was an occasional burst of artillery shell some distance away and the noises of the birds in a near-by tree.

A hundred yards or so on we reached an open gate leading into another field, paused another five or ten minutes to listen, then crouched low and passed through. As we crept along the edge of the field we saw evidence that Jerry had dug in a short time before for slit trenches and the dugouts still had pieces of equipment and clothing around.

Tense Moments

A few tense moments came when a machine pistol suddenly chattered 100 yards or so to the left of us, but evidently after someone else for no whine of bullets came over our head. Then as the moon started coming up behind us we started inching our way across the field. We knew we were inside Jerry land and the ground never had felt so good.

It was shortly after midnight when we slid down a ditch along the far side of the field, 300 or 400 yards from our starting point. Now came the job of finding our way through the thick hedgerow in front of us. Paul motioned us down while he made reconnaissance and then disappeared into the heavy undergrowth to the right.

Seems An Eternity

We lay hugging the ground for what seemed eternity; actually it was only 20 minutes. Suddenly the sound of a Heinie sentry moving along the road edge next to the field froze us to the spots wherein we lay. A few moments later Paul came back through the thicket and landed at our side with: "Did you hear that?" We moved back down the hedgerow to try another way through.

The artillery thundered all about us as we finally made our way through the break in the hedgerow then started down the grassy slope on our bellies toward the road that was our objective. To the left sat a farmhouse, one of several we had been warned to avoid.

Midway in the field Clapper came back along the line, told us we were too far north, that we would have to retrace our steps and follow along the hedgerow over which we had just come.

Shot Rings Out

As we turned we could hear the sounds of a German horse and wagon, probably a supply vehicle, passing along the road ahead of us. Fifty yards or so along the row we stopped to get our bearing, suddenly noticed the last man was not up with us.

When he caught up again we found the man ahead had evidently lost contact with Clapper for he was no longer in sight.

Suddenly a shot rang out from the direction of the farmhouse. A bullet whistled through the trees overhead, we all froze again where we were. As we watched the farm building only 50 yards away, suddenly we saw a flame flare up, coming evidently from a Jerry seeking to draw our fire for a few seconds and then die down.

Watching, Waiting

Then came the game of watching and waiting for what was to follow. There was no further movement or sound from the direction of the barn but noise on the other side of the fence separating us from the next field gave us a few tense moments until we saw a cow poking about.

We had hit the dirt at about 1.10 and at 2.15 we were still frozen at the same spot waiting for Clapper.

Once a few shots in the field to our left made us wonder if Paul was in trouble, whether Jerry was shooting at random or whether another patrol had run into the Germans. The only other sound was when another horse and wagon passed the road directly in front of us and occasional talking among the Germans somewhere off the left flank.

The artillery was still active all about us and a few Allied fighters flew low over our heads, spraying enemy positions with lead as they went. We failed to appreciate the ack-ack barrage Jerry sent up on these occasions.

Just as we were about to give up and head back we heard the sound of someone coming down the fence ahead of us. For a moment we wondered if it were a German patrol, then Paul Clapper flopped down beside us to report he had been to a few fields farther on and picked up more information about the movement along the road.

He too, had heard shots to the left and wondered if we were in trouble.

They Head Back

The moon had come up full behind us and looked larger and brighter than we had ever seen it as we headed back through the hedgerow and across the field.

This time Jerry had the advantage for we would show up directly against the skyline if we stood up. For some reason crossing the field on our bellies seemed a lot longer than when we came in, perhaps because it was slightly uphill. We reached the side across from our outpost just as another mortar barrage started landing in the area and hit the ground to wait until it was over.

Frightened Afterward

The luminous dials of our watches pointed well after 3 o'clock when we finally inched our way within hailing distance of the company outpost. Paul stood up and started walking when we were challenged by our own sentries who let us come in after an exchange of the password.

It wasn't until we had got well inside our own lines that any of us really felt scared. Then we all swore that was one job anyone else could have gladly.

THE EVENING SUN, TUESDAY, JULY 11, 1944

Normandy Hedgerows And Muck No Place For Tank Battles

By Holbrook Bradley [Sunpapers War Correspondent]

With the United States Forces on the Normandy Front, July 10 [By Cable — Delayed] — Our artillery has swung into action again tonight after a relatively inactive day marked otherwise along this sector line by exchanges of mortar fire and an occasional harassing by enemy snipers.

To our right we still can hear the thundering echo of batteries backing up other elements of the army pushing against the enemy along the Vire river. We learned this morning of the mauling they handed the Reich Panzer division which had swung in south and west in an attempt to stem the tide of battle.

No Place For Tank Fights

Although armored vehicles have been assigned to us in various stages in the drive inland from the beachhead, we have not yet engaged in anything that can be called a tank battle, for Germans as well as ourselves have found this section of Normandy far from suitable to mechanized warfare.

Several times during the progress of our push, forward elements of advancing infantry have been met by semi-armored enemy vehicles, a good many of which have been knocked out by bazooka anti-tank units. But in all instances these so-called tanks turned out to be a type of self-propelled gun, usually an 88 mounted on a light Czech armored car.

Hedgerows Hem In Fields

The principal reason for the absence of armor has been the continual hedgerows which hem all the small fields in this area. The only places these seem to be absent are in the scattered forests, which also present difficulties for operation of tanks, whether ours or our enemy's.

The same hedgerows which are a bane to tank crews now are affording a certain measure of protection against enemy fire, principally mortar, to infantrymen who are dug in this side of them along the front. Unless a mortar burst is very close to the soldier, the chief danger is from jagged pieces of metal, which knife through the air for a good many yards about. If a man has the protection of a hedgerow, added to the cover of his own slit trench, chances of his being hit by one of these fragments are considerably reduced.

Good Cover For Snipers, Too

But there are also difficulties attached to fighting among the rows. Jerry snipers, using high powered rifles, scope sights, find good concealment from which they can harass any of our men who show themselves even momentarily. By now most of us have learned never to take chances on walking in the open when we know snipers are about.

One thing about the French countryside we're fighting in that we all dislike most intensely is the mud following rain — and it's usually always raining. This mud is not like that at home or even in England. It has characteristics all its own, chiefly a gooey, sticky, consistency and a rather rank odor, making it far from a nice spot in which to live.

Drizzle Gums Up Travel

We waded through mud ankle high this afternoon on our way out to the battalion command post of one of our line regiments. A light drizzle, which had alternated occasionally with a heavy downpour throughout the day, still came down, making things even worse as a couple of us tripped down the straw-covered dirt steps to the dugout serving one section of headquarters.

Capts. William D. MacMillian, 12 East 28th street, artillery observer, and G. B. Hankins, 21 North Wickham road, sat at a rough table finishing their after-luncheon coffee as they talked over the general situation in their area. It was more comfortable than most dugouts; this one had a section of dirt left in it which forms a shelf for a bedding roll against one side, and there were a heavy timbered roof overhead and a couple of wooden boxes for chairs.

Had Quiet Night

There had been little activity during last night or today so far, with the exception of a few rounds of enemy mortar or artillery. Along forward platoons, men watching across no man's land took shots at Germans who showed themselves. Enemy snipers kept our men down behind our hedgerow.

We were just about to leave the dugout when a couple of dull explosions in the field ahead of us shook dirt down on our heads. Outside we saw clouds of smoke and dirt that indicated that Jerry was busy as usual with mortars. A few pieces of shell still hot lay smoking in a shallow hole 50 yards away, a spot where a mortar shell had landed.

Bumps Into Marylanders

One company's runners guided us across a trampled grain field, through a grove of broken and smashed trees, then up a dirt lane strewn with battle debris, as we went forward to a unit command post. From a deep slit trench, dug in against a protecting hedgerow, First-Sergeant Howard Jester, Centreville, called out that he and a few other Marylanders were still about, so we stopped for a few minutes' chat.

A few hundred yards to the left we found another Marylander, Pfc. James R. Byrd, Crisfield, who asked us to stop in his trench. As we talked, a sharp rifle crack zinged bullets overhead, showing that Jerry snipers were still on the alert. By now none of us had to be told to keep low.

THE EVENING SUN, WEDNESDAY, JULY 19, 1944

MARYLANDERS IN NORMANDY —
Two Maryland Men are mentioned in this dispatch.
In this dispatch Mr. Bradley tells how he rode in a tank which was one of the first to enter St. Lo and capture the city.

Riding In Attack Tank, Bradley Enters St. Lo With Doughboys

By Holbrook Bradley [Sunpapers War Correspondent]

With United States Forces on the Normandy Front, July 18 [Delayed] — We have taken St. Lo.

Hard-fighting American doughboys, spearheaded by armor and supported by artillery, tonight entered the battle-scarred Normandy town after a sudden drive from the east and north, penetrating the inner defenses and routing stubborn German infantry and artillery.

The first indication that the town was on the verge of capture came yesterday when one of our infantry battalions penetrated to the outskirts along the main Bayeux road. This morning the battalions were continuing the steady drive toward the inner city from the north and east in the face of continued resistance from the Infantry, increased activity from enemy artillery and self-propelled 88s.

General Meets with Aides

Early today the general commanding this outfit gathered with his aides to discuss sending a special supporting task force into St. Lo in accordance with plans formulated earlier in the week. As the map in the war room showed more than satisfactory progress in the battle for the town, units taking part in this combat raid were alerted, ordered to a rendezvous point.

With armor leading the force, a special combat group proceeded to a point north of St. Lo along the Lison road, then drove straight to the heart of the town in a swift jab. Tonight doughboys, tanks and supporting units continue mopping up the town that has been virtually leveled to the ground. The American flag and outfit's standard fly above the main square, placed there by the task force commander shortly after 6.30 this evening.

Plan Disclosed Saturday

The task force plan first came to light Saturday when the brigadier general and other members of the staff gathered to organize a swift-moving outfit which could deliver the final blow to capture the town that has been the center of battle for the past week. Leading components of this force, including the combat platoon, the infantry, the engineers, the tanks, the tank destroyers, the anti-tank, the civil affairs medical personnel, and others, were warned to be ready to move on three hours notice.

Shortly after noon today this alert was given, and units began assembling in the fields near the outfits' headquarters. As the hour approached, the force commander, Major Lloyd B. Marr, and the other ranking officers reported their units ready to move, stood by the final briefing.

"Always Be On Alert"

The commanders were told to assemble their vehicles in the order in which they would go into the town, and were warned in the event of a counterattack halfway through the town the mission would stand fast, consolidate positions. Artillery forward observers were told to bring fire on enemy positions which, undoubtedly, would zero in once our forces pushed through the outer perimeter.

Speaking in the shadow of a religious roadside shrine, under a brilliant July sky, the commanding brigadier general told the men:

"Plan on attacking immediately after the reconnaissance group takes up position. We expect to have some infantry in there but we don't expect to have to fight too hard. We must be ready for anything — don't let down one second, always be on your alert, on guard and do what you have to to carry out your mission."

Offered Ride In Tank

As the order was given to assemble for the attack, Private Howard T. Hill, Geary, Okla., tank commander of a medium armored vehicle, offered me a ride in with his assistant driver. It was taken up immediately.

Three other crew members included Private James Gavazzo, Buffalo, N.Y., gunner; Private Walter E. Hayfield, Princeton, Idaho, driver, and Private Edward Holler, Barberton, radio operator.

We had just time to adjust the headphone sets, set up a seat on ammunition boxes for the assistant driver, when the tank commander gave the order for us to pull out. We had a warning to keep a 100-yard interval from the next vehicle, our driver Hill remarked it would be a hellish job with the dust as heavy as it was, then we were off, lumbering over fields behind the reconnaissance force and a few armored vehicles.

Steady Cloud Of Dust

There was a steady cloud of whitish dust ahead as we rolled out on the side of the road, then headed over to the main Lison road. Our hatches were still unbuttoned, the tank commander with his head and shoulders movement was directing his vehicle.

Ahead was one of the most heavily shelled roads we had been along, burned-out German vehicles, shelled holes all about. Our quarters were already hot and cramped as Hill spoke over the interphone to give orders for us to button up. The last thing we saw was a sign in German telling of a steep grade to St. Lo 200 meters ahead. From then on we watched through periscopes.

Lumbering over the rough, torn road ahead, we felt almost apart from the rest of the war outside us. Through the periscope we saw medics alongside the road putting a wounded man on a stretcher; a few jeeps pulled up; one or two tanks were ahead of us.

No Sign Of Enemy Yet

It was 5.10 by our synchronized watches when we rolled up to the crowd of infantry crouched behind a few more jeeps on the side of the road. Sweat poured down our faces and into our eyes. As yet we had seen no sign of the enemy other than the occasional sounds of machine-gun bursts as we stopped to wait for the vehicles ahead to move on.

Then we were headed down the steep, winding hill that leads down into the town. Over radio sets we could hear the platoon commander calling us and the other tanks. Hill, our own commander, gave a few orders to Hayfield, who was having a hard time sticking to the road in all the smoke and dust.

The tank ahead suddenly stopped in its tracks, then swung its turret around over some sort of factory down to our left. We could barely see the few infantrymen and their officer crowded down in a ditch. There was a dull blast, a puff of smoke from the tank ahead and a shell burst outside the chateau.

Routing Out Heinies

By now we could see infantrymen all about us firing into the hills and building, evidently routing out Heinies. Hill shouted over the phone, "Here come three of the Germans," and we saw them running up toward us through the smoke waving white flags. A tough-looking infantryman, bayonet on the end of his gun, stood up to herd them to the rear.

Tank Commander Hill's voice came over the interphone system again: "Hayfield start a little ahead, we've got to move up." We were on again as another prisoner came through the smoke battle, a dazed expression on his face, hands clasped over his head.

The next moment we could hear heavy shell-bursting to our right and Hill said, "They are firing on us." Hayfield leaned over to the assistant driver's seat, noted we were stopped in a bad spot, with high ground on our left, and our right flank entirely exposed.

Hill swung the turret around in a complete circle to see if he could find an anti-tank gun.

Turn Periscopes On House

As we waited for it to land, we noticed a roadside sign, St. Lo. Evidently we were in the outskirts. Then came Hill's cry, "Hold the turret, I see something down there to our right, O. K., Gavazzo, put one in him."

We turned the periscopes in the direction of the house, then came the order to fire and the tank rocked almost as if it had been hit. "Good shooting, that one went right into the window — should hold him." We rolled on as smoke poured up from the red roof.

Our tank had turned into a hotbox as we lumbered up on the road, dust caked our hands, faces and clothing. Suddenly there was another burst near-by, smoke columned up from a spot 100 yards ahead of us.

"Artillery," Hill commented.

We moved on in through the dust, passing a few jeeps and tanks, evidently out of action beside the road.

Message Comes Over Radio

Over the radio came this message:

"At the other end of town. Can you get something in? It seems to come down Main street to my left. If I could get somebody up here to show me where to go, I could get down there."

Evidently our tank platoon commander was in town already.

There was a sudden burst of heavy machine-gun, artillery fire as we pushed on by another tank, a hail of bullets bouncing off our turret. A few seconds later a group of dusty infantrymen pushed on by us to flop in ditches on either side. Hill swung our turret around again, ordered the gunner to load when he gave the order to fire. The tank rocked violently again and brought the comment, "Okay, good enough," from the commander.

Then we rounded the last curve into St. Lo. Two more prisoners were coming from the buildings under the white flag as we ground over piles of rubble by infantrymen who stalked down ahead, looking right and left for snipers. We noticed that almost everything in sight had been blasted by artillery or tank fire.

Shells Landing Close

From the tank platoon commander inside the town came the order, "Four move into the square. We're in the town now — bring all our stuff in."

There was another blast behind us; we looked at each other, knowing Jerry was pouring it in.

"That shell landed 20 yards from us," came from Hill.

We were really sweating by now.

Our watches showed 6.55 as we rolled up to the main street.

Before turning directly ahead, we passed a group of buildings. We noticed they were gray stucco, top stories all missing. Along one side were a group of jeeps, and infantrymen hugged the buildings; at the corner stood the assistant commander and the group staff.

We could hear the sound of shells landing in the town ahead of us when the order came from the platoon commander ordering us to move on down Main street. The officer to one side of us stood looking at a map as we passed another tank and found ourselves the third vehicle in the column.

St. Lo Mostly Rubble

All about us was rubble that had been St. Lo. We could see a few buildings over two stories still standing about Main Square, twin church spires ahead, and the rest seemed leveled. Parked under the trees in the Main Square were three or four reconnaissance cars, a number of jeeps, and groups of infantrymen scattered about.

Our tank had ground to a halt just at the building line of the Square when there was a loud whine, bursting shells off to our right. We'd unbuttoned the tank, were wiping sweat from our faces and shaking dirt from our clothes when one or two landed in the Square. Hill, Hayfield and the assistant driver dropped the covers overhead in a hurry.

Down Main street, ahead, which was nothing but a pile of rubble, we could see a tank pushing through. Infantrymen following along suddenly hit the rubble at the intersection; the tank turned its turret to fire down the street. Then our gunner opened up with heavy machine guns to spray the buildings on our left.

Ordered To Move Up

The platoon commander's call came over again, ordered us to move up and support the infantry down the street. As our motors turned over, blast heat swept through the tank, dirt clouded up in front of us. We stopped at the intersection a moment, while Hill swung the turret, received a hail of white-hot machine-gun bullets which looked as if they'd come right on us but bounced off our heavy armor. Then we moved toward the cathedral and found ourselves heading down Main street.

Our tank drove into a cloud of dust through which it was impossible to see. From then on our driver guided the tank by compass. We all wondered when we'd bump into an anti-tank gun or enemy bazooka. All we got was a constant hail of machine-gun bullets, which were answered with blasts from our big gun and smaller machine-guns.

Infantrymen were climbing over rubble alongside of us when heavy enemy artillery started to land near by. We stopped on order from the commander. We could see the dirty, tough-looking soldiers looking the city over, ever watchful for snipers.

Stop For Breath Of Air

The next one came in closer and struck the road ahead of us, sending up columns of smoke, dirt and rubble, which fell back on our turret and forward gun deck. The infantry had hit shell holes and piles of rubble to get under cover. Then we were up at the church, almost out the other edge of town, as the platoon commander lumbered by us to take up his stand at another crossroad.

It was well past 9 when we unbuttoned to get a breath of air and drink of water. Shells from the high hills about the town were crashing into the rubble all about us, but Hill commented a Jerry couldn't get observation on us, so we didn't need to worry about more than a chance shot.

As we dusted dirt from our hair and clothes, a lull in the artillery gave me a good chance to leave the tank and get to the back outfits. The boys in the tank wished me luck and then buttoned up for the night. To the rear were a few more vehicles and infantrymen.

Building Still Burning

Enemy mortars landed in Main street as a group of three or four infantrymen clambered by over high piles of rubble. To right and left were still burning buildings, all about was the acrid smell of smoke, gunpowder and dust battle. Somewhere to the left a landing German shell sent up a huge column of black smoke, threw rubble skyward. Ahead, a few warned infantry-men ran by the intersection because Jerry snipers were busy a few hundred yards down.

Major Govers Johns, Jr., of Corpus Christi, commander of the first infantry battalion to enter the city, stood outside with a few officers, including Major Gordon Cauble, Atlanta; Major Asa B. Gardiner, Baltimore; Major Harold F. Donovan, also of Baltimore.

THE BALTIMORE SUN, TUESDAY, AUGUST 8, 1944

MARYLANDERS IN FRANCE —
Eighteen Marylanders are mentioned in the following dispatch by Holbrook Bradley from the Normandy front.

Heavy U. S. Artillery Barrage Precedes Drive Around Vire

By Holbrook Bradley [Sunpapers War Correspondent]

With the American Forces in Normandy, Aug. 7 [By Radio] — American infantrymen following along in the trail of spearheading tanks under cover of some of the heaviest artillery fire of this campaign reached a point about a mile from the important communications center of Vire tonight. They were astride the St. Sever-Calvados highway at this spot.

[An Associated Press dispatch reported that the Americans had captured Vire and were preparing for a push south from the city.]

Pushing steadily southward under continued German tank, artillery and infantry resistance, they have gained several miles of ground along this main rail and road link between Cherbourg and Paris. As darkness fell the drive was continuing with unabated fury.

Scores Captured

All along our sector there has been a steady pressure from tanks and supporting ground troops. Over highways pitted by earlier bombardments and down back-country lanes columns of men and vehicles of all descriptions are streaming toward the front, which rolls forward yard by yard, mile by mile as the hours pass.

German troops have tried repeatedly to make a determined stand, but have been forced back relentlessly. Scores of

Germans have been captured and marched or trucked back to the prison pen to stare in amazement at the ever-growing Allied strength.

A dust-covered MP waved us through Landelles and Coupigny today as we drove on to see how the action was going along the line.

Already French civilians in these villages are cleaning up debris left in the wake of war.

A few shops, cafes and other buildings were open. "Off-Limits" signs were posted, conspicuously warning GIs against entering certain areas except on official business.

Choked By Dust

Thick clouds of white dust choked and blinded us as we headed along the road. Blue skies and a bright August sun made it one of the hottest days any of us had known in France. Once or twice we saw Yanks bathing in streams or sunning themselves along the banks. We even found one bunch taking time out to try their luck at fishing.

Following the stream of traffic, we passed a long column of halftracks, and then six trucks loaded with troops and supplies. The closer we got to the zone of action the louder became the din of artillery fire. From all sides batteries were sending round after round into the enemy lines. As yet there was no sign of German retaliation.

Sound Of Battle Ahead

A halftrack carrying eight or nine German prisoners under guard passed us heading to the rear as we came in to Mesnil-Clinchamps.

To our right was a slightly damaged railway station with vine-covered archway leading under the tracks. Ahead of us was the sound of battle.

Major Albert G. Warfield, of the Earl Court Apartments, Baltimore, was busy on a phone located in a tent as we pulled into headquarters some distance farther along. He was getting the latest information on the disposition of the troops. Other officers were busy in other tents around us planning the next move. A few GIs were sunning themselves or catching a bit of sleep in the shade of the apple trees.

We learned that the battalion was pressing steadily on toward Vire, meeting some resistance from infantry and occasional bursts of mortar and artillery fire. The battle, however, was progressing on schedule.

An interesting phase of this battle was the increasing number of prisoners taken — something quite different from the entry into St. Lo, where only a few Germans surrendered.

Medical Vehicles Turn Off

One liaison officer was about to take off for a more advanced company, and there was a chance for us to see just how conditions were up there. Medical vehicles came down the road and turned off on a road running along the rail line. We noticed several dead Germans lying where they fell in a ditch a few feet off the highway, then a dead Yank covered with a blanket, waiting burial.

From a short distance on our right came the dat-dat-dat of a German machine pistol followed by the sharp blast of a machine gun. More vehicles and men were ahead of us as we rolled into a field dotted with burned-out enemy vehicles and dead.

Burned Out U. S. Tank

One of the spots where our boys caught hell lay a short distance away after we had crossed the railway bridge which showed only slight signs of damage.

A burned-out Sherman tank and a half dozen doughboys lying dead on the roadside were mute evidence of the tough fighting where we had been held up.

Then, as we headed up the dirt road, we were right in the front lines. Open fields marked by only a few hedgerows and occasional clumps of trees differed from the rough terrain about 15 miles back. Across the open space on our right we could see GIs digging in following the army routine of going underground whenever they stop.

Smoke Rises Suddenly

To our left in the direction of St. Martin-Tallevende, we could hear tanks firing into the enemy lines. As we watched them work, a column of black smoke suddenly rose alongside a church.

As a whine of incoming shells broke over the noises we hit the ditch ourselves. Three shells burst, one ahead, one 200 yards to the right and another on our left. The dirt, smoke and shrapnel looked familiar.

A group of dusty doughboys who were digging in along a hedgerow had been on the move for the last 10 days. Only occasional resistance and a fair amount of shell-fire from the Germans had necessitated an occasional letup for rest and reorganization. Then the tanks and the artillery would get to work and be on the move again.

In this relatively open country there has been none of the long periods of static action where troops have remained dug in for days at a time. Usually the advance has been during the day with slight rests after dark.

Seen about the front today were: Sergt. Miller Cassell, of Frederick; Sergt. Robert Bruchey, of 1714 Moreland avenue, Baltimore; Lieut. Col. Louis G. Smith, of 3508 Newland road, Baltimore; Lieut. Chester Bise, of Ridgley; Capt. George Paxson, of Thurmont; Sergt. Merl Riddlemoser, Sergt. Richard S. Minnick, Technician Jesse Scott, Private Roger Roberts, Technician Robert E. Bell, Private Arthur G. Zimmerman, all of Frederick.; Sergt. Otho Watson, of Pocomoke City; Technician Ralph W. Stauffer, of Walkersville; Capt. Eugene P. O'Grady, of Baltimore; Sergt. William T. Ryor, of Salisbury.; Private Joseph Wise, of Leonardtown; Sergt. Ned Lucas, of Rising Sun; Capt. Brooks Brown, of Washington, and Sergt. Philip Winborne, of Buckhorn, Va.

THE BALTIMORE SUN, WEDNESDAY, AUGUST 9, 1944

Mark S. Watson, Sunpapers military correspondent, in a radio dispatch, reported the manner in which Bradley was wounded, as follows:

Holbrook Bradley Wounded Slightly By Shell Fragment

Observed Proper Vigilance

He was apparently observing proper vigilance, but a cloud of dust raised by a passing vehicle attracted enemy attention, and several mortar shells were tossed into area where Bradley was passing.

He and his companion flattened out promptly, and when there was a pause, ran for better cover. Only when they stood again did Bradley mention that he had caught a steel fragment in his thigh. It did not reach the bone, and it disabled him so little that he walked to a dressing station for simple treatment.

He expects to be back with the troops in two or three days.

A WALL THAT FAILED — How thoroughly the Germans fortified the towns of Normandy against invasion is vividly portrayed by these photos just received from Sunpapers Correspondent Lee McCardell, now in Normandy. A Yank engineer uses drills on wall as civilians watch. AHO-230-BS

HARD WORK — The thick concrete of a fortification within the beachhead area offers stubborn resistance to Sergt. Ralph Wood, Rochester, N. Y., shown drilling holes for demolition charges. AHO-749-BS

McCardell Sees Normandy's Defenses Crumble

BEARING DOWN — Pfc. Don Spencer, Smyrna, N. C., member of an engineers unit, puts his weight behind a high-pressure pneumatic drill. AHO-774-BS

QUICK CLEANUP — Steam shovels like the one operated above by T/4 John Maione, N. Y., are facilitating debris clearance in Normandy. AHO-768-BS

ENGINEERS ON THE JOB — Compressor pick and shovels replace weapons in the hands of these Yank engineers. They are just finishing up the job of leveling a sturdy concrete barrier. AHO-753-BS

STAR OF INVASION is clearly visible on this steam shovel and army vehicles. This "shovel" is one of many being used throughout Normandy to remove wreckage of demolished Nazi fortifications. AHO-776-BS

Six days ago in Normandy

THE ENGINEERS TAKE CHARGE — American Engineers march into Montebourg to clear up the city streets after their doughboy and artillery buddies had chased the Germans out of the town. When the Germans refused to yield the city, Yank artillery blasted them out with a heavy bombardment wrecking the city. AHO-727-BS

SHATTERED CHURCH TOWER — The wrecked tower of the Church of St. Jacques in Montebourg shows the tough battle which the Germans waged to hold the Yanks off the Cherbourg peninsula. AHO-771-BS

With McCardell In Montebourg

The accompanying photographs were taken at the front by Mr. McCardell, Sunpapers War Correspondent, and were dispatched by air from Normandy in an envelope stamped "June 24, 1944, SHAEF — Field Press Censor," just six days ago.

A BATTLE SCARRED CHURCH — The interior of the Church of St. Jacques at Montebourg shows the signs of battle. German snipers and artillery observers used the church tower during the battle. AHO-780-BS

APPROACHING MONTEBOURG FROM SOUTH — American troops came into Montebourg along this road from the south to drive the Germans out of the city. Montebourg was one of the key points on a road to Cherbourg and the Germans put up a terrible battle to keep the Yanks from clearing the road to the north. AHO-767-BS

WINE FOR THE VICTORS — These young Frenchmen bring out bottles of wine to give to the Americans as they entered Montebourg. AHO-754-BS

FRENCH YOUNGSTERS ON TREASURE HUNT — Three small inhabitants of the city of Montebourg salvage a bit of loot from the wreckage in the form of a barometer, one of the kind where small figures either enter or leave the house as the weather changes. ABF-143-BS

ADDING ANOTHER SIGN — American engineers tack a mine warning under the road sign in German pointing the way to Cherbourg. AHO-779-BS

WHITE FLAG — Nazis surrender to Americans at Cherbourg. (Photo by Lee McCardell) AHO-724-BS

McCardell Along As The Old Man Leads Joes Of The 313th Into Cherbourg

YANKS BLAST PILLBOX — American anti-tank platoon works its gun at point-blank range as it reduces a German strong point in the fighting that led to the capture of the port of Cherbourg. AHO-720-BS

FIGHTING IN CHERBOURG STREETS — American doughboys of the 79th Division battle the Germans in the streets of Cherbourg as the Americans took the city after a battle all the way up the peninsula. As the tanks roll up the street to blast out Nazi strong points the GIs slip from house to house hunting stragglers. AHO-785-BS

ANTI-TANK GUNNERS BAG PRISONERS — In the final stages of the battle for Cherbourg, Germans were surrendering in great numbers to any Yank who would accept them. This anti-tank crew is taking charge of a group of Nazis, who have quit the fight. AHO-718-BS

SURRENDER AT PILLBOX — These German prisoners, with hands up, have quite the battle in the defense of Cherbourg and are emerging from their pillbox to give up to Yank doughboys lying in wait for them. The prisoner bag ran into the thousands. AHO-729-BS

NURSES' WASH DAY — Ropes strung between the tents in which they are living make clotheslines for Maryland nurses with invaders. AHO-766-BS

GOING TO THE WELL — Lieut. Alice (Fuzzy) Beecher, of Chevy Chase, a 1942 graduate of Johns Hopkins School for Nurses, draws water for her patients. AHO-789-BS

HELMET AS TUB — The smiling girl who is washing her hose in GI headgear is Lieut. Mary E. Andrew, of Federalsburg, who trained at Easton. AHO-787-BS

Marylanders in Normandy

Pictures on this page of Baltimoreans, men and women, and others from Maryland who are members of the American force pressing the Germans back in France, were sent by Lee McCardell, Sunpapers War Correspondent, who has observed some of the bitterest fighting on the Cherbourg peninsula. Some of the pictures were made by McCardell; the remainder he obtained from other photographers near the front.

AT FIELD HOSPITAL — Lieut. Virginia Lee Towers, Easton, and Lieut. Grace R. Boggs, of Baltimore, nurses. AHO-791-BS

WITH A FOXHOLE HANDY — Worse thing about war, reflects Corporal Alexander Iner, whose family lives at 1123 Haubert street, Baltimore, is the getting up at dawn. AHO-721-BS

HIDING IT FROM JERRY — Wallace L. Cannon, of Cambridge, an artillery truck driver, adjusts the camouflage net over one of the guns of his battery, which has just moved. AHO-784-BS

KITCHEN CLOSE TO FRONT — Mess Sergeant Robert Staiger, 1099 Virginia avenue, Hagerstown (he's with an infantry unit in Normandy), directs the erection of a field kitchen in a bivouac area near where the fighting is in progress. AHO-783-BS

STUDYING A NEW ARTILLERY TARGET — Artillerymen shown are, left to right, Leslie Hook, of Middle River; Richard M. Brown, of Catonsville and Major David C. McNeely, formerly of 5604 Bland avenue, Baltimore, who is battalion staff officer. AHO-758-BS

ANOTHER PRISONER — A German surrenders to two Americans, names not given but probably Marylanders. Captive keeps his hand high. AHO-742-BS

AT ARTILLERY COMMAND POST — Leonard Depser, of Baltimore, telephones a message from a shallow trench. He is a radio operator. Often in fighting in France artillery has been up with the forward infantry units. AHO-782-BS

GETTING READY TO FIRE — The cannoneers who are preparing the shell with its powder charge are, left to right, Private Pershing Holmes, of Lonaconing, Md., and Private John E. Carlisle, of Calhoun Falls, S. C. AHO-781-BS

Marylanders in Normandy

RADIOMAN — Corporal Bill Herrick, of Arbutus, Md., is a radio operator and driver of a radio car with a signal company. AHO-769-BS

ON THE CHERBOURG ROAD — While accompanying men of the 79th Division in the assault on Cherbourg, Sunpapers Correspondent, Lee McCardell encountered many Marylanders and snapped these photos in battle's interim. Above, a Hagerstown man, Sergt. Charles Jones (extreme right), tank commander, rests with his crew somewhere on the Cherbourg peninsula. AHO-762-BS

ATTACK MEN — T/5 Daniel Shattls, of Baltimore (right), and Private Bob Jameson, of Washington, watch for enemy aircraft. AHO-775-BS

MEDICAL TEAM — Among men of the Medical Corps winning high praise for their work in Normandy are Private Charles McMahan, of Detroit (left), and Private Charles Kinker, Baltimorean, whose residence is 2807 Frederick avenue. They are shown with litter used to carry wounded. AHO-788-BS

TWO OFFICERS AND A MAP — A battle map held the attention of Major John A. McConnell, of Fayetteville, Ark. (left), and Lieut. Col. Edwin M. VanBibber, of Bel Air, Md., when this photo was snapped in Normandy's brilliant sunshine. The men wear familiar battle jackets and netted helmets. The Cross of Lorraine shoulder patch of the 79th Division is visible on VanBibber's jacket. AHO-759-BS

CITY COLLEGE BOY with the 79th Division is Pfc. Harry Wilkins, of 3239 Lawnview avenue (left). He is showing a City College class ring just received from home to one of his army comrades. AHO-744-BS

YANK TANKS GO INTO BATTLE — One has been set afire; other creeps up behind cover for shot at Nazis. Photo by Lee McCardell, Sunpapers war correspondent, who has been often at front. AHO-765-BS

Grim contest in Normandy

COMMANDER — Major General Ira T. Wyche, commanding the 79th Division, studies a map. His unit has been prominent in the fighting. AHO-745-BS (Photo by Lee McCardell)

BRITISH HEAVY GUNS IN ACTION — Southwest of Tilly-sur-Soules men of British Royal Artillery work a 155-mm. gun, which stirs up dust as it fires. (British Information Services)

MOVING FORWARD — Seventy-Ninth Division infantrymen, with the marks of battle strain and fatigue on their faces, hike up a lane in Normandy for another go at the enemy. Note the hedges. AHO-716-BS (Photo by Lee McCardell)

AMONG FIRST PILOTS IN NORMANDY — Capt. Richard E. Leary, of Annapolis, was one of the first flyers of the Ninth Air Force to land in Normandy after the Air Corps established bases there. He is a graduate of Naval Academy. AHO-737-BS (Photo by Lee McCardell)

SET AFIRE BY GERMAN SHELL — An American ammunition truck burning not far behind the front line. AHO-732-BS (Photo by Lee McCardell)

POSTMASTER GETS READY FOR BUSINESS — Victor Wingate, a Marylander, who is attached to an army postal unit with Ninth Air Force, opens his field desk at a new location in Normandy. AHO-790-BS (Photo by Lee McCardell)

AID STATION OF THE 79TH DIVISION — The French farmhouse to which wounded of the 79th were brought on stretchers from the front at one stage of the fighting is shown in the picture above and the one at the right. AHO-735-BS (Photo by Lee McCardell)

DEBACLE AT ST. DENIS — A McCARDELL PHOTO — When American armor, operating in its first major test of war in France, touched off the recent Normandy break-though, Sunpapers Correspondent Lee McCardell obtained a remarkable pictorial record of the destruction of Nazi equipment at the town of St. Denis-le-Gast. In the above photo, shattered Nazi armor jams a road for a distance of a mile. AHO-719-BS

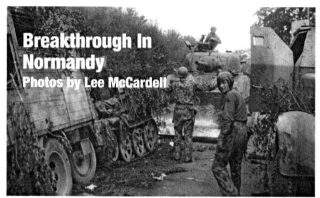

Breakthrough In Normandy
Photos by Lee McCardell

UNSTOPPABLE YANKS — Fleeing Germans left a burned-out armored car loaded with all manner of scrap on the St. Denis-le-Gast road, but it proved to be a poor road block when an American tankdozer came along clearing the way for the Yanks. AHO-736-BS

CLEARING THE TRACK FOR THE TANKS — American tankmen using tanks equipped with bulldozer blades shove wrecked German armor from St. Denis-le-Gast road so that they can effect their break-through and give the Germans a taste of Blitzkrieg. AHO-725-BS

A GIANT SUBDUED — This photo of a disabled Nazi tank was snapped by McCardell in the main street of St. Denis. The doughboy and French natives shared booty of the vanished crew. AHO-733-BS

RUMMAGE DAY — What Nazis left behind in their wild flight before the killing fire of Yank tanks and planes soon became the property of the French. These women of the town rummage among German equipment for articles of value. AHO-730-BS

CLOSE TEAMWORK — Operations of Ninth Air Force fighter-bombers supporting the tank attack was monitored by radio from jeeps at Second Armored Division headquarters. Here is the air force support party at work with radio and maps. AHO-734-BS

BATTLE BY-PRODUCTS — French refugees who fled the violence of battle at St. Denis trundled bicycles past wrecked Nazi armor as they made their way back home. The German tanks and other vehicles were smashed by American tanks and fighter planes firing rocket guns. AHO-786-BS

JULY 29 AND TODAY —
Map above shows American line in Normandy during the initial stages of the break-through when our armor captured St. Denis-le-Gast. It was here, almost precisely at the point of the break-through that Lee McCardell took the pictures on this page and the one on page 76. Map on above right shows the consequences of that break-through, with the American armored forces today overrunning Brittany and sweeping east beyond Le Mans toward Paris.

WARTIME SIGHT-SEERS — Twisted masses of once deadly German machines of war provided fascinating pastime for French civilians, photographed as they rummaged among wreckage. AHO-763-BS

THE YANKS KEEP DRIVING — The break-through at St. Denis-le-Gast, where American tankers roll on through the town past disabled German armor and a dead German (left foreground). The Yanks are headed southward chasing the forces of Field Marshal Erwin Rommel at the beginning of the offensive. AHO-717-BS

THE BALTIMORE SUN, AUGUST 13, 1944

WASH DAY IN FRANCE — American doughboys and Frenchwomen join in a washday offensive at the town pond in the square of a village now occupied by the invading Allied armies. A chance to put out a washing is one of the luxuries of warfare. Picture by Lee McCardell, Sunpapers War Correspondent. AGP-234-BS

THE BALTIMORE SUN, AUGUST 27, 1944

BREAKTHROUGH IN NORMANDY PHOTOGRAPH BY LEE McCARDELL — This exceptional picture of blasted German armor littering a country road was made at St. Denis-le-Gast by the Sunpaper's War Correspondent. It is impressive evidence of the firepower of United States tanks and artillery and the effectiveness of Allied rocket firing aircraft. In the center of the road is the ever present jeep. Photo by Lee McCardell AHO-741-BS

CHAPTER 4

BREAKOUT TO BRITTANY

THE EVENING SUN, FRIDAY, SEPTEMBER 1, 1944

This is the first dispatch to be received from Mr. Bradley since we was wounded in France August 8 by a fragment from a mortar shell. His dispatch mentions 19 Maryland men.

Bradley Finds Battle For Brest Unlike Fighting In Normandy

By Holbrook Bradley

With the United States Forces in Brittany, Aug. 28 — Allied dive bombers operating in support of the American ground troops closing in on Brest tonight are keeping up a steady attack against Nazi fortifications and naval installations as the forward elements of our infantry push on to a little more than two miles from the important French seaport.

From the PRO (Public Relations Office) tent, set up at the outfits headquarters north of the city, we can hear the steady drone of wave after wave of planes coming over, then a high-pitched whine interrupted by the bark of German ack-ack as the bombers head for the target areas and wheel off for another round.

Shooting On All Sides

The hills on all sides of us echo the continuous drone of artillery as our medium and heavy guns send barrage after barrage in to cover enemy troop and gun position with a curtain of steel. Farther south we can hear the small-arms fire as doughboys close in on the Jerries, who are retreating steadily, under growing Allied pressure, to the inner defenses of the Brest area.

Four days ago leading reconnaissance forces of this outfit passed through the small town of St. Renan, taken earlier in the campaign by United States armor and French Forces of the Interior, then swung due south toward the German troops holding the outer perimeter of the Brest defenses. Infantry and other elements following pushed on along the St. Renan le Conquet road.

Not Like Normandy

Late today some leading companies in our outfit, together with attached forces, have pushed to the coastal road from Brest to Pte. de Kermorvan, while others have continued south from St. Renan toward the high ground overlooking the city.

The troops fighting here in Brittany are finding the aspect of things far different from that of combat in Normandy. The terrain, while still broken up with some hedgerows, is easier to operate in, for the ground seems to be more open and there are few wooded areas.

From the gentle sweep of the countryside, and the wide, straight roads, we have seen immediately how General Patton's tanks were able to operate as swiftly as they did.

Meets Baltimorean

Three columns of grayish-black smoke were spiraling skyward from the direction of Brest this afternoon as we drove into the headquarters of the unit now moving toward the objective. Lieut. Col. Bill Purnell, of 3020 Fendall road, Baltimore, stood outside the staff tent with a razor in his hand, shaving.

A piece of broken mirror was propped up against a hedgerow. With his usual smile, Bill noted that things were going well, in fact, almost too much so, for the rapid advance of recent days has necessitated moving headquarters almost every 24 hours.

Has Meal Of Fish

Many familiar faces were at mess an hour or so later when we sat down to a meal, the main item of which was an excellent fish, obtained from the local Breton fishermen. As we ate, word came through that one of the forces on the right flank had captured 100 or so German prisoners who had been holding out for a number of days in one pocket of resistance, left behind as the armor moved through.

Characteristic of much of the fighting in Brittany, this pocket had been mopped up by a small United States task force that had surrounded the Jerries, cut off supplies, then forced them to surrender. Both American troops and French Forces of the Interior have concentrated on this job of cleaning up the area while the main effort is being launched against the German army, naval and marine garrison holding out in the outskirts and inside the fortified zone of Brest.

New Technique Used

As we advance nearer and nearer the port, the men are finding prepared steel and concrete positions far different from the rough and tumble hedgerow and apple orchard fighting of earlier days. New techniques have been developed and are now in use. And for almost the first time it is possible to see the battle unfold below as one watches from high ground north of Brest.

From one such vantage point we followed the progress of the battle this afternoon while on a tour of aid stations with Maj. Ed Beacham, of 2002 Eastern avenue, Baltimore. Directly in front of us, three miles or so to the south, the spires and taller buildings of the city stood out clearly against the bright blue summer sky. Columns of smoke seemed to rise from the eastern end of Brest, while a murky black pall hung over the ridge running parallel to us just north of it.

Sees Missiles Hit Nazi Lines

We could make out puffs from our artillery firing from positions among the hills on all sides, then we watched as the missiles crashed into the enemy lines. Once in a while, we could make out our own troop movements as we watched the intervening ground through field glasses. At times we could actually make out movement in enemy territory.

A few of those seen about today included Staff Sergeant Henry R. Waring, 813 North Fulton avenue; Technician Third Class William Burch, of Covington, Va.; Lieut. Col. Harold A. Cassell, Captain James D. Sink, Warrant Officer James B. Morris, Private Buford R. Howell, Pfc. William G. Dickerson, Technician Fifth Class James H. Rice, Technical Sergeant Charles L. Forbes, all of Roanoke; Major Miles C. Chorey, Round Bay; Sergt. Abe Sherman, 2106 Rupp street, Baltimore; Pfc. Joe Petty, Saltville, Va.; Lieut. Col. Arthur T. Sheppe, Staunton; Warrant Officer Nathaniel J. Cosby, Capt. Thomas D. Neal, Richmond; First Sergeant Walter R. Wilborn and Staff Sergeant William E. Wilborn, South Boston; Technician Fifth Class Clarence Clemmons, Waynesboro; Pfc. Charles Dimick, 904 South Bayliss street; Captains Henry J. Reed and James L. Hayes, Baltimore; Acting First Sergeant Orville G. Swartley, Cumberland.

THE EVENING SUN, SATURDAY, SEPTEMBER 9, 1944

MARYLANDERS IN FRANCE —
Five Baltimoreans and four other Marylanders are mentioned in the following dispatch.

Week's Battle To Capture Fort At Brest Described By Bradley

By Holbrook Bradley [Sunpapers War Correspondent]

With United States Forces in Brittany, Sept. 3 [By Cable] — American forces driving on the besieged port of Brest from the northwest tonight have seized a strategically located fort at the harbor's entrance and have consolidated the position gained yesterday in the vicinity of Hill 103 to clear the enemy from this highly prized point of observation.

Shortly after noon today, formations of B-26s and lighter fighter bombers wheeled in over German-held fortifications to drop tons of bombs, concentrated principally on the heavily fortified installations at Site Du Petit Minou. For the better part of two hours those of us watching the show from the ground saw the bombers come in over the target, peel off for attack and then nose over in a screaming dive to loose their loads as clouds of dirt, smoke and debris splattered skyward.

Rangers Attack

Even before the last bombers had completed their missions, the Ranger unit attached to this outfit pushed forward to attack from the vicinity of Kerveguen, knifed its way over some 2,000 yards of rough terrain to storm the fort before the German defenders could recover from the heavy aerial bombardment. By 3 P. M. resistance was entirely overcome and the heavy concrete fortifications with guns and 250 enemy garrison personnel were in our hands.

At the battle-scarred Hill 103, which the infantrymen of this outfit describe as a tougher fight than any they have come up against in the French campaigns, elements of the battalion regiment, commanded by a Baltimorean, Lieut. Col. William C. Purnell, 3020 Fendall road, pushed over the crest to drive the remaining German paratroopers from the entrenchments they have held for more than a week's fighting as other American troops completed forward encirclement of the southern slope.

Trip Made Up Hill

There was little evidence of any activity on the part of the Germans this afternoon as we drove up to the front-line position where a guard advised us to dismount and continue the remainder of the way up the hill on foot. Behind us was an occasional plop of mortars fired as enemy troops squeezed in a pocket between two regiments.

Farther to the rear and on our flanks we could hear a continued rumble of medium and heavy artillery as round after round was poured into the defenses of the French port, which is proving one of the toughest nuts to crack in this war.

Meets Baltimore Sergeant

Sergt. Frank Kruse, 1703 Lemmon street, Baltimore, section sergeant of the mortar platoon, stepped up to tell us he was on his way to the elements on the hill and offered to show us the best route. Even though regimental headquarters had pointed out details on a map, we felt it more expedient to accept his offer.

There were few signs of the heavy battle we'd heard about as we pushed toward 103. GIs sat on the edges of their foxholes cleaning equipment or catching a slight rest in the afternoon sun. Once or twice men carrying ammunition or returning with empty cases passed us. Here and there were craters made a few days ago when the enemy plastered the area with 88 and heavier stuff.

Encounters Destruction

It was only when we crossed the last few hundred yards to the crest of the hill that we began to see some destruction and desolation marking 103 as one of the heaviest battlegrounds of the war. Equipment of both sides littered the gully we were moving up and lined the side hedgerow that offered a slight measure of protection.

As we crossed the last 50 yards we could smell the sour odor of decaying flesh we'd become accustomed to back in Normandy, but had almost forgotten during the past few weeks. Hill 103 was the most desolate waste we've seen yet. As we looked over the area there was hardly a square yard that hadn't been hit by shells from ours or the enemy's guns. Barbed-wire entanglements, trenches and remains of concrete fortifications were blasted almost beyond recognition. Everywhere were pieces of discarded equipment, weapons and other materials of war.

GIs There, Too

So completely was the area devastated that we were surprised to see signs of life. But GIs were there. Dirty, grimy, tired but tough as they come, they poked their heads from the slit trenches and foxholes dug among the ruins to ask us how the war was coming or to offer us a drink of K ration coffee being cooked over fire fed from the remains of German ration boxes and wooden fortifications.

Our guide, Kruse, took us down into a quarry dug into the hilltop where some more difficult fighting had taken place. Descending along the broken, rubble-strewn path, we felt almost as if the trip was one into hell.

Firing Starts

Dead German paratroopers and equipment lay about us on the ledges and on the floor of the quarry below. There was still the smoke of battle, the smell of death about the area and we hardly felt like staying long. Then the shrill whine, whistle and carump which sent a shower of rock and dirt skyward 50 yards across the quarry made up our minds for us. A German 88 battery near Brest was at work again. We ran up the slopes seeking shelter, felt for a moment like a couple of clay pigeons when two more landed close on our heels and then dove head-first into the nearest slip trench when we reached the crest again.

As the dirt settled, Private Ignance Amshey, of Dubois, Pa., a rifleman who had been on the hill since it was taken, warned us to keep low and then gave us a slight idea of what the fighting had been like. Outside we could hear round after round from the 88 slamming about the area, occasionally ricocheting from a rock to land several hundred yards farther to the rear.

Attack Began Aug. 28

The attack on the Hill 103 began last Monday when elements of a rifle battalion moved into the area from the direction of St. Renan. Surprisingly enough, the men were able to walk up to within a few fields of the crest during this first day before they were held down momentarily by artillery and some small-arms fire.

Then, last Thursday, (August 31) the company, now led by Lieut. John C. Jones, of Winchester, Va., pulled into a position along the northern ridge of the hill, where they were met by heavy small-arms and grenade fire from the paratrooper elements entrenched only 25 yards away.

Enemy Out Of Site

All during the day our men hung on to their precarious perch while our own artillery pounded one side ridge and Jerry pounded the other. And during this time it was almost impossible to see the enemy because any movement brought on a fusillade of small-arms fire. This situation, with the Germans on one side and the Americans on the other remained the same until late Friday night, when a large body of Germans attempted a counterattack, executing a flanking maneuver that for a time completely cut off United States elements on the crest from the main force.

Mortars Turn The Tide

The battle, at this point, turned into a hand-grenade duel, each side afraid to fire heavier arms because of the danger of hitting its own troops. Only when mortars were brought in by Technical Sergeant Donald Hundertmark, 1223 Scott street, Baltimore, and the remainder of his platoon, did the Jerries decide the spot was too hot and withdrew. That was their last attempt to hold the hill.

Today units of another regiment succeeded in pushing forward to the southern base of Hill 103, thus effectively cutting off any enemy left in position and bringing one of the best observation posts this side of Brest completely into our hands.

A few others seen in the vicinity of 103 included Private Charles F. Rowe, Kansas City, Kan.; Staff Sergeant Henry F. Selmaggi, Brooklyn, N. Y.; Private Raymon Sprunger, Berne, Ind.; Staff Sergeant Arthur Humerick, Thurmont, Md.; Pfc. Richard O. Orban, 15 South Payson street, Baltimore; Lieut. Arthur E. Lomax, Nashville; Pfc. Thomas Coogan, Ellicott City, Md.; Pfc. William Bowden, Berlin, Md.; Lieut. Col. Roger S. Whiteford, Ruxton, and Capt. Guy Griffen, of Baltimore.

THE BALTIMORE SUN, WEDNESDAY, SEPTEMBER 13, 1944

Yank, In Captured Pillbox, Chats With Nazi Over 'Phone

By Holbrook Bradley [Sunpapers War Correspondent]

With United States Forces Attacking Brest, Sept. 7 [By Radio — Delayed] — American Rangers assigned the job of cleaning out nest fortifications guarding approaches to the harbor of Brest moved so swiftly during the last week that they sometimes were in control of positions before Lieut. Gen. Herman B. Ramcke's lieutenants knew they had fallen.

Late last night Capt. Edward Luther, company commander from Boston, stepped into what had been headquarters of one of these forts just as the telephone on the table started ringing violently. Luther hesitated a moment, picked up the receiver, and heard a guttural voice on the other end query, "Was machts?"

"Oh, We Couldn't Do That"

Unable to speak German, the captain tried a couple of sauerkrauts and a few other words that sounded Germanic; then he told the person on the other end that his forces were surrounded and had better surrender immediately. There was a moment of silence then a very polite voice asked in English if there were any German wounded and how they were being treated.

Luther again suggested surrender. "Oh, we couldn't do that," the German said. There was a click as the receiver was hung up; then the Rangers cut the line.

THE BALTIMORE SUN, FRIDAY, SEPTEMBER 15, 1944

48 Hours of Artillery Fire Leave Port Of Brest Ablaze

By Holbrook Bradley [Sunpapers War Correspondent]

With U. S. Forces in Brittany, Sept. 10 [By Radio — Delayed] — Brest this morning is ablaze. Even to those who have fought through France since D-day, the siege of this French port is one of the most awesome sights of the war.

Heavy artillery has been thundering about us continuously during the last 48 hours as thousands of tons of explosives were poured into the remaining positions of the German garrison. For more than ten days, medium and heavy bombers of the air force have dropped loads on these same targets, while fighters have dive-bombed and strafed the Jerry lines.

Smoke Clouds U. S. Camp

Early today, the skies above our camp were clouded with heavy black smoke from the direction of the besieged city, and as morning passed, we could see more evidence of huge fires burning throughout the port. In the hollows and lowlands about our area, smoke, clung near the frosty ground, and there was an acrid smell of burning wood, even though Brest itself is more than three miles away.

From the artillery post a quarter mile distant, we could see the entire city covered with a thick haze. Late last night, fires blazing in sections of the city gave indication of what we are seeing this morning, Brest burning from one end to the other.

Rangers Clean Up Le Conquet

As United States forces close on the city, American rangers and ground troops to whom the task force commander of this outfit has assigned the job of cleaning up enemy big gun installations on Le Conquet peninsula have swept across the area to capture main gun positions in Plougonvelin, St. Mathreu and Lochrist; and late last night, pushed on to rout out the stubborn defenders of Le Conquet itself. A German commander also was taken.

At 8 o'clock, H-hour yesterday morning, a battalion of infantry under Major Bill Puntenney, of Phoenix, Ariz., jumped off from a rendezvous near the main Brest highway to push an attack along the east coast peninsula.

Meeting little but scattered resistance from the enemy infantrymen and occasionally running up against fortified machine-gun or mortar emplacements, the battalion fought its way south to Plougonvelin, then swung west along the rocky coast toward St. Mathreu. By noon, Puntenney had reached the main objective, having sustained only a few casualties but having captured more than 600 enemy prisoners.

Moving out at the same time, two Ranger units headed directly across the neck of the peninsula, one keeping on to Le Conquet, the other striking south toward big guns in the central area.

Shortly before noon, a four-man patrol of the latter unit walked into the rear of heavy gun emplacements at Lochrist and forced the surrender of the garrison. The installation was found to consist of four 14-inch naval guns.

White Flags Found Flying

Less than half an hour later, a company unit commanded by Lieut. Col. James E. Rudder, of Eden, Texas, approached a heavily fortified position outside St. Mathreu, to find white flags, indicating that the commander was surrendering himself and all his troops in the area.

As the enemy forces on Le Conquet peninsula collapsed and resistance ceased, German marines, navy personnel, infantry and artillerymen surrendered by the dozens then by hundreds.

Late last night, the count at the prisoners' cage ran well above 1,500, including a lieutenant colonel, several majors and a number of subordinate officers. Today the only resistance reported is from a small force holding out against the Rangers and French Forces of the Interior along the coast north of the town of Le Conquet. Mopping-up operations continue this morning.

The commander of Lochrist and other peninsula garrisons was found to be Oberst Lieutenant (Lieutenant Colonel) Ramcke, who had been placed in charge of all troops in this coastal area.

A thin-faced, bespectacled Nazi, the typical German army officer, he was escorted yesterday to the commander of the forces effecting his capture, and then to a higher echelon for interrogation.

Late yesterday, Capt. Harvey Cook, of Narberth, Pa., an officer at the headquarters of the Ranger battalion, guided us through the position at which the German Commander had surrendered.

Station Of Steel And Concrete

Evidently a centrally located range-finder station for batteries in the area, it was heavily constructed of steel and concrete, many parts of it, such as watertight doors, evidently having been salvaged from warships. Intended primarily as a command post, its defense was mainly from near-by coastal batteries.

There was a dull rumble of heavy generators turning over as we entered the control center through a heavily fortified underground entrance. The Rangers told us that more than 70 prisoners had been taken from the structure. All about was evidence of how they had lived.

Rooms Like Ship Cabins

The rooms below seemed much like those aboard a ship. The bunks were in tiers, and there were ship-type washrooms. All about were piles of clothing, equipment, stacks of rifles and other arms. The mess hall was still set with the noonday meal, including a few half-finished bottles of wine. There was even a still-smoldering pipe.

The room on top of this structure commanded a wide view of the area all around, and contained some of the most intricate range-finding devices we have yet come across — all destroyed by Germans before surrender.

Most impressive about the surrender was that it was made while the Germans had plenty of food and ammunition still in their storerooms or gun positions. Military officials estimated that the garrison could have held out months longer on the basis of this materiel.

The reason for the surrender lay outside in the fort's ground, pockmarked with bomb and artillery shell craters. The universal complaint among the prisoners captured on the peninsula was that they could not take the constant bombardment of our ground and air forces.

As we watched the sunset from the lighthouse on the tip of the peninsula last night, the absence of battle noises seemed strange in the light of fighting that has taken place there during the siege.

From the ancient church, perched on the cliff's edge, came the chant of evening prayers of French peasants who already were returning to their homes, some of which were still smoking.

THE EVENING SUN, MONDAY, SEPTEMBER 18, 1944

MARYLANDERS AT BREST —
Ten Marylanders are mentioned in this dispatch.

House-To-House Battle In Brest Described

By Holbrook Bradley [Sunpapers War Correspondent]

Brest, Sept. 12 (By Radio — Delayed) — Doughboys of this United States infantry outfit, which first entered the eastern end of this battle-scarred port three days ago, tonight continue to push forward block by block in some of the fiercest street battles in France.

In what has become virtually house-to-house combat, the Yanks, who have had little sleep and no food other than K rations for days past, are stalking the enemy, who is resisting to the utmost as he retreats from building to building.

So close has the field of battle become that men on the ground floor may be firing at German snipers upstairs and those on one side of the street may be machine-gunning Heinies barricaded in the structure on the other side of the street.

Enters City With Baltimoreans

There was a constant rustling whistle of our artillery shells overhead this afternoon as we entered the city, with Lieut. Col. Lawrence Meeds, of Roanoke, Va., and Major Donovan P. Yeuell, of 5704 Loch Raven Boulevard, on tour from another front to see how his brother was making out. We found the fighting in this sector about the same as any we had been in, plenty being thrown both ways, the usual dirt, smoke and tension of battle.

Our jeep driver headed down the Rue Jean Jaures at the outskirts of the town and immediately we began to see evidences of past combat. A German blockhouse to our left, one of the strongest fortifications we had yet seen, was blasted into a pile of dirt, concrete, twisted steel and rubble, evidently the results of heavy concentrations of artillery and air attacks. Across the way was the twisted steel skeleton of what had once been a market or a large showroom.

Walk Down Streets

A military policeman at an intersection a dozen or 15 blocks ahead cautioned us to park the vehicle in a side street and walk the rest of the way, as the enemy fire down the main streets was liable to be heavy at any sign of movement.

There were scattered rifle and pistol shots toward the center of the city, occasionally interrupted by heavy bursts of the machine-gun fire. A quarter of a mile or so ahead we could see aerial bursts of artillery.

One of the things that surprised us most about the city was that the buildings weren't all flat, for we had had constant reports that bombardment and our artillery had leveled the city. There were few buildings not showing scars of battle, but many houses and apartments appeared to have a few broken windows and not much else damaged. Farther toward the center of town we saw evidence of heavier destruction — one, two, then a block of gutted and bombed-out structures.

Few GIs On Guard

There were only a few GIs standing on duty at intersections as we moved down the streets littered with rubble, broken glass and empty ammunition cases. Once or twice a group of FFI passed, usually dressed in civilian clothes, carrying Kraut rifles. One of the strangest things to us was the number of civilians who had apparently stayed in their homes throughout the siege.

Standing in the midst of the wreckage of their homes and personal belonging, they smiled as we passed and some waved the tri-color.

A grim-looking doughboy, standing in the middle of a small park at the intersection of two main streets, pointed out the direction of a forward command post of one company on the line, warned us to keep off the open highways as the Heinies had most of them covered with machine-guns. Two other Yanks were marching three German prisoners to a collecting point across from us when we took off, just as an enemy mortar shell broke against the side of a nearby building.

Find Command Post

At the command post in the basement of a building we found Maj. Louis Hamele, of Portage, Wisconsin, the battalion commander, and Lieut. Dan Manning, of Northampton, Mass., the company commanding officer. Stretched out on the floor or propped up against the walls were a dozen GIs, tired, dirty, most of them trying to catch a few moments of the well-earned rest. Through the open doorway came the heavy staccato sounds of machine-gun and rifle fire, occasionally the crack of a pistol.

From the company officer we learned that the Germans were resisting mainly with a force of infantrymen, paratroopers and marines armed with machine guns, rifles, pistols and mortars.

Their usual tactics are to cover all main and cross streets until forced back, then to set up at the next intersection. At the same time a scattered force of snipers is left in the buildings to harass the advancing Americans. As an added defense the Germans are using scattered mortar and heavy gun fire.

Nazi Strong Point Blasted

From a hole in the cellar of a building next to his command post Lieutenant Manning pointed out the wall across the way, a corner of which was blasted off, which had been an enemy strongpoint. Troops under him had taken it last night after a demolition crew first had worked its way up behind. A bazooka team and a tank destroyer had then finished routing out the Germans.

The toughest job in this close-quarters street fighting seems to be cleaning out each individual house, for if each house is not taken care of, there are apt to be a few Jerry snipers left behind who may cause a high rate of casualties among following troops. When the Yanks first entered the city they tried moving down a side street toward machine-gun emplacements at the corners. Then they found the doors of houses bolted, making it impossible to get in to chase out the snipers. The answer, which seems to be working well by now, is for a small group to climb over the rear garden walls, enter the house from the back and catch the Heinies napping. The score of some 4,000 prisoners indicates the success of this type of maneuver.

Two Baltimoreans Lead Attacks

Back on our own front we found that an infantry regiment commanded by Lieut. Col. Louis G. Smith, of Baltimore, had just jumped off in a new attack along the main Brest highway some 1,500 yards east of La Trinite. North of this sector an outfit commanded by Lieut. Col. William Purnell, also of Baltimore, continued to press on well past Hill No. 103 in the direction of Recouvrance.

A few of those seen in this area today included Private Charles M. Hough, of Pittsburgh; Staff Sergeant Elmer Wharton, Pfc. Louis Hickman, Technical Sergeants Kenneth Nelson and Henry Tyler, and Private Shad Crockett, all of Crisfield; Technical Sergeant Blair L. Crockett, of Salisbury; Capt. Christian Martin, of Lancaster, Pa., and Major James Morris, of Bel Air.

THE BALTIMORE SUN, THURSDAY, SEPTEMBER 21, 1944

Five Baltimoreans are mentioned in the dispatch below.

Brest Captured In 46-Day Siege – Enemy Also Cleared From Crozon Peninsula By Yanks

By Holbrook Bradley [Sunpapers War Correspondent]

Recouvrance, France, Sept. 15 [By Radio — Delayed] — Still fighting their way from house to house, patrols from this battalion have pushed past Fort Montbaray and have advanced well into this naval suburb.

From the north another outfit jumping off from the fortified gun range continues to hammer the retreating German paratroopers and marines back from Recouvrance covering 3,000 yards in their push.

To the east an infantry outfit is driving toward the heart of the city in a maneuver which places the retreating foe in a compact area in the heart of the old city wall.

Artillery Steps Up Pace

Tonight, as the sun sets in one of the clearest skies seen during the whole Brittany campaign, our artillery has stepped up its pace to an almost unprecedented peak. Thousands of rounds of medium and heavy artillery shells are pouring into the center of the city where General Ramcke's forces still hold out.

There is little smoke over the city, the fires evidently having burned out. The Germans evidently have finished demolishing supply dumps and other installations. As the prisoners continue to pour in by the hundreds, it becomes more and more apparent that the Nazi garrison is dwindling.

The troops surrendering are a mixture of paratroopers, marines and soldiers from World War I. They are generally dazed from the constant pounding of artillery and air bombing.

Defends Naval Guns

One of the few strong points still holding out is Crozon garrison, defending ack-ack and naval guns located across from Brest.

There is evidence that some of the forces from inside the city have been moved over to this garrison.

The enemy cannot hold out here much longer, but there is no indication as to just when he will decide to surrender. Hitler evidently intends to make this another Cassino, for an American mission sent into the city several days ago under a flag of truce to negotiate for the surrender of the port got the answer "Impossible" from General Ramcke.

Action Around Gun Range

There was still plenty of action around the rifle and gun range built by the Americans in the last war. An outfit commanded by Major Thomas Dallas, of Martinsville, Va., was engaging the Germans in a hand-to-hand battle.

Among the ruins of Fort Keranoux we met Lieut. Col. Bill Purnell, Baltimore; Lieut. Col. Lawrence Meeks, Roanoke, Va., and Lieut. Grant Darby, of Denver, Col., the latter commanding C Company which was the first outfit to scale this man-made hill.

Darby told how his outfit, which took Hill 103 earlier in the siege, captured this fort. After battling their way through a hail of machine-gun, rifle and hand grenade fire to the foot of the hill they halted for a moment, reorganized and then with Darby and his first sergeant, Alfred Harris, of Baltimore, in the lead swarmed up the 75-yard slope to the German trenches and in a hand-to-hand scrap blew the Germans out of their trenches with hand grenades.

Took 200 Prisoners

Before they knew it the Germans had surrendered and what was left of the Yank outfit went rolling on, taking pillboxes and the balance of the fortifications. By the end of the day Darby's outfit had taken 200 prisoners.

With the capture of the range, our officers have found the center of the German observation for their artillery.

From the top of this spot which much be a good 300 feet high one can see five miles in any direction. Among other things we captured some 88 guns on this hill centered on Hill 103.

Still Plenty Of Action

Late tonight there is little return enemy artillery fire but there is still plenty of action going on and one can hear the crack of German snipers' rifles.

Seen in this area today were: Lieut. Miller Kline, Strasburg, Va.; Technician Marion Hepner, Baltimore; Private John Rongyos, Baltimore; Sergt. Andrew Fisher, Baltimore; Capt. Charles Kinsey, Norfolk, Virginia.

THE 29th AT BREST

BIG ONE CAPTURED AT LE CONQUET — This was one of the heavy naval guns which the Germans had mounted on shore. Bradley mentions that when the picture was taken "town on peninsula burns in background as battle still rages." BKI-481-BS

BRADLEY'S CAMERA CROSSES FRANCE —

Last week's metrogravure section carried a page of pictures of the Blue and Gray Division fighting in Germany. Holbrook Bradley, Sunpapers' War Correspondent, attached to the division for many months, made the pictures on this page, which were long delayed. They are of notable events in the Maryland-Pennsylvanian-Virginia unit's career — events described by Bradley and other correspondents last summer. At that time the 29th, though well trained, was unseasoned. Since then it has been tempered in many battles, in all of which it has given a good account of itself.

PILLBOX — This was a heavily fortified position on the Le Conquet peninsula because it was a fire direction center and it was only taken by 29th troops after a stiff fight. BKI-483-BS

ANOTHER NAVAL GUN CAPTURED BY 29th — This heavy one also was taken by the division at Le Conquet. Note doughboy at left peering into huge shell case. BKI-482-BS

SURRENDER — Maj. Gen. Charles H. Gerhardt, Blue and Gray commander, accepts surrender of the German colonel who commanded the big guns of Le Conquet and its extensive system of fortifications. BKI-480-BS

CHAPTER 5

ASSAULT AGAINST THE WESTWALL

THE EVENING SUN, WEDNESDAY, OCTOBER 4, 1944

Bradley Describes Army Push From Holland Into Germany

By Holbrook Bradley [Sunpapers War Correspondent]

Somewhere in Holland, Oct. 2 [Delayed] — Elements of our troops have crossed the border into Germany and tonight are engaging the enemy along the southern bank of the river Saeffeler in the vicinity of the small town of Gangelt. The fighting as yet has not been stiff.

Other units, which have pushed north across the Gangelt-Geilenkirchen highway, have entered the towns of Kreuzrath and Birgden, where the leading companies carry on street fighting that has developed in recent hours to house-to-house, literally room-to-room combat, to knock the remaining Nazis from their positions.

Foe Lacks Tenacity

Throughout this area there has been no real show of tenacity on the part of the foe. Units of German riflemen, composed mostly of secondary troops, show a will to fight but as yet have not put up the bitter battle for the Fatherland expected of them. Their tactics so far have been continued with withdrawal as the steady pressure of the Allies increased, with only an occasional strong, determined stand.

The artillery used by the Germans had been heavier at times than much that has been experienced before, but again is nothing like what was expected. Seventy-fives, 88s and occasionally heavier shells are sent over, but usually in no more than two or three rounds stretched out over an interval. One annoyance we have met so far has been mobile mounts, both 75s and 88s, which have appeared to harass troops moving under observation.

The skies above us were clear and cold as we drove up towards one regimental command post this afternoon through the Dutch countryside. After the heavy rains of the last few days, the sunshine was a welcome relief to us despite the cold winds which made heavy underwear, extra coats and overshoes almost obligatory. Although we were only a few miles from the fighting, we were impressed with the fact that there is little feeling that we were so near combat until we reached the German border.

Dutch Children Call "Hello"

Blond Dutch children of all ages lined the streets as we passed to wave, call "Hello," dance delightedly as the jeeps bounced by. Their parents, most of whom seemed cheerful and happy, smiled or waved at us from yards or doorways of neat brick cottages and larger houses that seemed to be typical in this part of the country,

Once in a while we saw groups of armed civilians wearing a band of the national colors, members of Holland's underground and military movements, which are now fighting side by side with their liberators.

In the villages and fields alike, Dutchmen seem to be going about their normal pursuits, selling goods (not as plentiful as in parts of France and Belgium), and finishing their fall planting or harvesting. What has impressed us most about the people and their country is neatness — the neatness of their dress, their towns, houses and even the fields that make up the country.

Evidence Of Fighting

About us there is evidence of the fighting that took place when American armor and infantry poured across France, Belgium and Holland to chase the Nazis back across their borders. Here and there, buildings show signs of the fight, in some cases rows of buildings are blown flat, but often the damage is definitely old, sometimes apparently the result of the German invasion of 1939.

Along the routes leading to the front we passed burned-out enemy vehicles of all types — tanks, command cars, trucks, *volkeswagens*, even staff cars. There were a few pieces of wrecked American equipment, occasionally a burned-out Sherman tank, but little else. And so quickly did our troops pass by that in places we found German emplacements that never had been used, gun positions which appeared knocked out even before they could be brought into action.

We crossed the Dutch border into Germany for the first time along a narrow dirt road which was far from the main highway. Two stone markers showed us the exact spot where Holland ended and Germany began.

Warning To Dutch

Along one side — German — was heavy barbed wire entanglement bearing signs in German warning the Dutch to stay clear. We noticed a number of places where the wire had been torn or broken, placed where our medium tanks had forced their way through to push the Germans back. There were little other defenses.

The regimental command post was deep in a heavy forest of pine and birch, well back from any roads. Covered with heavy logs and sand bags, it seemed one of the most well-protected sites we had seen. Inside the dugout, a Baltimorean, Lieut. Col. Louis Smith, the unit's commanding officer, conferred with his aides and executive officers on the present situation. We learned the attack was going well, with the enemy still not stubborn in defenses, and with units on the way to their objectives.

It seemed the best move to follow down an echelon to the battalions and see for ourselves from a close spot how the outfit was doing, so we slogged out through the mud again to drive on toward the Ganglet road.

Feeling Different In Germany

The feeling as we pushed through the muddy lane in a jeep was far different from that of Holland. The houses seemed much the same type, all neat, orderly brick buildings, but there were no civilians about. Back at our outfit's headquarters we had learned from Civil Affairs officials that there had been some trouble with the German civilian populace. The policy so far was to remove all civilians from areas when the situation indicated any chance of their affecting military operations. In other spots, where more rural conditions exist, families allowed to remain are ordered inside. In any case, any suspicious civilians are taken into custody as a measure of security.

The battalion commander Lieut. Col. Randolph Milholland, of Cumberland, Md., was busy in a house taken over as temporary headquarters when we turned off down the main street of a small town. For the first time we had seen signs in German that had not been put up by occupying troops. One read: *"Achtung – Zivilischer Verkehr Streng Verboten."*

There was the sound of occasional artillery from some distance ahead of us, as the Germans now and then threw in a round of 75s, but enemy fire was almost entirely drowned out by the continuous roar or our own artillery in the rear. As we talked with Colonel Milholland about the location of his troops we could hear the echo of machine guns, dat-dat-dat, German "burb" guns (automatic pistols) and the crack of rifles.

White Flag Of Surrender

One other of our battalions had headquarters farther along the road, so we headed out for it, being careful to keep our speed down for telltale dust was certain to bring on hostile fire.

For the first time we saw white flags hanging from the houses of civilians. In France it had been the tri-color often with Allied flags; in Belgium it was a black, gold and red flag, again with those of the Allied nations; and in Holland it had been the Dutch national colors of blue, white and red. But here we saw no Nazi swastikas, nor the German eagle, instead the pure white flag of surrender.

Those few civilians still about were inside their houses or in silent groups waiting to be moved to the rear. There was no sign or cheering or waving of hands, no feeling of liberation. The houses seemed well made, the farms prosperous, and the few buildings we inspected were furnished with the latest and in many cases the best of everything — electric ranges, ice boxes, clocks; modern radios and latest plumbing and heating equipment.

Three shells from a German 75 landed near our town as we turned off the road to find the battalion command post where Major Al Warfield, of Baltimore, executive officer, was at a telephone talking with his commander. The streets of the village were deserted with only a few dogs and five or six work horses roaming about.

Major Miller Near By

In a forward command post not far away was Major Anthony J. Miller, 30 of Bernice avenue, a battalion commander who was up near the line observing the advance of his companies which had just pushed off into the woods nearby. So far, there had been only a couple of rounds of enemy artillery thrown into the area, and no small-arms fire or indications of enemy infantry resistance.

One of Major Miller's aides had sighted a telescope at an object in a field half a mile away or so, and he took it to be a mobile 75 mounted on a Nazi Mark IV tank chassis. Nearby was another, well camouflaged, and to the far left was a third that had obviously been knocked out of action, for it was blackened and burned.

Whether the first two were also out of action was not certain, but we rather suspected so, for they failed to show any signs of activity while we watched. As there still was some possibility of fire from them, however, all of us were wary of exposing ourselves.

Back in his command post we had a couple of peaches, a plum and a delicious apple from nearby orchards and then a drink of good Scotch from bottle saved a long time for the occasion of meeting in Germany. As we pulled out of town and headed back for our own command post, we knew well we were near the enemy, for a few parting rounds from apparently the same 75 landed a hundred yards or so away.

Down the road at a group of houses a unit of military intelligence personnel was arresting a young German in civilian clothes, who said openly he was a former SS man, but tried to impress us with the fact that the he was of the lower order and that he had given his uniform away four weeks before.

THE BALTIMORE SUN, FRIDAY, OCTOBER 6, 1944

SIEGFRIED LINE A SET OF FORTS — *Little Found Underground In One Captured Section*

By Holbrook Bradley [Sunpapers War Correspondent]

At the Siegfried Line, Oct. 4 [By Radio — Delayed] — A group of us this afternoon took time out to inspect some of the fortifications of the Siegfried Line which have fallen to an infantry outfit engaging the Germans on our right flank.

The countryside through which we passed on our way to the front looked much the same as that in which we were fighting. There were the same neat Dutch houses, cheerful, happy parents waving, and excited children shouting as we passed. Over the road we traveled there was a steady stream of armored vehicles moving toward the zone of fighting, and empty vehicles returning toward their bases.

Checked At Headquarters

As we crossed the German border for the first time we saw the barriers which were part of the pre-war customs systems. Now both the Dutch and the German gates were open as Allied convoys plowed through the mud and slush covering the roads. Once or twice we saw frail, old Dutch fortifications, built sometime in the late '30s.

Near the village of Marienberg, just inside the German border, a lieutenant, a member of the battalion engaged in attacking the German West Wall, advised us to check at his headquarters before moving any farther, and suggested that we might be interested in taking a look at the German fortifications from his observation post. As we followed him up the war-torn street lined with houses badly damaged by artillery fire on both sides, we noticed again that there were few civilians about, only a couple tending stock.

Post In An Attic

The observation post of the battalion was found to be in the attic of what appeared to be the house of a once-prosperous farmer. Now the house was a tumbled mess of furniture, broken plaster, and pieces of glass. A gaping hole in one wall was the result of German fire from the Siegfried Line, fire that had made the room a conglomeration of brick and debris.

From a window above we looked through binoculars out over a wide open expanse of fields, broken only now and then by clumps of trees and haystacks. In the distance were the smokestacks of Ubach, where another battalion of the same outfit was engaged in some of the fiercest fighting of this phase of the campaign. Columns of smoke billowing up to the north of Ubach showed where American armor was pounding German positions and emplacements.

Series Of Pillboxes

The lieutenant with us pointed out a portion of the Siegfried Line in front of us. We were surprised to find it only a series on unconnected pillboxes arranged for interlacing crossfire. Somehow, most of us had expected something on the order of the French Maginot Line.

A few moments later we headed out across open ground to the road running to Ubach. For the first time since being in Germany we felt as if we were back in the midst of the rough, tough type of war we have known since we first landed in France.

To our rear and on both of our flanks the constant roar of our artillery was almost deafening. There also was the less frequent whine, roar and explosion from the incoming "mail." The foothill in front of us as we bounced into the edge of the town of Palenberg was one of the strong points of the Siegfried Line. A few hundred yards to our left we could see black smoke, a yellow flash, and then hear the report of an enemy air burst. Somewhere to the far right the dat-dat-dat of a Schmeisser machine gun echoed back as clearly as if it were being fired a few yards from us.

Hotel Almost Destroyed

A large, modern-looking brick building bearing the legend of the Hotel Ernst stood across from the railway station that had been almost completely destroyed. We noticed gaping shell holes in the wall and could see part of an overturned bar with a few German beer mugs on the floor inside.

Then for the first time we noticed that we were looking into the face of a German pillbox across the way. Seized two days ago during the first heavy fighting as the line was breached, this pillbox had been one of the main strong points serving to back up other smaller forts we had passed earlier coming across the stretch of open ground.

From the GI on guard outside the pillbox we learned of an entrance through the rear of the sallyport, and inside we found Captain Richard J. Wood, of Minneapolis, operations officer for his unit, discussing the trend of the battle with the other staff members.

Equipment Litters Ground

Piles of German equipment and other debris littered the ground outside the fortification. Deep trenches — we noticed that they seemed recently dug — connected this structure with another similar one a few yards to the left.

Inside the fort seemed similar to many of those we have taken earlier in the campaign. There were two main rooms, evidently used as sleeping and messing quarters for the garrison. Heavy steel doors, very similar to those used on board a ship, separated each room, and we saw each door and large opening guarded by a small aperture and another vantage stop through which the entrance could be covered.

While we stood talking to Captain Wood, the phone on the wall rang violently. Four dead Germans lay where they had fallen in the trench outside the gun position of the pillbox as we left the living quarters to inspect this other section. From behind walls that were more than three feet thick, we saw a machine gun had been trained to cover the bridge over which we had come, the roads in either direction, and a large section of open fields. Similar positions at the other end of the fort were trained to sweep the approaches from this direction.

Taken From The Rear

Back inside the main portion of the pillbox we learned that the fort, which seemed virtually impregnable to us, had been taken as usual from the rear with a combination of pole charges and bazookas. Once the Americans had outflanked the pillbox, the Germans on the inside were reluctant to fight on. In this instance the six remaining in the garrison surrendered with no further show of resistance.

Before we left Palenberg we decided to take a quick look through the first town in Germany we had ever been in where there had been any real fighting. It seemed much like any of those towns in France that we had fought through.

Hears Crack Of Rifles

There were few buildings that didn't show some sign of heavy battle. As we walked through the streets piled high with broken tiles, glass, bricks, and the usual debris, we could hear the sharp crack of rifles, the staccato rattle of machine guns, and the interrupted fire of automatic pistols. Once in a while an artillery shell crashed into the building on one side of us.

As we were about to leave the building we had inspected, one of us noticed a package on the table bearing the label, "Maryland Tobacco, Fritz Hempleman, Berlin." It wasn't bad at all, even when we smoked in a German pipe.

THE BALTIMORE SUN, SUNDAY, OCTOBER 8, 1944

YANK DRIVE FACES STEADY BARRAGE — Bradley Describes Troops' Fight North Of Aachen

By Holbrook Bradley [Sunpapers War Correspondent]

Inside Germany, Oct. 6 [By Radio — Delayed] — American tanks and doughboys fighting through the breach in the Siegfried Line north of Aachen today continue to press slowly ahead against stiffening enemy resistance, which now has developed into an almost uninterrupted barrage of medium and heavy artillery.

In this outfit's wardroom this morning, where Lieut. Col. William J. Witte, of Catonsville, and Major James Porter, of Baltimore, were on duty, we learned that a battalion advancing east of the Siegfried Line supported by Sherman and light tanks, had pushed to the outskirts of Beggendorf, more than a mile beyond the battle-torn industrial center of Ubach.

Indications were that the unit was continuing to move despite constant heavy artillery resistance, wiping out pockets of Nazi infantrymen who were attempting desperately to stem the tide of the invasion.

Patrols Report Penetration

Elsewhere along our sector of the Western Front, other battalions of infantry continue their action against the enemy, who shows little desire to fight. Patrols which have been active along the entire front report penetrations a few miles north of Gangelt, on the Geilenkirchen highway, while a rifle company of a battalion commanded by Major Miles C. Shorey, of Round Bay, has indicated contact with German elements retreating to the Siegfried Line on the outskirts of the latter city.

In comparison with the Melle fighting area at the breach of the German main line, the small village of Birgden, one of our positions northwest of Geilenkirchen, seemed a most peaceful spot.

Lieutenants Alvin D. Ungerleinder, of Carbondale, Pa., and Dwight L. Gentry, of Roxboro, N. C., company commander and executive officer, told us this condition merely was a lull following the storm, for a few nights ago it had been one of the hottest spots along the front.

Describes Birgden Attack

A few nights ago the battalion commander, Lieut. Col. Randy Millholland, of Cumberland, gave the company orders to move out from the Gangelt road toward the objective of Birgden, with H-hour set at 1.30 A. M.

As the first elements began to move across more than 1,000 yards of open ground, the moon rose in a clear, cold sky dotted with thousands of stars.

There was no sign of the enemy as the troops moved out toward the town; the only sound came from small-arms fire in the distance and from occasional artillery passing overhead. Lieutenant Gentry, who led the patrol leading the element, entered the town still uncertain of what they were running into.

By 2.15, the troops were in the middle of Birgden, making a reconnaissance of the town. So far, everything seemed simple — too simple.

At 2.45 hell broke loose. A reinforced Jerry infantry platoon, supported by heavy machine guns, had closed in on the south side of the town, outflanked our patrols and guards, and was attempting to cut off our troops.

Gentry, who had been busy looking, with his men, for a place to set up a command post, was on his way back to the telephone when the German machine gunners opened up down the main street from a distance of only 30 yards.

As he gave his men orders to scatter, Gentry and a few others dived into a near-by doorway, out of the line of fire. By that time, intense street fighting had broken out all through the town. Doughboys were firing from house to house — in some instances from room to room.

Over 1,000 Yards Of Open Ground

With some of his men, the company executive edged his way to the outskirts of the town, then crawled back over the thousand yards of open ground to report the situation to his battalion.

It was decided to send in more troops under the command of Capt. Earle Tweed, of Fort Benning, Georgia, and the unit was ordered to start in at the crack of dawn next day.

For the next 24 hours the fighting developed into the toughest sort of house-to-house combat. The German garrison evidently was prepared to hold out at all costs, for the Americans literally had to go in and drive them out from the rooms of each house.

A few supporting tanks rolled up to blast enemy machine-gun nests and other strongholds which had been set up through the town. By late afternoon the last Heinie had been driven out, leaving more than 20 dead and three wounded behind.

Germans Reorganize

But it wasn't over yet, for just after dark the Germans reorganized to launch a furious counterattack. Moving up with a couple of supporting self-propelled 88s, mortars and heavy and light machine guns, the Jerries tried again and again to knock the Yanks out of their position. Five attempts were made before the enemy finally gave up, apparently realizing the trap he had laid was a failure.

Since Yanks have taken over the town there have been no further German attempts at a counterattack. Heine gunners lay in a nightly barrage of artillery, which so far has been anything but heavy, and otherwise there has been little activity other than the usual patrol tactics on both sides.

In company headquarters Technical Sergeant George H. Tyler, of Crisfield, told us he was about to make the rounds of the outposts, and asked if we'd like to come along.

Few Shell Holes In Roofs

Birgden seemed to have suffered much less than many of the towns where fighting has been going on in Germany. There were a few shell holes in the red tile roofs, some evidence of artillery fire on the brick walls of the buildings, but for the most part the houses showed only bullet holes made when the Yanks completed clearing up the town.

At a church near the town square we halted momentarily to take a look at the spot where Germans killed in the recent fight had been buried in a common grave. One of the few civilians left in the village passed, on his way to tend herd.

Tyler noted his company still was living on K rations, but pointed out that there were a good many German chickens, lots of fruit and other things about that made good eating no problem at all.

Chicken Stew For Lunch

Just to the rear of the command post we saw a group of four or five GI's preparing a lunch of chicken stew that looked a lot better than anything we'd see for a long time.

At the outposts there were few signs of any activity. Through binoculars we could see German machine-gun positions, and near a haystack a mile or so away a couple of the enemy were busy digging. But the men on guard warned us not to expose ourselves, for Jerry snipers across the way were waiting for just such a shot. And we were told we'd find it plenty hot, with the lines so close together, if we came back at night.

MARYLANDERS IN GERMANY —
In the dispatch below, Mr. Bradley mentions one Marylander.

BATTLE TURNS INTO GUN DUEL – Troops Fan Out After Heavy Fighting Around Ubach

By Holbrook Bradley [Sunpapers War Correspondent]

With the American army, Germany, Oct. 8 [By Radio — Delayed]. American ground troops operating east of the Wurm river sector of the northern breakthrough of the German line tonight have fanned out to occupy the strategic towns of Baesweiler and Oidtweiler several miles beyond Ubach.

After two days of fierce fighting in which the Germans made every attempt to hold on to the outer defenses of the Siegfried Line, the action has settled down to an exchange of artillery blows and occasional infantry engagements which drove the enemy from positions along the line.

During the last 24 hours we have heard little of the Germans' intensive counterfire which came from the screened pill-boxes during the early stages of our penetration.

Artillery Fire Continues

Our artillery continued to send out round after round of heavy and medium shells to soften up the resistance ahead.

Although it has been only a few days since we seized the concrete fortifications in and around Palenberg, there was little of the feeling of intense action of the opening days as we drove through the area this afternoon.

Army engineers had cleaned up the main supply route, filling in shell holes and bomb craters in the road and moving burned-out and blasted equipment as well as probing out the area for mines.

At the Wurm river a bridge blown up by the Germans had been replaced by an emergency structure over which tanks, six by sixes and other vehicles were moving to the front.

Towns Found Similar

Palenberg itself and the mining center or Ubach beyond looked much like the towns of France, Belgium or Holland through which our troops had just moved up.

Military police were directing traffic at important road junctions, others were on duty outside important installations. Here and there were a couple of GI's, tired and battleworn, poking through the ruins, rifles in hand.

We noticed soldiers who were occupying the town already making themselves at home. They were making themselves at home in courtyards and alleyways, preparing their evening meal, taking time out to clean up or grab a little rest.

Signs Of Tank Battle

Near one of the posts a young infantryman in his early twenties stood over a fire cooking a chicken stew in a huge iron pot. Sleeves rolled up, a pipe in his mouth and a tall silk hat on his head, he seemed a fantastic character amid the wreckages.

A few 88s and 105s landed somewhere off to our left as we drove into Baesweiler. On either side of the highway, lined with rows of tall trees, there were signs of a tank battle.

Along the road trees were either broken off just above the ground or had most of their limbs torn off just above the ground. In the field off to the left were two German, self-propelled 75s and a Mark IV tank, all burned out.

In the distance we could see the German-held town of Setterich, in which some buildings were burning. All about us were piles of empty shells and discarded equipment.

The guns of an American battery opened up with a roar as we turned off the road. Overhead there was the high-pitched whistle of out-going shells and the angry carrump as high-explosive shells landed among the enemy positions. The ground where the battle is taking place is so flat that we could see the columns of dirt rise where the shells hit.

Less Destruction Found

The town of Baesweiler seemed a bit better off than other towns we have seen here in Germany. The streets were littered with broken branches of trees and a few houses showed signs of heavy shelling, but generally there was less destruction than had been expected.

Elements of the battalion commanded by Major William Puttennay, of Phoenix, Ariz., had gotten only a few yards out into the open country when Tiger tanks halted them with direct fire at not much more than 200 yards. There was nothing that the Americans could do until the tanks were knocked out.

The artillery laid down a smoke screen and then followed with armor-piercing stuff which landed almost directly on the target. There was not further trouble from these. Four pillboxes half way across the open stretch were handled the same way; then the battalion pushed on over the open ground.

Germans Dug In

At the edge of the town the Americans ran into a tough scrap when they ran into 75 or 100 Germans who were dug in in World War I fashion. In the town behind them an 88-mm. gave supporting fire.

This pinned down a good bit of our attacking force for some time until a group of Sherman tanks and infantrymen outflanked the position. German tanks in the town found the going too rough and pulled out of town, leaving their infantry to be handled by the Americans. As a result most of the Germans were either killed or taken prisoner.

Still Held In Morning

As darkness fell, the Americans had taken the town and were spread out over the place. The enemy had fallen back into defensive positions several hundred yards outside and Baesweiler had been secured.

Then came the night and the heavy air and artillery bombardment. The German gunners evidently had exact coordinates on all parts of the town for they laid down fire over the whole area. The *Luftwaffe*, although few in numbers, added its bit by dropping a number of 200-pound bombs and strafing the streets. But despite all that we still held the village this morning.

Among those seen in Baesweiler today was Private Harper Tawes, of Cambridge, Md.

THE EVENING SUN, WEDNESDAY, OCTOBER 18, 1944

Taking A Very Close Look At Jerry — Down Gun Muzzle Of A Tiger Tank

By Holbrook Bradley [Sunpapers War Correspondent]

With the American First Army in Germany, Oct. 16 [By Radio — Delayed] — In a cold, driving rain which has cut visibility to a few hundred yards, American artillery and armor fighting on the edge of the Wurselen corridor today continue to exchange blows with an enemy who is putting up an almost fanatical resistance.

On the front running northeast of Aachen along the Alsdorf highway, doughboys and tankmen are slugging it out under some of the heaviest fire from German artillery and mobile mounts they have seen since the first landings on the continent.

Amplified by low-hanging clouds, the thunder of heavy gunfire echoes and reechoes through the wooded hills and valleys surrounding the battered town in which the battle rages.

Close To Enemy

While footsloggers of another outfit, which is moving up on Wurselen from the south, hold tight only 1,100 yards away, the infantrymen of one of our battalions have dug in against the enemy, in some spots only a street away.

German Mark V and Tiger tanks have moved up to cover the avenue's approach and have been sending heavy concentrations of harassing fire against the area occupied by our troops.

Combat in this escape gap has been so intense in the last few days that company and battalion commanders report gains of only a few hundred yards, in some cases only two or three houses. Despite every effort on the part of the

Germans, however, nowhere have our lines been pushed back.

Foe Knows Terrain

As in most defensive fighting, the enemy has the advantage of knowing the terrain over which he is retreating, and of being able to fall back to prepare positions that have been placed to cover all avenues of approach.

The Germans also have a decided advantage in terrain, for the high ground to which they have retreated provided observation of the movements of our attacking force.

There was little movement along Wurselen's wet streets as we drove up toward a forward battalion command post. A couple of GI's stood in the doorway of wrecked houses or hovered over fires inside, trying to dry out.

Incoming artillery shells were landing on both sides of the road along which we were moving and were exploding with a resounding crack that made them seem even closer than they were. On our left we saw what looked like a good place to park our vehicle, so we bounced in over a couple of broken rifles and other refuse the enemy had left behind.

Tanks Splatter Mud

Out on the street a couple of Sherman tanks lumbered by drowning out conversation and the noises of battle for a moment, and sending mud and water splattering over us. Up ahead there was a hollow "car-rump" sound as a few rounds of Jerry mortar fire landed amid buildings that already were battered and blasted hulks.

A number of German civilians still in the city seemed unconcerned about our appearance. Only a couple of times did we talk with any of these people and then they attempted to convince us that they were not Nazis.

The battalion commander, Major Thomas Dallas, of Martinsville, W. Va., shook his head when we asked about his progress, and pointed out the positions of a number of enemy tanks that had been spraying the area held by his troops.

Infantry, Tank Assault

Too close for air or artillery fire, the enemy's front lines have been attacked by a combination of infantry and tanks. Outside there was the almost continuous explosion of Jerry's shells of all sizes, indicating why our progress has been slow.

Our own artillery could be heard above the din of exploding shells, sending round after round into the enemy positions back in the corridor. With the situation plotted for us we decided to move up to a forward company holding buildings across the street from some Germans clinging desperately to the Alsdorf road.

Supported by a half dozen or so of Tigers, Panthers and halftracks, the enemy seemed determined to deny us any part of the highway. White smoke from phosphorus shells was rising from a row of buildings ahead as we took off from the apartment house where we had stopped for a few minutes.

Dash Across 50 Yards

Behind the company commander, Lieut. Loeb Adams, of Camilla, Ga., we dashed across 50 yards of open space, stumbling once in a wet, slimy shell hole, expecting that at any minute the next shell would be on top of us. Then we stood up to catch our breath in the shelter of the building line before a short run across the street to a cellar hole in which the CP was located.

A group of GI's stood about a couple of meager fires, trying to warm up their tins of K-ration to make them more palatable. In another section of the basement a few more men lay on mattresses trying to catch some sleep between shifts. One or two were reading letters just in from the States.

Adams asked if we wanted to take a look at Jerry, and then led us on a wild dash across a narrow street to a house opposite. Through a door and window beyond we could look right down the muzzle of the gun of a German Tiger tank sitting in the road not 75 yards from us.

Hard To Get

This tank was too close to our lines for artillery fire, one of the reasons why our army has been unable to move more rapidly. Because it was protected on all sides from our positions, we couldn't reach it with bazooka fire or our own tanks.

We could see now why the job of closing the gap has been such a tough one and we were amazed that our troops have made as much progress as they have.

Seen on the lines today were the following Virginians: Private Elmer Crawford, Harrisonburg; Private Roy Good, Harrisonburg; Private Ernest R. Rodes; First Sergeant Edwin Hering; Sergt. Ottoway Fore, Richmond; Staff Sergeant Howard Malet, Fairfax.

THE BALTIMORE SUN, WEDNESDAY, OCTOBER 18, 1944

GI's-Eye-View Of Wurselen, Where Aachen Lifeline Was Cut

By Holbrook Bradley [Sunpapers War Correspondent]

Wurselen, Oct. 15 [By Radio — Delayed] — Jumping to the attack in the vicinity of Aachen at daybreak, men in our companies moved toward their objective as their own artillery sent a supporting barrage smashing into the Jerry positions on high ground ahead. From the moment the first squad pushed out, the attack was one of moving a few houses, then getting under cover as Jerry gunners sent in counter-battery fire.

By noon today, the advance elements had battled forward more than 300 yards, scaling brick walls, moving from building to building in an attempt to stay off the main roads, which were under fire of mortars and machine guns.

The tanks up on the forward line were engaging the enemy in self-propelled and armored vehicles in a slugging duel that has been a feature of action here since we first chased the Jerries out of town.

No Army Seen

As yet, there has been no indication of Nazi attempts to withdraw men or materiel through the gap, nor have there been signs of the Germans massing large concentrations of armor, as has been reported during the past few days.

A group of GI's on guard on one of the streets of Bardenberg directed us to the unit that we were attempting to catch up with and warned us that the roads ahead were under constant fire from enemy guns.

At the crossroad ahead, a burned-out Sherman tank still smouldered amid a pile of equipment that lay scattered about the road. Out to the right we caught sight of a couple rounds of airburst that showered the ground below with jagged pieces of steel.

A Dead Jeep

German artillery and mortar shells were coming in from ahead of us as we bounced over the field criss-crossed with tank tracks. Midway was one of our jeeps that had received a direct hit; parts were scattered over the countryside, and a few hundred yards on we saw a knocked-out German halftrack and amphibious jeep.

There was a group of American soldiers standing around the entrance of a building near a coal mine as we decided to duck in and check the route forward and wait for a lull in the artillery fire. The mine evidently had been in operation only a short while before, for the steam still hissed from the stack overhead that had been pierced and broken by a direct hit.

Surgery By Firelight

In the basement of the building we found a medical side station where wounded from the morning's attack were being treated before evacuation. There was no electricity, but a couple of fires on the cement and brick floor gave enough light for the medicos to work by, and allowed the men off duty the chance to get warm and have a cup of coffee.

We could hear mortar shells landing on the street outside as we waited to talk with the medical personnel a few moments. The light from the fires cast strange shadows on the wall about us.

Staff Sergeant John T. Key, Fisherville, Va., offered to guide us forward. It seemed wise to accept his offer in a country as unfamiliar as this. The route forward had been pointed out on our map, but it is easy to take the wrong turn in the heat of battle, and we had no desire to run into enemy lines alone.

The Tanks Pass

The street forward had been chewed up into dirt and debris as we moved out with the sergeant. A couple of Sherman tanks rumbled up behind us on the way to the front and we cuddled into the doorway to let them pass, for it is almost impossible to hear the incoming artillery or mortars above the roar of tanks and we knew their presence generally draws fire.

Although the first infantrymen had passed over the same road as we were taking four hours before, there still was scattered small-arms fire and a good deal of artillery landing all about. The best method of moving up seemed to be that of running a hundred yards or so, always on the alert for an incoming whine, and then jump into the cellar of a building and wait to catch your breath while a few shells landed.

Colonel In The Cellar

Buildings thinned out as we moved up. Evidently we were passing the center of town to a more residential area, for the houses were now spaced apart with small gardens about each one. With typical white painted brick dwellings with black tile roofs, the development seemed to be one of the more recent undertakings. Like most of the city, there scarcely was a structure not hit by a shell.

Capt. Eccles H. Scott was giving the colonel the latest situation of his companies as we stepped into the cellar of one of these houses. Thundering explosions shook the walls and the roof over us, as rounds of heavy artillery landed all about the area sending up clouds of dirt and smoke, and knocking a few bricks down and a couple tiles off the roof.

Germans In Top Spot

We found out that the infantrymen ahead of us had moved up to the edge of town where they had run into a number of enemy self-propelled mounts and medium and heavy armor dug in on the ridge ahead. With the advantage of a defensive position, Jerry gunners were able to send harassing fire into the part of Wurselen we have occupied, while at the same time our tanks had the disadvantage of having to expose themselves whenever they wanted to strike back.

Despite heavy concentrations of German artillery, mortar and small-arms fire, the doughboys were moving along taking time out to clean out German positions in houses along the way and direct their own artillery fire on targets that could be picked up. The air above us was filled with the whine of shells from our medium and heavy batteries.

Up To The Very Front

Scott was on his way forward to pick out a better location and suggested that we come along to get a chance to see some fighting. We waited for a lull in the fire and then took off through back lots, jumping hedges and fences, dodging into buildings when the fire sounded too close, and then moving on toward the heavy small-arms fire some place ahead of us.

Once or twice we passed Sherman tanks parked in an advantageous spot where they could drop a few rounds on the enemy without exposing themselves unduly. A dead German lieutenant lay in a ditch on the side of the road which we crossed in a hurry as a machine gun cut loose to our left.

Line In Olive Drab

On the right flank we could see a line of olive-drab uniformed soldiers weaving their way forward through an apple orchard, rifles ready for instant action.

Once we stopped for a moment in a building used by cannon company observer, Sergt. Francis A. Kloske, Williamsport, Pa. From a vantage point on the roof we could see the field of battle ahead without being observed ourselves.

Three or four fields directly ahead a couple of United States tanks were firing into a patch of woods on the hill. Through the buildings near-by and behind a couple of hedges were small groups of attacking infantrymen. We watched as they moved a few yards ahead, then hit the dirt as machine gun bullets cut through the air over their heads.

A Kraut's Head

A good deal of heavy mortar fire had been coming from the direction of a deep draw to the west of us and we took the direction of the edge of the hill just in time to see a Kraut stick his head up over the edge of a roadside bank. He was a bit too far distant for one of our boys to take a shot at unless he had a sniper's rifle, so the cannon company observer called for fire from his guns.

As we watched the first rounds land, about all they could see was the German disappear in a hurry; they noticed the camouflaged pillbox that we hadn't seen before behind him. The next round of high-explosive shells landed right on the target and we watched as the dirt and smoke billowed up. There was no further sign of a Heinie observer. A light sprinkle of rain set in when we got moving again.

Overhead our bombers winged their way toward Aachen. Somewhere on the left flank we could hear the flights of Thunderbolts screaming down to strafe and dive-bomb enemy targets, probably the Tiger tanks still reported to be maneuvering along the Alsdorf road.

And we found going still rough, for a dozen or so mortar shells landed in an orchard less than 50 yards from us as we bounded over piles of dirt, cement, and debris. Down the street ahead of us we could see the doughboys of a leading company stalking the enemy, who still held out many buildings. The crack of rifle bullets with the chatter of a machine pistol warned us to keep our heads low.

Among Those Seen

A few of those about the area today were: Pfc. Paul Block, Baltimore; Pfc. John A. Tanko, 1321 Linden avenue; Staff Sergeant James J. Hogue, Silver Spring; Pfc. William T. Merriman, Martinsville; Major Victor Y. Gillespie, Centreville.

THE BALTIMORE SUN, THURSDAY, NOVEMBER 30, 1944

MARYLANDERS IN GERMANY —
Twenty-two Maryland men, including thirteen Baltimoreans, are mentioned in Mr. Bradley's dispatch below.

Simpson's Infantry Holding Area Within Mile of Julich

By Holbrook Bradley [Sunpapers War Correspondent]

With U.S. 9th Army, Germany, Nov. 29 [By Radio] — Forward infantry elements from this outfit operating southeast of Geilenkirchen tonight hold ground less than a mile across the Roer River from the important German rail and communication center of Julich.

A ceaseless downpour of rain for the past 24 hours has turned the field of battle into a sea of mud. Action of our troops has therefore consisted largely of consolidating new positions in the small towns of Koslar and Kirchberg seized yesterday by rifle regiments which advanced from near-by Bourheim.

Patrols Test Defenses

At night our artillery and that of the enemy exchange blows, while our patrols range along the west banks of the Roer testing enemy defenses and maintaining advance posts.

The present phase of the 9th Army's attack began last Thursday when the leading regiments jumped off from Baesweiler to break out of the Siegfried Line into the first stretches of the Cologne plain.

Striking southeastward toward the small settlements of Siersdorf and Schleiden, the infantrymen moved against stiffening enemy resistance consisting mainly of elements of the People's Grenadier Division and supported by heavy artillery fire and some armor.

Mud Often Knee Deep

Once the attack was under way the troops rolled through the mud, often knee deep to take the important rail center of Aldenhoven, fighting fiercely all the way.

The desperately resisting Germans brought artillery ranging from 75's to 240-mm. guns into action to harass the advancing Americans.

Even the added firepower, however, was not enough to stop our advance. As our troops break from the heavily defended Siegfried Line they find that the battle turns to cracking the defenses of the towns and villages.

The usual defense maintained by the Germans consists of barbed wire entanglements and trenches of the World War I type around the edge of the village. The open level ground of the approaches to these towns gives the Germans a wide field of fire, and makes leading a frontal approach difficult and costly.

Roer Floods Part Of Julich

The sea and mud occasioned by recent rains adds to the difficulties encountered by the advancing Americans and makes armored operations nightmares. We have the comfort, however, of knowing the enemy is having as much trouble from this same source. Reports coming in from the enemy lines indicate that the Roer River has risen to flood the southern part of Julich.

[An Associate Press dispatch said the Germans opened floodgates on dams of the Roer River, flooding the valley at some points to a width of nearly a mile, in an effort to combat the advance of Simpson's infantry. It added the enemy also blew up the bridge at Julich.]

A few bright intervals during the latter part of last week have permitted our air forces to go into action in close support of our ground forces. Thousands of pounds of high-explosives were dropped over this area, causing heavy damage to enemy installations and tying up his movements.

Late today flights of Mustangs swarmed low over the battlefield to dive-bomb enemy positions. There has been little activity on the part of the *Luftwaffe* over our area.

Farmers Return To Pursuits

Driving up to the front today through the rain and sleet we were impressed by the fact that the farmers of parts of Holland and Belgium through which we passed had returned to their normal pursuits as if the war were not still going on.

Some were finishing late fall plowing before winter freezes set in, others were gathering late crops.

In the towns through which we passed women went about marketing as they have done for centuries, children played in the streets and old men sat in the cafe windows and watched the world pass.

Only when one saw an occasional piece of destroyed Nazi equipment or a gutted house did we remember that the *Wehrmacht* had passed through here in disorganized retreat several weeks ago.

Picture Changes In Reich

The picture changed considerably after passing over the border of the Reich. It was colder and the general wetness more miserable. The roads turned into rutted muddy tracks. Everywhere there was the feeling of destruction and the smell of death. Buildings in the towns were partially or wholly destroyed and the few not in this condition were pockmarked by machine-gun and shell-fire.

Near Baesweiler we passed a coal mine being operated by Germans under the direction of American engineers. As we watched, the engineers blew up German pillboxes with an explosion that shook the surrounding area.

On all sides now one could hear the roar of artillery blasting away at German positions. Everywhere around were the sounds of battle.

At headquarters the men had moved out of their tents into the cellars of the blasted houses, where, at least, they sleep fairly dry. Two sections were lucky enough to have acquired stoves, and their cellars were by far the most popular for those off duty.

Tonight as artillery goes into more frequent action and the patrols prepare to cover their areas, other units are mopping up in Kirchberg and Koslar. Fighting from house-to-house, the hardened doughboys are rounding up the last Germans at this point of resistance.

Meets Maryland Men

Marylanders seen in this area today: Capt. Benny Cassell, 1156 Cleveland street, Baltimore; Lieut. Col. Robert Archer, Jr., 5301 Herring Run drive, Baltimore; Pvt. Robert Lansinger, 4403 Rokeby road, Baltimore; Sergt. Jack Archer, Bel Air; Sergt. J. Preston McComas, Bel Air; Sergt. Walter Beck, Garrison; Sergt. Charles Irwin, Bel Air; Sergt. Howard Pingree, Catonsville; George Bond, Laurel; Sergt. Raymond Everngam, Baltimore; TECH. 4/G Charles E. McLane, Baltimore; Sergt. Frederick Sturm, Jr., 2427 West Mosher street, Baltimore; Private Nelson T. Miller, 405 Rosecraft terrace, Baltimore; Sergt. Lloyd C. Gibson, Huntington; Sergt. Cornelius McQuade, 120 North Milton avenue, Baltimore; Lieut. Lawrence Brandon, 3 St. John's road, Baltimore; Staff Sergeant William T. Littleton, 3019 Overland avenue, Baltimore; Lieut. J. Victor McCool, Elkton; Lieut. Col. Howard F. Donovan, St. Dunstan's road, Baltimore; Lieut. Col. Lloyd Marr, Silver Spring.

9th Army Repelled Time And Again From Sportsplatze Outside Julich

By Holbrook Bradley [Sunpapers War Correspondent]

With U.S. 9th Army, Germany, Dec. 6 [By Radio — Delayed] — The United States 6th Infantry, supported by medium tanks and 30 Thunderbolt fighter-bombers today took another crack at a tough German resistance point, the Sportsplatze opposite Julich.

This is one of the toughest spots on the 9th Army front, and our men have been forced back from it time and again by the murderous fire of the Germans entrenched in the Sportsplatze and the near-by public baths.

Only Approach Over Fields

The position is located on the bank of the Roer River and is nothing more than an oval field surrounded by an 8 to 10-foot mound of earth. Of course this has been reinforced by concrete and steel pillboxes.

Our only approach to it is over open fields leading toward the river, and the Germans have these well covered with machine-guns. In addition to this the river is at flood stage, and many of the low spots in the approach are covered with water, which further limits the ground over which our troops can fight toward the Sportsplatze.

Today's attack began as four Thunderbolts swept in under the low-hanging clouds to make their first strafing run and then just at the end of it drop their bombs on the target area. They came in so low that they almost seemed to skim the houses and treetops.

This maneuver was one of the most finely co-ordinated that the air and ground forces have staged to date and one of the most difficult. Before it was staged, the air and ground personnel went over the ground carefully to work out the low-altitude problem of the action.

Crews Take Off

Once the details were worked out, the crews took off in weather which grounded most flying forces. German gunners were throwing their scattered rounds across the Roer into the fields surrounding Koslar as the first flight roared in low enough to come under the enemy flak.

The ground attack was scheduled for 2 P. M. First there was the low dull hum which grew to a roar as the first flight came in over our heads to throw a stream of flaming tracers at the target and then apparently bounce skyward at the river. Then they circled and came back to drop their bombs which went off with an earth-shaking roar that sent columns of black smoke, dirt and concrete soaring skyward.

For 50 minutes the ground forces under command of Major James Morris, of Bel Air, waited in the woods for their signal to advance as plane after plane swept in over the target and dumped its load. The last Thunderbolt pulled away and headed back toward its base and then our artillery took up the action with smoke and white phosphorus shells.

Smoke Billows Up

As the first rounds fell in the target area, white smoke clouds billowed up toward the low-hanging clouds, covering the whole scene with a man-made fog. Even the high-towers and buildings of Julich, about a mile away, were blotted out.

On the jump-off line machine-gunners with weapons zeroed to give support to the infantry crouched waiting for the troops to get under way.

As the clouds of phosphorous rolled over the river, the first squads got under way, moving across the wet terrain toward the right flank of the objective. Then one began to see black spurts of dirt and powder in the white fog as enemy gunners dropped mortar and high-explosives shells, trying to find the advancing men.

Machine Guns Start

The supporting machine-guns opened up with a deafening chatter. Our heavy artillery started to throw shells into the enemy position, and on the far right, when the fog lifted momentarily, one could see the first of the infantrymen moving along the levee toward the strong point.

From a distance the men who were leading the platoons looked almost a part of the ground over which they moved. Every once in a while one could pick out a man running from cover to cover and stopping now and then to fire his rifle.

As night fell, one could still see the flash of artillery pieces and the exploding shells in the direction of Julich, and one wondered if the attackers would get dug in close to the Sportsplatze during the night.

Three Marylanders Seen

Other Marylanders seen in this area today were: Lieut. Col. William J. Witte, Hunting Ridge; Major James Porter, Baltimore; Lieut. Thomas B. Jones, Baltimore.

Marylanders At The Front

Major Morris, whose wife and three children, Margaret, 8; James, 5, and John, 4, live in Delta, Pa., is the son of Mr. and Mrs. Walter W. Morris, of Pylesville, Md.

A graduate of the Highland High School, near Bel Air, he attended the University of Maryland for two years and then took a course in accounting at a Baltimore business college, later working for a Bel Air bank. For several years he was an investigator for the Harford County Welfare Board.

He was a second lieutenant in the Maryland National Guard when it was mustered into the Federal service and was promoted to captain while his division was in training in this country. He went overseas in September, 1942, and was promoted to the rank of major while in Europe.

Played Football At Poly

Major Porter, whose wife lives at 1 Poplar lane, attended the Polytechnic Institute, where he played in the backfield on the football teams of 1934 and 1935. He attended the Johns Hopkins University and later was a teacher of mathematics and English at Polytechnic.

He went overseas three years ago and participated in the invasion of Normandy, having been awarded the Bronze Star. Mrs. Porter said he wrote recently that he had been taking a course at the University of Paris in connection with educational work he is doing at the headquarters to which he is assigned.

Is Hopkins Graduate

Colonel Witte, whose wife and 2-year-old daughter live at 4720 Edmondson avenue, Hunting Ridge, is a graduate of the Johns Hopkins University and the Army's Command and General Staff School at Fort Leavenworth, Kan.

He enlisted in the Maryland National Guard while in college, resigned following his graduation in 1935 to accept a commission as second lieutenant in the United States Army Reserves Corps, gave up the commission a year later to accept a position as an engineer here with the Consolidated Gas and Electric Company and re-entered the National Guard as a private.

He was a captain when the National Guard was called into Federal service and was promoted to major while his outfit was in training in this country. He went overseas in October, 1942, and participated in the Normandy invasion, having been awarded the Bronze Star for his work in preparing plans for operations in France.

His daughter was born a month after he went overseas.

Holds Presidential Citation

Lieutenant Jones, son of Mrs. Lillian Jones, of 3005 Elgin avenue, has been overseas for two years. He holds a presidential unit citation and the Purple Heart for wounds suffered on August 6 in Normandy.

THE LORRAINE CAMPAIGN

From Bradley Back to McCardell

THE BALTIMORE SUN, SUNDAY, SEPTEMBER 24, 1944

Many people have been wondering what has happened to Lee McCardell — so have the Sunpapers. After a period of 12 days during which his whereabouts were unknown, he suddenly turned up with the American infantry in the Alsace-Lorraine area. In a series of dispatches, of which the accompanying one is the first, he describes the activities of the division to which he is attached.

Destruction Of A German Infantry Division — A Day-By-Day Account

McCardell Strings Along With "The Old Man's" Outfit Across France And Sees A Lot Of Action

By Lee McCardell [Sunpapers War Correspondent]

With a United States Infantry Regiment Somewhere in Alsace-Lorraine, Sept. 16 [By Radio — Delayed] — The corps commander drove up in his jeep to where the Old Man was standing in the crossroads village of Ramecourt yesterday morning, returned his salute, and said:

"As we piece the situation together, this is what has happened:

"We have destroyed the entire German infantry division that was screening preparations for the tank attack from the south on the Third Army flank. They had assembled about 200 tanks. While we were finishing off the infantry, one of our armored outfits hit the tanks from behind and knocked out 80 of them."

Medics Got No Souvenirs

The main road through the village, from where they were standing to the outskirts of the next little town, a mile or so beyond, was strewn with burned and battered wreckage of one German infantry column's cars, trucks, caissons, wagons and bicycles, with the carcasses of dead artillery horses and the dead bodies of German soldiers.

At the aid station across the road, American medics were patching up a score of wounded German prisoners, most of them litter cases.

"The trouble with being a medic," grumbled Capt. Maurice Lazarus, of Buffalo, N. Y., a former Johns Hopkins student now commanding one of the Old Man's battalion medical detachments, "is that we never have a chance to pick up any souvenirs."

A Luger For The General

"I wouldn't mind having one of those German Lugers myself," said the corps commander.

"Here you are, sir — I'll be glad to give you this one," said Capt. Emmett Creighton, of Cambridge, Maryland.

He handed the general the Luger (a German automatic) which he'd been lugging around for the last two months.

"I've been meaning to send it home to my father," the captain said, "but it's all right — I'll get another."

"Something Wrong," Old Man Says

Today the Old Man's outfit is resting in another village miles closer to the German frontier. The probabilities are that it won't rest long. It never does.

"Something is wrong," said the Old Man after lunch today. "We've been sitting here six hours now and no orders yet to move."

Since landing in Normandy last summer the force of which his regiment is part has traveled approximately 1,000 miles to establish what is believed to be this war's record for long-distance movement by any American outfit in France.

Direction Of Attack Changed

Crossing the Seine after the breakthrough and rout of the German armies along the coast, the regiment appeared headed for Berlin via Belgium when the direction of its attack was changed to this sector.

The easiest way to tell the story of the destruction of the German division in this attack, as we watched it last week while stringing along with the Old Man's unit, is in modified diary form. The Old Man, incidentally, is the regimental commander. We can't mention him by name. We shall therefore refer to him throughout as the "Old Man," just as his own officers and men do, with profound respect and admiration.

Sunday, September 10

Bucking convoys and guns and trucks moving east from Paris, we overtook the Old Man's outfit in a French farm village, like hundreds of other French villages whose earthy, unpaved streets are banked with manure piles, and whose principal traffic problems before the army's arrival was the departure of the villagers' cows for the surrounding pastures every morning, and the return of same every evening at milking time.

The general advance in this section is now getting under full steam. Engineers are rebuilding bridges destroyed by the retreating Germans. Quartermaster truck companies are hauling rations, ammunition and gasoline to newly established dumps. Field hospitals are being set up. Generally unravished by the war, the countryside is beautifully rolling, moderately prosperous farmland.

It's Eggs The GI's Want

As usual the GI's are shopping it thoroughly for one thing. They go from door to door asking the farmers' wives:

"*Madame, havez yous daze erfs?*

"*Pas des oeufs.*" madame usually replies with a shrug of the shoulders. Meaning some other Joe has beat them to it if she had any. Eggs are none too plentiful here. The farmers seem to have more cows than chickens

Troops On Move Everywhere

It wasn't easy to catch up with the Old Man's regiment. We had battled around for three days, in and out of towns whose names were by-words in the last war. Everywhere troops were in movement. Fighting still centered on Metz, where we dodged one midday air attack by a small force of German planes.

We finally found the division headquarters temporarily installed in a dismantled chateau recently evacuated by the Germans.

Anticipating a day or two's rest there, Lieut. Harry Seevers, division G-1, was arranging municipal bathhouse and movie-show schedules for the division's troops when orders came down from the corps commander to push on toward the Moselle river.

Off for a Better CP

The order reached the Old Man just after he had returned to his CP (command post), in the village *mairie* (school house), from inspecting the defenses of his battalion bivouac areas. The troops had pulled in only that morning.

"Oh, well, it wasn't much of a CP anyway — we'll find a better one where we are going," said his adjutant, Capt. Tommy Lyons.

We will sleep tonight in the chateau with the divisional CP. It isn't as fancy as it sounds. The beds are German wooden bunks in a dirty upstairs chamber which the Germans used as a barracks room.

Encounters Private Sciuto

At meal time, the division staff lines up with mess gear at the kitchen truck in the chateau part for 10-in-1 rations. There, I happened upon Private Nino Sciuto, of Collington avenue and Biddle street, Baltimore, a member of the division band. Sciuto hasn't seen his saxophone since he landed. The band has been doing guard duty with the security platoon at division headquarters.

The only other Marylanders we've seen the last day or two have been Lieut. Col. Charles Lydecker, of Baltimore, with an armored division near Metz, and Sergt. Charles Blankenship, of Dundalk, with a Third Army engineer group.

There are lots of Virginians around, however, Pvt. David Loan, of Clifton Forge, is here with a division G-3 section. Pvt. William McAllister, of Portsmouth, and Pvt. Garnett Hardy, of Danville, are with the division motor section, where we drew a precious supply of gasoline to keep our jeeps going.

Monday, September 11

The Old Man's regiment marched this morning, and we trailed along. At noon, artillery and quartermaster trucks picked up some of the infantry. Others climbed up on tank destroyers, trailers, guns — anything they could hold on to, and the column rolled on until its point met "enemy opposition of unknown strength," according to the radio report from a mechanized cavalry reconnaissance unit near Olleville, a few miles west of the Moselle.

One unit of the division, traveling by motor truck, had turned south to attack Neufchateau. Another had gone north to secure the Moselle river bridgehead below Nancy. The Old Man's outfit stopped for the time being, bivouacked in cow pastures several miles west of the Moselle, where the Germans held several small villages among the hills.

German artillery tossed a few shells toward his moving column this afternoon, but the day's progress has been more or less of a triumphal march, the villagers turning out along the way to greet the Americans with flowers and flags, and whenever the troops halted, with baskets of fresh tomatoes and bottles of homemade wine.

One Unhappy Nazi Officer

A few prisoners, mostly stragglers, had been picked up. One German officer had been brought in ignominiously seated on the hood of his captor's speeding jeep. The French loved that. They hooted and jeered as he swept past, clutching the engine hood with one hand and holding his cap with the other. He was trying desperately to sit erect, his boots on the bumper. He looked unhappy.

[It was later discovered that the entire division had marched right across the front of a German defensive line which here stretched from west to east at that time, in order to protect the Belfort Gap, through which other German troops were trying to withdraw from southern France before the Seventh Army could catch them.]

Tuesday, September 12

It was a quiet night from a military viewpoint. Nobody bothered to dig a foxhole and, weather remaining fine, few pitched shelter tents. But nobody got much sleep.

All night, American tanks, trucks and tractor-drawn artillery, some of it heavy stuff, clanked noisily along the narrow, dusty road winding through the bivouac area.

At Jeanne d'Arc's Birthplace

We took time out today to pay respects to the village of Domrémy-la-Pucelle, the birthplace of Jeanne d'Arc. The Old Man's columns by passed Domrémy yesterday by three miles, but an antiaircraft battery had been there, and Sergt. E. E. S. Connor, of 128 Augusta avenue, had signed the visitors' book in the little stone house where the Maid of Orleans was born some 500 years ago.

Connor and two others of his battery — Lieut. John Piribek, of Allenport, Pa., and Sergt. Joseph Rosso, of McKeesport — had been the first to sign the register since *Madame la custodienne*, the French Amazonian in charge, had returned the book to the shrine from the *mairie*, where it had been concealed during the German occupation.

Petitions To The Maid

The tragic years of 1941-42 saw the register inscribed with prayers as well as with names:

"*St. Jeanne d'Arc, rendez-moi mon Papa cher*," signed "Jacqueline."

And countless anonymous petitions to the maid to "*Sauvez la France*" and "*Rendez nous nos prisonnieres.*"

In Domrémy's pretty valley, where the maid first heard her "voices," the Catholic brothers living at the magnificent basilica above the village were enjoying the greatest rush in their souvenir shop for postcards and medallions that they had known since pre-war days.

A Message For The Kovacs

At Attigneville, where we stopped for lunch at the village café, Mme. Theresa Kozic, a Yugoslav waitress, implored us to try to pass on word to her brother, Joseph Kovacs, 66 West 71st street, New York city, that his wife and son in Yugoslavia are both safe and well, according to the last letter she had from them. They haven't been able to write to him since the German occupation.

In the meanwhile, one of the Old Man's battalions had been feeling out the defenses of the village of Poussay, near Mirecourt. The place appeared strongly held by the Germans dug in on the surrounding wooded hills.

A cavalry reconnaissance patrol reported 500 in one woods. We got back in time to hear Lieut. Carl Ness, of Portsmouth, Ohio, a cannon company forward observer, call the report in by radio to the Old Man.

"How many did you say?" the Old Man called back from his CP on another hill.

"I did not say," said Ness, who used to be a newspaper reporter, "I said *they* said '500.'"

Stopped for a moment, the Old Man grinned, then told Ness:

"Well, don't lose 'em — get some fire in on 'em."

Regimental headquarters moved up last night to another cow pasture on the outskirts of Frenelle-la-Petite (not to be confused with the next village of Frenelle-la-Grande, equally smelly).

Outfits Hospitality

It was colder, and looked like rain. We were glad to accept the invitation of Capt. Harie Keck, of Charlotte, N. C., to unroll our sleeping bag in his shelter tent.

This morning Capt. Jack Matthews, of Riverton, N. J., headquarters commandant, picked us up on his strength report for rations. Privates John D'Alessio, of Staten Island, N. Y., and Dan Bieze, of Chicago, who drive the headquarters' overburdened three-quarter-ton truck, squeezed our bedroll in with the rest of its baggage. Our jeep went back to Paris with another correspondent.

For all practical purposes, we are *pro tem* members and proud of it.

His third battalion, commanded by Lieut. Col. Roy Porter, of Grand Rapids, Iowa, attacked a village above Poussay, and took it by the book.

Thanks To Timmons' Company

In that attack, they suffered only one casualty — one man slightly wounded — thanks in large measure to the cannon company commanded by Capt. John Timmons, of Baltimore.

Two Jerry machine guns, which dug into the hillside hedgerows, had been holding up the advance, were found silenced, with three dead Germans by each, after one of Timmons' forward observers had laid fire on them. The crew of the German anti-tank gun near the center of the village took off, leaving the gun behind them.

Last night Lieut. Dennis Sullivan, of Buffalo, led a platoon into town on a reconnaissance mission. Every man in the platoon, except Sullivan was killed or injured.

Note To Company Commander

To one wounded man whom he bandaged, and then sent back, Sullivan gave a scribbled pencil note to his company commander:

"I am in town alone. Advise what to do. No radio. Send aid for wounded in open field we crossed."

Sullivan hid all night in the bushes on the edge of the village, met and helped guide other infantrymen of his battalion coming in this morning to attack.

The 150 Germans who had been in the village for the last ten days were pretty well demoralized, depending upon the local telephone systems for communication with other units in the neighboring villages. Despite the artillery fire, the outposts seemed to be asleep when the Americans closed in for the final assault.

The Jerry Wasn't Asleep

Down through a hillside vineyard into the village, Lieut. Harold (Little) Roberts and Private Arthur Apodaca almost stepped on one Jerry lying beside a mined lane.

"Is that guy asleep? asked Apodaca.

The German started up, pulled back his rifle's bolt.

Apodaca shot first.

"*Nicht! Nicht!*" cried two other Germans cowering in a foxhole with upraised hands.

The German company cook was still at work at the kitchen stove in one village house when Capt. William McKean, of Boston, walked in. The cook didn't argue, McKean cut himself a slab of mirabelle plum pie, sitting on the kitchen table. Lieut. Maurice Kelly, of Boston, split a bottle of *biere de charmes* with McKean, and the battle was over.

A colonel whose name we cannot mention, member of a well known old Maryland-Pennsylvania family, led the Old Man's jeep-mounted I and R (Intelligence and Reconnaissance) platoon across the bridge and around the roadblocks toward the next village.

Its shutters were closed, its streets empty when the little task force entered the town cautiously. Two of three old Frenchmen poked their heads out one doorway to tell the colonel there were Germans with two cannons near a chateau at the far end of the village.

The colonel and three men went around the back way on foot through the villagers' gardens, captured half a dozen prisoners and two machine guns without firing a shot.

Private Earle's Jeep

Other jeeps of the I and R platoon, one driven by Private John Earle, of Baltimore, sneaked up the road beyond the church and started around the corner by the stone wall of a chateau on the grounds when a knot of Jerries scampered across the highway ahead of them.

"There they go — get 'em!"

Pete Heffner, riding in the first jeep, cut loose with a 50-caliber. From trees and shrubbery on the chateau grounds the German machine gun came back at him.

Pete Sticks To His Gun

The platoon scattered to find cover against walls of the nearest houses. But not Pete. He stuck to his 50-caliber mounted on the jeep standing there in the middle of the road and sprayed away.

The platoon's leader, Lieut. C. L. Swope, and the colonel ducked through the gate of the stonewalled enclosure in which the Germans had parked a halftrack and planted an anti-tank gun commanding the highway. Others were still firing from the chateau shrubbery. Swope started to jump into the foxhole, found two Germans ahead of him.

Around the corner of the halftrack ran another German with a rifle aimed at Swope's back. Jim Lusk, another I and R Man, got him with one shot.

Jerries Yell "Kamerad"

"*Kamerad! Kamerad!*" yelled two Jerries in a foxhole.

Two more I and R men, Rush Allen and Neil Sinclair, tried to work their way around the chateau and across its tennis court. The Germans, still firing from the shrubbery, flung hand grenades at them.

"I'm afraid they got Sinclair," panted Allen when he got back to the road. "He's lying over there near the tennis court. I can't get to him — he don't answer when I call him."

The sheet-iron covered gates of the chateau's stable yard burst open and a frightened Frenchman ran out with hands up.

Sergt. Bill Donaldson and Doc Seller, I and R platoon's spunky little aid men, tried to get through the stable yard to the tennis court. German fire was too hot.

"Sinclair!" Donaldson yelled over the stone wall, ducking machine-gun bullets, "Sinclair!"

About that time one of Porter's platoons came up the road. They doused the chateau's shrubbery with rifle, grenades and mortar shells. The Germans stopped firing, disappeared. Sinclair, whose home is in Philadelphia, picked himself up near the tennis court and limped out. He had been struck in the back by a German grenade fragments, but not wounded seriously.

And that was the end of the battle of one more village.

A Scared Polish Boy

I and R platoon swept up another prisoner, a scared Polish boy in a German uniform wounded in the knee by Heffner. Private James (Smokey) Henthorn, of 1238 Carroll street, Baltimore, one of Porter's company runners, pedaled up and down the road on a captured bicycle shouting:

"Fastest runner in the regiment now!"

All told 73 prisoners were captured today, along with enough abandoned German trucks and automobiles to make the Old Man's service company, given the job of hauling them back to a company area, thoroughly sick.

The Sunpapers correspondent was offered the use of one car if he'd drive it away, but he elected to ride on with Jim Lusk and Privates Abe Coveney and Ray Zwolinski in one of the I and R platoon jeeps.

THE BALTIMORE SUN, TUESDAY, SEPTEMBER 26, 1944

This is part of a series of dispatches by Mr. McCardell recounting the activities of an American infantry regiment in Alsace-Lorraine. In it he mentions eight Marylanders he encountered.

A Division Dies Between Midnight And Dawn

By Lee McCardell [Sunpapers War Correspondent]

With Infantry Forces Somewhere in Alsace-Lorraine, Sept. 15 [By Radio — Delayed] — At Poussay, the billet where we tried to sleep last night wasn't as roomy as we had first thought.

It seems that the two old French women and man who own the house and live there had locked up most of the second-floor bedrooms. We were late in staking out a claim on floor space. The only spot we could find for our bedroll was a patch of cold, tiled floor, in the downstairs center hall, under the staircase by the door, at the head of the cellar steps.

We shared this piece of floor with Lieut. Jeff Collins, of Richmond, Va., who, like us, was hotel-less when the time came to go to bed.

Awakened At Midnight

We were awakened around midnight by a loud and alarming babble of French, to find ourselves lost in a dimly lighted forest of hairy shanks and wooden shoes, which we presently identified as those of the two old ladies and the gent. They were standing over us in their nightgowns. One old girl held an oil lamp. Another clutched a sleepy pet dog to her bosom. They were obviously in trouble, but neither Jeff nor I could make it out at first.

Finally, we caught on. Stretched out on the floor as we were at the head of the cellar stairs, we were blocking the path to their *abri*, their cellar shelter. From off in the direction of Ramecourt, about a mile away, we could hear machine-gun fire. The three old people were frightened.

They asked if we thought the Germans were coming back.

We did not.

Did we think there was any danger?

We did not.

In our best French, which is lousy, we advised them to *restez content*, go back to bed and forget it.

Wooden Shoes Cellarward

They shuffled off in their wooden shoes, unlocked their bedroom door farther down the hall and disappeared inside, locking the door behind them. We went back to sleep on the floor.

But not for long.

"Pardon, M'sieur. Pardon, M'sieur."

Again the air was full of hairy shanks and wooden shoes. Stampeding for their *abri*, the old folk were walking right over Jeff. We helped them open the cellar door. They plunged through.

"Lock it," said Jeff, "so they can't change their mind again."

The Old Folks Leave

The sound of firing near Ramecourt was louder. Through the wall beside us we could hear our own "Old Man" on the radio in the dining room. He was calling Major Sam Gooding, commanding officer of the force which took Ramecourt yesterday, and was posted there last night.

The artillery was coming down strong around Ramecourt now. We could hear one concentration after another.

Wooden shoes clumped up the cellar steps behind us. The door was pushed open.

"Pardon, M'sieur. Pardon, M'sieur."

Again Jeff was run over. The old folk were taking off for keeps this time, pet dog and all. Evidently they had lost faith in their *abri*. They left the house by the back door, and we didn't see them again until this morning.

Artillery And Champagne

Our Old Man sleeps in an upstairs bedroom. He had been awakened by the call of "Urgent! Urgent!" over the radio in the downstairs dining room. He had come down and got on the horn himself, to find out what was going on. He was told that an enemy column had tried to barge through Ramecourt.

Three trucks had made it as far as Mirecourt, where they were stopped. The rest of the column had been caught in Ramecourt. Then Gooding called for artillery. The guns had been surveyed in yesterday afternoon, on the road beyond Ramecourt.

Neither the Old Man nor his staff, gathered in the dining room, could understand exactly what had happened, but Gooding seemed to have the situation in hand. The bottle of champagne which the artillery last night had presented the Old Man was still sitting on the side table. The Old Man suddenly remembered he had forgotten to open it, so he and the staff killed it then and there.

When he got out to Ramecourt at daylight this morning, the Old Man understood why the situation had seemed confused last night. The wreckage of enemy columns, burned vehicles, many of them towing artillery, stopped up the road to the next village of Domvahler.

Two hundred and fifty-three Germans had been captured. Lying along the road were uncounted German dead. Wounded Germans were still being carried into the aid station. No Americans had been killed. Ten had been wounded in the weird battle-royal fought in the darkness between midnight and dawn.

Here's the story:

About midnight, a jeep came speeding down the road from the direction of Domvahler. An American anti-tank gun crew, posted beside the road just outside Ramecourt, let the jeep pass. They must have been mistaken. The next thing they knew, a convoy of German trucks and German soldiers pedaling bicycles were highballing past them.

"One Hell Of A Mess"

"When the shooting woke me up, there were Jerries all over the place — one hell of a mess," said Corporal Walter Hubbs, 2007 Girard avenue, Baltimore, an anti-tank gunner off duty when the fighting began.

A few minutes earlier a Frenchman had walked into the medical aid station in a house at the other end of the village and asked Capt. Maurice Lazarus, of Buffalo, N. Y., a former Johns Hopkins student, to come over to his house on the other side of the road and take charge of a GI who had too much to drink.

Lazarus went over and was bringing the GI back across the road to the aid station when they were almost run down by a motor truck. The captain angrily flashed his light to see who was driving and was told, in German to put it out.

Grinke Opens Fire

He didn't have to be told a second time, because he saw another truck, loaded with German soldiers, behind the first. He beat it for the aid station, got the force commander's CP on the telephone, and told the officer who answered that a German convoy was passing the aid station.

"Nuts," snorted the officer, and hung up — just as a burst of machine-gun fire whipped past the front window of the aid station.

Lieut. Louis Grinke, of Rochester, Ky., an anti-tank unit commander, bedded down for the night at Capt. Emmitt Creighton's house farther up the road, had seen the Germans. He had backed his jeep, armed with a 50-caliber machine-gun, out of the covered alleyway where he had parked it earlier, and opened fire.

Convoy Piles Up

He hit a truck loaded with gasoline and ammunition. The truck stopped and burst into flames, blocking the road. Other vehicles of the convoy piled into the burning truck. The blaze lighted up the road. The troops in the jammed column scattered, trying to get out of sight, and away from Grinke's 50-caliber. They headed for the nearest houses on either side of the road.

They didn't know that the men of Gooding's force were quartered in almost every one of those houses.

"I never saw such a mixup," said Private Norman Jenkins, of Mount Airy, Md., who was also in Captain Creighton's combination farmhouse-barn.

"Kamerad!"

"There were Jerries inside and out. One crawled in under Lieutenant Grinke's jeep and got up in the haymow. I made him holler 'Kamerad.' Others sneaked in the back way. There must have been a dozen in here at one time.

"We couldn't tell who was who in the dark. They were lost and didn't know who we were. One German shook hands with a man in our anti-tank unit."

Another walked up to Private Ira Baker, of Somerset, Ky., a radio operator, and "kept jabbering at me in German until I knocked him cold," Baker said.

"Dullest, Damn Bayonet"

"I grabbed hold of somebody in the dark and asked, 'Who are you?'" said First Sergeant Ralph Elrod, of Minneapolis.

"'Kamerad,'" he says.

"Kamerad, hell," I said. "We got no Kamerads in this outfit, and I knocked him down. He got up, and I knocked him down again. Then Baker finished him off with a bayonet."

"Dullest damn bayonet I ever saw," remarked Baker.

"We had to feel the ends of each other's rifles to make sure of our own men in the dark," Elrod said. "If we felt a cleaning staff — our rifles don't have any — we knew he was a Jerry."

Disconnected Telephone

Captain Creighton, a Maryland Eastern Shoreman, had been talking over the field telephone when the shooting began. He ran outside and joined the open-air fight of rifles, machine guns and hand grenades. Some of the machine guns talking now were those which Sergt. George Maerz, of Baltimore, had posted farther up along the road.

One group of Germans blundered into the front yard of Gooding's CP. Two boxes of German hand grenades captured yesterday afternoon were sitting in the yard, and the staff expected them to come through the windows any minute. The switchboard operator didn't dare talk above a whisper. When the Old Man came on the radio, demanding to know what was going on, it wasn't safe for anyone to talk loud enough to tell him.

Captain Lazarus and his medics also had Germans in the front yard of their aid station. The medics disconnected their field telephone for fear it would ring and give them away.

Sounds Funny Now

The crocked GI whom the captain had navigated across the road, through the German column, revived every now and then to break the strictly observed silence with a loud bellow:

"Gimme a carbine. I'll clean up the lousy Jerries!"

The another aidman would sit on him.

The French civilians living upstairs, and always helpful, came down with a light to inform the blacked-out medics that les Boches were out front.

"It sounds funny now, but it wasn't funny last night," Lazarus said this morning.

One soldier was using a rifle to pry open the front door of Lieut. Ralph Scott's house farther down the road when Sergt.

Stanley Whitten, of Detroit, opened up from the inside with a submachine gun.

"Had The Joint Cased"

"I was coming down from the loft, where I had been sleeping," Scott said, "and he almost took me off that ladder."

(Scott received another letter from Baltimore this morning. It contained a photograph of his newborn son who, much to his father's satisfaction, already has hair on his head).

Other Germans managed to break into other buildings along the road, including the village café, which Corp. Henry Zorn, of Orangeville and Pvt. Wm. Vieweg, 2703 Bayonne ave. Baltimore, had almost settled on as a good place to sleep last night. Their final choice had been Gooding's CP.

By this time, Major Beadell's artillery was dropping the first of its concentrations.

"We had the joint cased," said Capt. Clifford Couvillon, of Louisiana, an artillery officer with Gooding's headquarters.

Column Wiped Out

"He was referring to the fact that the guns, surveyed in yesterday afternoon, had registered fire on either side of the road.

"While the infantry was mopping up the head of the column within the village proper, our artillery wiped out — and I mean wiped out — its tail, a string of cars, trucks, towed mortars and horse-drawn artillery which was detouring the road block between Ramecourt and Domvahler. We've never seen a more completely destroyed column. It looked like an air corps job."

When the artillery shells first began coming in last night, the Joes weren't sure whose they were. In the field outside Ramecourt, where he had bivouacked, one Joe started to dig himself a foxhole. Just across the fence another soldier was digging like mad. Not until the soldier in the neighboring foxhole surrendered this morning did the Joe know he was a Jerry.

The Morning After

At daylight, 15 or 20 Jerries climbed out of the stack of American bedding rolls in which they had been hiding beside Creighton's billet since the midnight blowoff. One came forward to surrender the lot. From a ditch across the road where he was hiding, some fanatical Nazi threw a hand grenade at his *Kamerad*, killing him.

The other Germans still alive were willing enough to be taken prisoner. They crawled out of cellars, bushes and even the Americans' motor pool, 200 strong.

A wounded German first lieutenant lying in front of Scott's billet haughtily asked Sergeant Whitten to get him a clean pair of pants and a pipe from his pack in one of the cars of the blasted column.

No Chance At Souvenirs

The Joes, followed by the inevitable French scavengers, had pretty well picked over everything in that column. Its burned wreckage had been shoved to one side of the gory, ash-covered highway. The live artillery horses had been cut loose from their traces and turned loose in the fields. Caissons had been hauled away, and captured bicycles stacked up.

French farm carts filled with bloody Germans still were coming down the road from Domvahler when we got into Ramecourt this morning. Captain Lazarus, his own medics, a captured German major — a medical officer — and German aid men had been working with the wounded for the last five hours.

"What burns us up is that we medics never have a chance to gather souvenirs," said Lazarus, who was taking time out for a canteen cup of coffee.

End Of The German 16th

Then another ambulance and another wagon load of wounded mostly litter cases, pulled up. Lazarus handed a canteen up to another medic.

"Keep it hot for me," he said.

"Get me a water can to put under the foot of that litter over there. Get me a bottle of plasma."

The destruction of the column last night marked the end of the 16th German Division, of which this force has been whittling.

Saturday, September 16

We have another CP in another muddy Alsatian village of cows and manure piles, but the house we are in is clean and cowless. It was vacant when we moved in. We are told it is the home of a collaborator who has moved on to parts unknown.

The Old Man has a bed upstairs and there is enough empty floor space for the rest of us. Our good friends of I and R platoon, billeted down around the corner, in the village schoolroom, offered me a mattress there. I and R platoon has a way of arranging such matters as soft beds and fresh eggs. But we had already bedded down on the floor beside Capt. Tim Timmons, safely removed from entrances to any *abris*, and thought we had better stay there.

Old Man Has A Car

The Old Man has a real car for the first time since he left the States. It's a brand new 1942 Mercury, just like the one he drove at home. He picked it up among the snazzier German sedans captured by his outfit during the last couple days.

A general ran off with it after the Old Man had placed it under guard. And being gifted with a rare sense of humor, the Old Man promptly reported it as "stolen" to the military police.

He got it back yesterday, and hopes to ride in it tomorrow, if it is still here. But he doesn't expect to keep it very long. You can't buck a general in this man's army until you can match him star for star.

The Rooster That Grew

Which reminds us that another colonel, whom we saw at headquarters a few days ago, had acquired the only thing he said he ever wanted in France — one of these sheet metal chanticleers that roost on every French church steeple, a weather vane. The only trouble is that when he got it down on the ground, the bird proved to be much larger that it had appeared on the steeple.

It stands about six feet high. Now that he has it, the colonel says, "What the hell am I gonna do with it?"

The movement here was uneventful, and on the theory we may stay put a day or two, Captain Kecke today jeeped back to a rear echelon for a moving-picture machine, and he hopes for a final okay on a tentative engagement for Bing Crosby and his troupe to put on a show for the outfit.

Back To Three Squares

We are back on three regular meals per day. The cooks have set their gasoline-burner unit at the top of the kitchen's green tile stove, and on this cold, rainy day it was right cozy down there at chow time.

Among the staff mail received today was a letter from Lieut. Col. Ed Van Bibber, of Bel Air, in a hospital near Paris, sweating out the slight injuries of a jeep accident.

Colonel Van, who takes an exceedingly dim view of hospitalization, wrote in his characteristic style:

"My injuries include numerous bruises, which are unimportant. I figure I can get out of here if I work it right. Suffice it to say, they'll regret every day they keep me. I see by the papers you're in Holland." (Note: He reads the wrong ones.)

"I feel badly not being with you. I hope I'll be in at the kill."

Sunday, September 17

We have a house guest, Lieut. J. M. McCaughlin, of Decatur, Ill., a heavy bomber pilot, shot down yesterday. He was unhurt, but is lying in today for a rest. He's occupying the only real bed in our room, thereby suspending a bitter dispute between Capt. Tommy Lyons and Lieut. Ben Westervelte as to which of them should sleep in state.

Although it's still raining hard, Captain Goodwin has kindly volunteered to drive us back to Third Army press headquarters so we can dispatch such portions of these notes as the censors may be good enough to pass.

This "Is Their Story"

The notes are necessarily incomplete, because it is impossible to list all the incidents and name all the individuals fighting in the past week's operation.

But because so many who receive little public credit in this war have made it possible, in one way or another, to compile this record, which is their story, not mine, we append a few of their names, in the hope that some friends or member of their families may know what they are doing:

Sergeants: Sidney Hall, Richmond; William Beynon, Pittsburgh; Stanley Stokowski, Pittsburgh; Stanley Kulys, Philadelphia; James Croasdale, Philadelphia; William Gikson, Dalton, Ga.; Eddie Kirkland, Springfield, Ohio; Philip Hanson, Muskegon, Mich.; Ronald Fuller, Hampton, Iowa; Frank Brighton, New Orleans.

Corporals: Robert Warrick, Washington, Pa.; Jacob Labor, Philadelphia; Grover Waldron, Bluefield, W. Va.; James Stokes, Maywood, Ill.; T/3 Ralph Etter, Philadelphia; T/4 Hank Grzylowoki, Pittsburgh; Elvin Lee, Picayune, Miss.;

Goodrich Gamble, St. Louis, Mo.; T/5 James Manganello, Vandergrift, Pa.; T/5 Connie Lane, Durham, N. C.

Privates: Edward Martin, Washington D. C.; Ernest Carter, Charleston, W. Va.; John Geary, Wheeling, W. Va.; Lonnie Trivette, Logan, W. Va., Charles Young, Altoona, Pa.; William Gerrity, Mount Carmel, Pa.; Ray Zwolinski, Ambridge, Pa.; Eddie Tyszka, Pittsburgh; Frank Treatta, The Bronx, N. Y.; Stig Stabe, Bernardsville, N. J.; Al Jaeger, Farmersville, Ill.; Edward Kelly, Fall River, Mass.; Lewis Barnes, Litchfield, Ill.; Joe Monohan, Troy, N. Y.; Theodore Kallelis, Peabody, Massachusetts; Rudolph Leesha, West Hartford, Connecticut; Charles Schiel, Bayport, Long Island, N. Y.; N. J. Kincaid, Dalton, Ga.; Lawrence Bernhardt, New York; John Delessio, Staten Island, N. Y.; Daniel Bieze, Chicago; William Farrel, Akron, Ohio; William Riley, Travers City, Okla.; Newton Spitsfaden, New Orleans; Alvin Asberry, Windy, Ky.; Carlee Robinette, Taylorsville, North Carolina; Kenneth Campbell, Detroit.

THE BALTIMORE SUN, MONDAY, OCTOBER 9, 1944

This is part of a series of articles on the American Third Army's battle for Fort Driant.

MARYLANDERS BEFORE METZ —
Five Maryland men, including one Baltimorean, are mentioned in the dispatch below.

Fort Driant Battle Held Unique In War – Yanks Fight From Cellar To Cellar To Clear Out Post Of Metz

By Lee McCardell [Sunpapers War Correspondent]

Outside Fort Driant, Oct. 8 [By Radio] — Early in the morning the mist lies thick in the valley of the Moselle between Pont-a-Mousson and Metz. Someplace down along the river our engineers keep a couple of white smoke generators going from dawn till dark so the Germans in forts farther up the river cannot see what's going on here. This artificial smoke dopes up the river's natural autumn morning haze until a thick gray fog overflows the valley's brim.

When the upper valley clears, the city of Metz and the spires of its cathedral stand out distinctly in the broad flat plain beyond their ring of hilltop forts.

Like Upper Potomac Valley

The deep narrow valley of the Moselle below Metz reminds you of the upper Potomac river country between Harpers Ferry and Cumberland. Its western wall, high plateau rolling up gently toward the river, falls off sharply in the thickly wooded slopes. The hilly eastern banks are under cultivation except for the higher humps covered with trees and tangles of undergrowth.

Upon the tops of the higher hills east and west of the river the French built a ring of forts to defend Metz 100 years ago. After the Franco-Prussian War of 1870 when Metz was surrendered and Alsace-Lorraine ceded to Germany, the forts were enlarged and strengthened by the German army engineers. When France regained Alsace-Lorraine at the close of the last war the French reoccupied the forts and modernized them.

One Of War's Strangest Battles

Since the fall of France in 1940 the forts again have been garrisoned by German troops. The southernmost of the forts on the eastern bank of the Moselle is Driant, actually a group of forts inclosed by a moat and a broad belt of barbed wire and connected by an underground of tunnels.

Inside Driant's barbed wire one of the strangest and bitterest battles of the war is now in progress. The Americans have broken through the outer defenses. They have fought through the corridors into the underground tunnels linking up the fort's separate works.

From neither observation planes nor forward observation posts does Driant bear any resemblance to the conventional ideas of a fort. It looks like a neglected hilltop overgrown with scrub growth. You have to search this natural camouflage closely with high-powered glasses to pick out its semi-subterranean pillboxes and steel turreted, three-gun batteries.

Other Forts Rake Surface

Day before yesterday this correspondent entered Driant riding in a tank. Upon close examination he found the fort to be pretty much the same as it appeared to be from a distance. The interior is filled with trees and bushes masking its pillboxes and batteries. Since the Americans entered the fort the Germans have buttoned themselves up in its underground defense while the other German forts around Metz, rake Driant's surface with covering fire.

Of Driant's hilltop area, roughly the same as that of Baltimore's Patterson Park, the Americans now hold only a small part. The battle to clear the remainder has become a highly specialized sort of cellar-to-cellar fight in which the Americans are using tanks, dive bombers, flame throwers, acetylene torches, pole charges, bazookas, mortars and hand grenades.

Comparatively Small Force Used

Under fire from other German forts of the Metz system it has been impractical for the Americans to storm Driant in large numbers. The troop commanders have decided the most economical method of reducing the fort is a simple delousing proposition for a strong and specialized, but comparatively small task force, according to moving-picture standards. It is slow but it is the safest process, this correspondent decided after spending about 24 hours with the American troops in Driant.

Earlier last week we had watched Ninth Air Forces dive bombers blast away at Driant and two sister forts on the hilltops east of the Moselle. On Wednesday American troops which had been knocking off Driant's outpost and reconnoitering its approaches for the last three weeks finally crossed the moat, broke through the outer barbed-wire entanglements, captured several pillboxes within the fort area and cleared two underground barracks of the enemy.

First Message Misunderstood

The commander of the attacking force sent back a terse message to the effect; "We are in the fort." In transmission through the routine military channels to higher headquarters, this message was misinterpreted to mean the entire fort had been captured.

Interested in seeing what effect the aerial bombardment had on the fort, we hurried forward the next day by jeep. At the advance command post we were informed that while the American troops had entered the fort, the greater portion was still being defended by the German garrison.

Not Safe For Sightseeing

It would not be safe to try to go sightseeing in Driant that day. Driant's own big guns had ceased firing, but those of the other German forts were peppering its top and its approaches.

The next day we paid a visit to Lieut. Joseph Schaech, of 2933 McElderry street, Baltimore, who commands an infantry cannon company which has been shelling Driant. One of the first selectees to enter the army from Baltimore, Schaech was inducted at Fort George G. Meade from where he was sent to officer candidate school to be commissioned a second lieutenant of infantry.

Tall, broad-shouldered Joe Schaech — he's 6 feet, 6 inches — was too big a target for German snipers to be leading an infantry company, his regimental commander decided.

Took Over Cannon Company

Schaech was transferred to the regiment's cannon company. When the company commander, Capt. Pete Smith, of Lexington, Ky., was attached to the task force investigating Driant, Joe took over the company.

Other Marylanders in the cannon company are Corporal William Duncan, of Salisbury, company clerk; Corporal Aubrey T. Ford, of Hyattsville, gunner on Company No. 5 gun, and Private Earl Moats, of Oakland, who drives the lieutenant's jeep.

Not far away we met another Marylander, Lieut. John A. Filbert, of Joppa, anti-tank executive officer, whose wife lives at 3012 Westfield avenue, Baltimore.

We spent Thursday night and the better part of Friday with the cannon company. Through glasses and the BC scope at the company's forward observation post we watched the day's operations against Driant. The cannon company had silenced the fort's "battery Moselle" built into the shoulder of the hills below the fort proper overlooking the Moselle river.

Dive Bombers Hammer Fort

Our dive bombers hammered Driant again this afternoon. Their target was the fort's most prominent structure above the ground, concrete barracks above the battery Moselle, which is just about the closest air support fighter bombers have ever given ground forces over here.

Like all troops attacking Driant, the cannon company was well dug in. To keep out of sight from German observation posts which overlook the greater part of the Metz area, soldiers moved about through the system of old trenches. Nobody knew whether the trenches had been dug during this war or the last. Similar trenches zigzag over scores of hills between Verdun and Metz.

The cannon company's chow is cooked at the field kitchen away back in the hills and trucked forward in Marmites at meal time. We learned to appreciate the chow prepared under the direction of Mess Sergeant Noah "Deacon" Bailey, of Alabama, a character known throughout the regiment for good cooking and ability to quote from the Holy Scriptures in times of stress.

Few Dugouts Waterproof

Heavy autumn rains have made the entire battle area here pretty muddy. And few dugouts are entirely waterproof. But we slept warm and dry in the concrete dugout which houses the cannon company's fire-direction center. It was a little crowded. There wasn't room to open another sleeping bag so we shared the blankets of a hospitable soldier from Wisconsin, Private Jack Jacobson, an infantryman of the heavy weapons company.

Our hosts were many. They included, besides Jake and Joe, Lieutenants Charles Roggenstein, of Rockville Centre, N. Y.; Francis J. Robinson, Milwaukee; Jerome Glickman, of Chicago, and John Bedell, of Elizabeth, N. J., all of the cannon company, a heavy weapons company officer and about half a dozen enlisted men.

Added attractions of the dugout were two August issues of *The Sunday Sun*, which Joe had received that day and the first full-grown *Sunpapers* we'd seen since June. As usual, when two Marylanders get together, we sat around until bedtime chewing the fat. Joe told us his brother Dan, Air Corps officer, had shown up recently in Cherbourg.

It was difficult to tell next day by watching the fort just what the situation out there was. Because our own troops were in Driant our artillery has ceased firing on that fort but were plastering other German forts firing on Driant.

Jeeping back with Joe and his driver to the regimental command post that afternoon we stopped along the muddy road to talk with Capt. Harry Anderson, of Morgantown, W. Va., who had just come back from Fort Driant.

Anderson is better known to the men of his outfit as "G. I." Anderson. He acquired the nickname when he interrupted a college career before the war to serve one year in the regular army as an enlisted man.

"G. I." Anderson had led his infantry company which was one of the units in the first attack on the fort at noon Wednesday. He'd had only four hours' sleep in the last three days.

40-Foot Belt Of Barbed Wire

"We didn't have so much trouble getting into the fort," Anderson said. "We'd picked our spot in advance reconnaissance. The moat wasn't too deep where we crossed it. There was a 40-foot belt of barbed wire, but we broke through that with bangalore torpedoes and with H. E. (high-explosives) fire by one of the tanks that went with us. We had five tanks in our unit.

"We caught the enemy by surprise in the first pillboxes. I didn't like the looks of the first when it didn't fire. I threw a hand grenade in. One Jerry came out. I figured where one was there must be more, so I threw another one in — a smoke grenade — and three officers and two men came out. I told them we'd kill 'em if they moved. So they sat down there and we went on.

"I imagine a number of Jerries in the part of the fort we attacked had us outnumbered, but if they did they didn't know it. They held us up in two underground barracks, slammed steel doors shut and we couldn't get in.

Torpedoes Down Shaft

"Big guns in the fort couldn't fire on us. They couldn't depress 'em low enough. But they went after us with machine guns and small-arms. It was the worst I have ever seen.

"Sergt. Robert Holman — he comes from Minneapolis and isn't scared of anything as far as I've been able to see — is the man who really ran 'em out of those barracks. He fused a bunch of bangalore torpedoes and dropped 'em down through the ventilators shafts. We could hear Jerries hollering down there when they went off. Then we ran a tank around and went to work on the doors.

"When we got inside we went from room to room and down through the corridors cleaning them out with rifles and hand grenades. The electric lights had been burning in the first pillbox we took but they cut the lights off in the barracks and we had to fight in the dark.

Few Prisoners Taken

"Those who got out of the barracks — we didn't take many prisoners — ran down a tunnel leading into the rest of the fort. They closed steel doors behind them.

Tired "G. I." Anderson sat down on his bedding roll in the mud beside the road and drew a plan for Fort Driant on a page of a pocket notebook.

"I'll show you just how it was," he said. "Here's the moat and here's the barbed wire. Here are the first two pillboxes and here are two underground barracks that were our first objective. After we had secured them we posted a unit for security here outside the main fort, another along this line in front of two gun batteries and another between two batteries.

"We weren't able to take them or reach this building we've been shelling in the far corner."

Tanks Run Around In Fort

"They had two or three tanks running around in the fort and they threw a lot of big stuff on us from other forts. We were pinned down and couldn't get any farther. We had some losses. We knocked out a couple of their tanks, but they got several of ours."

An enlisted man of Anderson's company, who had come up while he was talking, put it:

"The Jerries got one of those tanks of theirs back this morning, sir. We thought we had knocked it out, but while we were watching it a couple of Krauts come along and one hopped in and stepped on the starter and backed it off before we knew what was going on."

Hours After Dark Worst

The worst hours in the fort for the attacking force had been those after dark. It was difficult to know for sure who was where. Infantrymen outposting the captured area dug in for the night. The Jerries counterattacked shortly before dawn, an operation which became a sort of daily standard procedure with them thereafter.

A German bazooka team crawled out of their underground defenses and hunted our tanks in the dark.

"My men were great," said Anderson. "They really did a job. Four of my sergeants especially — Holman, Troy, Ernest Reeder and Charlie Jackson. Reeder's from Gary, Ind. I don't know about Key and Jackson."

American troops within the fort had been reinforced during the night. Rations, water and ammunition had been carried into the fort by American tanks.

From what Anderson told us and from what we heard later at the regimental command post we thought that maybe we could go up that night.

"You can go up if you want to," an officer at the advance command post told us. "We call it the tank freight line and offer no guarantees of any sort."

We left all our equipment except a camera with the cannon company's First Sergeant William Jones, of Ann Arbor, Mich. As it turned out we might as well have left the camera behind, too, because the situation in the fort was not favorable enough for photography.

We walked up the muddy trail through the woods to where a red crayoned notice tacked on a stick read:

"Supplies going forward to fort by tank here."

A couple of spools of telephone wire, a stock of radio batteries and five soldiers were waiting for the next trip.

"Every now and then," said one soldier, when we asked him how often the tanks ran.

"Unless," he added, "you want to call a cab."

THE BALTIMORE SUN, TUESDAY, OCTOBER 10, 1944

This is part of a series of articles on the American Third Army's battle for Fort Driant. In it, two Baltimoreans are mentioned.

Yanks Hold Fort Driant Underground Barracks – McCardell Witnesses Attempt to Drive Through Tunnels Barricaded By Nazis

By Lee McCardell [Sunpapers War Correspondent]

Outside Fort Driant, Oct. 8 [By Radio — Delayed] — It wasn't like any other fort we had ever seen. When the tank which delivered us pulled up inside Fort Driant and we piled out, we alighted in a small, bashed-down clearing amid a thick clump of bushes and young trees.

Scattered about on the ground were wooden cases of K-rations and boxes of ammunition. We had landed in a supply dump at Driant, the terminus of a tank freight line.

Moat Not Particularly Deep

In the gathering dusk behind us lay a moat, not particularly as deep as Capt. Harry (GI) Anderson, of Morgantown, W. Va., had said. Rains must have washed away its sharper slopes. Beyond the ditch were twisted steel stakes and tangled scraps of broken barbed-wire.

There wasn't much time to look around. The soldiers with whom we had ridden out to the fort were unlashing spools of telephone wire, a field telephone switchboard and radio batteries which were fastened behind the tank's turrets.

A Captain Kelley, a communications officer, tossed a couple of cartons of radio batteries into our arms. Other soldiers grabbed up the rest of the load and took off at a run through the bushes and over a massive concrete dugout, where they dumped the wire and paused a minute to catch their breath.

Lugs Switchboard At Run

The next moment they were off again on the run through a brick-covered ditch, a long semi-circular one overgrown with more trees and bushes. The last man in the line, lugging a telephone switchboard, had a hard time keeping up with the rest of us.

As far as I know our tank had not been fired on during the course of our trip to the fort. But now Jerry dropped a few bursts over the fort area. The man ahead of me ducked and leaped agilely over some broken tree branches in the path. I surprised myself with equal agility and kept going.

The ditch ended at a high, broken, spiked-steel fence like that around lion cages at a zoo. Through its smashed gate a short flight of stone steps led down into a rectangular well. The well's western wall was faced with yellow stone.

There was a door in the wall and we plunged through from the day's fading twilight into the gloom of underground barracks. My guides vanished and I was lost in the semi-darkness.

We were in a long, casemated corridor. At one time windows had opened onto the rectangular well out front, but now they had been closed with masonry and strapped with short lengths of steel railroad rails stacked solidly edgewise and held into place by huge steel uprights anchored in the wall's heavy stonework. Narrow slots at the top of each window panel were covered with sliding steel shutters an inch thick.

In two or three places the walls and steel rail straps had been punctured by direct fire of a German self-propelled gun or tank which had rolled up on the opposite edge of the well the previous day to shell the barracks at point-blank range.

Only Light Through Holes

Through these holes, by which infantrymen were stationed, came the only light entering the gloomy, battle-battered corridor.

Doors opened from the wall into dark, windowless underground casemates littered with rubble, empty K-ration tins, filth and rubbish. The corridor's broken floor was strewn with more rubble. Thick dust, the sour smell of stale burned explosives and the stench of war were everywhere.

Through similar corridors and casemates of this barracks and another like it, buried out of sight under six feet of earth in another well but connected to the first by a long underground tunnel, Anderson and his men had fought their way.

Every hole and embrasure in the two barracks' face was posted now with American riflemen and machine gunners. Mortars had been set up wherever practical, but everybody tried to stay under cover. Other German forts were still shelling Driant and could be depended upon to continue firing off and on all night.

Lines Outside Uncertain

Beyond the barracks area where outposts had been established in captured pillboxes things were still pretty well mixed up as to where our lines ended and the Germans' began.

Shortly after we reached the fort, Yanks at one outpost nabbed an 18-year-old German who had walked into the pillbox they occupied. He thought it was still in German hands.

"Oh well, the war is over anyway," he said. He had been wounded once in Normandy, and still carried in his pocket a shell fragment recovered from his thigh.

A tank was waiting to take Captain Kelley back. He turned over the equipment and four men he had brought out to Lieut. Paul Church, of Saluda, S. C., communications officer. One of the four was Private Gerald Branam, of West Franklin street, Baltimore. Another was Corporal Thomas Davis, of Simpson, W. Va.

Phone Line Runs From Fort

All four were headquarters wiremen. They had just run the first telephone line from the fort back to the advance command post. Their next job was to run lines to the company command posts and get the telephone switchboard into operation.

They worked at this for the better part of the night, the lieutenant himself taking his turn at the switchboard so his men could catch a little rest.

To find Major Wilfred H. Haughey, Jr., of Battle Creek, Mich., commanding our troops in the part of the fort (others were pushing into Driant from the opposite side), we stumbled through more dark corridors, felt our way down a dark stairway and through more dark casemates into a small, breathless underground vault dimly illuminated by candlelight.

The major was busy with his company commanders, who included Lieut. Francis L. Carr, of Leesburg, Va.; Capt. Robert E. Todd, of Providence, Ky., and Capt. George Polich, another Michigan man, his artillery liaison officer. They were laying plans for the night's defense and a renewal of the attack on the rest of the fort in the morning.

A company commander, Capt. Pete Smith, was idle for the moment. The first thing he asked was:

"What did Deacon Bailey put out for supper tonight?"

We hated to tell him — corned beef, baked potatoes, stewed tomatoes and canned peaches. Smith groaned and tore open a box of K-type rations. In another casemate, less crowded, where two Joes had built a tiny fire on the stone floor, he warmed a can of potted meat and a canteen cup of instantaneous coffee. The little fire inclosed the casemate with smoke, but the light it made in the darkness was worth any discomfort.

Groggy From Loss Of Sleep

Smith was groggy from loss of sleep.

"I'm so sleepy right now it sure doesn't matter whether I sleep or not," he said.

But when the fire burned out we turned in on the best beds the dark, smoked-filled casemate offered, a wooden door and three flat boards on the concrete floor.

Jerry was still shelling the fort. Sometimes the blasts shook the casemate, but we were so far underground it didn't matter. Nobody slept very soundly. People kept stumbling in through the darkness to find the other people in the dark and awaken them.

Guide Litter-Bearers

First it was two men to guide litter-bearers to the forward command post. Then it was two to look for something else. At 4 o'clock, somebody awakened Smith to take over the command post telephone.

Around daylight, non-coms began pouring into all the casements to arouse soldiers sleeping on the floors. You'd never have known it was daylight down in the dark underground casemates, but somebody who had been up on the top said it was.

There were no latrines working in the barracks. The fort was still being shelled and nobody wanted to go outside. Nobody did. There was no water.

Bleary-eyed soldiers, unwashed and unshaved, covered with dust and grime, kindled a fresh batch of fires on the concrete casement floors to warm up K-rations for breakfast. Everybody was smoking. The atmosphere in the lower casements couldn't have been much heavier.

Got Into Wrong Fort

Somewhat out of breath, Corporal Clarence Wilkinson, of Aurora, Ill., an artillery runner at the forward observation post, blew into the command post to report his safe return from the main fort of the Driant group. The main fort was still in enemy hands. Wilkinson hadn't intended going, but like everybody else, he was none too sure of his way around this joint.

"I'd been told by one of my officers to report back to the command post," the corporal said. "I had never been here before and didn't know the way. He said it was in a fort and told me how to come.

"I came along till I saw four other guys in a foxhole with a machine gun. I asked them if I was going the right way. They didn't know, so I kept going until I came to a fort. It was kinda beat up and it looked like the place I wanted.

"I looked in the first door. The room was empty. I went on to the second and there was nothing in there but a lotta machinery. So went to a third. Its steel door was blown off the hinges and I saw an American Garand rifle leaning up against the wall inside.

"I was sure that was the place, and I stepped inside. Somebody shouted something in German. I looked up and there was a Jerry grabbing that Garand. I could have shot him where he stood, but I didn't realize he was a German at first. I thought he was one of our boys — I was so sure I was in the right place when I saw that Garand.

"I ducked out just in time. They opened up on me with machine guns from two directions."

Wilkinson described in detail the route he had followed from the observation fort and the fort he had entered by mistake.

"You were in the fort all right — the main one we haven't taken yet," said Captain Smith.

"Gosh, it kinda makes me shaky to think about it now," said the corporal.

He was all for trying to sneak back and lob a couple of rifle grenades through that third door. Captain Smith himself inclined to the belief that "when one man goes the whole platoon could go," but other plans had been made for the day's attack.

The captain got an empty wooden box and started through the barracks to pick up any spare ammunition or hand grenades that might be lying around. I trailed along to get a look at the place by daylight.

Fitted As Laboratories

Two or three casemates I hadn't seen last night were fitted up as chemical and physical laboratories, and so designated by red-lettered signs painted on white walls in German and Russian. Another big casemate was equipped with brand new engine lathes.

In the course of that tour we met another Baltimorean, Corporal Louis De Stefano, formerly of 2404 North Calvert street. Once a big shot in his local roofers' union — he said he also drove a cab in the hard times of the depression years — Louis is a radio operator now. He was holding down a radio telephone in one of the barracks' shell-torn corridors when we saw him.

Troops were moving about the barracks now, taking up positions for an attack timed to be coordinated with the arrival of fighter-bombers which would strafe the rear slopes and approaches to Driant. There would also be artillery preparation.

To Try To Open Tunnel

Engineers were strapping on their back packs of flame throwers and arranging pole charges and "beehives" of explosive. While one artillery force pushed out above ground with the tanks toward the northeastern end of the fortified area, another force with engineers would try to open the underground tunnel leading from the barracks into another part of the fort. Gun batteries were still being held by the Germans.

This was the tunnel down which the Jerries had fled from Anderson's men. Our own troops had blocked its entrance temporarily with stones, chunks of concrete and heavy timbers to prevent the Germans from breaking out. It was the same sort of tunnel as that which connected the barracks. This meant it would probably have the same type of steel doors and gates. Engineers were prepared to blow them.

The fighter-bombers were on schedule, but from down where we were you could neither hear nor see them. You couldn't hear our artillery, either. Jerry was shooting, too, that morning, and closer to where we were. Assaulting infantrymen climbed out of the well and that was the last we saw of them.

The barricade at the tunnel's entrance was cleared away quickly. Infantrymen moved up the pitch-black corridor cautiously. About 300 feet from the entrance they found what they had expected — a steel door barred on the other side. Engineers laid a charge to blow it, and ran wires back to a detonator at the tunnel's mount.

We were standing back in the second tunnel midway between the barracks when they set it off. The concussion almost knocked us down. Dust filled the air, shutting off the faintest flicker of light from either end. A soldier staggered past us in the dark muttering:

"Is the other end closed?"

Warned Against Matches

Somebody was shouting:

"Steady — hold it — everybody all right? Don't strike any matches!"

"Medic!" somebody else was shouting.

And for a moment we had the sickening feeling that the Germans had blown the tunnel in which we were standing. But they hadn't.

The engineers' charge had blown open the other tunnel's door, all right. But when the smoke cleared away they discovered the Germans had blocked the far end of the tunnel with machinery, old artillery pieces and every other heavy piece of junk they could lay hands on.

Regular Mining Job

It would be a regular mining job to clear away all this stuff. The tunnel is so small only a few men could work at one time on the barricade. There was no room to pile the stuff aside. It would have to be carried out piecemeal.

The advance of infantry across the top of the fort had met with strong opposition. Lieut. Lee Town, of Louisburg, Kan., tank officer, came back to the command post to report another of his tanks knocked out. The Jerries had shot off one track. The disabled tank was in such a position that it would have to be towed back before another tank could advance over the same route.

That was the general situation in Fort Driant when we left yesterday afternoon. It hadn't changed materially today.

Aid Station Not Overcrowded

We noted with some satisfaction before coming away that the advance aid station set up in one casemate was not overcrowded with patients. Most of the injuries being treated there seemed to be slight. The medics were handicapped by darkness, working by lantern light.

We left the fort's enclosure with Captain Smith, Lieut. Col. Charles Dixon, of Lake City, Fla., staff operations officer, and four German prisoners. We ran for it again because the other German forts were still firing on Driant. There was no tank to take us back. We raced across the moat, through broken barbed-wire and across an open field to the first protective patch of woods

When we saw Captain Smith again later in the afternoon, he was back at his cannon company's forward observation post, spooning sliced peaches out of a big pan on his lap, his eyes glued to a BC-scope.

"I'm slaughtering Germans," he said grimly. One of his observers had spotted a platoon of Jerries climbing out of a battery on the Moselle and starting up the hill, evidently to join and reinforce Driant's main garrison. The captain himself was adjusting the fire. The cannon company's guns were thundering.

"What excellent shooting!" said the captain.

THE BALTIMORE SUN, SUNDAY, NOVEMBER 19, 1944

3d Army Driving Through Metz

By Lee McCardell [Sunpapers War Correspondent]

With U. S. Third Army Nov. 18 [By Radio] — Third Army troops have entered Metz, fighting their way toward the center of the city, but they have not yet reached its heart — the Great Cathedral Square, in which Marshal Petain reviewed French troops when they made their solemn entry into Metz, November 19, 1918.

The American Infantry tonight occupies one of four islands over which the western half of the city sprawls. The infantry is still fighting in southern outskirts around the airfield and in the locality of Fort de Queuleu on the southwestern edge of the city.

Three more Metz forts have fallen; another has been surrounded. The Germans' only road of escape from the city is not yet actually held by our troops, but is under American artillery fire. The so-called escape gap has been narrowed to about one mile, and our fighter-bombers have been watching the gap hungrily all day.

Perl Occupied

In the Third Army sector north of Metz, armored cavalry elements have occupied the little town of Perl, just across the German border, east of Moselle, while other armored elements have advanced southeast as far as Bouzonville, the road junction on one of the two main roads from Metz to Saarlautern.

Farther south the 19th Infantry Division has advanced eight to nine miles over the ten-mile front to new positions, generally along the Metz-Bouzonville road abreast the armor to their left. The 95th Division has filled out its salient by moving up and taking Fort de Saint-Julien, one mile northeast of Metz.

Other elements of the 19th have taken Fort Kellerman and Fort Lorraine to the northwest of the city and surrounded Fort de Plappeville in the same general locality. Forts Driant and Jeanne d'Arc are still firing.

A 19th Division patrol last night crossed the Moselle river bridge into the city of Metz, and during the day more infantry of the same outfit occupied one of the four islands formed by a network of Moselle river canals within the city limits and laced together as part of Metz by a dozen bridges and viaducts.

26th Gains Half Mile

East of the Moselle, below Metz, the infantry of the Fifth Division had surrounded the Forts Saint Blaise and Romy, reported by prisoners of war to be occupied by a German garrison of 100 men with food and ammunition for ten days.

The die-hard force was still holding out tonight with rifles, machine guns and mortars. Its big guns were silent.

On the southern sector of the Third Army front, the 35th Division had advanced five miles northeast to the town of Bertring on the main highway beyond Morharq. The 26th Yankee Division had made about half a mile progress on the four-mile front above Dieuze.

The 19th Tactical Air Command took advantage of the fair weather to fly more than 350 sorties. They dive bombed and strafed enemy columns moving through the narrow Metz escape gap. At times the road traffic was bumper to bumper.

Tank Depot Attacked

They also ranged far behind the enemy lines shooting up railroad trains, tanks, gun positions and transport columns. Near Rastaat, beyond the German border, they attacked a tank detraining depot — a loading platform, eight tanks and 20 flatcars. The only aircraft encountered in force was a flight of 40 ME-109's near Dieuze, one of which was shot down.

It was impractical today for noncombatants to enter Metz. It wasn't exactly healthy for American soldiers to penetrate the city too deeply. Enemy fire was still brisk south of the city where the defenders used small-arms, mortars, tanks and artillery to prevent infiltration of their lines by American infantry.

The main road into Metz from the south through the town of Verny is now open as far as Magny which according to the black and yellow sign post is *Matz-Stadtteil Mannigan*, the Magny district of the city. Magny's civilian population had not yet been evacuated when we were there this afternoon.

A young German soldier who had died with his hobnailed boots on still lay where he had fallen, opposite the Schenkwirtschaft whose shirt-sleeved proprietor stood in front of the door of his establishment regarding the body with mixed curiosity and distaste.

Children peeped around the corner of a modest villa's garden wall to look at a dead man, probably the first they had ever seen. He lay doubled up, his helmet still on his closed-cropped head. You wouldn't have known he was dead except from the crimson stain running from his check to the rusty grating of the gutter's sewer.

Nobody Interested In Beer

Tacked up beside the open front door of the *Schenkwirtschaft*, a large, clean, white building, was a red and white metal sign advertising a popular Metz brew. The sun was shining brightly. It was rather warm in Magny. But nobody seemed interested in beer this afternoon.

The mothers of Magny stood in the open front doors of their homes, hands tucked under their elbows. They kept one eye on their children and one on the muddy American tanks rattling up the streets, as if uncertain what to do. The other men and women of the town stood around the burgermeisters house waiting for something to happen.

Our troops had entered Magny last night, taking about 40 German prisoners. They parked their jeeps and trailers in the front yards, courts and alleyways. They strung telephone wire up and down the street. Half a mile beyond Magny they were still fighting.

Gray Haze On The Flats

Down the railroad tracks behind Magny in a cemetery back of a couple of warehouses a battery of German 88's fired at any Americans who showed themselves. American mortar shells were dropping around the cemetery.

Farther east a gray haze hung over the flats where the Germans and Americans were still fighting. Shells were dropping on the mountain top crowned by Fort Driant across the Moselle. American fighter-bombers were noisily peeling off from overhead and diving and strafing unseen targets hidden by the hills east of Magny.

But for the debris of war you might have been out along the railroad tracks on the edge of an American city of about

100,000 population. The city into which the tracks curved was silent and lifeless except for one thick column of smoke rising from its heart a mile away. The Germans must have fired an ammunition dump there.

Somebody Shot A Dog

The black muddy lane through the underpass in the railroad embankment behind Magny led uphill toward Fort Queuleu. You couldn't see the fort. The hillside was covered with brown vineyards, leafless orchards and small garden plots. Each had its little black wooden tool shed.

The lane petered out when it reached a couple of ordinary two-story houses at the foot of the hill. They had been deserted by their occupants. Somebody had shot a black mongrel dog chained near the back door of one house.

There GI's had moved into the cellar of another. They had brought a jeep load of rations and water cans that far and were waiting for the company runner to tell them what to do next.

Mud Sucks Shoes Off

He was up on a hill some place around the fort. The Germans were still shelling the old-fashioned star-shaped fort with underground casements. Our infantry was on the top casements. The Germans were still inside. It was not a good idea to walk around the fort unless you wanted to draw the enemy fire.

You could go on up the hill if you wanted to, following the muddy path through the vineyards and the orchards. The mud was thick, heavy stuff that threatened to suck your shoes off at every step. The soldiers who had gone up the hill ahead of us had dug themselves foxholes at every halt.

Fort 200 Yards Away

When we reached the top of the hill we could see the brush-covered parapets of the fort some 200 yards away. The Germans had evidently planned some kind of an outer defense for the hilltop. They staked a line for barbed wire. Big rusty coils of the wire were scattered all around the hill crest. But there wasn't a soldier in sight.

A little farther on we met two muddy, unshaven telephone lines men returning to battalion headquarters from an unsuccessful search for their company command post up around the fort. They had been shelled by enemy artillery and didn't think much of it.

But they told us where you could find Major Wilfred H. Haughey, battalion commander, and some of the others in a house a little farther on. So we went on slipping and sliding and splashing through the mud. In the valley below the houses and the tall, slender church spire of Metz stood out like a toy village in the afternoon sunshine.

Name Misspelled

The major, who had commanded an infantry battalion last month in an attack on Fort Driant, said he didn't have much hopes of getting into Metz this afternoon.

With him was Lieut. Paul Crouch, of Saluda, S. C., battalion communications officer, who said that when his name was mentioned in a story about Fort Driant, it was spelled wrong. It came out in the Sunpapers "Church." You said you hoped the mistake would not occur this time.

Crouch's Notes

Lieutenant Crouch was writing out memoranda on a page torn from his notebook to be taken back by another runner. He checked and double checked each item:

"Tell the jeep driver to stay in Magny . . . hand grenades for each man . . . both thermite and phosphorous . . . rations for three meals . . . water . . ."

The only Marylander up there was Private Francis M. Passarelli, aged 19, of Frostburg, assistant gunner with G company's mortar section.

Like everybody else, he was pretty tired after a long advance up the roads toward Metz. His only bedding was his raincoat, his only food K rations.

"But I got a package from my mother today," he said, "candy — it didn't last long."

18 More!

Another mortar section, not Pasarelli's, was trying to knock out those 88's in the cemetery down by the railroad tracks. A young lieutenant who was spotting the mortar bursts through field glasses and calling back corrections by radio finally got the mortars on the target.

"Beautiful" he yelled, "now — 18 more right in the same place!"

They came down one after another, kicking up a cloud of black smoke, and the noise of their blasts echoed up the hillside.

Then the Germans dropped a couple on the hilltop and everybody ducked. Jerry was not inclined to give up Metz tonight.

THE BALTIMORE SUN, MONDAY, NOVEMBER 20, 1944

BALTIMOREANS IN METZ —

Two Baltimore men are mentioned in the dispatch below.

American Troops And Guns Battle In Metz In Force

By Lee McCardell [Sunpapers War Correspondent]

With the United States Third Army, Metz, Nov. 19 [By Radio] — American infantry and self-propelled guns are in Metz tonight in force.

Hundreds of the garrison of this fortress city have surrendered, but a few fanatical Nazis are still holding out in the Storm Trooper and Gestapo headquarters, near the main railway station, and in other isolated buildings.

As this is written the northern portion of the city is aglow from the flames of the burning railway warehouses and the barracks of Fort Bellacroix – renamed Fort Steinmetz by the Germans during their occupancy of the city. The northern corner of the fort was blown up this afternoon a moment after its garrisons had marched out to become prisoners of war.

Blast Knocked Troops Down

An American infantry column was moving down the road around the corner of the fort when the explosion, a triple blast, went off. The infantry on foot were knocked down and those riding in jeeps were blown out of their vehicles by the concussion.

The cause of the explosion, which occurred after the fort had surrendered, has not been explained.

The last hope of the Metz garrison to escape by the one highway leading east to St. Avold, vanished this morning when the infantry of the 95th Division attacking from the north, and the troops of the Fifth Infantry Division, attacking from the south, joined up at the village of Vallieres, just east of the city's boundary.

Artillery Fire Continues

Artillery fire from the center of the city and from Fort Driant west of the Moselle river below Metz continued. Other small German commands surrounded by our troops kept on fighting with rifles, machine guns and mortars.

Some of these diehards were fighting from behind the walls of the city's minor forts, others from improvised defenses. Tonight our artillery is shelling the southern edge of the city in an effort to wind up the battle without further delay.

This correspondent entered Metz with the 95th Division. The infantry and self-propelled guns encircled Fort Steinmetz, the largest and one of the oldest defenses within the city proper, crossed the Seille river bridge into the arsenal and began fighting their way toward the cathedral and the city's central plaza.

Reach Square Beyond Gate

At dusk the self-propelled guns had reached the large square beyond the medieval castle gate of the Port des Alemands — the Germans called it "Deutches Tor" — and were in position to begin blasting the Storm Troopers and the Gestapo out of their holes, but the final operation was postponed until daylight.

The approaching night was crystal clear, but neither the bright stars nor the sickle moon rising behind the cathedral spire provided enough light to see who was who in the dark narrow streets of Metz. The American commanders were unwilling at this late stage of the battle to risk shooting their own men.

The French population of Metz, and there still seemed to be a large number in the city, was coming out of the dark, silent, shuttered houses to kiss the Americans and pour quick passing glasses of wine. The FFI appeared in the streets, wearing its tri-colored armbands, to lead the Americans to the Nazi hideouts.

Enters By Back Way

This correspondent circled Metz and entered the city by the back way, by way of the St. Avold road, littered with the charred bodies of German soldiers and the burned wreckage of the German artillery, trucks, personnel carriers and other vehicles bombed, strafed and shelled in their efforts to escape before the Americans closed the last exit.

The city itself did not appear badly damaged and there were few signs of American losses within its boundaries. We turned a corner in the road around Fort Bellacroix, alias Fort Steinmetz.

The fort is a long, narrow work whose bastions face eastward and whose rear is a series of three storied stone barracks heavily constructed parallel to the railroad tracks and the Seille river, just above the junction of the Seille and the Moselle.

First Thought Road Bombed

At first we thought that the bend in the road had been bombed. We thought a German column had been caught there. Vehicles and equipment had been caught in some sort of an explosion which had blasted limbs and bark from the trees growing on top of the parapet of the fort. The road was covered with loose dirt, stones and debris.

Then we saw that the vehicles were American jeeps and that the helmets lying in the debris were American helmets.

We heard the story of what happened when we reached the rear of the fort. Some of its buildings including the post bakery, were in flames. The explosion had been set off after the fort had surrendered, we were told.

Described By Baltimorean

"We were about 300 yards behind the infantry column when it happened," said Private Neftal Tarsi, 3035 Northern Parkway, Baltimore, anti-tank gunner with a tank destroyer outfit. "There seemed to be three explosions, one after another, right along the road."

Tarsi had not been hurt. He and a friend, Sergt. Stephen Schwab, of Pittsburgh, ("Schwab often had spaghetti at my home in Baltimore," Tarsi said), were safe in the shelter of one of the fort's remaining garrison buildings when we saw him. There were no other Marylanders in his outfit and only one man from Delaware, Private Malcolm Chambers, of Wilmington, another anti-tank gunner.

It was after 11 o'clock, Tarsi said, "The fort had surrendered and the column was moving up. The concussion of the blast was terrific. It pushed the skin back tight on your face and there was a thick column of black smoke.

Suspects Mine In Road

"The Germans must have had something planted along the road. That's where some of the explosions came from. And they had ammunition piled up on the parapet of the fort that went off."

"We had passed the corner and had reached the bakery," said Sergeant Leo A. Moreau, of Minneapolis, an infantryman caught in the blast. "There was one explosion from the building across the road from the bakery and two in the fort itself."

"I think it knocked all of us down. They tell us 200 Germans had surrendered in the fort. We counted 84-coming out just a few minutes before the explosion. They were laughing and walking fast — and to think that I bandaged-up one of those skunks who was wounded."

Colonel Last Man Out

"The last man out was a Kraut colonel. It wasn't 15 minutes after he had left when the explosions went off. Some of the GI's who saw it think that the Germans must have set it before they came out, probably with a time fuse."

Colonel Bacon, of Harlingen, Texas, force commander, later told us he didn't know how the explosion had been set off but suspected it had been fired by remote control.

The only Marylander we could find among the infantrymen was Sergt. Hall Sullivan, of 2365 North Charles street, Baltimore, but Lieut. A. K. Bott, of 3421 Massachusetts avenue, Washington D. C., had come into Metz with Colonel Bacon as liaison officer.

It wasn't a particularly convenient time to be looking for people from home. We caught Sullivan by chance while he and his unit were advancing at a run to keep up with the tank destroyers, self-propelled guns and some light tanks rumbling through the gap in the old city walls of Metz to carry the attack into the downtown district.

Surprised To Find Bridge

Colonel Bacon had been surprised to find the stone-arched bridge across the Seille river still standing between the rear of the fort and the old French arsenal which the Germans had called "Moltke Kaserne." He had expected all the bridges in the city would be destroyed.

Most of them have been and, because Metz is built on a narrow neck of land between the Moselle and Seille rivers and on the five islands formed by a network of interlocking canals, the American penetration of the city proper has been delayed. But the colonel took his force across the Seille river bridge to the largest island.

Drew Artillery Fire

Before they crossed they had drawn enemy artillery fire, possibly from the self-propelled guns in the Cathedral Plaza. Once across they occupied the arsenal area and some of its buildings. These and other buildings of the city's closely built heart protected them momentarily from everything except the fire of German snipers.

The Americans set up machine-guns around the building, used by the Germans as barracks. The infantry fanned out through the adjacent streets. FFI's pointed out the safest and shortest routes by which the self-propelled guns could reach the remaining German strongholds.

The soldiers made the most of the short pause to reorganize for this attack. They had been living for three days on field rations. In the railroad warehouse opposite the fort they found large supplies of tinned fruit, honey and bottled beer. The Kaserne was apparently stocked by the Germans before they abandoned it, for it yielded a large supply of fresh apples.

Each With White Handkerchief

The Germans surrendered to the Americans soon after they resumed their advance into the city. The largest group of these marched up wearing full field equipment without rifles, each one carrying a freshly laundered white handkerchief in his hands clasped over his head.

The French civilians who began venturing out to greet the Americans said that the other Germans had tossed their rifles into the Seille river and scattered to find shelter in the Metz basements after the Americans had entered the city.

Near the breach in the old city wall through which the Americans advanced lay the bodies of a French man and woman shot down earlier in the day.

THE EVENING SUN, TUESDAY, NOVEMBER 21, 1944

Metz Yields Prize Nazi Captives In Final Phase Of Battle

By Lee McCardell [Sunpapers War Correspondent]

With the American Third Army, Nov. 20 [By Radio — Delayed] — East of Metz, in both the north and the south, General Patton's army advanced today. The battle for Metz itself was as good as over. The city's German military commander had been taken prisoner while trying to escape across the Seille river. The head of Himmler's secret police for Lorraine and the Saar basin had been captured hiding in his office near a brewery.

Five German fortress groups around Metz were still in German hands tonight. A few German snipers were still fighting from barricaded buildings around the prefecture in the old French quarter of Metz, in barracks on the northern edge of the city and down around the gashouse and railroad yard of the city's southern industrial section.

Fighting On Two Islands

[An Associated Press dispatch dated today said remnants of the Metz garrison still fought on on Sauley and Chambiere islands in the northern portion, but American troops wiped out all large-scale organized resistance. The German commander in the northern part of Metz spurned an ultimatum to surrender.]

The Metz military commandant, Col. Constantine Meyer, 44, had tried to get out of Metz last night by automobile. He and his orderly were picked up on foot this morning along a road near the Seille river by an infantry patrol of the Fifth Division.

Refuses To End Fighting

Taken to divisional headquarters, Colonel Meyer was asked to end street fighting in the city and to order the evacuation of its remaining forts by ordering his men to surrender. He replied that "as a soldier" he must refuse.

Gen. Maj. Anton Dunckern, 39, boss of the Gestapo for the Metz region, also was caught by Fifth Division infantrymen. They said they had swept him up "with a lot of other trash while cleaning out a brewery last night in the dark."

Disorganized Units

By "trash" they meant non-descript German soldiers of various ranks and disorganized units. The Gestapo boss was not actually in the brewery. He was in the office of a near-by warehouse, one of several buildings the infantrymen had been searching for snipers along the railway tracks in south Metz.

The warehouse formerly had been occupied by the Metz branch of International Harvester Corporation. Dunckern occupied an office there, although his police had their city barracks and administrative headquarters in an old seminary building of downtown Metz, captured this morning.

Refuses Interview

He too was taken back to divisional headquarters where he declined to waive an immunities guaranteed him as a prisoner of war by the Geneva Convention. It had been suggested that a man of Dunckern's importance might consent to be interviewed but his reply to this request was:

"I surrendered as a soldier and I'll discuss only military matters with the military."

One question that remained unanswered was why a Gestapo official holding Dunckern's high rank which makes him responsible directly and only to Himmler, should apparently have ignored Himmler's broadcast orders that no member of the Gestapo should surrender.

Typical Gestapo Official

A Hollywood casting director needing a caricature for a Gestapo official type would have been delighted with Dunckern. He was short, fat, blond, close-cropped, red-faced, pop-eyed.

Dunckern's uniform was immaculate, although his jacket strained a bit at its buttons over the bulge of his generous stomach. He spent his first few hours as a prisoner of war in a casemate of a captured Metz fort, puffing a German cigar. When informed that his lunch was ready, he called for soap, hot water and towel. Unfortunately, none was available for anyone in the fort.

The normal Metz population of about 80,000 has been increased by 10,000 or 15,000 refugees from the city's surrounding villages since the battle for Metz began. Hundreds of these people, including children and grownups, came out of the doors to talk on the streets and watch the soldiers this rainy afternoon as the fight to clear Metz of Germans dragged toward its conclusion.

All Shops Closed

Modern Metz is a German city with broad boulevards. Old Metz is a congested French city with narrow, winding streets and two-foot sidewalks. All shops were closed. Their windows were shuttered, boarded up or smashed. Hotels and restaurants were closed. Even the doors of the great cathedral were locked.

The caretaker unlocked a door to permit Americans to climb to the spire from which the streets of the city presented a sort of Sunday calm. He led the little group of soldier sight-seers through the cathedral, unused for several weeks. He took them down into a bomb-proof vault in the crypt to show them the wooden cases in which the cathedral windows' older stained-glass panels have been packed away.

Cathedral Undamaged

The cathedral has not been damaged beyond the loss of one modern window. The rest of the town has also come off lightly. Its wires are down and its windows smashed. A few of its streets have been ditched and barricaded for German defense. But the Germans still holding out this afternoon were indoors.

German police who last night had shacked up in the old seminary building, their Metz headquarters near the main railway station, came out and surrendered this morning after an American self-propelled gun had drilled one hole by way of warning through the corner of the building. The seminary chapel yielded the largest stock of souvenir pistols yet uncovered in any single action this war.

The police had dismantled the chapel as a place of worship. They had piled the side altars, altar ornaments, chandeliers and other chapel fixtures in its sanctuary. The remainder of the building, aisles and pews, were packed with wooden cases of pistols — pistols of all ages and descriptions.

Pistols Of All Types

There were baby automatics and horse pistols, pearl-handled revolvers and dueling pistols, French army issue pistols and ancient flintlocks. The collection, running into thousands of small firearms represented French compliance with the German police order to surrender all arms in their possession.

The police had packed the pistols in boxes and stored them in the chapel, where some pistol-lover found them this morning. Pistols, particularly German lugers, are highly cherished by American soldiers as souvenirs. There were few lugers among this lot, but there were pistols.

Soldiers Take Pick

News of this find circulated among American troops in Metz quickly. Hundreds of soldiers found some excuse to visit the chapel. The pawed over the pistols, took their pick and, in some cases where they found the gun was suited to captured German ammunition, tried out their selection in the seminary yard.

All American soldiers in Metz today were tired and weary from the long, hard fight to take the city. Many fell asleep in easy chairs in deserted hotel lobbies. Even in those parts of the city cleared of Germans there were few signs of rejoicing. A few French tricolors were hung out. There was little drinking. Liquor seemed scarce.

THE EVENING SUN, THURSDAY, NOVEMBER 23, 1944

Part of the dispatch by Mr. McCardell below appeared in The Evening Sun yesterday. The remainder was delayed in transmission. Because the dispatch gives such a remarkable picture of modern battle as actually fought, The Evening Sun is herewith printing it in its entirety.

Eight Marylanders are mentioned in the following dispatch.

Metz Called Battle Of Strategy

By Lee McCardell [Sunpapers War Correspondent]

With the American Third Army, Nov. 22 [By Radio] — Now that Metz, the most formidable fortress in western Europe, has fallen, we have the feeling that we have told the story of its fall very poorly.

London newspapers arriving here speak of the front being "aflame from the fire of thousands of guns," of infantry "storming Delme Ridge . . . under the shattering thunder of a terrific artillery barrage."

In text as well as in headlines the papers dress up the battle for Metz in terms of "smashing attacks," "slicing lunges," "pulverizing blows," "grim bids," "bludgeoning forward," "in paths blasted by massed artillery."

No Adjectives In Pictures

It is easy for us to appreciate the complaint voiced a few days ago by the newsreel cameraman whose home office was concerned about a lack of dramatic action in his pictures.

"Dammit," he said, "It's all very well to write about this war, but the story just doesn't stand up for the movie camera."

"In other words, you can't improve upon photography with adjectives."

Easy To Be Wrong

Well, we've used some adjectives ourselves these last ten days. In the haste to get off our dispatches, we've often snatched up the wrong word.

Now we are beginning to wonder exactly how distorted may be the average American's mental picture of Patton's capture of La Pucelle, as the French like to call the Virgin Fortress of Metz, impregnable for the last ten centuries.

Phony Pictures

Is it a picture of American infantry storming up Delme Ridge with fixed bayonets? Of them fighting with the Germans hand-to-hand or artillery lined up "hub-to-hub," gun muzzles blazing? Is it a picture of American tanks charging across the fields of Lorraine like herds of galloping horses?

If you have any such pictures in your mind, they are phony. The battle for Metz hasn't been spectacular in any such sense. The infantry doesn't go storming up any ridge with fixed bayonets. Hand-to-hand fighting is extremely rare. Modern artillery never lines up hub-to-hub. Tanks don't go charging across open fields in mass formation.

Surprise Element Important

The battle for Metz has been a cautious, carefully calculated military operation employing troops, tanks and artillery dispersed widely over a broad front. It has been as much a battle against the weather as against the Germans.

Military historians probably will weigh the element of surprise as a contributing factor to Patton's victory. Even now it is obvious that the Germans did not expect him to attack when he did. It had been raining for a week before the battle began. The Moselle river had reached the highest flood stage in its history. The countryside across which Patton had to launch the attack was a series of lakes and bogs and mudholes.

November 7, the day preceding the opening of the attack, was raining and overcast. The bombers were unable to take off, so there was no heavy aerial preparation for the drive. But the attack was set for November 8 and it began November 8.

Jeep Around In Rain

The correspondents whose job it was to report the progress of the Battle for Metz were briefed twice daily on the American military situation. The first briefing was at 10 A. M.

They filed their early dispatches as quickly as possible, with the army press censors, then hurried out to the front. At 7.30 P. M. they were back for the second briefing. They then filed urgent bulletins and more complete dispatches.

They travelled by jeep and, allowing time for the journey out to the front and back (as the front advanced, a round trip sometimes required a six-hour ride), they didn't have much time to spend in the actual battle zone. There has probably been a lot of sloppy reporting.

But one thing they learned to appreciate while jeeping around the front was the terrific beating the ordinary GI was taking from the weather. Correspondents came back from the front cold, wet and covered with mud, but they had dry quarters in which to change and dry out. Cold, wet and muddy, GI Joe often spent the night in a foxhole, bailing water out of it to keep from freezing.

GIs Seldom Grumble

The American soldier loves to grumble, or "bitch," in his language. Lack of bitching in this battle has been remarkable. Men in combat have complained less about having to sleep in foxholes than the average soldier in garrison complains about sleeping in an army cot.

"Many of these men were trained for this sort of weather in the Tennessee maneuvers," an officer told us. "I doubt if this weather has been as bad on the whole as what they went through in Tennessee."

Just outside Metz one cold rainy evening we picked up an infantryman and gave him a lift in our jeep. We asked him how he was making out.

Cold But Not Bitter

"Gets mighty cold in a foxhole on a night like this," he said.

And it was seldom that we heard any comment stronger than that.

The most obvious characteristic of this battlefront was its mud, and there was mud everywhere. The movement of most of the troops and supplies was by road. Tanks, tractors, trucks, ambulances and jeeps moving up and down these roads splattered and sprayed each other with mud. They splattered and sprayed the files of foot soldiers trudging forward on either side of the road. They splattered and sprayed the engineers repairing the culverts and rebuilding bridges blown up by the Germans.

Trees lining the roads are splattered with mud. Village house fronts are sprayed with it. Carcasses of dead cattle, tangles of telephone wire and dead German soldiers lying in roadside ditches not yet reached by burial parties, acquire the same muddy patina.

The soft and gummy mud clings like dirty, wet snow to vehicles churning it up, to trailers and artillery pieces towed behind them. Drivers keep their windshield wipers working so they can see. In an open jeep, mud is at its worst when the winds are blowing; it beats into your face like sleet, blinds you.

Trace Progress Through Mud

You can trace the war's progress by those mud-sprayed routes and by the deep ruts in muddy fields where tanks and trucks have pulled off the road, and by water-filled foxholes. There is no solid or continuous front line. "The front" begins at that point where muddy GIs and jeeps and trailers and field telephone wires disappear from the roads.

There are no mass formations of troops. They are strung out in scattered groups and except when advancing they are under cover, out of sight. There are no bayonet charges in the classic tradition. The firepower of modern small-arms prevents troops from closing in for hand-to-hand conflict except in small patrol actions.

Bayonet Almost Useless

Infantry mortar is probably the infantryman's favorite weapon in this war. With it he can lob shells over onto his enemy's head, even though his enemy is protected by a wall or ditch against direct fire. His bayonet, for the most part, is a useless antique.

There is little direct artillery fire. Most of it is adjusted by forward observers. Cannoneers rarely see the target at which they are shooting.

Swift, massed tank attacks are few and far between. Tanks creep forward cautiously, usually at the pace of infantrymen who precede or follow them. Light armored cars of the mechanized cavalry do patrolling and reconnaissance for the armored columns.

Guns Usually Scattered

Massed artillery fire comes from countless scattered gun positions. All shells may be timed to hit the target at the same instant. Artillery salvos are uncommon. Only during the heavy artillery preparation or when barrages are being laid down is there anything approaching a steady roar of guns. Only during an infantry attack is there a continuous rattle of the small-arms.

The ordinary tactics of modern advance are a methodical process of eliminating the enemy gun positions. It's a slow and tedious process. It moves most rapidly when the enemy has been driven from commanding positions on the high ground by a flank attack or superior fire power.

Few Mass Slaughters

This doesn't mean that war is any less deadly than it used to be. It's simply more calculated. But the veterans of the last war do tell us that mass slaughter which characterized the bitterest fighting 25 years ago hasn't occurred very often in this war. Casualties mount slower.

Metz, the most formidable fortress in western Europe, fell because it was outflanked. Its roads and highways were cut. The weakest and oldest forts in the city's famous double ring of them were reduced largely by modern infantry tactics. Fighter-bombers harassed the Germans, but even without their assistance the foot soldiers and their supporting artillery probably would have taken Metz in time.

Fighter-Bombers Help

There are no indications around any of the Metz forts we've seen that the aerial bombardment caused any serious damage. But fighter-bombers did help isolate the forts. They chased German army transport and supply columns off the road whenever the weather was good enough for fighter-bombers to fly.

They protected our own troops and transport from German air attack to a point where camouflage was of little importance and tank and truck columns could jam roads for miles behind our own lines by day as well as by night without suffering serious losses.

The city of Metz, without its forts, is just another French city overburdened with arsenals, caserns and barracks.

The capital of German Lorraine, its most famous native son probably was Paul Verlaine, French poet. Its chief sentimental interest for Americans lies in the fact that Lafayette set out from Metz for America in 1776.

We were impressed chiefly by the names of its streets, which seem to change every time Metz changes hands. Under German occupation, for instance, Place de la Republique became Platz des Fuhrers; Avenue Foch was Herman Goering Strasse and Rue de Verdun was Adolf Hitler Strasse. Street signs probably will be changed back tomorrow.

Much of the credit for the capture of the city belongs to the hardworking, unglamorized truck drivers and engineers of the army. Engineers replaced demolished bridges overnight. They drained flooded roads, dug up mines, cleared away road blocks. That indispensable engine of modern warfare, the bulldozer, again performed miracles.

Supplies Kept Going

Over those muddy, flooded roads — cleared, rebuilt and maintained in the roughest of wintry weather by the army engineers — American truck drivers kept convoys of food, water, gasoline and ammunition rolling forward. Only American drivers, with sturdy American transport, could have done that.

The Third Army also owes a debt to its signal companies, linemen and telephone men and radio operators who tied the operations together with a radio network, who built poles and lines under fire and strung hundreds of miles of telephone wire with interlocking switchboard systems — another task not easily performed in the midst of rain and snow, cold and flood.

Eight Marylanders Named

There were a lot of Marylanders among these unsung heroes. In the 26th Yankee Division alone, for instance, there were Lieut. Douglas P. Campbell, Jr., of Owings Mills, executive officer of a combat engineer company; Andrew A. Tyrie, Jr., of 3200 Clarence avenue, Baltimore; Edward E. Wise, of 2720 Lauretta avenue, Baltimore; Jess W. Jenkins, of 1248 South Ellwood avenue, Baltimore, and Donald M. Bernard, Jr., of Chevy Chase, all members of the division signal company.

And there were T/5 Harold Adkins, of Cheverly; Pfc. Harlow J. Thomas, of Baltimore; T/5 William Finkelstein, of 2809 Keyworth avenue, and several others in the infantry regiment service companies of the same division.

THE EVENING SUN, THURSDAY, NOVEMBER 23, 1944

Patton's Forces Advance 4 Miles In Saar

By Lee McCardell [Sunpapers War Correspondent]

With the Third Army, Nov. 23 — Thanksgiving Day was no holiday in General Patton's advance to overtake the retreating German forces before they reached the Siegfried Line, but Quartermaster Turkey has gone forward and every Joe on the battlefront has been promised a piece, hot or cold, before nightfall.

Armored elements of the Third Army today pushed closer to the Saar river, making gains up to four miles, while infantry and mechanized cavalry sealed off enemy pockets.

There were indications that fresh German troops had been brought into the line to oppose Patton's advance, but four counterattacks against the Americans yesterday failed. The heaviest of these was made by a force of eight German tanks with SS infantry against the 27th Yankee Division in the area of the village of Munster, east of Morhange.

Railway Guns In Action

The Germans also brought heavy railway guns back into action on the Third Army front, but their fire was not effective. Yesterday's count of German prisoners was 1,622.

The farthest advance by the Third Army armor was a drive four miles toward the town of Fenetrange, about eight miles north of Sarrebourg. Mechanized cavalry patrols had screened and sealed off an enemy pocket formed by the salient in our front around Foret Domoniale de Fenetrange.

Armored Drive Gains

Another armored column made two and a half miles' progress toward the village of Saint-Jean-Rohrbach on the road to Morhange and Sarreguemines and about ten miles from the German city. The infantry was a short distance behind this point near the villages of Lexviller and Insming, on either side of the Morhange-Sarreguemines road.

With all organized resistance in the Metz area ended, Fifth Infantry Division elements moved east to seal off another enemy pocket around Bionville-sur-Nied on the main road to Saint Avold. North of the German border, just east of Luxembourg, where more of Patton's army is operating, another advance of a mile toward the village of Kesslingen was reported.

THE BALTIMORE SUN, TUESDAY, NOVEMBER 28, 1944

MARYLANDERS IN SAAR —
Four Maryland men, including three Baltimoreans, are mentioned in the dispatch below.

3d Army Front In Saar Extended To 19 Miles

By Lee McCardell [Sunpapers War Correspondent]

With the U. S. 3d Army, Nov. 27 [By Radio] — American forces today edged their way deeper in the Saar Basin. Nineteen miles of the 3d Army's front was north of the German border. Along the 20-mile sector of northwest from St. Avold, troops were within sight of the border. Farther south armor and infantry were still pushing forward.

The little factory town of St. Avold, strategic road center beyond the Maginot Line, was captured this morning by an infantry battalion commanded by Lieut. Col. Hiram D. Ives, of Baltimore. To make that advance possible another battalion, commanded by Lieut. Col. Elliot B. Cheston, of Annapolis, had fought its way yesterday through the Maginot Line.

Other Divisions Advance

The 10th Armored Division north of the German border advanced about a mile northeast to the vicinity of the town of Faha. The 90th Infantry Division gained up to a mile and half of enemy territory along a six-mile front beyond the border near the towns of Kerprich-Hemmersdorf, Niedwelling, Furweiler and Oberesch.

The 95th Infantry Division crossed the Maginot Line and pushed ahead as much as six miles on a three-mile front in rough, wooded country dotted by pillboxes and the villages of Téterchen, Coume, Hargarten-Aux-Mines, Dalem, Varsburg and Procellete.

Obstacles Overcome

South of the Nied River the Germans had dug a fifteen-foot anti-tank ditch across the country as the first obstacle in any approach from that direction. Then they blew bridges over the river at Faulquemont and Pontpierre. But neither of these devices stopped the 80th, which crossed the river and took Faulquemont several days ago.

Beyond Faulquemont the hills rise sharply, their slopes bare and their crests wooded. Richly veined with coal, these hills are southern bastions of the famous Saar Basin, whose industrial towns of Saarlautern and Saarbrücken form a triangle from the apex of St. Avold.

St. Avold itself is a rather charming little town in the elbow of these hills. It reminds you of the little English towns nestling in the hills of Devon. But St. Avold's yellow streetcars, bulbous church towers, high-pitched gables and baroque facades are German, not British.

From 1870 until 1914 it was a German cavalry post. When France recovered Lorraine and surveyed its Maginot Line across the hills facing the German border from behind St. Avold, the little town became a French *ville de garrison*. Its 5,000 inhabitants speak both German and French.

Aside from the barracks, a few small factories and some hillside villas which attracted summer week-end vacationists, St. Avold's importance lies in the fact that it is the hub of a network of good roads. Its strategic possibilities as a communications center appealed so strongly to the Germans that they located an army headquarters there when they reoccupied Lorraine.

St. Avold is out of sight from Faulquemont, five miles to the southwest. But you can see one of the Saar coal mining towns from Faulquemont. It doesn't look like a Pennsylvania coal mining town. It is spick and span and has a model housing project of modern stucco dwellings with high-pitched red tile roofs, strikingly clean and Germanic for Lorraine.

Mine Heads Well Ordered

The mine heads behind this landscaped housing development, constructed by the French with German reparations money after the last war, are equally modern and well ordered. They look like up-to-date American public school buildings of red brick and concrete with clock towers and generous windows. The largest of these mines produced 1,500 tons of coal daily for Germany's industrial war machine.

Along the backbone of hills in which the mines are located, runs part of the French Maginot Line. The Germans dismantled the big guns of the larger forts after France fell. The embrasures faced the wrong way — toward Germany. But when the 3d Army swept west across France last August, the Germans strengthened the rear of the Maginot Line with anti-tank ditches, rifle pits and road blocks. These were some of the fortifications the 80th had to pass to take St. Avold.

In Face Of Heavy Fire

Colonel Cheston's battalion, the 3d, of the 319th Infantry Regiment, went through them yesterday in the face of heavy enemy fire from mortars and machine-guns. The anti-tank ditches were not serious obstacles. American bulldozers bridged them quickly with earth fills.

After the infantry had reached the village of Longeville, three miles west of St. Avold, the retreating Germans tried to reorganize for a counterattack to regain lost ground. American artillery concentrated on the Germans each time they reformed, some of its airburst falling close to our own front lines.

Tactics Seemed Foolish

Some of the German infantry tactics during the battle seemed foolish as well as ineffectual to the Americans.

"They came at us with machine-guns, pistols and hand grenades," said a headquarters staff officer, "many of them belonged to a German division we had chewed up pretty badly when we crossed the Nied.

"We tried to account for one battalion when we were rounding up prisoners later. We located 80 men in one company, and two officers and two enlisted men of another. That was all of that outfit we could find."

Many of the Germans manning the forts and pillboxes of the Maginot Line quit fighting and took refuge in underground galleries, which in the case of some forts are seven layers deep. An American artillery sergeant making a rubber-neck tour of one of the fort's underground galleries after its capture found 70 Germans hiding in one tunnel.

Enter Without Opposition

Colonel Cheston's battalion was unable to enter St. Avold last night. The town's western approaches were too strongly defended. But early this morning, Colonel Ives's 1st Battalion, of the 319th Infantry, tackled St. Avold through the village of Valmont, lying to the south, and about 10 o'clock entered the town without opposition.

The townsfolk said the Germans had started moving out of St. Avold about 8 o'clock last night and that by 8 o'clock this morning all had gone except a few stragglers whom the Americans rounded up.

The fighting was all over when this correspondent reached St. Avold this afternoon. The guns were silent, and the soldiers welcomed the interlude.

"We fought our way past every manure pile this side of France," said one GI.

If you had ever tried to count the manure piles of Lorraine alone, you would appreciate what he meant.

Day Sunny And Cold

It was a clear, cold, sunny day for a change. The shady spots were white with frost. The black mud of the country roads was still with ice. The army was rolling on over those roads with tanks and trucks and guns and jeeps.

And the fast-working Signal Corps linesmen were almost abreast of the combat troops in the construction of a double crossarm pole line of sort whose copper telephone wires now trace the course of every American advance across France.

The route of the advance also was marked with the usual roadside litter of smashed German trucks, assault guns, overturned caissons and dead artillery horses. But, on the whole, the German retreat, in the general direction of Saarlautern, was said to have been fairly orderly.

The village of Faulquemont had recovered from the initial shock of the war. Civilians were cleaning the streets. Almost every house had hung out a French flag with the Cross of Lorraine on its white panel. Some kind of French Government commission had arrived to inspect the recaptured mines beyond the town.

Flags For Americans

We thought that tricolors might have been hung out for them. But a Frenchman whom we questioned shrugged his shoulders and said the flags were simply out for the Americans.

There was grave concern about those mines, however. The Germans had apparently left them intact except for their electrical power plants. If power could be restored, the mines might help solve the winter problem of fuel which faces Paris and other large French cities.

The broad flat of the Nied River valley was still flooded. From the crest of hills above Faulquemont, the river valley looked like a long chain of muddy lakes.

Tanks Never Left Road

Then the road passed the first of the German anti-tank ditches north of the river. It was a pitiful sort of defense. The tanks had never moved off the road here. Our engineers had either bridged the ditch or shoveled in a fill of earth and stones and the tanks had rolled right along.

The Maginot Line beyond Faulquemont, as elsewhere, is simply a scattered hilltop outcropping of concrete pillboxes and gun emplacements as far as you can see from the road. Each emplacement had a carefully cleared field of fire — in the direction of the German border.

Connecting rifle pits and communication trenches had been constructed with the usual German exactness. Each road entrance to the successive villages along the way had its stout barricade of logs and stone. In the village of Valmont, the town crier was ringing a hand bell prior to shouting a military pronunciamento — in German — ordering civilians to stay indoors from dark to dawn.

Banged By Guns And Bombs

Saint Avold had been banged about a bit by artillery but apparently appeared to have suffered its worst damage from an American aerial bombardment about two weeks ago. The town was still full of civilians but the shops had been looted or were deserted.

The noisiest spot in town was the wrecked bar of the Hotel Aubert on the public square where Private John Di Gaudio, of Newark, N. J., had found one beer pump in working order and was filling glasses for any thirsty Joe who came along, until the keg ran dry.

We found Colonel Ives in a home which he had taken over as a temporary command post. Colonel Ives had talked by telephone with Colonel Cheston a few hours before and reported him all right. Ives apologized for not having more time to "chew the fat" with the newspaper correspondents. His battalion was moving on and he was moving on with it.

Other Baltimoreans There

There were two other Baltimoreans around his headquarters, Privates Joe Deming and Russell Foltz, but in the general hubbub of the advance nobody knew where they were. They were safe.

The 328th Regiment of the 26th Yankee Division today occupied the village of Honskirch, which it had captured last night. Armor had cleared most of the Foret De Bonfontaine and was working east of Saar.

Yesterday's prisoner count in the 3d Army area was 708, making a total of 22,125 for the operation. Four more Metz forts had been abandoned by German garrisons.

The 19th Tactical Air Command flew more than 200 sorties yesterday in support of the 3d Army, its fighter-bombers destroying two enemy aircraft in three encounters with the *Luftwaffe*.

Was Awarded Bronze Star

Colonel Ives, in a letter received yesterday by his mother Mrs. Mary Dudley Ives, of the Ambassador Apartments, said he had been awarded the Bronze Star.

He was a member of the Maryland National Guard when war was declared, and after training with the 29th Division and 80th Division in this country, went overseas last July. He attended Polytechnic Institute, Cornell University and the Johns Hopkins University.

His wife, Mrs. Constance Morley Ives, lives in New York. A brother, Major Walter Ives, is serving with the air forces in France.

Went On Active Duty In '41

Colonel Cheston, a reserve officer, was called to active duty in 1941 and went overseas last June. He is the son of Colonel and Mrs. D. Murray Cheston, of Annapolis. His wife, the former Miss Ann Cary Robinson, and 18-month-old son live in Chestnut Hill, Pa.

A brother, of Lieut. Col. D. Murray Cheston, Jr., is on General MacArthur's staff.

THE EVENING SUN, FRIDAY, DECEMBER 1, 1944

MARYLANDERS IN FRANCE —
One Marylander is mentioned in the following dispatch.

Just Ahead Lies The Rhine — Wide, Swift And Formidable

By Price Day [Sunpapers War Correspondent]

An Outpost on the Rhine, Nov. 30 [By Radio] — Across the Rhine from here, pillboxes of the Siegfried Line squat partly under water.

They are big pillboxes with wide black embrasures. Their sides are built up with grass-covered sod and their concrete tops gleam wetly. They are spaced about 75 yards apart. In my limited field of view I can count seven.

Nearest To River

Behind them stands a line of young leafless poplars with their delicate uplifted branches. Then there are clumps of darker trees beyond them and the red roofs of a German village made pale by the mist.

Out of the mist rises a thin stone tower marked with vertical slits. Our men in this outpost, the closest of the American positions to the river, call it a "water tower," but another theory that it was built for observation seems more likely.

Come From Howitzers

The drab woods behind the pillboxes are marked by four sharp orange flashes. Then after an interval, four more make the river's edge bright. The latest four appeared at one end of a boat landing where a few minutes ago a small group of Germans — four or five or six — climbed out of a motor boat and went up the bank.

We know about those flashes because they come from 105-millimeter howitzers.

The Germans may know or guess something, too, because the air in this large building is still moted with smoke and dust from direct hits fifteen minutes before we got there. No one was hurt.

The best guess would appear to be that the German shell was a 150. Smaller stuff comes now and then, too. A machine-gun slug through one of the windows almost made its way through the sheet of steel behind the window. It bulged the steel inward over an area the size of a quarter and cracked the bulge, but didn't go through.

Five Enemy 88's

About as far as the centerfield bleachers there is a two-story wooden structure painted green. It is in a factory yard and marks the limit of our patrol activity. Beyond the building sit five enemy 88's. The Germans have abandoned the guns but we haven't captured them yet.

From a window on another side of the building I can look up the river to the left where the Strasbourg-Kehl bridge still stands intact and two other spans, a railway bridge and a recently-erected steel bridge, still lead from the Germans' tiny Strasbourg bridgehead into the Reich.

In that direction there is the thin stream of the Little Rhine making its way between Strasbourg proper to flow again into its broad gray formidable stream before us.

Very Wide, Very Swift

Here it is reported to be about 800 feet wide and to have a current from eight to ten miles an hour. I cannot see this bank and can only say that the Rhine is very wide and, judging from its wash at the corners of the Siegfried pillboxes, it is very swift.

The men here have been looking at the river since yesterday and are more interested in the artillery fire going and coming. Lieut. Budd Sturzl, of Rhinelander, Wis; Private Louis Matuzewski, of Erie, Pa., and Sergt. Clarence Jones, of Kansas City, Kan., who led the way through the tunnel to this post, watch bursts in the mists and trees of Germany.

Then sharp heavy firing breaks out among the buildings to the left and they look that way but see nothing.

Marylander In Platoon

Jones says there's a Baltimore man in the platoon. He turns out to Pfc. Clyde Miller, who now lives in Westernport, Md., but worked for three years in Baltimore. Miller says it looks to him as if the pillboxes were half flooded,

"When we were dug in along those railroad tracks on the other side of the Vosges Mountains," he says, "I never thought I'd be looking at the Rhine this soon."

He is looking at it now and he is one of the first American soldiers to do so in this war.

Overseas Since Spring

Private Miller, 23, the son of Mr. and Mrs. Robert Miller, of Westernport, has been in the Army two years and overseas since last spring, going first to Africa and from there into France.

Formerly a resident of Barton, Md., where he attended school, Private Miller was employed at the Celanese plant there prior to joining the service.

He has two brothers also serving with the armed forces. John, 32, is a seaman stationed with the Navy in Florida, and Staff Sergeant Harry Miller, 28, has recently returned from Burma, where he was with Merrill's Marauders for fourteen months.

THE EVENING SUN, MONDAY, DECEMBER 4, 1944

Marylanders Take Big Part In Bold River Crossing Feat

By Lee McCardell [Sunpapers War Correspondent]

With the 3d Army in Saarlautern, Dec. 3 [By Cable — Delayed] — At 5 o'clock this morning when December's first full moon was high and veiled by scudding clouds of mist, American troops led by a 27-year-old lieutenant colonel paddled across the Saar River here in assault boats.

Before the sleepy German outposts were aware of what was going on, the Americans had cut behind them to seize the northern abutment of Saarlautern's principal highway bridge across the river.

Unorthodox Attack

The attack was absolutely contrary to the book — the sort of thing that military tacticians are schooled never to attempt. The Germans held the river banks at either end of the bridge. But perhaps because of its audacity the operation tonight appeared to have been completely successful.

American troops held the bridge intact. The Germans had prepared it for demolition. They had not yet withdrawn all of their troops from that part of Saarlautern south of the bridge. But even if they had planned to sacrifice these men they had no opportunity to set off explosive charges that would have blown the bridge. The Americans got there too quickly.

For almost a week the 3d Army had been closing in on Saarlautern. The progress had been slow and cautious. Troops had to fight their way past the old Maginot forts and over the new anti-tank ditches. The soldiers had to cross the German border and reduce, one by one, each of the solidly built farm villages whose closely bunched stone barns and houses guard every road that winds over the hills from Lorraine into the valley of the Saar.

Felsberg Taken

Day before yesterday troops of the 95th Division took Felsberg, the last of those villages on the main road from Metz to Saarlautern. From the crest of the bluff on which Felsberg stands, they could look down into the misty valley of the Saar.

Four miles away, where the river makes a broad U-loop in the valley, were factory chimneys and church spires of

Saarlautern. We went up there yesterday afternoon. Felsberg's last German sniper lay dead in a muddy alley near the village church. Some loyal German villager had laid a paper wreath of pink and white flowers on his body.

Now the villagers had taken to their cellars. German artillery, some of it emplaced in the Siegfried Line beyond Saarlautern, had shelled their town. Some of its ruined houses of dirty brown stone and plaster were still burning. Its white goats and yellow-spotted cattle wandered through the hillside streets.

Smoke Over City

American troops had followed the Metz road down the bluff and across the valley to Saarlautern. They were fighting in the western outskirts of the city. Saarlautern, also shelled, had hatched its brood of fires whose gray smoke thickened the river's haze hanging over the city.

The head of another American infantry column, scheduled to join the attack on Saarlautern today, had halted in Felsberg. This column had been crawling along the road from the village of Tromborn, five miles back, since early morning. The troops were fed up with their slow progress.

It was a cold, damp day. During the long halt in Felsberg some sat in muddy ditches on either side of the road looking down the valley. Others had moved into vacant barns and houses along the road to munch apples and warm themselves at small wood fires they'd kindled on the stone and dirt floors of their temporary shelters.

No Haste To Evacuate

Col. Robert L. Bacon, of Harlingen, Texas, regimental commander, said the Germans appeared to be in no haste to evacuate Saarlautern. The original plan had called for the column halted in the village to attack the city and try to cross the Saar River that afternoon.

With Colonel Bacon was Lieut. Col. Tobias R. Philbin, 27, of Clinton, Mass. This young lieutenant colonel is the brother of James T. Philbin, of Catonsville. He intends, if the war ever ends to marry Miss Anne Scarborough, 716 Wyndhurst road, Roland Park.

Philbin is so young and so youthful in appearance that when we first saw him beside the white-haired colonel we took him to be a second lieutenant. It was a surprise to learn he was in command of the column of infantry which had halted in the village.

We walked along a muddy road that is Felsberg's main street, asking soldiers if any of them were Marylanders. We found five within five minutes. There were Privates Weston Emmart, 708 St. Johns road; John Rademacher, 33rd street and Hamilton avenue; Raymond T. Floyd, 211 Scott street; Norman Leverton, 324 South Macon street, Baltimore, and Wellwood Putnam, of Reisterstown.

Red Cross Girl From State

Sitting in the hallway of a house beside the road a little farther on was Lieut. Stanley Kummer, of Relay, Md., a University of Maryland graduate who reported having seen another Marylander, Miss Peggy Maslin, in a Red Cross doughnut wagon near the front a few days ago.

There were at least two other Baltimoreans in the outfit that had halted along the road. Private Charles Sussman, another rifleman, and Private George Hyman, headquarters company switchboard operator, but we didn't have time to look them up.

Colonel Philbin came along in a jeep with orders for the column to start moving. We fell into line and hiked on toward Saarlautern with his infantry. It was less than five miles into Saarlautern, but the column moved slowly, halting frequently.

Couldn't Strike Matches

Night came on and it started raining again, fine, cold drizzle, long before we reached the outskirts. The infantry shuffled along wearily, weighted down with packs, bazooka ammunition, mortars and machine guns.

The soldiers griped as soldiers will each time they stopped for another wait. Blackout regulations were strictly enforced. They couldn't strike matches to light cigarettes. The only light in the dark and mist and rain was the red glow from the burning houses along the shelled road. German artillery still shelled the road every now and then. When bursts came too close, the waiting columns scattered into wet muddy fields.

An officer finally came back up the road from the direction of Saarlautern with the word that the German barracks west of town had been cleared of the enemy and the column would shack up there for the night.

The troops cut across the backyards of suburban Saarlautern, because the Germans still held the center of town, and turned into the gateway of a large modern Kaserne where doughboys stood guard at a striped German sentry box.

Most of the window panes of the Kaserne's large brick and concrete buildings had been shattered by shell-fire and the aerial bombardment of Saarlautern and earlier in the day by fighter-bombers and Martin Marauders of the 9th Air Force. The doors of its cold, drafty rooms banged dismally in the darkness as the soldiers groped around with a few shaded flashlights to find themselves the most comfortable spots for billets.

Facing the Saar

There were beds with mattresses in some of the upstairs rooms but the bare basement rooms, whose small windows had been constructed to serve as rifle ports, were popular with the Americans. The Kaserne faced the Saar River, less than 200 yards away, and the Germans were on the river's opposite bank.

Germans were also in the town proper, immediately south of the barracks. And in their examination of the Kaserne for sleeping space, the Americans found six Germans still hiding in its barracks.

Three were in one room trying to use the telephone. They surrendered without fighting and were sent back under guard.

We moved into a cellar room with Colonel Philbin, Lieut. Kummer and the rest of the HQ staff. It was a concrete casemated room whose ceiling was reinforced with timbers of telephone pole proportions. The medical officer, Capt. Ormond Haynes, of Marietta, Ohio — his wife lived in Richmond, Va., where he graduated from medical school — provided us with a couple of spare blankets.

Called To Conference

By the light of a gasoline lamp we were eating supper of hot chow brought up by jeep when the messenger arrived with orders for Colonel Philbin and Lieutenant Kummer to report back immediately for HQ conference. They groaned and took off, sending back word a half hour later to Major Edward P. von Derau, Philbin's executive officer, to assemble all company officers.

Some sort of special mission was plainly afoot and while sitting around the basement room awaiting Colonel Philbin's return, the company officers speculated on what it might be. They'd drawn tough assignments before, including frontal attack on Metz forts when, cut off from other American troops, they'd been supplied by air by liaison planes.

"At 0500 tomorrow morning," the colonel announced on his return, "it will be the mission of command to cross the Saar River and capture the northern abutment of the highway bridge, which is still intact."

He went on to explain that the higher command had information that the bridge had been prepared for demolition and it was hoped the attacking force would reach the northern abutment in time to prevent the Germans from blowing it. The engineers would provide assault boats in which the infantry would cross the river.

Artillery Shells Bank

During the remainder of the night German artillery shelled the western bank of the Saar around the Kaserne but the noise didn't keep the officers awake. They had too many other considerations to keep them busy. First, they had to go out and reconnoiter the river's western bank to pick the most suitable point for the crossing. The artillery liaison officer had to work out plans for supporting fire missions. They'd never been across the river. They'd never seen it by daylight except at a distance of five miles through the afternoon's haze. Maps and aerial photographs showed that its eastern bank and bridge abutment were protected by a fort they'd never seen.

"We will cross in two waves, 13 men to each assault boat," the colonel said. "I will be in the fifth boat of the second wave."

No one remarked aloud during that council of war that that plan of attack violated the first and universally accepted military precept governing all standard orders of procedure for a river crossing. That precept is that an attacking military force never should attempt to force a river crossing until it has secured the bank of the river from which the effort is to be launched.

American troops had by no means secured that bank. The plan of the impending attack was a bold and daring bid to get into the enemy's rear at a time and at a point where he would not be expecting an attack. Upon the measure of surprise depended the entire success of the maneuver. If the attacking force were cut off it would probably be annihilated.

After the infantry officers had agreed upon the general details of the attack, engineer officers arrived. The remainder of the night was spent working out boat loading schedules, choosing the exact spot for the crossing and the point at which the engineers would attempt to build foot and light vehicle bridges after the assault troops had been boated across the Saar.

Engineer trucks came up under cover of darkness with loads of nested little assault boats and bridging materials. The engineers were commanded by Lieut. Col. James I. Crowther, of 2824 East Presstman street, Baltimore.

With Colonel Crowther, as one of his staff officers, was Capt. Richard J. Meise, 3118 Northern drive, Baltimore. A platoon of engineers from the company commanded by Capt. Walter Koppelman, Jr., 101 Millbrook road, Guilford, was detailed to accompany the infantry and try to cut the wiring of the German demolition charges on the bridge.

Planning Continued

Still another engineering officer, Major Haig Jackson, of Lonaconing, Md., arrived later to help plan assistance by another corps engineer unit in the construction of the river bridges. Planning and revised planning continued until within a few minutes of the time set for the actual jump-off.

Luck favored the assault on two counts. First, the rain ceased and a full moon came out, enabling the engineers to get a fairly good look at the opposite bank of the river. Second, it was discovered that the river, out of its banks during recent floods, was almost back to normal.

The moon was still fairly bright but occasionally was blotted out by shifting clouds when the infantry filed out of the Kaserne silently shortly before 5 o'clock, each boat party of the first wave carrying the little craft in which they would paddle across the river.

American artillery went into noisy, vivid action, firing the first of the prearranged concentrations behind the German lines and by way of giving the Germans a bum steer if they should suspect anything, a deceptive concentration father north.

Screen Of Woods

Infantrymen carrying their assault boats moved out quickly, following the river road a short distance west of the Kaserne to the point which had been chosen for the crossing, the point which would land the troops around a bend in the river screened by a patch of woods about 1,000 yards from the bridge abutment.

Though the artillery thundered, all orders along the river bank were issued in whispers. The only full-fledged sound was the gentle grating of the boats' bottoms on the edge of the high river bank, about ten feet above the water level, as the assault craft were eased into the stream.

The wet paddles of the boatmen in the first wave glistened as they dipped the blades into the smooth but swift-running stream. The men who were to cross in the second wave knelt in the shadows while the boats disappeared in the gloom of woods and the opposite bank. The boats returned and the second wave crossed silently.

Not A Shot

Not a single sound of a shot had come from the opposite bank of the river when the engineers set in work at the somewhat noisier task of fitting together sections of a foot bridge, floating them out into the stream one after another and joining them up. One faulty center section broke when the bridge was almost completed, but the engineers finally got a footway across — 228 feet of it from bank to bank.

A few minutes before they anchored this floating footway with steel stakes and rope cables there was a short burst of small-arms fire from the direction of the fort guarding the northern abutment of the highway bridge. We assumed then that the attacking party had been seen.

But German artillery did not open up until daylight. The enemy's big guns and snipers made things pretty miserable after that for the engineers. Sectional rafts which they were fitting together for a light vehicular bridge suffered three hits and the engineers were eventually driven back from the river bank, but the footbridge stayed in.

14 German Prisoners

Meanwhile, Colonel Philbin had sent back fourteen German prisoners, including a wireless section. The engineers had found explosives on the highway bridge and started to remove them. One prisoner stated the bridge had not been blown up because the electric generator used to provide the power for the detonator had been knocked out of commission either by American artillery or by the previous day's aerial bombardment.

We do not yet know the full story of the capture of the highway bridge abutment. Philbin and his men are still on the far side of the river, and it is not safe at this time to cross. German artillery and snipers are too active. All we know has been contained in concise reports Philbin has made by radio.

These reports state that he and his men have beaten off two German counterattacks and taken 100 prisoners. Other American infantry forces and tank destroyers have reached the southern abutment of the captured highway bridge and late this afternoon were awaiting clearance by the engineers, still demining the bridge, before crossing.

Retreat Cut Off

Seizure of the bridge has cut off the retreat of the German snipers and machine-gunners still fighting from house to house in downtown Saarlautern this side of the bridge. How many Germans have been cut off is unknown. The prisoners say the largest part of the defending garrison remaining in Saarlautern is one of Himmler's Volkssturm units.

It will probably require at least another day to clear the city of snipers. How long the German artillery will continue to fire on Saarlautern is another matter. The city is within short and easy range of the guns in the outer defenses of the Siegfried Line directly behind the town.

THE BALTIMORE SUN, TUESDAY, DECEMBER 5, 1944

MARYLANDERS IN GERMANY —
In the dispatch below, Mr. McCardell mentions two Marylanders

Saar River Bridge Taken 10 Minutes Before Germans Planned to Blow It — Four Enemy Soldiers Shot While Wiring Captured American Bombs For Detonation

By Lee McCardell [Sunpapers War Correspondent]

With the U.S. 3d Army in Saarlautern, Dec. 4 [By Radio] — Lieut. Col. Tobias R. (Toby) Philbin's 1st Battalion of the 379th Infantry yesterday captured Saarlautern's main highway bridge over the Saar River less than ten minutes before the time set by the Germans to blow it.

This postscript to the story of bridge was related today at regimental headquarters. Colonel Philbin had come back last night to report the capture of the bridge officially to his commanding officer, Col. Robert L. Bacon. He'd taken off again to rejoin his battalion before this correspondent saw him, but here's the authentic second hand version of what happened.

Passed German-Held Fort

Philbin's battalion, which contains several Maryland men, crossed the Saar River by assault boat in the dark at 5 o'clock yesterday morning. They crossed below the bend in the river about a half mile west of Saarlautern, circled a patch of woods to avoid German outposts and approached the bridge from the rear of the German lines.

They moved silently down the road, past an old fort held by the Germans, and arrived at the northern abutment of the river bridge. Not one shot was fired before they reached the bridge. Five or six astonished German soldiers whom the Americans encountered along the road surrendered and went along quietly with their captors.

Find Nazi Radio Car

When the head of the American column reached the northern abutment of the bridge, a sturdy, old-fashioned, hump-backed, masonry structure, they found an armored German radio car parked along the gloomy road. One German in the car surrendered, but another — a lieutenant wearing radio earphones — refused to obey the command to give up and get out.

Fearful that the German officer would broadcast an alarm and give away the secret of the surprise attack, and not daring to risk sounding an alarm himself by firing an unnecessary shot, an American infantryman bayoneted the lieutenant where he sat in the front seat of the radio car.

Colonel Philbin, farther back in the column, which had been moving forward in single file on either side of the road, anxiously hurried ahead with his tommy-gun to find the cause of the delay. It was 7.21 A. M. when he reached the bridge abutment. Dawn was breaking.

Four German soldiers were busy with something in the middle of the bridge. There was no time to argue. The Americans opened fire, killing all four. From the opposite side of the bridge a voice called out in German, asking what the shooting was about.

Out of the shadows appeared another German lieutenant and three more German soldiers. A German-speaking American infantryman with Colonel Philbin called to them to surrender. The lieutenant came on at a run, reaching for his pistol.

Colonel Philbin opened fire with his tommy-gun, killing the lieutenant and two others. The fourth man surrendered.

Engineers who had crossed the river with the infantry ran out onto the bridge and discovered the Germans had laid four 500-pound American aerial bombs on the bridge deck and apparently had been fusing them when they were surprised. Back along the bridge floor lay electric wires to detonate the bombs. The engineers clipped the wires in short order.

The attack on the bridge was no longer secret. From the far side of the river the Germans began firing at the engineers with rifles and machine-guns.

"It was the most murderous small-arms fire I have ever seen in my life," Colonel Philbin said later, "My hair actually stood on end as I watched those engineers of ours working under that fire."

Too Heavy To Carry

The four bombs, which the Germans evidently had salvaged from some wrecked American plane, were too heavy, too ponderous for the engineers to manage with their bare hands. Though the electrical detonating system had been disconnected, the engineers were afraid some unlucky German rifle or machine-gun bullet would set them off.

They dare not roll the bombs over the side of the bridge into the river. The impact of the fall might cause the bombs to explode. Near the northern abutment of the bridge lay a wooden ladder. The engineers broke the ladder in half and used each half as a sledge on which to drag the bombs clear of the bridge, one at a time. And all the time they were sweating over that ton of high-explosive, the Germans continued firing at them from the opposite end of the bridge and the far side of the river.

After the wire to the bombs had been cut, other engineers followed the clipped ends into an old fort beside the road north of the bridge. The wires led to a room in which they found another German soldier waiting at the plunger for the orders to detonate the charge. He surrendered without any argument.

Planned for 7.30

From their prisoners the Americans learned that the Germans had planned to blow the bridge at 7.30 — nine minutes after Philbin reached the northern end. They had delayed blowing it before then because they needed it to supply and maintain contact with other German troops still in Saarlautern south and east of the river.

The four German soldiers shot down in the middle of the bridge had been preparing the bombs for detonation. The original firing system, set several days in advance, had been thrown out of kilter either by American artillery shells or the air bombardment of Saarlautern by Marauders the day before yesterday.

250 Germans Captured

Meanwhile, other units of the 379th Infantry and self-propelled guns of the attached tank-destroyer battalion, which had been fighting the Germans through the streets of Saarlautern this side of the river, had reached the southern end and captured the bridge.

More than 250 Germans had been captured in street and house-to-house fighting. Some 500 others, according to the prisoners, threw away their arms and escaped across the river above the captured bridge by boat, raft and swimming. They made their way to the line of German pillboxes farther back along the Saar's eastern bank.

Early this morning the Germans counterattacked the Americans east of the river. Philbin's original battalion had been reinforced during the night. Five tanks spearheaded the German counterattack down the same road Philbin's men had used in their surprise assault yesterday morning.

German infantry and machine-gunners rode forward on the tanks, jumping off and scattering on each side of the road as the tanks broke out of column formation to deploy. An American infantryman armed with a bazooka knocked out the leading German tank. A tank destroyer knocked out a second, and American artillery is believed to have scored a direct hit on a third. The others pulled back and, with the enemy infantry, retreated.

Saarlautern Found Dead

This afternoon I went down through the main streets of Saarlautern with Lewis Hawkins, Associated Press correspondent. We were both eager to cross the river, see Colonel Philbin and his men and get the story of their exploit from them directly.

Saarlautern was a dead city, its lifeless streets littered with bodies and debris. German artillery, some of it emplaced in the Siegfried Line defenses beyond the city and the Saar, had been shelling the town all day yesterday and again last night. Hawkins and I got as far as the southern abutment of the captured bridge. The bodies of seven German soldiers still lay where they'd been shot down in yesterday morning's fight.

But just as we reached the bridge, German artillery resumed its fire. We ducked into a shattered doorway of a blasted shop to get out of the shrapnel which came rattling down in the street. The third burst discouraged us from trying any further.

They Turn Back

We turned back and contented ourselves with the version of the story as I have written it from accounts given us by Lieut. Col. Aubrey W. Akin, of Newport, Vt., executive officer of the 379th Infantry, and Major Byron Doll, of Los Angeles, executive officer of the 320th Engineer Battalion, both of whom had talked to Philbin last night; Staff Sergeant John Michael, of River Forest, Ill., a member of Philbin's Battalion Headquarters Company, and Pfc. Raymond Ferguson, of El Paso, Texas, a member of the company's 1st Platoon, which had been "the point" of yesterday morning's attack. Michael and Ferguson had driven back across the bridge in a captured German radio car.

The 320th Engineer Battalion, commanded by Lieut. Col. James I. Crowther, of Baltimore, provided the engineers which participated in the surprise attack. Crowther's battalion also constructed a foot bridge across the Saar and tried to build a light vehicular bridge until driven back from the river bank by heavy German machine-gun and artillery fire.

One Error Noted

From Major Doll we learned we had erred in one detail of our early report on yesterday morning's attack. The platoon of engineers which crossed the river with the infantry was not from the company commanded by Capt. Walter Koppelman, Jr., of Baltimore. It was drawn from another company and commanded by Lieut. Edward Herbert, of Montgomery, Ala.

Koppelman's company provided assault boats and a three-man crew of engineers for each boat, which made two trips carrying loads of ten infantrymen across the river at each trip. The crossing was completed in record time of eleven minutes. Later the engineers, driven back from the river, took cover in abandoned German trenches this side of the river to return German small-arms fire.

THE BATTLE FOR METZ

MYSTERY EXPLOSION EFFECTS — McCardell told on November 20 of a terrific triple blast which occurred as a Yank infantry column moved past Fort Bellacroix, just after its garrison surrendered. ADX-772-BS

Lee McCardell's Camera Covers The Metz Front

The story of the capture of Metz, most formidable fortress in western Europe, by Lieut. Gen. George S. Patton, Jr.'s Third Army was related in detail day by day for Sunpapers readers by War Correspondent Lee McCardell, who entered the city with the 95th Division. McCardell's camera was busy, too, as these pictures prove.

IN FLANDERS: TWO MARYLANDERS — In the door of this communications truck at an airfield are Pfc. Tony Zamer, of Brandywine, and Corporal John M. Lanza, whose address is 4124 Kershaw avenue, Baltimore. ADX-761-BS

BALTIMOREAN SUPERVISES WELDING JOB — The man who is bossing the man with the torch on this job at a Flanders airfield is Sergt. George Kruelle, of 2201 East Oliver street, Baltimore, who is a top sheet-metal worker. ADX-765-BS

YANKS FOUGHT THEIR WAY THROUGH HERE — The wreckage of war fills this street in Moyenvic, captured by 26th Division. ADX-760-BS

WITH HANDS HELD HIGH — Picture above of Germans coming in to give themselves up under the guns of an American tank at the village of Puilly, which was among points captured by Fifth Division. ADX-774-BS

FOE'S BARRACKS — Another view of the effects of the explosion which followed the surrender of Fort Bellacroix, which had been renamed Fort Steinmetz by the Germans. Many buildings there went up in flames, too. ADX-757-BS

ROAD OF DEATH — Sunpapers Correspondent Lee McCardell procured the photos in this space while proceeding with American forces in the Metz sector of the Western front. The road into Metz, near Fort Bellacroix, presented this devastated scene after a terrible explosion. ADX-768-BS

A STREET IN JALLACOURT — Motorized equipment of the 3d Army stands in this street of Jallacourt, near Metz. The town was captured by the 39th Division in heavy fighting. The town church is in background. ADX-763-BS

FIGHTING YANKS — These doughboys helped take Fort Bellacroix. Left to right: Sergt. Stephen Schwab, Pittsburgh; Pfc. Neftal Tarsi, 3035 Northern parkway, Baltimore and Private Angelo Guerra, Trenton, New Jersey. ADX-769-BS

THE INFANTRY MOVES UP — Battle-weary Yanks of the 3d Army march into Fort Bellacroix. ADX-771-BS

BARRACKS UNTENABLE — Concentrated fire of American artillery smashed the barracks of Fort Bellacroix on the road to Metz. Buildings gave off smoke and flame as Yanks pushed through. ADX-762-BS

AFTER THE BATTLE — The smoke-blackened walls of Fort Bellacroix stand bold in the sunlight in this photo, snapped after brisk fighting in the sector. Yanks at left pause before the ruins. ADX-764-BS

WITH MARYLANDERS NEAR FRONT

Third Army Life As Seen By Lee McCardell's Camera

The hard-hitting Third Army, conqueror of Metz, has a larger proportion of Marylanders than the run of the American armies in France, and Lee McCardell, Sunpapers War Correspondent, who has been reporting its achievements, has had little difficulty in finding Maryland men, whose names are scattered through his dispatches, as targets for his camera. Not lack of subjects, but lack of good photographic sunlight, lately has been the greatest obstacle in his camera work, but as the pictures on this page indicate, he has managed to add to his photographic record of the campaign on the western front.

YANKEE DIVISION CHOW LINE — Men of the 26th with their cups and mess kits file past the steaming pots that their cooks have set up in the village of Lohr. Not like home cooking but it beats cold rations. ADX-756-BS

THIS BALTIMOREAN DOESN'T LOOK DOWNHEARTED — The broad smile of Pfc. Andrew Boland's face as he tucks away his chow, indicates that things go well. His address: 2043 Annapolis boulevard, "Westport." ADX-766-BS

CAN'T STOP A JEEP — Roads like this have slowed the American advance but jeeps can take the going. ADX-770-BS

ENGINEERS — Another Third Army unit gets it hot from the cooks, who are doing business in mud. This picture of alfresco dining was made near the town of Dieuze. ADX-773-BS

BOMBERS PASSED THIS WAY FIRST — To enter the town of St. Avold, the Third Army had to negotiate a huge bomb crater, on the rim of which stand a number of civilians, looking down into the hole. ADX-758-BS

BUSY CORNER IN METZ ON DAY FORTRESS FELL — In front of the barracks at Fort Bellacroix, with foot soldiers slogging forward, a gun and tank momentarily halted. Shattered glass in nearly all windows shows that there's been action here. ADX-767-BS

BALTIMOREAN AT ST. AVOLD — Lieut. Col. Hiram D. Ives (with field glasses) shortly after battalion under his command occupied town. ADX-759-BS

CHAPTER 7

SNOW AND COLD MAKE A TOUGH FOE

THE BALTIMORE SUN, SUNDAY, JANUARY 7, 1945

MARYLANDERS AT FRONT —
Three Marylanders are mentioned in the following dispatch.

'Bloody Bucket' Division Lives Up To Its Jerry-Bestowed Nickname — Full Force of Rundstedt's Plunge into Luxembourg Caught By The 28th Division

By Lee McCardell [Sunpapers War Correspondent]

With U.S. 3d Army, Jan. 6 [By Radio] — It was the 28th Infantry Division, a former Pennsylvania National Guard outfit and sister organization of Maryland's own 29th Division, which caught the full force of Field Marshal Rundstedt's line plunge across the Our River into Luxembourg last December 16.

When the 28th Division, also known as the "Keystone Division," from the red keystone its officers and men wear as a shoulder patch, was fighting in Normandy last summer, a captured German officer said:

"You are either picked troops or madmen. We call you Die Blutig Eimer — the Bloody Bucket — Division."

It's unlikely the Germans have changed their opinion.

Commanded By Cota

The 28th landed in Normandy late in July. Since mid-August it has been commanded by Maj. Gen. Norman D. (Dutch) Cota, a North African campaign veteran who was assistant division commander of the 29th when the Marylanders hit the beachhead on D-day, and who remained with the 29th until wounded at the battle of St. Lo.

When attacked by von Rundstedt's forces, the troops of the 28th were stretched thinly along the Our River. They'd been withdrawn from the 1st Army front for a holding operation after hard fighting in the battle of the Hurtgen Forest.

Start Of The German Influx

Early on the morning of December 16, German infantry began pouring across the river, as one division officer later described them, "floods of infantry, screaming, shouting, laughing and acting as no other German infantry had acted before — until the men who faced them swore they were doped or drunk, or both."

The defense put up by the 28th, some of whose scattered units subsequently were overrun and surrounded, is now credited with having delayed the German advance long enough to enable the 101st Airborne Division and elements of the 9th and 10th Armored divisions to occupy and hold the vitally important crossroads town of Bastogne.

Fired At 50-Yard Range

One of the first units of the 28th to be hit by the advancing Germans was a heavy-weapons company near the village of Reisdorf, on the Our River, 20 miles north of the city of Luxembourg. Well dug in, the Americans held their fire until the oncoming enemy infantrymen were within 50 yards, then "racked 'em and stacked 'em until the Nazis were clambering over their own dead."

Farther north, another heavy-weapons company, unable to reach the river bridge and blow it to halt the German tanks, stood off German infantry supporting the tanks for 36 hours with mortar, machine-gun and small-arms fire on the main road from the city of Luxembourg to St. Vith, fought two columns of German tanks all night and the next day. At midnight, the American commander radioed his battalion headquarters that the situation was critical, his force outnumbered, surrounded and almost out of ammunition. He was ordered to withdraw, if possible.

But They "Made Them Pay"

He replied, "We can't get out, but we'll make them pay!"

The major commanding the battalion didn't speak directly with the company's captain after that, explaining when he told his story later: "He knew and I knew. What can you say to a man at a time like that?"

At 4.30 Monday morning a young lieutenant came to the radio to report his men fighting from house to house with no ammunition except hand grenades.

"We've blown everything there is to blow except this radio — it goes next," he sobbed. "I don't mind dying. I don't mind taking a beating, but we'll never give up to these bastards!"

The radio clicked off and shortly before 10 o'clock went dead.

"Closer! Closer — Closer!"

From the village of Walhausen, 3 miles south of Hosingen, where another unit of the 28th was beating off repeated German infantry attacks, a nameless private called urgently for artillery fire.

"Jerry multiply 20 millimeter, tank, another vehicle and a lot of infantry coming down the road!" he yelled over the battalion radio. "Pour it on!"

"Closer!" he shouted after the first salvos landed. "Closer — closer!"

The rounds were landing within 30 yards of the advance observation post from which the solider was calling for fire. The roar of the exploding shells could be heard over the radio telephone at the artillery fire-direction center.

"Let me speak to your commanding officer," said Major Harold F. Milton, of Jasper, Fla., the artillery commander.

"Bring It In On Top Of Us"

The lieutenant came on the phone and confirmed the private's judgment.

"Bring it in!" he said. "Bring it in on top of us, Goddam it! We'll duck!"

Two miles farther south, at the village of Weiler, a 28th mortar squad blew their guns and fell back into the town after they'd exhausted their ammunition. With the company cooks, clerks, truck drivers and riflemen, they held Saturday and all day Sunday, then slipped out of the town after dark, rejoining the battalion command post to reorganize and fight again.

Cannoneers of a field artillery battery set up on a hill outside Weiler fired their guns at constantly decreasing elevation, and when the Germans threatened to overrun their position they grabbed rifles and carbines, jumped into foxholes and fought as infantry. They beat back five attacks before all their ammunition had been expended.

Jerries "Close Enough To Touch"

The full tide of the German advance was now sweeping across the Luxembourg border between Vianden and Clervaux — *Panzers and Volks Grenadiers*. The American officer at the village of Marnach, east of Clervaux had reported "Jerries — hundreds of Jerries!" And when the battalion command post inquired how far away the enemy was the answer came back:

"Just take it from me, they're close enough to touch!"

The Marnach garrison was ordered to hold out at all costs. It held out until Sunday afternoon against repeated assaults by German halftracks and infantry. That afternoon a radio man had called in from Marnach to report a German half-track in front of his command post, when he suddenly stopped talking, then whispered, "Gee, there must be a million Jerries outside."

Then the radio went dead, and from the distance came the sound of firing.

Bazookas And Tiger Tanks

Three American tanks attached to the 28th climbed a hill behind the village of Urspelt, 2 miles north of Clervaux, and poured fire into the advancing German columns for three hours. American officers armed with bazookas fired at German Tiger tanks.

Farther south in the triangle formed by the villages of Munshausen, Marnach and Drauffelt, other American tanks commanded by Lieut. Raymond Fleig, an Ohioan who had just been awarded the Silver Star for gallantry in the Hurtgen Forest, plugged another front-line gap while the battalion and regimental headquarters were battling Germans at their front doors.

Suddenly It's No Rest Center

The peaceful, picturesque little Luxembourg town of Clervaux, 30 miles north of the Grand Duchy's capital had been the 28th Division's rest center. The battle-weary GI's who had survived the Hurtgen Forest fighting had come to Clervaux to sleep, eat, enjoy daily movies and forget about the war.

But at 5 A. M. on December 16 Clervaux ceased to be a rest center. German artillery began shelling the hotels and private houses where the GI's were sleeping. Infantrymen were rounded up and organized into improvised rifle companies with signal corpsmen, cooks, clerks and drivers.

That afternoon 30 German tanks clanked down from the height beyond Clervaux toward the town and by nightfall German Tigers, guided by men in civilian dress, had reached the center of the town, halted at the doorway of one Clervaux hotel and poured round after round into the hotel lobby.

Cut Off Five Times In Three Days

Headquarters personnel, rear-echelon typists, military police, waiters from the officers' messes, engineers, stragglers and other scattered groups fought something approaching guerrilla warfare for the next three days. One command post was surrounded and cut off five times during those three days, but each time it filtered out to reorganize and fight again.

Communications were disturbed. Occasionally artillery units had been separated from the infantry. Ammunition was running low. The best that some groups could do was mine and block roads as they were driven back slowly.

Finally orders came to withdraw toward Bastogne, where the 101st Airborne Division was beginning to close. One column of 28th troops, forming a convoy of tanks and vehicles, had to fight its way through enemy roadblocks. A few stragglers drifted in behind them for days after, suffering from hunger, exhaustion and trench foot.

The "Task-Force Rabble"

Lieut. Glenn Peterson, of Olivia, Texas, who led one last group of 50 rear-echelon riflemen out of Wiltz, was almost drowned crossing an icy stream. This little group thought themselves cut off. The bridge on their only route of withdrawal had been captured by the Germans, but they were shown another way through the German lines.

Many stragglers who made their way to Bastogne fought there with an improvised task force known variously as the Task-force Rabble and the Team SNAFU. Said one sergeant who had fought from Clervaux to Bastogne, speaking with considerable satisfaction:

"We laid some tanks, five or six machine guns and some rifles in on some Heinies in one thicket outside Bastogne. We fired all day. Then we went in. There were only thirteen left alive. Man, they were piled up there three deep. I never saw such a mess in my life."

German Column Ambushed

Around the towns of Diekirch and Ettelbruck, on the south of the 28th's front, the fighting had been equally severe. Between the villages of Grosbous and Feulon, a German artillery column with vehicles and horse-drawn artillery was ambushed by the Americans and 2,000 German corpses littered the road when the fighting ceased.

This was the area in which troops of Lieut. George S. Patton's 80th Infantry Division, including three battalions commanded by Maryland officers, eventually passed through the remnants of the 28th to relieve them.

Golden, Ives And Cheston

The battalion commanders are Lieut. Col. John Golden, of Cumberland; Lieut. Col. Hiram Ives, of Baltimore, and Lieut.

Col. Elliott Cheston, of Annapolis.

The 28th fought its last engagement in the battle of Bastogne, near the little village of Sibert, while falling back from Bastogne toward Neufchateau. It was here that the division's staff officers fought on the lines with the headquarters enlisted personnel.

The next morning in Luxembourg I was talking with an American Red Cross girl, Marion Conley, of Boston, who had been with the 28th in Wiltz. We knew what the 28th had been through, but the security considerations of the press censorship forbade any mention of the division by name. The girl from Boston was pretty blue, and she was close to tears.

She wailed, "Nobody gives them any credit. They've taken an awful going over — but they're grand!"

THE BALTIMORE SUN, SATURDAY, DECEMBER 23, 1944

'Nazi Tanks Have Entered Bastogne'

By Lee McCardell [Sunpapers War Correspondent]

With American Forces, Dec. 23 — The military situation at this front as described at noon today by official statement may be summarized as follows:

"The enemy, having previously surrounded Wiltz, now has control of the town and his tanks have entered Bastogne.

"In the thrust west from Bastogne enemy tanks have reached the area of Saint Huber. South of Bastogne they have cut the Bastogne-Arlon highway, and in the north the enemy has reached the Laroche area.

"Northerly drives are still being contained in the Stavelot sector. Enemy troops are known to be concentrating on this area.

"Enemy attacks with tanks and infantry east of Malmedy was repulsed in the Faymonville and Bullingen area."

THE BALTIMORE SUN, SUNDAY, DECEMBER 24, 1944

This letter was written by Mr. McCardell, Sunpapers war correspondent with the United States 3d Army, to his young daughters Mary Ann, Abby and Tillie.

Lee McCardell's Christmas Letter
Luxembourg, December 23, 1944

Dear Children:

The real name of the town where I am is Luxembourg, but on Christmas Eve I'd rather call it "toyland." With its funny little houses, its sharply pointed twin church steeples and its tiny trolley cars no bigger than Gleason and Lutts's delivery truck, Luxembourg really looks just like toyland.

Luxembourg is built on steep hills overlooking a river valley, just as Ellicott City overlooks the Patapsco River. But Luxembourg is much, much older than Ellicott City. There are ruined castle towers on some hills. The little river winding along their feet is crossed by beautifully carved stone bridges standing on high, slim, graceful arches.

Christmas Garden Town

Yesterday it snowed, and now Luxembourg, with its funny houses, sharp church steeples, ruined castles and high arched bridges looks exactly like a little town in a Christmas garden under a Christmas tree.

It looks as if it had been covered with dabs of white cotton and powdered with the same kind of sparkling, artificial snow we used to buy at the 10-cent store for our Christmas garden. The tiny trolley cars look just exactly like the little trolley car we had in our Christmas garden at grandfather's long ago at Christmas time — except our trolley car was red and yellow, and those of Luxembourg are green and yellow.

Once upon a time, a happier Christmas time, we all went to Keiths on Lexington street to see a moving picture called

"Babes in Toyland." It had a song, "Toyland, Toyland, Little Girl and Boyland." Do you remember? It keeps running through my mind.

Abby Hid Her Face

The people who made that moving picture put some things into it which I do not think Mr. Victor Herbert, who wrote the song, would have liked. There were some robot soldiers who frightened the people in Toyland. They frightened you too, Abby. You were a very little girl then. You hid your face and held my hand tightly. Do you remember?

Well, on this Christmas Eve some real robot soldiers of Hitler, grown men old enough to know better, are frightening the people of Toyland — I mean Luxembourg. They are only 20 miles away, and the people of Luxembourg don't like it at all!

But I don't think the German soldiers will ever get here, because our American soldiers are fighting hard to keep them out of Toyland.

Tree On A Cannon

This isn't a very happy way for anybody to be spending Christmas Eve, especially when they are so far from home. It's cold and wet and muddy, and tonight it will be dark and lonely out there where our soldiers are fighting. There will be no Christmas candles, no Christmas music, except perhaps a little that a few soldiers may hear on the radio.

When I was out there yesterday, I saw only one Christmas tree. Some soldiers posted along a road had set it up on top of their cannon which was aimed toward Germany. They had no Christmas bells and no tinsel with which to decorate it, but I think it was the bravest Christmas tree I have ever seen.

Until a few days ago it didn't seem at all like Christmas. Even in the bigger towns of Lorraine, like Metz and Nancy, there were no holly wreaths, no red ribbons, no bright shop windows. Somebody told us they saw one Christmas tree in the window of one store in Nancy, but we never saw it. Big balls of mistletoe grow wild in the tree tops of Lorraine, but nobody seemed to take the slightest interest in it.

Battered Baby Carriage

In the majority of the poor little country villages where the armies have been fighting there aren't even any shop windows. They've all been smashed to pieces. Houses have been burned and blown to bits. Their broken furniture is scattered all over the streets.

The other day I saw a little girl about as old as you, Tillie, wheeling a battered baby carriage out of the wreckage of one house in a ruined village. I wondered if she'd expect a new one on Christmas morning. I hope not, because I am afraid if she does she will be disappointed.

And the poor little village churches! They were the prettiest building in most of the villages. Many of them have been knocked down. All the colored glass windows, which would have glowed so softly when the churches were lighted up tonight for the midnight services, have been shattered.

Church roofs have been blown off. Their pews and pipe organs and altars have been smashed. Their steeples have been knocked down. But there was one little village named Mittersheim where the churches are still standing and where the church bells, silent last Christmas, will ring tomorrow morning.

Church Bells Taken By Nazis

A few days before Christmas last year, Nazi soldiers took all the bells out of Mittersheim's church steeples. They took the bells to the railroad station at the next town, Fenetrange. People think they meant to put the bells on the train there and send them back to Germany, probably to melt them and make bullets out of them.

But something happened and the bells never were sent to Germany. Maybe our airplanes bombed the railroad so badly the trains could not run. Anyway, when some American tanks captured Fenetrange, the bells were still at the railroad station. The American general sent the bells back to Mittersheim.

Letter Of Thanks

The other day the general got a letter from the Mayor and two village pastors of Mittersheim. They wrote:

"For all of us, Catholic and Protestant, it is the most beautiful Christmas gift imaginable. This Christmas we shall again hear the chimes which we missed for so long a time, and which, thanks to the 4th American Armored Division under your command, have this day been returned to us. Please accept as the general of the division, the thanks of a grateful community."

Perhaps because he's so busy in America on Christmas Day, Santa Claus works in France and Belgium on the Feast of St. Nicholas, which this year fell on December 5. That was the day on which he delivered a limited supply of toys to luckier children in those two countries.

We've forgotten to ask exactly how Santa operates in Luxembourg, but from the looks of this toy town, he'll be doing the best he can tonight. Not that there are many toys in the shops, but the shop windows are the gayest and brightest we've seen this side of the ocean in the last three years.

There are little pasteboard Santa Clauses. There are red candles and paper cornucopias stamped with pine and holly. And little packages of ginger cakes tied with colored ribbon, and sprigs of evergreen and tinfoil Christmas stars.

Down in the square near the railroad station there's a man selling Christmas trees. A short while ago I saw a woman hurrying home with a little bunch of red-berried holly. Of course, the soldiers haven't been fighting in the city of Luxembourg as they've been fighting in the little villages of Lorraine. The stores, houses and churches haven't been knocked to pieces.

Fortunate To Be There

I am most fortunate to be in Luxembourg on Christmas Eve. So many other homesick fathers will be in muddy foxholes tonight. It makes me ashamed to look around, my hotel room, clean and tidy, with white painted woodwork and carpeted floor. My bed has clean white sheets and a soft white pillow. However homesick I may be, I will not be cold or wet or hungry.

In a world of miserable men this Christmas Eve, who am I that I should be comforted by the knowledge that my three children will sleep this night in warm, dry beds; that you'll awake tomorrow morning, bright-eyed, in a cheerful house with a roof and all its doors and windows?

Good Night, God Bless You

So many, many other children of Europe will sleep tonight in houses without roofs, without doors or windows. Many will sleep on straw in cold, damp cellars where Santa Claus, even if he should extend his continental activities from St. Nicholas Day through tonight, will never find them.

In fact, though this is the third Christmas I have been away from home, I think it will be the happiest I have spent. Not the merriest, mind you, but the happiest. Happiest because God, by being so very good to you, is being good to me. At least there is peace this Christmas Eve in your world of men of good will. Good night. God bless you as bountifully as he has blessed me. And a Merry Christmas.

Dada

THE BALTIMORE SUN, MONDAY, DECEMBER 26, 1944

Yule Spirit Absent At Front As American Troops Fight On

Lee McCardell [Sunpapers War Correspondent]

With the American forces, Dec. 25 [By Radio] — This has been one hell of a Christmas.

It has been a magnificent winter day of bright sunshine and freezing temperatures along the pine-clad hills of Ardennes, white with snow where the American troops are fighting to beat back one of the main thrusts of the German counteroffensive. But there is no Christmas spirit out there so far as the soldiers are concerned.

The snow-covered hills and the deep little valleys among them have been noisy all day with machine-gun and artillery fire.

Dirty brown smoke from burning villages bombed and strafed by our fighter aircraft smear the blue horizon of the Christmas sky.

Fighting Confused

The fighting is slow, and confused by the fact that many Germans still are wearing American uniforms, driving captured American trucks and using American tanks.

"You don't know exactly what to do when you round a bend in the road and find an American tank in front of you —

unless you see it is manned by Jerries in German uniforms," said one Joe we saw this afternoon up near the front beyond Martelange.

A squadron of fighter-bombers had just been overhead bombing and strafing a small village to the right where the Germans were trying to halt our advance. Infantry was fighting over there now.

Wounded Yanks Limping Along

Across the white field from the direction of the battle came two wounded American soldiers, one limping on a shrapnel-injured foot, the other holding a forearm struck by a German bullet.

Enemy mortar and machine-gun fire had been particularly heavy, but the Americans were making slow progress. The only Germans we saw were two prisoners riding on the hood of a jeep which flashed past us bound for the rear. They wore the green mottled smocks of German snipers over their gray uniforms.

The country over which the battle now is being fought is extremely rugged, with high wooded hills and steep ravines. It is distinctly not what a soldier of a tank division would call "good tank country."

Still Held By Germans

In the first swift stages of their offensive, the primary objective of which was to disrupt communications behind our lines, the Germans seized many road junctions and still hold them with strong forces. Several American units have been cut off from each other, notably those troops supplied day before yesterday by air transport planes.

One of our principal objectives now is to clear those road blocks, link up the separated forces and re-establish a fixed front line in those areas now described officially as fluid.

Field orders issued to American troops are grim instructions to simply "advance and destroy the enemy," and it was to that end our ground forces were operating today with the close support of the 9th Air Force Martin-Marauder medium bombers and Thunderbolt fighter-bombers.

Marauders Roar

Flock after flock of Marauders roared overhead early this Christmas morning, and when we were at the front line this afternoon the cold blue December sky was streaked with the vapor trails of other aircraft.

Our supply trucks had brought up frozen turkey for the GI Christmas dinner, but only those troops farther back had any hopes of tasting any turkey today.

The Christmas dinner for the men on the front line was cold canned C rations of meat and beans.

As of 2 o'clock this afternoon, we had seen only one American soldier with turkey in his possession. He was warming a small sliver of frozen white meat on a pointed stick over a little fire which he had built beside the road where his truck was parked.

Freezing Along The Road

"I got it from the cook a little while ago when I was back at the company kitchen," he said. "I guess the rest of it will keep all right until the boys get it — in this kind of weather."

It was freezing cold along the road. Another soldier, Private Earl Swaine, of Norfolk, Va., was using a penknife to break the ice on the top of his canteen to get water, he hoped, unless the canteen was frozen solid.

We saw only two Marylanders, Corporals Anthony Ariko, of 201 North Hammond's Ferry road, Linthicum Heights, Buster Sines, of Oakland. Ariko is a headquarters staff corporal of an armored artillery battalion. Sines recently was awarded the Silver Star for gallantry in action at Conthil, where he operated a radio under fire. Now he drives the battalion commander's car.

Both corporals are married. Ariko to a sister of Miss Dorothy Klingenburg who was "Miss Maryland" of 1944.

Sleeps On Potatoes

"What a Christmas!" said Ariko, "I went to sleep last night on top of a pile of potatoes in the cellar of a house up the road. I had to get up at 5.30 this morning to stand guard.

"We have been sweating out dinner now for almost two hours, but don't mind, since we think that they are going to bring it up to us. We understand it's turkey. They've got it back at the company mess with all the trimmings."

Sines had been luckier than Ariko in the matter of a Christmas billet. He slept in an upstairs room.

The corporals said there were at least two other Marylanders in their outfit — Sergt. Donald Roe, of Oakland, and Private Arthur Christ, of Baltimore, a member of the battalion reconnaissance section.

Meets Virginians

Farther up the road we met an infantry unit containing another Marylander, Sergt. Roger Sheriff, of Landover, and several Virginians, Sergt. Durwood Robertson, of Richmond; Corporal William McAllister, of Munstog, and Privates Swain, Warren Bowling and Fred Naff, of Roanoke.

The only member of this group we talked to was Swain. The others were scattered among the black fir trees that cover the hilltops and sides of the deep ravines extending on the other side of the road.

"We got here about 10.30 last night and slept in the snow under the pine trees," said Sergt. Irving Goodwin, of Raleigh, N.C. "We had our sleeping bags with us, so it wasn't too bad."

Many detachments of enemy infantry supported by self-propelled guns and tanks had concentrated forces in the small villages, from which the Americans were trying to drive them.

THE EVENING SUN, THURSDAY, DECEMBER 28, 1944

McCardell Finds Bastogne Defenders Calm, Confident

Lee McCardell [Sunpapers War Correspondent]

With American Forces, Dec. 27 [By Cable — Delayed] — This afternoon I was flown into Bastogne, still held by American troops who had been encircled by enemy forces since last Wednesday.

Other American units fighting up from the south to relieve the beleaguered city made contact with its defenders shortly before 5 o'clock last night.

The field hospital that normally served the troops defending Bastogne had been captured by Germans early in the siege and the evacuation of the seriously wounded was one of the garrison's most pressing problems. By noon today all wounded men had been removed by truck and ambulance.

"Perfect For Defense"

"I think we were much less excited about being cut off than were the people outside," a headquarters staff officer in Bastogne told us. "Bastogne is a perfect spot for defense and we could probably have held the Germans off indefinitely."

Fighting was still in progress east, north and west of Bastogne and the city had been damaged by night raids by the *Luftwaffe*, but bombing casualties were not high and at the time we were in the town none of the Americans we saw and talked with seemed the slightest bit concerned over either the progress or the outcome of the battle.

From the airfield we drove into the town by jeep without any serious difficulty and even while we were approaching the city a huge formation of American transport planes that had been supplying Bastogne by air by dropping rations, ammunition and medical supplies almost daily for the better part of last week, was roaring overhead toward the city on another supply mission — a mission that was really not necessary.

Value Of Air Supplies

"Three days before Christmas our artillery ammunition was down to eleven rounds per gun," the staff officer told us. "We had eaten the last meal of rations we had brought with us and were checking up on the town's food supplies. But the next day we were supplied by air, and since then our situation has never been critical."

"What kind of Christmas did we have? Great! We knocked out 28 tanks and I would say the Germans have been suffering decidedly heavy losses. As we count the score since the battle began, we've knocked out 148 tanks and 25 halftracks. We've also taken about 600 prisoners."

We had seen some prisoners coming out of town as we went in. We counted six army truckloads. They were all in German uniform. But other prisoners captured south of Bastogne wore American Army winter clothing.

Battalion With U.S. Gear

We were told by an officer of American forces fighting south of the city that his troops had captured one German artillery battalion completely equipped with American gear. When they crossed the German border at the beginning of the offensive ten days ago they were a horse-drawn artillery outfit.

When captured they were completely motorized with captured American trucks, burning captured American gasoline. They wore American uniforms and had been living for several days on captured American rations.

The weather is still wintry in the battle area. The sun shone brightly again today but the countryside is still white with snow and the ruts on muddy country roads that we traveled into Bastogne were frozen hard. Fighter-bombers were out again and the horizon was still banked with brown smoke from their bombing and from fires started by their bomb explosions.

Life Goes On

We were stopped once on our way into Bastogne. German artillery shells had fallen across the road injuring an American infantryman riding in a halftrack ahead of us. A medic was bandaging him. But when we crossed the top of the next hill we felt ashamed of our hesitancy. Up the road ahead of us, arm in arm, walked a Belgian country swain and his girlfriend, apparently oblivious of the battle being fought along other roads in the little villages around them.

The road we followed was lined with charred skeletons and smashed wreckage of German trucks, tanks and captured guns. Some of our own halftracks that carried some of our troops in to relieve Bastogne last night also had been knocked out along the road.

"We had pretty stiff rear guard action after the head of our column had gone into town," said Tech. 5/G Lester Smith, of Rome, N.Y., whom we saw in the municipal plaza of Bastogne, our first stop after entering the town. "We knocked out at least two German halftracks, two 88s, two tanks and two motors with fire from our 50 caliber machine-guns. Don't ask me how you can knock out German tanks with a 50 caliber machine gun. I only know you can set it on fire if you hit it in the right place."

Smith had picked up a bottle of cognac in the course of his advance into the city and borrowed our corkscrew to open it.

Smith shared his find with another member of his outfit, Pfc. William Bean, of Lexington, N.C., introduced as a veteran of "seven campaigns, beginning with North Africa," and with four of Bastogne's relieved defenders, Privates Kenneth Hemics, of Milwaukee; William Matay, of Forest Hills, Long Island and Charles Carillo and Jack Harris, of Brooklyn, N.Y., who happened to be strolling through the plaza.

A field hospital captured by the Germans had been set up in what the city's defenders regarded as "their rear area" until last Thursday, when they found themselves encircled by the enemy. The Germans gave the hospital personnel 30 minutes in which to move casualties into trucks and ambulances behind their own lines.

Hospital Set Up

With a handful of medical men who escaped and doctors and surgeons of other units, another emergency hospital was organized within the city.

Stragglers from various other combat units who had become separated from their own outfits and who had made their way into Bastogne were organized into special provisional combat units designated as "Team Snafu." "Team Snafu" did valiant service in building roadblocks and in defending one sector of the city's perimeter.

Although enemy tanks once infiltrated the defenders' gun positions from the rear and one complete battalion was temporarily cut off from the main defending force, "we rigged up a plan by which we got them back," a staff officer told us. Bastogne's fall never appeared imminent to American forces holding it.

Civilians In Cellars

In most of the town civilians are still in the cellars of their homes. As a matter of military security they are permitted to leave only between the hours of 12 and 2 P. M. The civilians we saw did not appear to be any more worried than the soldiers with whom they were talking and laughing in doorways of their homes.

City streets are littered with debris from German shelling and bombing. Some of its buildings are in a sad state. But Americans had everything well organized, even to printed directional signs pointing to water points and that inevitable proscription which reads "No parking on this street."

THE EVENING SUN, FRIDAY, DECEMBER 29, 1944

McCardell Describes Events During Nazi Breakthrough

Lee McCardell [Sunpapers War Correspondent]

With U.S. 3d Army, Dec. 28 [By Radio — Delayed] — Because of the recent news blackout, it has been impossible for correspondents to give the home front anything but the sketchiest generalities regarding the situation.

After an interval of liberal censorship which had permitted transmission of the very latest military news, even to the naming of the military units involved, that blackout must have been the source of considerable anxiety and apprehension at home.

Day-By-Day Account

After December 16, those of us accredited to Patton's 3d Army were no longer permitted to use a 3d Army dateline on such meager dispatches as we were permitted to file. We were forbidden even to mention that there was any movement of American troops within the battle zone. Perhaps a day-by-day account of one correspondent's impressions and reactions during that time may now help clarify the situation.

It was a tense, exciting time for all concerned. We heard more rumors than the home front did, but we enjoyed the reassurance that came from the sight of confident troops in action to meet the emergency.

A Correspondent's Record

Here is one correspondent's diary:

Saturday, December 16 — Germans began counteroffensive. Tonight's situation map estimates up to fifteen divisions as having crossed the German frontier into Belgium and Luxembourg between Malmedy and Luxembourg city. Weather here has been fair today, and we anticipate our air force will give the enemy a pounding.

The sector on which the Germans have launched a counteroffensive lies between the two main fronts on which we have been attacking and probably was picked because the German general staff concluded it would be the more lightly held position of the American line. But it is not in this area. Therefore our interest is largely academic.

Nazis Massed 15 Divisions

No wonder it was possible for the Germans to mass the fifteen divisions thrown into the attack without our army's intelligence having been aware of the concentration. Our air reconnaissance recently has reported considerable lateral movement behind the German front.

The only explanation of the surprise would appear to lie in the fact that general weather conditions have not been favorable for complete air reconnaissance recently. The Germans may also have taken advantage of the rough, wooded country from which they launched the attack to conceal their troops by day and to move only by night.

Still "Innocent Bystander"

Sunday, December 17 — The Germans are still going — or coming, whichever way you want to look at it. But they are not coming in our direction — yet. The battle of the Saar goes on and our concern with the enemy offensive farther north is still that of an innocent bystander.

More German divisions have been identified. We have heard more details about paratroopers dropped behind the lines and fresh reports about Germans in the attack wearing captured American uniforms and using captured American equipment.

Tonight the situation map is a rash of scattered red marks indicating points at which the German troops have been encountered. Forward elements have advanced about 30 miles or more since the jump-off. Some appear to have been cut off.

Objective Not Known

There is considerable speculation here tonight as to the objective of the offensive.

Was their main thrust toward Liege, north or south? Is this the last desperate gamble on the part of a defeated army? Will it prolong the war? Or does it offer an opportunity to end the war sooner than we dared hope, now that the enemy has left the protection of his Siegfried Line to meet us in the open.

For those of us accredited to the 3d Army the battle of the Saar still holds our attention. But conscious of the probable shift in public interest, our dispatches tonight are shorter than usual. We anticipate news of a German advance will push the 3d Army off the front pages of tomorrow morning's American newspapers.

Go To Sarreguemines

Monday, December 18 — Jeeped out to Sarreguemines today with Lew Hawkins, of the Associated Press. It has been another cold, rainy day, and the Germans have been making hay while the sun was not shining. Fighter-bombers cannot operate in force over the area of the offensive. The heads of their advance columns have made about 40 miles.

Excitement over the drive is increasing here. So are the unfounded rumors, including one that Eisenhower paid a hasty visit to Patton's headquarters. Other reports in circulation are to the effect that certain 3d Army troops have alerted to move.

Press File Cut To Minimum

Tuesday, December 19 — All interest of the correspondents here in the Saar battlefront has ceased. The nightly press file has dropped to a minimum. Jimmy Cannon, Stars and Stripes correspondent, returned tonight from Paris with the news that there was considerable alarm there after another correspondent on the Northern front had used the word "chaotic" to describe conditions of certain areas in the path of German advances.

Well, there's no chaos here; no signs of it. "Serious but not critical" is the way the army officers here size up the offensive. They're reluctant to admit the Germans have made anything approaching a breakthrough.

Ominous red lines have appeared on tonight's situation map pointing toward Liege and others as possible German objectives. Overcast skies, preventing much flying, are still in their favor. There have been several headquarters conferences today, but tonight when we attended the 19th Tactical Air Command briefing everybody present took the situation very calmly.

Orders To Move Northward

Wednesday, December 20 — Patton has received orders to move some of his troops northward, but the news blackout on operations quite properly prevents any of us reporting the fact. For the last several days both the British and American newspaper correspondents attached to the 3d Army have been taking off to Paris and London for Christmas vacations. News of the blackout has discouraged them. They can't write anything about impending operations. They figure this is a good time to take a rest.

Having nothing better to do, Collie Small, of the United Press, and I took off for Luxembourg. We figured we might as well take a rest too. It was bitterly cold and cloudy.

We travelled by way of Metz, where we noticed the townsfolk were taking down old German street signs. Metz plainly was not alarmed.

Germans 16 Miles Away

But things were different in Luxembourg. Streets were lined with people. We wondered what occasion, what event, what personage had brought them out. We soon found out, Germans were within 16 miles of the Grandy Duchy's capital city. Luxembourgers wanted to see what the United State Army was going to do about it.

At least parts of the Army were moving. All along the road we'd been bucking military convoys. Long columns of trucks and tanks were rumbling and clanking through Luxembourg.

Civilians Skeptical

But Luxembourgers were skeptical. They'd also seen small groups of refugees coming into the city from small towns to the north and east of the city. Refugees had arrived by truck, wagon, bicycle and on foot, carrying bundles of bedding, clothing and food with them. Luxembourg had taken down all flags it had flown since the liberation of the city last September.

"People here have been on their ear for the last two days," an American officer told us at the hotel where we spent the night. "We've had air raids every night — not many planes, but just enough to annoy you, like a couple of mosquitoes in your room when you're trying to sleep.

Terrific Ack-Ack

"Ack-ack has been terrific. I put out my bedroom light last night and opened a window to watch it. I didn't watch long. There was a streak of tracer bullets right down the street so close I could have reached out and grabbed a couple. I came in and closed the window.

"I hung around the hotel lobby until late last night waiting to see what might happen. About every half hour the telephone would ring. The clerk at the desk would jabber for a few minutes, always saying the same thing, and then hang up. He talked German and I couldn't understand.

Hotel Owner Anxious

"I got curious after a while and asked him what the hell all those calls were. He said they were from a woman who owned the hotel. She was calling him up to ask whether the Americans had started to leave Luxembourg, whether the Germans were in the town yet."

Collie and I went down the street just before dark to a building where refugees had been assembled. They sat around quietly, surrounded by their bundles, and their children eyed us inquiringly, but asked no questions. If they were frightened, they didn't show it.

Rest And Cleanliness

Thursday, December 21 — This was my first day of rest in many weeks. I spent an hour in a steaming tub of water in the hotel bathroom. I cleaned two months accumulation of Lorraine mud from my combat boots.

I oiled my camera. I put a new ribbon on my typewriter. At supper time Merley Cassidy, of the Philadelphia Bulletin, came back from Vaux-les-Rossiere, a little village on the road from Neufchateau to Bastogne. He wasn't very happy over what he'd seen up there.

Cassidy Pessimistic

He'd seen division headquarters' staff officers, cooks and clerks, separated from the rest of their troops, fighting rear guard action, with German tanks and infantry coming down from Bastogne. He'd watched the blasting down of trees to make roadblocks. He was pretty pessimistic about it, thought the German offensive would prolong the war for possibly six months more than he'd previously figured.

I am ashamed to say I slept very well in my hotel feather bed again that night. Luxembourg's air raid sirens kept tooting pretty steadily — as they had the night before — and ack-ack banged and thundered at Jerry planes buzzing over the city. But there was a comforting racket all night in the streets. It was the racket of American armored columns moving up toward the battlefront.

We could hear our artillery firing, too, out beyond the city.

Off To War Again

Friday, December 22 — Collie announced at breakfast that our vacation was over. It was time we were off to the wars again. We got out our jeep after breakfast and headed for the nearest divisional command post. From there we started toward Echternach, still held by American troops but cut off from the main forces. The weather was still cold and it had begun to snow.

We spent the better part of the day talking with officers and soldiers in the Echternach area. Fighting out there was rather spotty now. But there wasn't the slightest sign of panic, although the city of Luxembourg had had a pretty close call.

Situation Improves

On one sector of the front where the line had been stretched pitifully thin, they'd sent cooks, clerks and division military police into action. But things were better now. The first elements of one 3d Army unit had gone into the line now to reinforce it.

We passed Patton himself on the way back through Luxembourg to the 3d Army press camp, where the censors and the press radio station are located. The Old Man was riding his jeep, the top down, bundled up in a heavy coat against the oncoming night's cold. His escorting body guard, trailing and tooting horns like mad to clear the way, waved us aside. He wasn't any novelty. We'd seen him often before. But that night he gave us a bit of a thrill. He was the man who'd been called on to turn the tide of battle.

Big Surprise

The officer who was at Patton's headquarters when orders were issued to move some of the 3d Army troops into the battle area later told us:

"Another officer in the room took the phone call. It was the Old Man himself. When he heard the Old Man say we must move, he almost fell off his chair, and me — I almost died!"

Troops were moving with vengeance that night. On the long icy hill on the way back to our camp we came up with a convoy of heavily loaded ammunition trucks. The trucks were stalled, their wheels spinning, their rubber tires smoking from friction.

GI's And Shovels

A military policeman came running down the hill from the head of the stalled convoy.

"One GI off every truck!" he bellowed. "One GI off every truck with a shovel! Shake it up — let's get rolling!"

One GI crawled down from each truck with a shovel. They went along the column, shoveling dry dirt from the roadside and scattering it over the icy roadbed under spinning wheels of stalled trucks. The trucks were in a solid line, literally bumper to bumper, those behind pushed those in front.

Their spinning wheels finally caught, gained traction on the dry dirt the GI's were flinging under the hot tires. They caught and the convoy began to move. It moved painfully, slowly, with a mighty groaning and a mighty panting, but it moved up the icy road toward the battlefront miles away.

Tide Changes

Saturday, December 23–Two days before Christmas and the day, I imagine, from which the military historians may date the turning tide in Germany's winter offensive of December 1944. The weather has cleared after yesterday's heavy snow and the fighter bombers of the 9th Air Force took off in great strength to hammer the Germans' supply lines, tank columns and gun positions.

"Wonderful!" said an officer of the headquarters of the 19th Tactical Air Command early this afternoon when we asked him how the first sorties of the day had made out in their operations.

I don't have the figures in front of me now, but I know the day's score of damage and destruction was something to write a story about. Here we had only the toll of one tactical command. Totals for the entire 9th Air Force were much greater.

Moving Day

Sunday, December 24 — Moving day for McCardell of the Baltimore *Sunpapers*; Cyril Ray and Stanley Unwin, of the BBC. We decided to move on to Luxembourg for a few days, loaded our gear into the BBC sound-recording trailer, piled into the jeep that towed it and took off.

Luckily we'd phoned ahead for hotel accommodations. Otherwise we might have slept in the streets. I think every war correspondent in Paris headed for Luxembourg. All the notables were there. Leland Stowe and Ernest Hemingway and Martha Gelhorn and Charlie Wertenbaker and Emaree Bess and the Lord knows who else.

We made the sad mistake of turning over to the central management a small stock of wine, whisky and liquor which the three of us, who drink very little, had been hoarding for Christmas Eve. The entire stock was opened up about 6 P. M. and by the time the notables were through with it McCardell had had exactly one small glass of brandy.

We must be pretty much of a heel to note this even in passing. God knows we're well off this Christmas Eve, even if Jerry dogs come abombing as usual after dark. The 3d Army isn't having much of a Christmas Eve. It's out there in the cold, frozen snowy hills of the Ardennes, fighting its way toward Bastogne.

Too Late For Mass

We had hoped to go to midnight mass tonight in Luxembourg, Notre Dame. But too late we discovered that midnight mass had been held at 4 o'clock this afternoon. The 8 o'clock curfew is not being relaxed here tonight. And double guards of military police are patrolling the streets to see that it is observed.

Monday, December 25 (Christmas Day) — It has been a glorious sunny day and picturesque Luxembourg has been at the height of its glory with frozen snow on its funny roofs and baroque steeples and high arched bridges.

Townsfolk were out early to promenade with their children. We got rid of our Christmas candy in a jiffy and took off in a jeep for Martelange on the road to Bastogne, where some of Patton's armor and infantry are fighting northward. We did a story about it tonight and another about the air force, which certainly had the biggest Christmas in history.

The tide of the battle, if there ever was any question about it, has definitely turned now. Our troops are still rolling forward, and rear installations, including one divisional headquarters which spent Christmas billeted in one of Luxembourg's several breweries, are rolling behind them.

Experts Satisfied

Tuesday, December 26 — Most of the military experts from Paris went back there today, satisfied that the war was under control and convinced they could foretell the date of its end. Such are the wages of fame. We had hoped to get into Bastogne today, but only got as far as Vaux-les-Rossiere after reconnoitering about 25 miles of the southern front.

The armored command with which we spend the greater part of the afternoon was expecting momentarily to make contact with Bastogne's defending force when we had to leave it and start back to Luxembourg. Just before we got in the liaison officer whisked back with word that contact had been made, but the press censors can't pass the news tonight.

Incidentally, one of the visiting experts who knows a general got it straight out of the feed box yesterday that Bastogne had been relieved Christmas Day. We trust he bases his forecast of the date the war will end upon more reliable sources.

Reach Bastogne

Wednesday, December 27 — We got into Bastogne this afternoon. Early tonight a BBC news broadcast announced that the city had been relieved and about 10 o'clock the press censors agreed to clear press copy giving more details. The complete story cannot be told until later.

Thursday, December 28 — The story we've been waiting for broke tonight — the story of how Patton's 3d Army hit the Germans hard from the south. We had planned to write a "hold for release" story tomorrow and now we've been caught with our pants down and no copy. So I filed a diary instead.

THE EVENING SUN, SATURDAY, DECEMBER 30, 1944

MARYLANDERS AT THE FRONT —
The names of three Marylanders are mentioned in this following dispatch.

McCardell Tells How 3d Army Stopped German Drive

Lee McCardell [Sunpapers War Correspondent]

With U.S. 3d Army, Dec. 29 [By Radio — Delayed] — The speed with which Gen. George S. Patton's 3d Army threw both infantry and armor into the battle a week ago to halt the German advance can now be revealed.

The first 3d Army elements to go into action, the 4th Armored Division and the 80th Infantry Division, each moved a distance of more than 100 miles in less than 24 hours to attack the Germans from the south.

Break Bastogne Ring

Units of these two divisions were the first to break the enemy's ring around Bastogne and join up with the American troops holding that city, the 101st Airborne Division, with small elements of two other armored divisions and stragglers from various other outfits.

The 80th Infantry Division was some distance east of Sarreguemines when it was ordered to move into Luxembourg and support another division under orders to hold a defensive line in the Echternach area "at all costs."

The first regiment of the 80th Division to get rolling was the 317th Infantry. Loading into motor trucks at 1 P.M. on December 20, the regiment had reached the Junglinster in Luxembourg by 4 o'clock the following morning after a journey of 150 miles.

Weather Very Cold

The trip was made in bitterly cold weather. There were no halts for hot meals, not even for a warming cup of coffee. In many instances soldiers wrapped blankets around their heavy winter overcoats.

At dawn the regiment's supporting artillery fired for registration and by early afternoon all three of the division's infantry combat teams were in position. There had been a scramble to bring up the last outfit. Twenty-two motor trucks of the convoy which moved it had temporarily gone astray.

Shifted Farther West

On the morning of December 21 the entire division was shifted about ten kilometers farther west. The infantry covered this distance on foot. Because of last-minute changes in orders, part of the regiment moved into new positions, back to the old line and then back to the new position again, marching and countermarching a total of 30 kilometers.

At 6 o'clock, an hour before dawn, on the morning of December 22, the 80th Division began its advance northward. The infantry moved across country, over rough, wooded hills and through deep ravines in the midst of a heavy snowstorm. The advance continued day and night for the next 48 hours, the weary, sleepless soldiers gaining 14 miles.

Fire On Nazi Infantry

They went into action shortly after 9 o'clock on the first morning of their advance. Scouts reaching a hilltop between the towns of Merzig in Luxembourg and Ettelbruck spotted a German infantry column with horse-drawn artillery marching south in the general direction of Luxembourg city.

The 80th opened fire with every gun in the division. The Germans marching along the road in a column of two's, were taken by surprise. The attack in the vicinity of Merzig was made by the 3d Battalion of the 319th Infantry commanded by Lieut. Col. Elliott B. Cheston, of Annapolis, Md.

Captured Two Towns

Another part of the enemy column nearer Ettelbruck was attacked by the 3d Battalion of the 318th Infantry, commanded by Lieut. Col. John C. Golden, of Cumberland, Md. Cheston's force drove the enemy through Merzig and Golden's battalion captured Ettelbruck. Neiderfuelen, midway between the other two towns, also was captured during the day.

The road above Merzig was strewn with slaughtered Germans, dead horses and smashed German artillery pieces. Two German regimental commanders were wounded and from prisoners taken the Americans learned the column they had virtually destroyed had been moving south with the intention of attacking Luxembourg from the west.

Heiderscheid Captured

That night the 1st Battalion of the 319th Infantry, commanded by Lieut. Col. Hiram D. Ives, of Baltimore, moved up the road from Neiderfuelen to take the next town of Heiderscheid, light tanks spearheading their advance. Fighting continued all next day, Cheston's battalion capturing the towns of Tadler and Ringel, northeast of Heiderscheid.

In addition to knocking off a projected flank attack on the city of Luxembourg, this battle resulted in final dispositions of American forces over territory which prevented the Germans using the main highway west from Diekirch to Bastogne, the road which the German command probably had hoped to use as the main supply route for their offensive in the south.

Join Drive To Bastogne

On Christmas Eve, with the weather still freezing cold, the 1st Battalion of the 318th Infantry, 80th Division, commanded by Lieut. Col. Glenn H. Gardner, of Parkersburg, W.Va., moved another 40 miles west to join the 4th Armored Division in its drive to relieve Bastogne.

Like the 80th Infantry Division, the 4th Armored had been doing some fast moving as Patton swung elements of his army north to strike the German offensive. On short notice, tankers had moved out of the area near Fenetrange at 8 o'clock on the morning of December 19, reaching the area around Arlon at 8 o'clock the same night. They, too, had a bleak journey through the rain and cold.

Cold Aids Armor

Christmas Eve found them advancing toward Bastogne along a front running generally from Vaux-Les-Rosiere to Martelange. Snow and freezing temperatures had been to the advantage of the armored units. The cold snap, hardening muddy fields, had enabled tanks and tracked vehicles to leave the roads and maneuver across open country.

While a German infantry division was attacking encircled Bastogne from the south, a German paratroop unit tried to hold back the armor. The Americans' main effort was along the highway from Arlon to Bastogne until Christmas Eve, when the 4th Division's reserves, commanded by Col. Wendell Blanchard, of Lowell, Mass., was switched suddenly from the extreme right to the left flank resting on the road from Neufchateau to Bastogne.

This sudden change of armored weight, coupled with an attack by Gardner's infantry battalion through the little town of Chaumont on Christmas Day, overran the paratroopers and brought the Americans close, enough to fire on the enemy artillery that was supporting the German infantry attack on Bastogne. The armor made contact the next night with American forces defending Bastogne.

Tank Unit Gets There First

The first element of the 4th Armored Division into Bastogne was the 37th Tank Battalion, commanded by Lieut. Col. Creighton (Old Abe) Abrams, of West Newton, Mass. Next morning, Gardner's battalion was the first American infantry force to link up with the 101st Airborne Division in the city.

I saw them slogging along their last mile into Bastogne. They looked tired. But they didn't look half as bad as the demoralized German paratroopers they had rounded up as prisoners on their way in. They got their delayed Christmas dinner when they lined up for chow at supper time on December 28.

THE BALTIMORE SUN, MONDAY, JANUARY 8, 1945

MARYLANDERS With 3d ARMY —
In the dispatch below, Mr. McCardell mentions two Marylanders

Ardennes Heights Taken By 3d Army — 80th Division Crosses Sure River In Steep Gorge

By Lee McCardell [Sunpapers War Correspondent]

With the U.S. 3d Army, Jan. 7 [By Radio] — The fir-clad hills rise to a height of more than 1,500 feet where the main highway from Ettelbruck to Bastogne crosses the Sure River in the heart of the Ardennes. The river flows through a narrow gorge. The road zigzags down one steep side of the gorge, crosses the river on a high, double-arched stone bridge and forks just before it begins to climb again.

The right fork zigzags up a steep mountainside, then strikes off across a high plateau toward Wiltz. This plateau commands the high ground of the battle area in that sector. Captured yesterday by the 80th Infantry Division, it is held tonight by the same men who took it — the troops commanded by two young Maryland officers.

The Germans counterattacked them fiercely at 3 o'clock this morning. They shelled them again this afternoon. The snow was black and grimy from the smoke of exploding shells. From the hills on either side of the Sure River you could look down into the deep river gorge and see the pattern of shell bursts, black against the snow.

Little Other Activity

Little other activity was reported in the 3d Army zone. West of Bastogne our infantry had advanced about 1 mile northward on a 3-mile front near the village of Flamierge. Southwest of Bastogne, the 35th Infantry Division had thrown back a counterattack by a German battalion with twenty tanks, knocking out six of the tanks, near the village of Harlange.

But the Sure River crossing was the day's big news. We jeeped out to look at it. The icy roads were still frozen hard and the fir trees were still burdened with snow and sleet. More sleet was falling in fine white, frozen pellets. It reminded us of pictures we used to see of the Russo-Finnish War.

Preparations for the river crossing began the day before yesterday. Engineers sanded the icy, zigzag road leading down to the bridge whose two high stone arches had been blown up by the Germans. They took up the mines which our infantry had planted this side of the bridge as a protective measure in the early days of Field Marshal von Rundstedt's winter offensive.

Started To Build Bridge

When it first became dark the night before last, a company of engineers commanded by Lieut. Joseph Lelevich, of Kulpmont, Pa., began putting a Bailey bridge across the first of the two broken arches of the old span. Half an hour later the Germans began shelling the engineers and finally drove them back up the road from the bridge abutment.

Most of the engineers were New Englanders, but there were a few Southerners, among them Tech 5/G. William G. Rose, of New Castle, Va., a bulldozer operator; Pfc. Paul Rash, of Pulaski, Va., a platoon runner; Private Charles Walls, of Narrows,

Va., and Private Robert Williams, of Charles Town, W. Va.

"It was pretty hot for a time when all that stuff was coming in," Rose said today. "I hit the ditch."

The German artillery was zeroed in on the bridge site. One shell hit the center pier of the ruined double arch.

Went Back Later

Later that night, the engineers went back to the river with steel treadways for another type of bridge. They thought the construction of the treadway would be less noisy than the building of a Bailey bridge. But the Germans kept dropping timed fire on the bridge site. They were still shelling the site this afternoon.

The Sure River isn't very wide here, not more than 90 feet, but it is deep and swift. And it looks mighty cold down there in its gorge.

Meanwhile, two infantry forces, one commanded by Lieut. Co. Hiram Ives, of Baltimore, and the other by Lieut. Col. Elliott Cheston, of Annapolis, had rendezvoused in the village of Heiderscheid, 2 miles south of the river. They were scheduled to cross the Sure at 4 yesterday morning. They crossed about two minutes late.

Used Secondary Road

Ives's infantry climbed the opposite heights, using a narrow, secondary road whose hairpin turns make it a series of steep switchbacks. So narrow was the road and so sharp its turns that some of the American tanks which tried to follow the infantry slipped over its edge. One had to be abandoned.

A mile beyond the river is the village of Goesdorf. It was Ives's original plan to deploy his force when approaching the village and enter it only after the American artillery, firing from below the river, had worked it over.

"But it was getting late," Ives said today. "It was almost 7.30 when we reached the point we were to deploy on either side of the road. We talked it over and decided to try to slip in without any artillery preparation. Luck was with us.

Moved In From West

"Our force moved around and in from the west side of the town. The rest of us went up the main road, entered the town, turned east of the crossroad at the village church, and had almost reached the eastern edge of the town before a single shot was fired. The other force drew fire as they entered. It took us about two hours to clean out the Germans from the place."

Of the force of about 50 Germans within the village proper, Ives's men killed eight or ten and took most of the remainder prisoners. From the talk of the prisoners we later learned that the American attack came at a time when the Germans holding that sector of the enemy line were being relieved by other troops. As a result, there was considerable confusion and disorganization.

While Ives's force was advancing on Goesdorf, Cheston's infantry was moving parallel to the Bastogne road, up the narrow stream's valley along the foot of the wooded hills. A mile or two upstream it turned northeast, climbed the snow-covered cliffs and struck out for the village of Dahl, 1 mile north of Goesdorf.

Took Germans By Surprise

"It was a little rough making that climb in the dark," Cheston admitted today. "But we spread out when we reached high ground and took the Germans in the village by surprise. The villagers told us there were only 36 Germans in the town itself and when we finally counted up the dead, wounded and prisoners, we had exactly 36."

Five German tanks or self-propelled guns north of Dahl were destroyed by American artillery fire. Our infantry had neither tanks nor tank destroyers with them in the initial assault. The only road by which armored vehicles could follow our troops was under enemy observation and they caught one tank destroyer.

About 3 o'clock this morning enemy artillery opened up on Dahl with everything. Something like 400 rounds fell on the village within a period of one hour when we were there this afternoon. The snow-covered streets and surrounding fields looked like week-old snow in Pittsburgh. It was black from shell explosions.

One Reaches Town

After heavy artillery preparation, the enemy infantry tried to rush the village from three sides but were driven back. The only German who actually succeeded in reaching the town probably was the one who charged into a house on the northwestern edge of town.

He was tackled around the neck by Lieut. Mike Mikatinac, of Ontonagon, Mich., commanding a machine-gun platoon which was holding the house, and shot. While fighting at close quarters continued, Mikatinac hurried back up the road for American tank destroyers, personally led them back and pointed out two German tanks, which were destroyed.

Later today the Germans made another counterattack, this time against a column of infantry which Lieut. Col. Paul Bandy, of Hillsboro, Texas, was leading into Goesdorf. Like the earlier attack, it failed.

Tired But Cheerful

When I saw and talked with Ives and Cheston in Dahl this afternoon, both were tired but cheerful and optimistic. Cheston had recovered completely from a slight shrapnel wound he received near St. Avold several weeks ago, and Ives was still happy over the visit which his brother, Maj. Walter Ives, of the 9th Air Force, paid him at the front.

The only things they wanted, they said — aside from going home, of course — were gas mantles for their Coleman gasoline lamps. You can't buy gas mantles over here. The army's supply of them is slow in coming up, and as Ives explained, his troops haven't yet fought their way into the electric light country.

"I am using my last mantle now," he said, looking anxiously at the fitful, uncertain glow of the lamp on the table of the blacked-out room in which we were working.

Staff All Writing

"Tell the folks at home to rush me some more by mail — special delivery!"

Cheston said he had all his staff officers writing to their wives and girl friends for gas mantles.

Coleman gasoline lanterns, it might be explained, provide just about the only illumination soldiers have, except for occasional candles, in the dark, windowless cellars where they take cover from the shell-fire and find billets when they're lucky. Any winter nights over here are still long and dark.

THE BALTIMORE SUN, TUESDAY, JANUARY 16, 1945

MARYLANDERS WITH 3d ARMY —
In the dispatch below, Mr. McCardell mentions eleven Marylanders

Snow And Cold Make A Tough Foe For 3d Army GI's In The Ardennes — Troops Dig Foxholes in Frozen Earth, But Some Say Even That Is Better Than Mud

By Lee McCardell [Sunpapers War Correspondent]

With the U.S. 3d Army, Jan. 12 [By Radio — Delayed] — You have to see it to believe it.

If you can imagine an army fighting its way through the mountains of Garrett county in mid-January, with ten to twelve inches of snow underfoot, the trees encased in frozen sleet, the temperatures 4 or 5 degrees above zero, the skies overcast with a constant threat of more snow — if you can imagine this, you'll have some idea of the ordeal through which the American troops are passing in the battle of the Ardennes.

Tanks Crawl Over Fields

But that's only part of the picture. You must blacken the snow with greasy 500 where enemy shells have burst. You must drop frozen bodies with waxen faces in the drifts along the back roads, where burial parties have not yet passed. You must people in the pine forests with cold soldiers in shallow foxholes, their fingers numb and their toes frostbitten.

You must picture tanks crawling across unbroken fields of snow, the dull clank of their tracks over the snow-caked bogie wheels muffled and remote. You must see infantrymen, gloved and bundled against the stinging cold, weighted down with ammunition and weapons, toiling across the hill across the hilltops, knee-deep in snow.

When the dreary winter afternoon's cold, unfriendly half-light fades across these frozen hills, you must see the infantry-men drop their gear in the snow, get out their shovels and dig in for the oncoming night — dig through a foot of fine, dry, sifting snow and another foot of hard, frozen earth. You must feel the bite of the icy Ardennes mist that rises now from the snow to fill the hollows among the hills and cling to their heights like thick, gray, frosty mildew.

Feel Sting Of Snow

You must feel the sting of the drifting snow that the winds whip across the hilltops, over the improvised snow fences the engineers have built along the roads with fallen pine trees. You must get stuck in one of those drifts, get out and push, or shovel a path for your jeep while the snow beats into your face like a desert sandstorm.

You must watch the signalmen stringing telephone lines in that swirling snow. You must watch infantrymen dragging wooden sleds loaded down with rations and ammunition. You must watch the aid men struggling along with their stretcher cases or hauling litters — as they occasionally do now — mounted on ski runners.

Try Keeping Warm

You must try keeping warm in mid-January in a freezing countryside whose houses have been stripped of their doors, window glass and roofs. You must try keeping warm in unheated truck cabs, tanks, halftracks and open jeeps.

The correspondents attached to the 3d Army average eight or nine hours a day in jeeps, getting up to the front and back again to town where the press censors and radio station are located. We live the life of Riley compared with that of the average GI in combat on the battlefront. I wish we could do half justice to his fortitude and heroism.

Warmer Than GI's

To keep my own aging bones warm, I go forward wearing heavy GI winter underclothing and a woolen uniform re-enforced by two woolen sweaters, a wool-lined combat jacket, felt-lined flying pants, a wool-lined trench coat, a muffler, two pairs of heavy woolen socks, felt-lined galoshes, a fleece-lined helmet and two pairs of woolen gloves.

No GI is so warmly dressed. I don't have to sleep in the snow or eat cold rations. And I never return to my own warm, lighted quarters at night without a deep sense of my unworthiness and shame.

After dark there's no light in the cold, lonely foxhole in the pine forests. There's no warmth except that of the bodies of the living men who sleep there in their overcoats or lie awake waiting for the dawn. It's a long wait.

The winter nights in the Ardennes are still two hours longer than the winter days.

Good For Pleasure Ride

Come up the road from Arlon toward Wiltz, through the 26th Yankee Division sector. If you were out for a pleasure ride, you'd call the country magnificent. The 1,500-foot fir-clad hills drop almost sheer to narrow, winding valleys, eerie ruined castles tower on rocky crags. The snow and sleet looks as if it had been applied to the wintry landscape by some giant's paint spray gun.

But there's nothing pretty about the Ardennes when you are a soldier fighting there in midwinter. It's a cold, Godforsaken country in which your canteen freezes, your C-rations freeze and your feet are blistered with frost; where you can build a fire only when well behind your own lines, and then only during the light of day.

The MP's on duty at the Bailey bridge across the half-frozen Sure river are dancing around a little fire in the snow, trying to keep warm. The road beyond the bridge is an icy, one-mile ramp to the snow-covered hilltop. On another near-by crest there's a battery of 105-mm. guns. These guns have been painted white to camouflage them against the snow.

"Could Be Worse"

"Things could be worse," grins the battery commander, Capt. J. E. Cheatham, of Appomattox, Va., a graduate of V.M.I., class of 1942. "We'd rather have snow than mud any day."

Like the other men of his battery, Captain Cheatham wears a knitted cap pulled down over his ears under his helmet. He hunches his shoulders a little in his GI overcoat. He takes the weather a little easier than some of his cannoneers, whose noses are berry-red and whose eyes water a bit from the cold.

Most of them have pitched their shelter tents in the snow, close to their gun positions. They've spread straw under their blankets and built windbreakers by piling ammunition boxes around their tents.

More Elaborate Dugout

Lieut. Frank Pryor, of Pensacola, Fla., battery executive officer; Tech. 5/G Ignatius Rascas, of Lynn, Mass., and Corporal Maurice Miller, of Westminster, Md., share a more elaborate dugout — a pit six feet square with a superstructure of wood and tin. They carry their wood and tin with them when the battery moves. The bottom of the pit is covered with straw.

"We got four blankets apiece," says Miller. "We roll up and sleep close together. I am doing O.K."

In the next village up the road Pfc. Charles Kraemer, of Baltimore, a driver in an anti-tank platoon, and Pfc. Woodrow Schaeffer, of Brunswick, Md., cook for an infantry battalion headquarters company, have found shelter in the battered buildings. Schaeffer sleeps on the floor behind the field range of the company kitchen set up in an abandoned bowling alley.

"I use five blankets — and more, if I can get 'em," says Schaeffer.

Along comes Sergt. Larry Hadden, of Lawrence, Mass., with a new recipe for ice cream:

"You take some of this powdered milk and some evaporated milk and mix it with the canned fruit and snow."

"Who wants ice cream in this kind of weather?" shudders Schaeffer, his breath steaming in the frosty air.

"I don't know," says Hadden, who runs the artillery headquarters battery mess in a barn across the road. "But they told me to try it. I'm gonna melt some cake chocolate and cover the ice cream with that — sort of like an Eskimo pie. See?"

Not Interested

Private Francis Fuss, of 1236 Light street, Baltimore, says he sees, but isn't interested. Fuss, an assistant gunner in a mortar squad, has just returned to duty from the hospital, where he was sick — not a battle casualty. He's another lucky one with an indoor billet, a sleeping bag on a bare floor.

"The thing I could use best right now is a quart of whisky," he says drearily. "Sometimes people manage to slip them into packages."

The battalion aid station, in another barn farther up the road, is the warmest place you've struck yet. A blanket hangs across the drafty double doors and Capt. Robert Burton, of Rochester, N.Y., battalion surgeon, has set up a small tin stove in one corner.

"We have to keep the blood plasma warm," he says. "Some of it, probably improperly processed, doesn't run any too well."

Hard On Litter-Bearers

The winter weather is hard on litter-bearers. It's hard enough when they have to carry their wounded men through deep snow. It's harder when their fingers stiffen with cold. The battalion is not in action right now, so the aid men have no battle casualties. But daily sick calls bring them patients suffering with colds, sniffles and frostbitten feet.

"I'm getting 'truck foot'" pipes up one soldier, and when the medics laugh, he says: "I mean it! Not trench foot — truck foot. You think it's funny, but haven't been driving around this country with cold feet as I have."

The battalion headquarters and rifle companies are bivouacked in the woods on either side of the road beyond the village. The soldiers have dug themselves foxholes among the trees, covering the holes with roofs of logs, pine boughs, frozen earth and snow.

Hard Digging In Dark

"The ground isn't too hard to dig," they say. "It's only frozen about one foot down. But it's tough when you've got to dig in the snow and the dark, when you don't see the tree roots, and you're pinned in with machine-gun fire and can't stand up."

They try to sleep together, two or three, or as many as six, in the largest foxholes, so as to keep each other warm. Most of them have sleeping bags.

"But you've got to keep your head under and covered up until you practically suffocate," says Lieut. Harold Smith, of Manassas, Va., a V.M.I. graduate of the class of 1943, one of the officers of K Company.

"When you wake in the morning your blankets are frozen around your face where you've been breathing through them."

Church Services Held

Capt. Grover B. Gordon, regimental chaplain, of Dewey, Okla., comes into the woods and asks if there's any objection to a church service. There isn't.

"Then we'll hold it over on the other side of the kitchen, in about ten minutes."

The chaplain has a hard time working in the church services when the battalion is in combat. The men are too widely scattered. It is rare that he manages to get one in on Sunday. He just holds services whenever and wherever he can.

Tech. 5/G Otho Wines, of Naylor, Md., company jeep driver, says he is fairly comfortable in his foxhole with six blankets and an old GI comforter that he picked up somewhere along the line and wouldn't part with at any price.

Shares Eleven Blankets

Pfc. Wallis Bratton, of Roanoke, Va., shares eleven blankets in another foxhole with Corporal Arthur Hels, of Uniontown, Pa., and Russell Durant, of North Adams, Mass.

Some soldiers are drilling over toward the other side of the woods. Bratton goes over to them. Chaplain Gordon is passing out little paper-backed hymnbooks. The soldiers stand in the snow, ankle-deep under the pine trees. They form a semi-circle around the chaplain and sing "What a Friend We Have in Jesus."

Pfc. Henry Linstig, of 617 North Appleton street, Baltimore, L Company headquarters platoon messenger, is raising a beard and mustache, but his whiskers aren't lush enough yet to afford much protection from the cold. And it was so cold last night that when Private Ellis Young, of Charleston, W.Va., tried to write a letter to his mother, Mrs. Lydia Young, of Charleston, his fountain pen would not work because the ink was frozen.

Just Beginning To Thaw

Tech. 4/G Arthur Smallwood, of 609 Sixth street, N.E. Washington, is still in his foxhole with his overcoat on, trying to keep warm under three or four blankets and a green German comforter he acquired way back at Sarre Union.

"We're just beginning to thaw out," says Linstig. "We were out on the line for three nights without any blankets, sleeping two men in a foxhole, with two overcoats between them. We'd dropped our bedrolls when we went up, and the Jerries captured them. When we got back, there were only nineteen rolls in the whole company."

For days, L Company commanded by Lieut. Sam Thomas, of Tucson, Ariz., a full-blooded American Indian, lived on cold canned C-rations — meat and beans, meat hash, meat and vegetable stew — often frozen to a hard, snowball consistency. The life is much easier here in the pine woods, with hot chow and three men to a foxhole with blankets.

Wants Are Few

Standing around the wood fire, hands in their pockets, they take it all pretty matter-of-factly. They don't like it, but they don't whine. Short of going home, there isn't much they want.

"We could use some candles," says Linstig; "and I wouldn't mind having a pipe."

"And some candy — good, fancy candy, not this hard stuff the Army gives us," somebody else chimes in. "Or, better yet, a shot of whisky to warm you up inside."

Others around the fire were Sergts. Wilbur Charles, of Lancaster, Pa.; Robert Hauer, Harrisburg, and Patsy Macioce, of Pittsburgh; Privates Richard Labin, of Uniontown, Pa.; Joseph Tingen, of Roxboro, N.C., and Terry Martin, of Denver, Col.

Lieutenant Censors Mail

In a cold command post pitched in the next patch of woods up the road Lieut. Clifford Huhta, whose wife lives at 2900 Ailsa avenue, Baltimore, was censoring mail.

"Mail from the States is coming in fairly well," said the lieutenant, battalion communications officer. "But we could still use more letters from home."

"And more packages," said Private George Swope, 3737 East Lombard street, a cannoneers with the headquarters anti-tank platoon.

Swope, who wears the Purple Heart, has also been awarded the Bronze Star for a fight in which his gun recently fought off a German patrol. He was a little low in spirits, having just learned of his mother's death two days after Christmas. He asked to be remembered to Paul Menton and the staff members of *The Evening Sun* sports department, where he worked about ten years ago.

Two-Man Foxhole

Like everybody else in Headquarters Company, Swope sleeps in a two-man foxhole. His blankets were riddled with shrapnel a few days ago when a shell burst over his gun truck, but they are the best he has, and he says they will do. He is thankful to get away from frozen chow for a change.

The other Marylanders in his company are Privates James Dawson and Wallace Tavenner, of Silver Spring. Wallace is a member of the ammunition and pioneer platoon.

Across the road Lieut. Dave McGill, of Richmond, Va., and other officers of I Company were sitting around a log fire in the snow under the trees censoring V-mail.

When out of action, these forward soldiers haven't much else to do except write V-letters. Two men with a deck of cards sit on empty jerricans with an ammunition case across their knees and solemnly play gin rummy. The majority just sit around the wood fires and wait for chow.

Missed Mickey Rooney

Mickey Rooney was up this way a couple of weeks ago, but they didn't get to see him. Nobody in the Yankee Division saw him. The whole sector was under heavy German artillery fire, and the division commander thought it too hazardous for any large group of solider to congregate. Dispersal is still the order of the day.

There are no movies. There isn't anything except cold, snow and battle. Fortunately, the days are not too long. They have supper early so the cooks can get their stuff cleared away before dark, because there are no lights after blackout.

The only Marylander we found in I Company this afternoon was Private Clarence Godlove, of 4028 Fairfax road, Baltimore. There may be others, but they are scattered around through the woods and it's time for chow. We did, however turn up three Virginians: Privates William Hopkins, of Portsmouth; Joe Thompson, of Newport News, and Archie Pargen, of Hillsboro. Sergt. James Connor, of Wilmington, Del., and Private Carl Newcomb, of Washington, were present.

Connor suggests that although it is cold they could all enjoy a good barrel of beer. "Maybe we could warm it up a little," he says.

THE BALTIMORE SUN, FRIDAY, JANUARY 19, 1945

Defiance of Germans' Gunfire Brings Baltimore Private 3 Stripes Fast

By Lee McCardell [Sunpapers War Correspondent]

With the United States 3d Army, Jan. 18 [By Radio] — For knocking out two German machine gun nests and taking twenty prisoners the first time he was in combat, a feat of arms which enabled his infantry company to continue its advance toward besieged Bastogne, Private Paul J. Wiedorfer, of Baltimore, was made a sergeant on the spot.

Wiedorfer is a member of Company G, 318th Infantry, 80th Division. His company was a unit of a battalion commanded by Lieut. Col. Glenn H. Gardner, of Parkersburg, W.Va., the first infantry unit to establish contact with the enemy-encircled airborne division holding Bastogne.

The Story Revealed

We got the story from Lieut. Berney Didinsky, public relations officer of the 80th Division. Didinsky did not have Wiedorfer's Baltimore address, but here is the story:

A newly arrived replacement assigned to the 80th Division, Wiedorfer went into battle for the first time with Colonel Gardner's battalion, when it was pushing through the snow-covered Ardennes toward Bastogne on Christmas Day.

Encountered Fire

Coming into the clearing in skirmish formation, Wiedorfer's company was met by the direct fire of two well-placed German machine guns scarcely 50 yards away. The company hit the ground like one well-trained man — except for Private Wiedorfer. He kept going.

He kept going on the run, zigzagging across the snow toward the nearest machine gun nest, while the veterans of Company G, like other replacements, watched breathlessly. The German machine guns were kicking up little plumes of snow within a few inches of Wiedorfer when he hurled a hand grenade.

A Bullseye, And Then —

He scored a bulls-eye, killing three Germans, but the second gun, barely ten yards away, kept chattering. Wiedorfer leaped into the hole of the crew he had just knocked out, aimed his rifle at the second nest, fired one clip and killed three more Germans.

Twenty other Germans, dug in around the two machine-gun positions, stood up in their foxholes, their hands over their heads and shouted *Kamerad.*

Then and there Wiedorfer's company commander promoted him to the rank of sergeant. After the relief of Bastogne, Wiedorfer was the subject of special commendation sent into division headquarters.

Overseas Since September

Sergeant Wiedorfer, the husband of Mrs. Alice Wiedorfer, of the 1900 block Bank street, entered the Army in the Summer of 1943 and was sent overseas last September.

The son of Mr. and Mrs. Joseph Wiedorfer, of 2431 McElderry street, the 24-year-old Baltimorean attended St. Andrew's School and is a graduate of Polytechnic Institute.

Prior to entering the service he was employed at the Gas and Electric Company.

THE EVENING SUN, MONDAY, JANUARY 29, 1945

This is part of a series of dispatches by Lee McCardell describing the activities of the 26th (Yankee) Division. Two Baltimoreans are mentioned.

Snow Covers Battle Scars In Ardennes

By Lee McCardell [Sunpapers War Correspondent]

With the Yankee Division in the Ardennes, Jan. 20 [By Radio — Delayed] — It's snowing again this afternoon. It seems to snow almost every day now up here on the windswept crests of the Ardennes. But troops are moving. Armored cars, armored jeeps, halftracks or mechanized cavalry are rolling through the crooked main street of this battle-ruined village, bound for the Wiltz River, 6 miles farther north, where the Germans are retreating from the southernmost shoulder of their withered Bastogne bulge.

Snow Drifted Deep

We've stopped for the night in this village, Eschdorf, a hilltop crossroads hamlet of possibly 500 people in peacetimes. There isn't much left of Eschdorf now. Some of the bitterest fighting in the early phase of the battle of Ardennes raged over these hills.

The road from Luxembourg city to Eschdorf has been drifted eight or ten feet deep with snow. Hills out here, 1,500 or 1,600 feet high, are bare of pine forests which cover other parts of the Ardennes. Snowdrifts cover German tanks knocked out along the road a few weeks ago. Engineer bulldozers have plowed the road open, piling snow ten or fifteen feet high on either side.

Snow Like Whitewash

Stark chimneys of Eschdorf's fire and shell-gutted houses come into sight above these snowbanks. Snow conceals the dirty litter of their ruins. Snow turns stacks of empty shell cases into white pyramids. Snow half buries army trucks and trailers parked in fields around the village. What a mass of hidden battle scars spring will bring forth this year in the Ardennes when the first warm sunny days melt this merciful snow!

Our jeep turns into Eschdorf. Cold wind flings snow against the battered faces of its smoke-blackened walls. Snow clings to those faces like whitewash. It clings to the rim of a helmet and to the shoulders of a military policeman who gives us the come-on signal.

It's good to get out of your open jeep after the cold two-hour ride and feel the warmth of the village Gasthaus in which you'll spend the night. Army blankets have been nailed over its blownout windows and you could sleep tonight on its kitchen floor. But there's a wood fire burning in the kitchen range and it's a warm dry room.

Sound Is Muffled

You go outside again in the snow. Mechanized cavalry columns are still passing though the village. Vehicles, daubed white with calcimine camouflage, make very little noise as they move through the snow. The road's soft, thickening white carpet muffles all sound except the chainy clanky of halftracks whose long fishpole radio antennae wave silently and majestically over the snow-covered tarpaulins as heavy vehicles weave and sway down the crooked, uneven street.

Cavalrymen are still cavalrymen even though they do ride jeeps (they call 'em "peeps") instead of horses in this mechanized era. There's something about the easy loose-jointed way they ride, sitting deep and solidly in their seats. And something about the way the snow clings to them now, as dust clung to them last summer. You can't mistake a cavalryman, mechanized or otherwise.

Few Still In Village

Few villagers are still in Eschdorf. An old woman sweeps snow from her doorstep. An old man hauls a load of firewood down the street on a child's sled. Half a dozen children hang over the iron railing in front of the village church, watching the mechanized cavalry stream past.

Infantrymen billeted in the town and off duty filter into the church where a Catholic army chaplain is saying low mass. It is freezing cold in the church. Some of its shattered windows have been covered with straw. But through another still open, snow blows in, powdering the wooden pews and the carved confessional.

Waiting For The Chaplain

You stop in a cramped little vestibule to talk with two soldiers standing there. They're waiting for the chaplain to come out. One has a camera. He says, nodding toward his companion:

"Zeigler here is a new convert."

When the chaplain comes out he and Ziegler have their picture taken in the snow.

You eat supper in a patched-up shell of a house around the corner from the church. You eat because the day ends at dark. After supper you drop around to another house behind the church where the 3d Battalion Headquarters Company of the 104th Infantry, which you haven't seen since Thanksgiving, has shacked up for a day or two of rest.

Story About Baltimorean

They tell you the story of Charles Shutz, of Baltimore, and Fred Winkler, of Erie, Pa., two privates of headquarters company, who were digging themselves a foxhole when Winkler looked and saw a German soldier standing on the edge of the hole.

"You American soldiers?" the German asked gravely.

Shutz and Winkler stood there with only their shovels in their hands. They'd laid their carbines aside.

"Ja," said Winkler.

The German raised his hands above his head.

"Me prisoner," he announced.

Praise For Baltimorean

Capt. Harley Langdon, of Faribault, Minn., artillery liaison officer with the battalion, tells you:

"We've got a man from Baltimore in my battery who's just been made a sergeant and made a forward observer — a job that usually calls for a commissioned officer. Nelson A. Wright is his name. He was a buck private last July, was made a corporal after he landed in France, and now he's a sergeant and a damn good one."

No Marylanders are around the house right now, but there's a chaplain from Boston, Capt. John F. Smith, who five years ago was stationed at Sacred Heart Church in Highlandtown.

Everybody is interested in the latest news of the Russian advance. It's become the big topic of the day on this front.

The room in which you talk, an old-fashioned farm parlor with a reed organ in one corner, is pleasantly warm from the heat of a small wood stove. But it's freezing cold and still snowing when you go outdoors again, on your way to the Gasthaus kitchen where you're billeted for the night.

The kitchen's back door opens into the barn. You can hear the cow lowing at the other side of the door. But the kitchen is still warm from its stove and bright with electric light from the portable generator humming in the trailer parked outside the blanket-covered window.

Shells May Come

"Windows are closed up with concrete blocks on the outside so you might as well stay in your sack if Jerry starts shelling us during the night," you're told. "He throws in a few now and then, but you're as safe here as anywhere. They'll come from the other side and you've got a couple of good stone walls between you and him."

A captured German radio sits on the deepest window sill. You wait up with several others billeted in the same house to hear the late BBC news broadcast for the last word on the Russian advance. Then you unroll your bedding on the kitchen floor and crawl into your sleeping bag. If Jerry shells Eschdorf tonight, you do not hear him.

THE EVENING SUN, WEDNESDAY, JANUARY 31, 1945

This is part of a series of dispatches by Lee McCardell describing the activities of the 26th (Yankee) Division. Four Baltimoreans are mentioned.

It's A Cold, Uncomfortable, Uphill March

By Lee McCardell [Sunpapers War Correspondent]

With the Yankee Division in the Ardennes, Jan. 22 [By Radio — Delayed] — It snowed again last night, once over lightly, the Ardennes version of a midsummer night dew. And it's still freezing cold this morning.

By the morning light you get your first good look at Noertrange, another village broken on the wheel of war. Here are some old shattered, hollow-eyed houses, a few gaping doors screened with timbers leaned up against the outside walls by the German occupants before they abandoned the place.

Wreckage Buried

Here, half-buried in the snow, are the same old wreckage and rubbish of battle — German helmets, German ammunition boxes, German bicycles, German potato peelings and dirty straw that German soldiers have used for bedding.

There are still four Germans in the town. Their bodies frozen stiff, are stretched out on the floor of the ruined village church under the little font of frozen holy water just inside the door. Wooden Stations of the Cross, blown off the wall, and snow, sifting through the broken windows, cover their heads. The boots of three of them are missing, probably taken by other Germans who lived to retreat. Two are wearing plundered American army socks of thick gray wool. There's something decidedly dead about a rigid corpse in stocking feet on the cold, stone floor, powdered with snow.

Good Observation Point

From the high, bare hills on which Noertrange stands, you can look south for miles across the tumbling humps of the Ardennes. What observation the Germans had here! No wonder they were able to pour artillery fire on any American who poked up his head.

Tank destroyers, draped with white sheeting and parked so closely to the snow-covered straw stacks that you haven't noticed them until they start pulling away, take the road down the hill into the town of Wiltz, whose houses and factory chimneys are plain enough in the hazy river valley a mile below Noertrange. You follow the tank destroyers, taking care to stick to their tracks when they swing away from mined stretches of the snow-drifted road.

Wiltz Is Battle-Scarred

Wiltz is another battle-bashed town. It was the divisional headquarters of the 28th Infantry Division when it was captured a month ago in the German offensive. Many old divisional signs are still up. The Germans never bothered to take them down. There are more American than German helmets lying in the snow around Wiltz. And there are a good many smashed American Army vehicles with "28" in white paint on the OD bumpers.

Down near the half-destroyed bridge across the river you see a bareheaded American master sergeant with the red keystone shoulder patch of the 28th Division on his field jacket.

There For A Month

"How long have you been here?" you ask.

"Since the eighteenth of December," he answers coolly.

He is one of seven or eight men of the 28th Division who either escaped from the Germans after the town had been captured or eluded capture to hide out in the cellars of Wiltz through the enemy occupation of the town. Like the civilians who stayed in the town, he subsisted on potatoes and apples. Even so, he did almost as well as the Germans, because they had nothing better to eat, he says, after they'd gone through the captured American Army supplies.

Praises Luxembourgers

"Say a good word in your paper for the Luxembourgers of Wiltz," he asks you. "They've been magnificent. Even though most of the damage to their town was done by American artillery, they've been waiting for days for the Americans to return and they haven't the slightest hard feeling against us."

He is anxious to get back to his outfit and make a report on the captured field hospital personnel taken in Wiltz by the Germans and evacuated as prisoners. The Germans were short on transport, he says, and it was several days before they got trucks to take their prisoners out.

Baby Covered With Sores

Col. Walter Scott, of Washington D.C., regimental commander of the 101st Infantry, comes along. You leave the sergeant at the bridge repeating his story to the colonel and start back up the hill toward Noertrange. You pass a man carrying a baby wrapped in a white blanket. He has stopped to talk to an American soldier who is examining the baby closely. The infant's head and face are covered with sores.

"He wants a doctor," says the soldier. "I guess I can find one all right. A month in a cellar ain't much good for a baby, is it?"

Shells Overhead

A shell or two go screaming overhead, and a woman appearing at the front door of a shattered cafe with a broom in her hand — she has been sweeping out broken glass and debris — searches the sky anxiously and calls to you:

"*Americain ou Allemand?*"

You don't know. You shrug your shoulders, look around and wait to see. She doesn't wait. She hustles a man, presumably her husband, and three or four half-grown girls out of the building and through an outside doorway into the cellar.

Photograph Of Baltimorean

D Company of the 101st Infantry has posted a section of machine guns along the street farther up, on a high hillside curve overlooking the lower town. You make a picture of one crew, including Private James J. Moudry, of 2825 East Madison street, Baltimore, who says there are at least two other Baltimoreans in his company, Vincent Lohran of 2902 Berwick avenue, and William Kolb, of 5210 Catalpha road. But they are in the second platoon, not here.

When you get back to Noertrange a little after noon, you find that the 3d Battalion has been ordered to Eschweiler, another village 2 miles to the northeast, where the Germans withdrawing from Noertrange and Wiltz are reported to have rendezvoused.

Probably Are Gone

It isn't very likely that they are still there. According to the best information Lieutenant Hillman has been able to pick up, those who left Noertrange had been ordered withdrawn all the way to the West Wall. Anyway, the 6th Cavalry is already working up toward Eschweiler and has taken 25 or 30 prisoners.

L Company of the 3d Battalion is already on the march to Eschweiler. You hurry out along the road to overtake them. Just outside Noertrange you meet the 6th Cavalry's prisoners, miserable looking as prisoners always look. You step off the road to let a cavalry jeep and the little column of prisoners, on foot, pass by. A cavalry halftrack trailing the column stops when it comes abreast of you and a GI leans out and says:

"Stay in the road buddy. Those krauts have lined it with shoe mines. Two of our men just lost a foot farther up."

Catch Up With Company

You catch up with L Company slogging along the road in the next pine woods. It really isn't a road at all. It is just a trail through dry sandy snow 18 inches deep on the level, 2 to 3 feet deep where it has drifted.

The march is a repetition of yesterday's advance, up hill and down. The infantry overtakes the rear of the cavalry elements near the hamlet of Erpeldange-Wiltz. The route to Eschweiler is a roundabout one, about 5 miles to cover 2 miles as the crow would fly it — if there are any crows in the Ardennes. We've never seen one.

More Junk In Snow

Beyond Erpeldange-Wiltz, where the road winds and twists up another of those everlasting icy hills, you come upon another heap of torn and rusty junk in the snow — more unhappy halftracks of the 28th shot up last month by the advancing *Panzers*. There's a good deal of junked German vehicular equipment along the road, too, where our fighter-bombers have been working.

Now the infantry leaves the road and strikes straight off across the snow. They've reached another of those mined stretches. The 3d Battalion's pioneer platoon hasn't cleared the road beyond the next bend. They've got one hell of a job, feeling around in the snow for hidden mines which they can't see, can't locate with their mine detectors.

Some Hard To Find

They can pick up teller mines with detectors, but they have to get down in the snow on their hands and knees and probe with bayonets for wooden-shoe mines and other non-metallic mines of concrete and plaster.

"Looks to me like the Jerries just shoveled 'em off the end of a truck as they pulled back," says a lieutenant. "There's no pattern to them. They've scattered them all around."

The infantrymen, plowing across country through snow knee-deep, have to break a path as they go. They don't move very rapidly. They haven't drawn any fire yet. The only noise has been behind them, where the engineers are blowing up mines uncovered along the road.

Snipers Start Shooting

But snipers' bullets whistle when the head of the column, single file, reaches the next hilltop.

"We're under fire — pass it back."

We're under fire from Jerry burp guns by the time word reaches the end of the column. It doesn't matter. We're under fire.

"Spread out — five-yard intervals — pass it back."

Line Stretches

The long file thins and stretches out across the snow.

"Wait for the mortars — pass it back."

The column halts in the snow and nobody is sorry, except the mortar squad men, hand-carrying their heavy weapons up the hill through the snow. Uphill, always uphill, the route seems to run.

Stumbles And Falls

"I can't go any farther," pants a soldier carrying a machine gun. He stumbles and pitches headlong into the snow. "I just can't go any farther! I gotta rest a minute."

"You gotta get up forward," says the squad leader. "You ain't worth anything back here with that gun."

"And I ain't gonna be worth anything if I ever get up there," says the soldier in the snow.

"Gimme that gun — I'll carry it again."

Hands Over Gun

The man lying in the snow makes a weak effort to hand it over.

"Why didn't I join an outfit where I could ride?" he groans.

"Why didn't you?" grumbles the squad leader, jouncing the gun back onto his shoulder and ploughing ahead.

Sees Church Steeples

It's getting dark again. Over the crest of the next hill the infantrymen catch sight of Eschweiler's church steeple. But the next minute they lose it. The column strung out through the snow is sticking to defilade. It crawls up to the brow of another hill and slides down into another hollow through the trees and brush and brambles. It comes to an open field.

"Four men at a time — pass it back."

"Four men at a time — pass it back."

"Plenty of distance — pass it back."

"Plenty of distance — pass it back."

Cross By Fours

They cross the field four at a time, quickly, keeping wide intervals. They reach another steep, wooded hillside. They have to help each other up, men ahead reaching down their rifles by the shoulder slings to haul the next man up behind them.

They slip and slide and fall and stumble and finally (Thank God!) reach a narrow path between high snow drifts. The path stops at a house beside the road into Eschweiler. It is dark now. It is cold. The column halts. The men sink down into the snow. A woman opens a door of a house and looks out. She smiles and closes the door again.

Go In To Get Warm

"Any heat in there?" asks a soldier.

Two or three get up and go inside to see.

The cavalry patrol is already in Eschweiler, a heap of black silent buildings in the darkness. Infantry officers and two or three non-coms go into town to look over billeting possibilities. You follow them.

A knocked-out American tank sits by the road beyond the village church. Covered with snow, it evidently is another casualty of last month's battle. Even in the darkness you can read the white lettered name painted on its side: "American's Answer."

Find Deserted House

Lieutenant Brown goes from house to house looking for a suitable battalion headquarters. The doors of one house are locked. No one responds to vigorous knocks. He takes out his automatic and tries to shoot the lock off the front door. It is old-fashioned, too sturdy. Then he boosts a sergeant through a front widow. The sergeant unlocks the back door. Fire is still burning in the kitchen stove but the house is deserted.

It is none too clean and smells of Germans. He decides that the house of the village padre, farther up the street opposite the church, is better. The padre isn't around. His housekeeper, with the family next door, says he has gone to Belgium. The Germans left two days ago. She has kept the fire going in the padre's kitchen. The study and the dining room are fairly clean.

Stop Next Door

You go into the house next door with a couple of artillery forward observers who have lugged a portable radio up to Eschweiler with the advance infantry. The rest of the battalion is still moving up back there some place from Noertrange, through the cold and the dark and the snow. You sit in the front room with the family that lives here — a man, his wife, his sister, two small boys and a baby.

You just walk in and sit down. You ask no questions. It is too cold to stay outside. There is no light in the padre's kitchen. There is light here, one small candle. You don't notice the baby at first, although you smell its damp, steaming diapers hanging on a string above the stove to dry out. Then the baby begins to gurgle, and sits up in a carriage in a shadowy corner of the room and you notice it for the first time.

Men Tired And Sleepy

The two forward observers, tired and drowsy, slump in their chairs and cuss the weight of the army's portable radios and wonder what the latest news is from the Russian front. The wife and sister clear the supper dishes from the littered table. The two little boys, recovering from their shy initial awe, grow coyly playful. You try to talk with the man of the house, but your French and German are both bad and he, apparently a man of few words, doesn't help you any.

So you just sit there in the dim candlelight and watch him change the two little boys' gingham pinafores and get them ready for bed. You sit there until the room becomes a little too stuffy from the steaming diapers over the stove.

Go To Padre's Kitchen

Then you go back to the padre's kitchen in the house next door and strike matches and look around for scraps of candle and find one melted down on the wainscoting ledge. You light it and feed the dying fire in the padre's kitchen range with pieces of a broken wooden chair lying among old meat bones and empty bottles and straw that the Jerries have left on the kitchen floor.

Two or three cold soldiers wander in and you take turns sitting close to the stove. The candle scrap burns out and you sit in the dark. You wonder what the latest news from Russia is and what time the rest of the battalion will come up and whether the bedrolls will come with them.

Colonel, Captain Enter

Colonel Peale and Captain McLean come in after a while. The man next door is called over to see what he can do about the missing pipe for the stove in the padre's study.

He fiddles around with some odd lengths and elbows and finally fits a flue together by the light of the colonel's electric torch. A fire is started in the stove. It smokes badly. The room fails to warm up. The colonel discovers the trouble. There is no glass in the study's only window, incompletely covered by a heavy wooden wardrobe.

The wardrobe, filled with the padre's books, must weigh a ton and a half but the three of you finally drag it out. You help to cover the open window with an army blanket and move the wardrobe back again.

Huddle Over Stove

The battery of the colonel's torch begins to fail. You huddle over the stove, still smoking so badly that your eyes smart with tears. You wonder if the engineers will get the road open tonight; if the rest of the battalion will ever get here.

Captain McLean, once stationed at Fort Meade, muses:

"Baltimore — Miller Brothers — the Oasis — wonder how the Russians are doing."

Road Is Open

You doze — until Captain Christie comes in and announces that the road is open and that the other companies of the battalion are moving into the village. They take over houses assigned to them and find two Germans hiding in their billets. Lieutenant Hillman says to hell with them, he doesn't want to bother with any more prisoners tonight, but goes out to question them just the same.

Lieutenant Staiger comes in and says the kitchen trucks are up.

"And the blanket truck?" asks the colonel.

Blanket Truck Comes

"Blanket truck, too," says Staiger. "What a road! The cavalry's moving up, too. And tanks. Everything. It's jammed. And slippery! One vehicle gets stuck in a snowdrift and everything stops."

Pfc. Sidney Hoffman, of Baltimore, Sergeant Major Daley and Colonel Peale's jeep driver, Fred Eisler, of Somerset, Pa., bustle in with a portable electric light system. Somebody starts the generator outside and the padre's study is presently bright and habitable and filled with people.

Put In Telephone

The wire section runs in a telephone. La Rocca shows up with a kettle of hot chocolate. Captain Christie winds up the padre's big clock hanging on the wall and sets it by his watch. Everybody listens as it chimes 3 o'clock. Sergeant Daley digs up the latest report on the Russian advance. The bedrolls are brought in and everybody gets ready to turn in for what is left of the night.

Your roll is covered with snow. You shake it off, open it up and spread it on the floor of the dark dining room beside the padre's study. You take off your shoes and your mackinaw and your helmet, but you keep your knitted cap. You crawl into your sack, icy cold again on the inside. But you sleep.

SNOW IN THE ARDENNES — These pictures by Lee McCardell, Sunpapers war correspondent, show American tank destroyers moving into the town Wiltz after its occupation by Yankee Division infantrymen, ADX-451-BS and the Yankee Division infantry as it resumes its march through the shell-torn village of Berle toward the Wiltz River in pursuit of retreating Germans after battle in the snow-covered Ardennes Forest region along the Franco-Belgian border. ADX-441-BS

CHASING FOE FROM ARDENNES

INFANTRY MEN ON MARCH TOWARD WILTZ RIVER — Snow is hard here and the men can step out, although all of them appear to have heavy burdens of ammunition and weapons. First or second man on right is Private Robert Gunther, probably a Marylander. ADX-453-BS

UPHILL — Above: The going is hard through snow with loads such as this infantry man is carrying and the heavy grade and undergrowth make it even tougher. ADX-434-BS

IT'S A RUGGED COUNTRY — Typical view of this part of the front, where the hills are steep and in many cases rise to 1,500 feet or more. ADX-425-BS

McCardell Pictures Of Yankee Division

That the pursuit of the retreating Germans after the Battle of Ardennes, reported by Lee McCardell, Sunpapers War Correspondent, in his dispatches, was accomplished under difficult weather conditions, this page of photographs made by McCardell is proof. The men shown are members of the Yankee Division, prominent in the struggle in this area and a unit which, despite its name, contains many Southerners. Photographs of Marylanders encountered by McCardell at about the time today's pictures were made will appear in a subsequent Metrogravure issue. Terrain as well as weather was against rapid progress by the Yankee Division in this sector, study of the pictures here will make plain. It is a hilly country, well wooded and consequently offering a retreating army numerous points at which a pursuing force could be delayed by small but skilled and determined rear guards, particularly when the weather was such that they were not likely to be cut off by armored forces of the pursuers. The difficulties which tanks and other heavy motor vehicles met at this time because of the heavy snow was frequently stressed by correspondents.

WELL SPACED FOR SAFETY — Above: Clinging to a gate of millrace while crossing frozen Wiltz River. ADX-449-BS.

Below: T/5 Walter Zoloski, New Yorker, drinks from frozen canteen. ADX-429-BS.

CAMOUFLAGE — The lace curtains wrapped around this tank destroyer's main weapon are to fool the enemy-if he didn't see the gun he might think the vehicle less formidable than it is. AGT-952-BS

SNOW IS EVERYWHERE — Above: Tired Yankee Division doughboys reach the crest of a ridge north of the Wiltz River. ADX-439-BS. Right: Mortar squad digs in on side of railroad embankment, getting ready to cover a crossing of the Wiltz River. ADX-431-BS

PART OF THE BOOTY — Guns of various sizes abandoned by the retreating Germans near the Wiltz River because of lack of horses or prime movers to haul them out of reach of Yanks. ADX-444-BS

McCARDELL'S CAMERA IN ARDENNES

Lee McCardell, Sunpapers war correspondent, accompanied the Yankee Division when it helped to erase the deep salient driven by the Germans in the Ardennes region in a midwinter drive that for a time appeared to imperil communications of the Allied armies all along the northern part of the Western front. In hard fighting the Yankee Division, which includes many Marylanders, and other veteran units, threw the Germans back and imposed on them losses that served to more than balance what the Wehrmacht's surprise attack had cost the Americans in early stages. Previously published McCardell pictures showed the nature of the terrain, hilly and wooded, and how the heavy snow and severe cold made difficult the Yank counteroffensive. The severity of the weather also is apparent in the pictures on this page, which show more of the Yankee Division's men including some from Baltimore, as they broke the German hold on the region.

Drawing water at Noertrange; on left is Sergt. Wayne Kiser, of Hagerstown; on right Pfc. D. C. W. Finney, Baltimore. ADX-443-BS

MARYLANDERS — Circle: Pfc. Sidney Hoffman, Baltimorean, interprets for Eschweiler villages. ADX-427-BS.

HAVING A LOOK AT THE ENEMY'S WEAPONS — Soldier in center peering at the mechanism of this captured German cannon, one of many taken in counteroffensive, is Private Charles L. Boarman, of 822 North Augusta avenue, Baltimore, member of a Yankee Division headquarters company. ADX-445-BS

SET UP FOR BUSINESS IN WILTZ — Private James L. Moudry (left), of 2825 East Madison street, Baltimore, and a fellow machine gunner, have placed their weapon to command lower part of city. ADX-428-BS

KEEPING WARM DURING HALT IN VILLAGE OF BERLE — Soldier who is standing in group at left is Corporal Paul D. Long, of Cumberland. Town in which this picture was made is on the crest of the Ardennes. Cooks seem to be operating from the trucks. ADX-433-BS

WEARING RED CROSS BRASSARD — Pfc. James H. Buckler, of Upper Marlboro, member of ambulance crew with medical battalion. ADX-446-BS

Sergeant Henry Hoffman, New York City, lines up captured German paratroopers in village Eschweiler during Yankee Divisions pursuit of retreating Germans after fall of Wiltz. ADX-454-BS

Snow In Ardennes
Photos by Lee McCardell

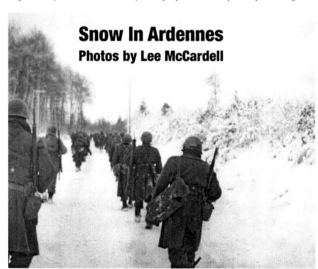

Yankee Division Infantry on march toward Wiltz River in pursuit of retreating Germans after the Battle of Ardennes. ADX-422-BS.

Two Yankee Division Artillerymen break up wood to feed captured German stove in front of their dugout in pines. Left to right: T/5 Robert H. Mitchell of Normal, Ill., and Pfc. Tom Gannon, of Congers, N. Y. ADX-450-BS

Chow line in town of Berle where infantry of Yankee Division halts briefly before crossing Wiltz River in pursuit of retreating Germans after battle of Ardennes. Pursuit continued day and night regardless of freezing, wintry weather. Left to right: T/4 Rudolph Nilosa of Philadelphia, and Private Richard Downey of SHAEF. ADX-456-BS.

Field hospital collection station set up in snow in Ardennes. Note icicles hanging from edge tent, caused by heat inside tent, heated by small coal stoves. Outdoor temperatures have remained below freezing for weeks. ADX-442-BS

CHAPTER 8

RAID ACROSS THE RIVER ROER

From McCardell Back to Bradley

THE BALTIMORE SUN, SUNDAY, FEBRUARY 25, 1945

Bradley In Crossing Of Roer River

By Holbrook Bradley [Sunpapers War Correspondent]

Julich, Germany, Feb. 24 [By Radio] — American 9th Army troops have crossed the Roer River under cover of one of the heaviest Allied artillery barrages of the war and are fighting in the well-torn streets of this battered fortress city.

To the north and south of the German river stronghold, other elements of General Simpson's command have gone into the attack from Dueren to a point above Linnich, where the doughboys have already gained over 2,000 yards against slight resistance.

Fire Thousands Of Rounds

The first indications that the offensive was under way came at 2.45 A. M. when division corps and army artillery battalions unleashed some of the heaviest cannonading of the war to send thousands of rounds of high-explosive shells into enemy positions in the town itself and to cover communications and other vital spots in the Germans' rear.

For more than four hours howitzers, Long Toms, mortars, tanks, 8-inch guns and smaller weapons belched forth ton after ton of steel that literally saturated the ground for miles around Julich. The buildings and the banks of the river itself shook for hour after hour as cannoneers worked overtime to soften up Jerry positions and personnel for the attack that was to follow.

Current Chief Difficulty

Fifteen minutes after the artillery first opened up, combat troops covering the platoon launched assault boats to cross the swift Roer River current, then secure a bridgehead on the opposite bank so that the engineers could begin to string a series of pontoon foot bridges over the water and make way for the infantry companies that were to follow.

The chief difficulty encountered in the operation was the swift current, for there was little enemy counterbattery fire, a surprisingly small amount of resistance from the German troops holding the city. A few self-propelled guns brought a harassing fire down on personnel and equipment immediately behind the men on the initial phase line.

Two and a half hours after H-hour, which had been set for 3.30 A. M., the engineers had the first pontoon footbridges over the Roer and construction at two more crossing points was nearly completed. By 6 o'clock two platoons of infantry were across the south main Aachen-Julich highway bridge and a third had pushed over the river on the floating bridge.

All three then were engaged in the first phase of the operation cleaning out buildings and emplacements along the river bank and started to push east into the main section of town.

Co-Ordinated Operations

Co-ordinated with the assault on Julich, itself, other units moved out and early this morning the first elements succeeded in crossing heavily wooded, flooded lowlands in amphibious Alligators to reach eastern riverbank objectives, only encountering minor opposition.

There was little indication of the impending operation. Equipment moved into the area had been backed off onto side roads, camouflaged or put under cover, and the artillery carried on its normal activities of sending over a few rounds every hour, as had been its custom for the past two or three months.

Some slight activity came during the evening meal, when a low-flying ME-109 tangled with a flight of P-47's overhead, came out the loser in the fracas and went down in a trailing column of smoke to crash behind our lines with a thundering explosion that sent flames sky high.

Pull Out At 6.30

Major John Geglein, of Westminster, battalion commander, and the officers of his unit were putting on their gear, issuing last-minute orders as we landed in the command post and found it about to close.

The message center clock read 6.30 A.M. as the first elements of the battalion command post pulled out onto the highway, moved slowly in the direction of the Roer and Julich.

Along the road we could see the dim figures of doughboys marching toward the front in columns down both sides of the highway. Half an hour later we had stopped at a road intersection, where the battalion commander stood checking the units of his command as they passed.

In the bright moonlight, which made the surrounding area almost as visible as day, the faces of the boys moving up could be seen clearly, as could the weapons and equipment they carried.

For the most part the men moved silently, even walking so as to avoid unnecessary noise. Occasionally a platoon leader would caution his men to slow up, space out, as a precaution against excessive casualties should some rounds of enemy artillery land on the road.

German Gun Pinpointed

Those of us who were more spectators than participants, who wondered how many of these Yanks would be killed or perhaps wounded in the fighting to come, found the men moving into battle a strange contradiction to the hellish noise to follow shortly.

A mile or so down the road, Major Geiglein, Capt. Ben Pollard, of St. Dunstan's road, Baltimore, and the rest of the group dismounted from vehicles for the slight protection offered by a farmhouse. Numerous other vehicles showed advance parties already up on the line. The line of heavy trucks carrying boats and bridging equipment indicated the size of the operation to those of us still not acquainted with all the details.

An orange-red flash first in the air above the town to our right, followed by the sharp crack of explosives, warned the Jerries to be on the alert, as did the short sharp blast of automatic weapons that followed.

Trail Across Open Field

The trail forward to the point where the troops were moving out led across several hundred yards of open, muddy field, then a stretch of swamp bordering the road near some demolished houses. There was a tense feeling of anticipation of enemy fire as we crossed that stretch, but we reached the building link without drawing a single shot.

It wasn't until we had crossed the back of the houses and had entered the muddy vegetable garden that the Krauts suddenly opened up. Pollard hit the ground instantly and the three of us behind him followed automatically as a hail of lead cracked and whined through the air a few feet over us to smack resoundingly into the brick wall at our backs.

Evidently Jerry had seen us coming, for the moment we tried to move he opened up again. Pressing our faces into the dirt seemed hardly enough protection, but there was little else to be done.

Diversionary Fire Helps

A few moments later diversionary fire from one of our outposts gave us the break we needed, and the four of us were on our feet in a flash, stumbling over barbed wire through mud and knee-deep water to reach the forward command post.

In the basement, taken over for the night's operation, a warm fire glowed cheerily from the stove and gave us a chance of partially drying out our soaked clothing.

Wiremen already were installing the command post phones, closing out the old switchboard. Artillery observers and a group of liaison officers were on hand to co-ordinate all phases of the attack. The message center and aide-room had been set up in adjoining basements where personnel not on duty were trying to catch a little sleep prior to the jump-off.

The comparative quiet of the riverfront was suddenly shattered at almost 8.30 A.M. as all hell broke loose. We waited a moment, then made out the sound of enemy aircraft swinging low over the front and bringing up a hail of ack-ack and machine-gun fire.

At nearly the same time a call from a company further up the river reported that a German machine-gun was definitely pinpointed in the second story of the house across the Roer.

Command post and attached personnel attempted to catch a few hours of sleep in cramped quarters and succeeded remarkably well under the circumstances. At a table at one side Major Geiglein and Captain Hollard played a fast game of gin-rummy by the light of a lantern. The phone rang to interrupt them as companies reported in "All quiet."

Those of us who managed to get some sleep awoke shortly before 2.30 A.M. as a Kraut machine gun across the river sent a stream of lead ripping through the upper stories of the house above us. At almost the same time heavy enemy mortar fire dropped in our rear, exploding with its characteristic dull thud and causing little appreciable damage.

Big Guns Open Barrage

Then as we checked our watches at 2.45, the first of our big guns began to open up with the artillery barrage. In a few moments it was barely possible to hear the man next to you because of the terrific noise. The continuous thundering roar echoed and re-echoed from the guns behind us, the hills ahead and both banks of the Roer. For hours on end the barrage shook the building and the ground about us.

Even to those of us who have seen a good deal of this war during the past eight months, the artillery fire this morning seemed more intense than anything before. One doughboy sitting in a corner commented:

"This will be one day Jerry will always remember."

Patrols Across River

Major Geiglein made a quick grab for the phone as it rang two minutes past 3, and received the A Company report covering the patrols already across the river in assault boats. Outside we could hear the continuous chatter of machine-guns and small-arms, then the heavy, sharp report of the tanks which had rolled up to take part in the action.

Seven minutes later the phone rang again in the midst of the infernal racket of war going on around us and the A Company's executive Lieut. Robert D. Nelson, of Chicago, reported that his men had secured the bank and had pushed on to the building line, where they were routing the Krauts out of cellars, already having knocked off a few manning river-line trenches.

Pontoons Swung Into Line

The command post held an air of silent expectation as we waited for the report of progress, which came a few minutes later when the engineers sent back word that cables were already across the river at the middle bridge site, that pontoons were being swung into line.

Outside the skies were being lit up with the steady glow of repeated flashes of explosions throughout Julich and along the ground behind the city. Almost in front of the house we were in, a Sherman tank stood firing round after round into a house across the Roer where the Jerry machine gun had been reported. Overhead, streams of red tracers glowed through the black night to cover what was left of the network of roads in the town.

There seemed to be little opposition and only occasional incoming rounds of artillery and scattered resistance from Kraut automatic weapons stations along the far bank. Thirty feet in front of us could be seen the dark forms of the combat engineers who were carrying up pontoons, wading out into the ice-cold water to get them lined up.

Another Platoon Across

Reports came into the command post that another platoon had crossed the river in assault boats as we headed upstream to inspect the second crossing site.

Shortly before 4.30, the moment came when it looked as if the worst had happened. A large assault craft paddled by seven men, suddenly swept downstream by the swift current, drifted into the nearly-finished bridges, bucking the midsection. For a few tense moments the engineers dropped everything and clung to the cables as the current almost carried the whole works away.

The bridge was saved with only the loss to the time schedule.

Third Platoon Crosses

Enemy artillery and machine-gun fire had increased slightly shortly before 6 o'clock when the footbridge finally was completed and the infantry was allowed across. Our own batteries were still sending rounds overhead by the hundreds as the third platoon of Able Company trotted down to the water's edge, then moved across the swift current at a dogtrot.

Up on the banks ahead the doughboys dodged low, leaped across the haze and mist rising from the cold waters. There was little time to worry about enemy mines or booby traps, and one assumed because the man ahead got through, he would too. And the line coming across behind made hesitation impossible.

Almost Steps On Germans

A moment later we jumped the width of the trench, almost stepped on the face of a dead Kraut and stood alongside a demolished building — panting slightly. Around us were elements of three platoons who were across and back on the other side there was a slow-moving column as the battalion filed up to the crossing point.

A couple of GI's stood in the shelter of a building to direct us along the street and prevent crowding up. We took off again, dodging shell holes, bomb craters and a good number of dead Germans. Once or twice we had to put on an extra burst of speed to get by the end of an open street for in the gradually increasing light, Germans snipers in the town were beginning to take pot-shots.

Seven prisoners, mostly men well up in their fifties, stood against a wall of one building while doughboys searched them for weapons while a medic was bandaging the wounds of two of them who had been hit earlier. A short while later two more came down the line, their hands clasped behind their heads. Out in a trench a wounded Kraut moaned audibly but we didn't investigate.

Baltimorean Leads Squad

Staff Sergeant Chester Ruby of 840 West Thirty-fourth street, a squad leader, was about to move up the street to take a building held by the Germans as we moved in. He took a few seconds to say "hello," then pushed out ahead of his men to a low brick wall and moved on up the road as a Kraut with a Schmeiser machine pistol opened up to send dirt and debris flying across the road from the squad.

Up ahead where the platoons were spreading out through the blasted town, small-arms fights broke out as the doughboys moved up, hit the enemy strong points and began to wipe them out systemically. Back at the crossing sites, more raftmen began to pour across the bridges and a few casualties moved over to the aide stations on the west bank.

For the first time we had a chance to take a close look at Julich, and found it almost a complete pile of rubble, dirt, debris and scattered German equipment, the result of continual artillery and aerial pounding during the past months, with the added effect of last night's barrage.

Marylanders Encountered

Marylanders seen during the night's engagement were: Major Jack Lawton, Baltimore; Major Jack Reed, Baltimore; Capt. John King, West Lanvale street, Baltimore; Lieut. Donald Hundertmark, Baltimore; Tech. Sergt. Clarence Shaw, Baltimore; Staff Sergeant Joseph Finn, Frostburg; Staff Sergeant Paul S. Cooley, Halethorpe; Tech. Sergt. Emory Y. Burk, Phoenix; Lieut. John S. Insley, Frederick.

THE BALTIMORE SUN, SUNDAY, FEBRUARY 25, 1945

29th Takes Julich's Citadel

By Holbrook Bradley [Sunpapers War Correspondent]

With the 29th Division, Feb. 24 [By Radio] — Blue and Gray Division riflemen have captured the fortress citadel of Julich and are continuing to mop up the few snipers left in town, while other elements, pushing along have fought within a mile of Stetternich.

North of this Roer River stronghold a battalion of the 115th Infantry has pushed a mile beyond Broich, which was taken after a tough fight yesterday, and another battalion, commanded by Major Al Warfield, of Baltimore, has secured a high ridge dominating the whole approach.

Resistance Less Than Expected

Enemy resistance at this stage of the attack has been more moderate than was anticipated, with the principal opposition from a few self-propelled guns, single artillery pieces and scattered small-arms fire. There have been harassing mortar and occasional rocket bursts in the area.

Throughout the initial stages of the operation, which have been carried out under better weather conditions than anticipated, there has been little indication of anything but a token show of enemy resistance.

During the initial crossing yesterday morning when the 175th Infantry spearheaded the attack in assault boats, the doughboys first ashore ran into a few Krauts holding out in the river-bank trenches, basements of houses and scattered through the town.

They're Very Young Or Old

These German troops were for the most part very young or old enough to have been on the high draft side during the first World War. There has been the usual sprinkling of *Wehrmacht* noncoms, officers and medics. The indication that there is a comparative light sprinkling of true Heinies through the area is gained from the fact that only 299 prisoners were taken in the first 36 hours in which 3,000 yards of ground was gained.

One of the principal difficulties of this phase of the offensive has been getting a sufficient number of bridges across the Roer to accommodate supplies and reinforcements.

Bulldozers were busily engaged in clearing piles of rubble and debris [from Julich] that littered almost every street.

Rolling Steadily Eastward

This morning, despite enemy artillery and air activity, the crossing sites are firmly in place, and both men and materiel are rolling toward a steadily eastward moving front.

Elsewhere along the Roer, where the lack of high banks and flooding in the past few weeks have made crossing more difficult, army amphibious alligators and weasels are on the job ferrying.

More truckloads of doughboys, equipment and supplies were rolling toward the front as we headed for Julich and the battalions making the attack east of the city. In the bright morning sunshine Allied Thunderbolts, Mustangs, Lightnings and other fighter-bombers roared toward the enemy's supply lines and the rear or patrolled the river and frontline area. At an early hour the score was one ME-109 that had ventured in too close.

Roer River Scene Changed

Down at the Roer River the scene had changed considerably since the hours of darkness yesterday when the first troops moved up on the line for the jump-off.

Now heavy trucks and a stream of smaller vehicles moved along the river road to the crossing sites and bounced up the other bank to push on through the town. Ack-ack gunners strategically located around the edge of the river scanned the skies for Jerry planes.

On the east bank of the river six dead Krauts still lay where they fell during the fighting yesterday. They seemed almost unnoticed by the men busy at the job of fast-moving war.

For the first time since the attack began, we had a good chance to see how badly Julich had been pounded. To those who remember St. Lo, Vire and Brest it looked vaguely familiar.

Few Evidences Of Jerry

There was the same evidence of heavy artillery, air and mortar pounding, the same fallen buildings, piles of rubble, smoke-filled, dirt-littered streets and the smell of battle, but there seemed to be a decided lack of evidence that the Jerries had been there lately.

A couple of doughboys stood outside the remains of the old gate. The wall dates back to the Middle Ages and once was the boast of Julich.

A near-by bulldozer scraped loose dirt and bricks from the roadway down over which two riflemen were marching a column of twenty German prisoners. On both sides of us could be heard the occasional sharp crack of rifles that told that the Kraut sniper was still in action.

Moving Along On Schedule

The command post of Major John Geiglein was found in the basement of a house not far away, and here we learned the attack was moving along on schedule with the company already approaching Stetternich, another unit occupying another town and others holding the high ground running west parallel to the river.

Casualties were reported to be light and prisoners taken relatively high for a total division score.

Across from Geiglein's headquarters a German medic, still wearing the large Red Cross chest shield, was attending wounded Germans on litters while Yanks stood by, rifles ready, for they have learned never to take a chance with the enemy, no matter what the circumstances are.

Doughboys Search For Snipers

We had found our location by company and battalion and set out across the rough terrain toward the northwestern end of the city. There were few GI's about. The doughboys moved through the battered buildings searching for snipers and Jerries hiding out in the cellars. A couple of times we hit the bricks and dirt as a few rounds of enemy artillery whined overhead.

We located B Company in a brick yard near the edge of town and we found them almost ready to shove off.

Lieut. William C. Cook, of Irvington, N.J., a platoon leader, told of running the Krauts out yesterday with little opposition other than occasional rounds of artillery.

A View Of The Battlefield

From the hillside near by it was possible to see a good deal of the battlefield, but the only activity at that moment was the concentration of our artillery landing around the farmhouses and woods ahead and a couple of incoming shells from self-propelled guns hitting over to the south.

Back in Julich itself, Lieut. Col. Stuart G. Fries, of Washington, the battalion commander, stood with Lieut. Col. William Puttennay, of Phoenix, Ariz., planning an assault of the citadel where some of the enemy had been left when the main body pulled out.

The citadel, which dates back some hundreds of years in the town's history, recently has been used as a military school. Built of brick and stone, it has withstood countless sieges through the ages. Now it shows a considerably changed aspect as a result of our artillery and air activities.

Plan For Taking The Citadel

The plan evolved by the commanding officers was for flame throwers to spray the main entrance to the area and shell it for a few minutes while the artillery zeroed concentrations into the central part of the fort. Then the dirt-eating doughboys would climb out of the shell craters and come from the near-by building to do the dirty work.

Snipers' fire from the citadel made the open area immediately in front of it rather unsafe so we crossed over the piles of brick and masonry along the rear of the building line to a house from which observation was possible. Machine guns were already at work on the entrance and a few seconds later the heavy grilled doorway collapsed under a barrage of a couple of rounds from 75-mm's.

The run across the park to the shell holes where GI's crouched ready for the take up seemed more than the 50 yards it was, but the protection of the dirt thrown up around the rim seemed to bring some measure of security. Almost as the fire ceased, the order came over the radio for the assault platoon to take off.

Lieut. Clay S. Purvis, of Charlottesville, Va., from K Company of the 116th Infantry, yelled "follow me," and took off through the smoke and dirt toward the bridge over the moat.

At the same time other doughboys moved in from the holes on our right, with bayonets fixed, and running close to the ground. Even as the first men hit the bridge another artillery barrage landed inside the fort and a couple of snipers' bullets kicked up dirt at our feet. Then we hit the main gate and were inside the tunnel.

On Through The Tunnel

There was a constant clatter of machine guns and the occasional carrumph of larger guns as we moved on through the tunnel. Up ahead, a Yank fired a tommy gun into the gunslit, someone dropped a grenade down the cellar stairs, while rifle fire echoed and re-echoed in the courtyard beyond.

Inside the fort we found the buildings — once a part of the school — almost complete piles of rubble, broken bricks and masonry. Three German staff cars stood at one side — blown to bits. One was still burning. Over on the other side of the citadel the Yanks hugged the wall and kept out of the way of snipers as they searched through the buildings and walls.

No Sign Of German Defenders

Less than ten minutes after the first man had entered the citadel, a patrol had already reached the far side and checked the rear exit. So far there had been no signs of German defenders, but a maze of catacombs below the buildings and inside the walls was still to be searched and would probably reveal the company of prisoners reported to be holding the area.

There still was very much of the sound of battle as we pulled out of the citadel. Overhead the outgoing and occasional incoming mail whined through the sky to crash in the distance of carrumph somewhere behind. Off to the right front the sounds of automatic weapon and rifle fire told of fighting in that sector. Already the eyes of the artillery, the division Piper Cubs, wheeled and turned over Julich and beyond, spots they never would have flown over two days ago.

THE BALTIMORE SUN, MONDAY, MARCH 5, 1945

Holbrook Bradley As GI's See Him

By Lee McCardell [Sunpapers War Correspondent]

With the U.S. 9th Army. March 4 [By Radio] — The current issue of Twenty-nine Lets Go; mimeographed front-line publication of the 29th Division, tells its readers:

"Don't be surprised if an unarmed correspondent jauntily comes at you from the enemy sector inquiring 'Anyone here from Baltimore?' It'll be 'Brad,' Holbrook Bradley, Baltimore Sunpapers, who Saturday got out ahead of our right flank, got back safely and then was the fourth man into the Julich citadel, dashing in with the first squad."

THE BALTIMORE SUN, FRIDAY, MARCH 2, 1945

Bradley Sees Rheydt Attack; Is Knocked Down By Shell

By Holbrook Bradley [Sunpapers War Correspondent]

With the 29th Division, Rheydt, Feb. 28 [By Radio — Delayed] — The fast moving elements of our infantry battalions have stormed into this southern suburb of the industrial and communications center of Munchen-Gladbach and tonight pushed forward block by block to drive out the enemy who still doesn't seem inclined to put up any determined show of resistance.

Near a rail junction to the north a battalion of the same regiment has crossed four kilometers of open ground and is engaging the Germans on the edge of Rheydt, a part of the main city area itself, while to the east companies of another unit are hitting *Wehrmacht* troops below Giesenkirchen.

Barrage Almost Continuous

In this six-day operation the doughboys, supported by an almost continuous barrage of heavy and medium artillery, armor and air forces, have shoved more than 16 miles northeast toward the Rhine from the Roer. As the foot sloggers continue to bear the heaviest burden of the attack, more and more supporting units and equipment are pouring into the steadily deepening penetration as the enemy falls back mile after mile.

AMG Men Busy

So rapid has been the advance during the past 24 hours that the situation of the German civilians is now entirely charged and towns captured are found to be full of people who were unable to move out ahead of our advance. Military government officials are finding more work than they have had since entering Germany.

The highway north of the battle ground was virtually untouched as we rolled up it this morning in the wake of tanks, trucks and other vehicles bound for the front.

Doughboys who had moved up from Keyenberg in the morning already were preparing to jump off when we pulled into Wickrathberg shortly before noon. In an attic, Lieut. Col. Roger S. Whiteford, of Ruxton, was checking over the ground his troops were about to cross to secure a toehold on the Rheydt-Odenkirchen, which even then was under heavy artillery fire preparatory to attack.

Plans Gone Over

To the north other elements could be seen moving through the built-up area where they would provide flank protection. An hour before 12.15 P. M., the hour set for the push, Colonel Whiteford and his company commanders went over the situation again from a vantage point on the ground, checking up on the disposition of the units, routes covered, initial and final objectives.

The riflemen were moving up along the side streets in single file, spaced apart so that casualties would be lessened if the enemy artillery landed. The platoon and squad leaders warned their men to spread out, told them to keep moving over the open ground in the event that the Jerries put up a fight and gave words of encouragement that the tanks would be along to take care of the big stuff.

Up at a command post at the edge of town we could look across the whole width of the field and see the other battalions of the regiment already on the high ground to the north.

Then as the watches pointed to 12.15 and the artillery continued to pour into the objective area, a long line of infantry began to fan out from the orchards in front of us to push onto the level ground and on up toward the rail tracks in the distance.

Germans Surrender

Almost as the first wave broke clear we saw one of the strange sights of war, when one, then a dozen and then more Germans stood up in the trenches, hesitated a moment, then dropped their weapons and started toward our lines, hands held high above their heads.

Soon there was a line, more than 60, moving at first slowly, then almost at a run to our men who stood with their rifles waiting to see what happened. The German first-line defenders gave up without firing a shot.

By 12.30 the companies were well out on the fields and the tanks were moving across the terrain south and west of us, and as yet there was only scattered small-arms fire, a few weak rounds of artillery landing ahead.

He Almost Got It

We stopped worrying about what lay out there and turned to talk to the man at our side, probably partly to make sure someone was there with us.

The next moment a shell from a Jerry self-propelled gun somewhere in town smacked into the ground not ten yards away with no warning at all. The three of us nearest the concussion were hurled to the ground at the impact, the man on the left yelled that he had been hit, and as we moved away we saw that he had half a shoulder torn away, his collarbone broken with the jagged edges showing.

There were a couple of more shells, but it was evident that Jerry was trying to knock out one of the tanks for they kicked up dirt a couple of hundred yards to our left. The man on the ground was already being bandaged, the medics who moved with the company calling for a litter squad to evacuate him before too much blood was lost.

Artillery Lifts Fire

The tanks were sending round after round into particularly stubborn sections as the riflemen pushed on to the east, crossed the railroad tracks and started cleaning out the edge of town.

Behind us more and more infantry poured out over the field, moving steadily toward the objective. The tanks moving in past us looked like a good way to cover the ground, so we hopped on the back of one, bounced over the tracks and then rolled into the first row of houses where civilians stood dubiously in the doorways.

A few Marylanders around were: Major Jack Lawton, Baltimore; Tech. Sergt. Edward J. Greenlow, Holbrook street, Baltimore; Tech. Sergt. Wilbur Graham, 414 South Bouldin street, Baltimore; Pfc. Charles Dimick, 904 Bayliss street, Baltimore; Lieut. William Milhouse, Hagerstown; First Sergeant Joseph L. Staley, Williamsport; Staff Sergeant Calvin Q. Walters, Savage.

THE BALTIMORE SUN, SATURDAY, MARCH 3, 1945

29th Chased Foe Out Of Bed In Taking Munchen-Gladbach

By Holbrook Bradley [Sunpapers War Correspondent]

With the 29th Division at Munchen-Gladbach, March 1 [By Radio — Delayed] — The first Blue and Gray unit to reach Munchen-Gladbach was a battalion of the 17th Regiment of the 29th Infantry Division, which kicked off its attack seven days ago with a jump across the Roer River at Julich and then pushed out along the Cologne road to seize Stetternich.

[The 175th Regiment is composed of elements of the old Dandy 5th of Baltimore.]

In a well co-ordinated drive, forward elements of the division sprinted over 1,000 yards of ground to enter the southern section of the largest German city yet reached by the Allies, and occupied virtually all the building area as the weak German resistance collapsed entirely.

Resistance Light

Contrary to expectation, the enemy resistance in this important rail, communication and industrial center was even lighter than that at Julich, or other towns occupied along the push, and the main sections were taken almost without a fight.

Only a few strong points and a handful of Tiger tanks remained to put a token show of resistance and the prisoner count for the operation ran well under 100 men.

So fast was the American advance across the last score of miles that thousands of German civilians were still left in the town as the doughboys moved up toward the northern boundary.

Although no exact count has been made as yet, the Reich police and other officials have estimated that between 15,000 and 20,000 of the more than 126,000 inhabitants remained behind when the *Wehrmacht* hauled out.

Germans Try To Be Friendly

Although it is far too early to make any estimate of the German people, there is a definite feeling of apprehension mixed with an attempt to appear friendly.

At house after house, old men, women and children stood in windows and doorways waving white flags, making attempts at conversation and smiling at the troops in an obvious approach to the Yanks' softer side.

Tuesday afternoon, a battalion commanded by Major John Geiglein, of Westminster, jumped off from Keyenberg in a move to take Borschemich, which fell half an hour later with a count of three prisoners, and no resistance whatsoever.

On Wednesday the battalion moved north to Wickrathberg, following the 2d and 3d battalions, to secure the town and head across toward Munchen-Gladbach at Guedderath.

City Is Entered

The leading elements jumped off at 7.30 in the morning from Odenkirchen to cover open ground leading up to the building line of the city itself. Attacking with companies abreast, the battalion rapidly advanced and an hour and a half later had crossed into the city with practically no resistance encountered.

Our artillery, which had been plastering the lower end of the town for hours preceding the jump-off, continued to fire round after round into the northern sector of Munchen-Gladbach to neutralize the German defenses there and catch the enemy troops attempting to escape back toward Neuss and the Rhine. There was little sign of enemy counter battery or other fire during the whole operation.

Enemy Guns Open Up

As Capt. Charles E. Norris, of Montrose, Col., brought B Company along the western edge of the town, there was little sound of fighting only occasional rounds of mortar and some artillery fire from the ground to the northwest.

Over to the right, C Company sent back word that it was getting some enemy fire from self-propelled guns located up the street ahead.

From the time the men first crossed into the main building area until the companies buttoned up for the night, there was just the same story of only isolated cases of resistance from the enemy ground troops and a brief burst of fire from three Jerry tanks still left to guard the main access to the roads.

A Dead City

The first night in the city the doughboys and tankers attached to the units held tight where they landed just before dark, while patrols pushed on to the northern suburbs of the city to report no sign of any German elements left there. There was no sign of incoming artillery or that the *Luftwaffe* intended to make things hot.

Munchen-Gladbach, one of the primary targets of the Allied air attacks since the first days of the war, is literally a dead city. Although there are a good number of civilians scattered through the area, they seem lost amid the thousands of buildings making up the town and its suburbs.

Few Buildings Undamaged

In the dull light of a half moon there is little or no sign of anything alive. The doughboys standing guard around the battalion's positions step from black shadows to challenge anyone moving over the streets.

Everywhere is the evidence of terrific punishment the city has taken during the few years past, and more recently, in the preparation for the Allied seizure.

Block after block of the industrial and residential areas lie in crumbled heaps of blasted masonry and piles of rubble, bricks and dirt. There are few buildings which have not been damaged.

Traces Of Recent Occupation

In many places there is evidence that the German troops pulled out from the town in a hurry, and this could only mean they were hit faster than they had expected. Many buildings are full of clothing, equipment and other traces of very recent occupation.

One building, which evidently had been the center of both the military and civil activities of Munchen-Gladbach, still has running water, electric lights powered from wet-cell batteries, elaborate steel-doored living and working wards in which the bed clothing was thrown back as if the occupants were in bed when the Yanks hit town, and operational maps brought up to date a few hours before the Germans hauled out.

Throughout the operation from the Roer, the casualties in this battalion have been extremely light, with fatalities fewer than had been anticipated, even in the most conservative estimates.

THE BALTIMORE SUN, TUESDAY, MARCH 6, 1945

MARYLANDERS IN GOEBBELS'S CASTLE —
Mr. Bradley mentioned eight Marylanders in this dispatch.

29th Drinks Goebbels's Wine, Officers Sleep In His Bed

By Holbrook Bradley [Sunpapers War Correspondent]

Munchen-Gladbach, March 4 [By Radio — Delayed] — The high-raftered ceilings of the Schloss Rheydt, which a few days ago echoed to the *Sieg Heil* of German Storm Troopers, last night rang with the toasts of the 29th Division, as the Blue and Gray's 115th Infantry celebrated their victory in the castle which the grateful citizenry presented arch-Nazi Joseph Paul Goebbels.

As massive logs burned in the huge medieval fireplace over which the light flickered about a life-sized portrait of Hitler and gleamed on a newly painted *Kaput*, the officers of the regiment and their guests dined at a long table, formally laid with shining china and glittering goblets.

Baltimorean Toastmaster

The toastmaster for the occasion was Lieut. Col. Anthony Miller, 30 Bernice avenue, Baltimore, regimental staff officer, who welcomed the divisional generals, Gerhardt, Sands and Watson, and then proposed a series of salutes to the personnel present and those men, wounded or dead, who have left the outfit.

While the doughboys served a meal that ran from a fruit cup as a first course through Southern style ham, apple pie and constantly flowing wine, the regimental orchestra played off to one side, starting out with "Roll Out the Barrel" and running through songs old and new as the hosts and guests joined in.

Fell Without A Shot

Captured Thursday when advance elements of the 115th flanked the city from the east in rolling up to the northern limits of Munchen-Gladbach, the Schloss Rheydt fell without a shot being fired, the only people there being the German caretakers and the Polish slave labor.

Spotlessly clean, the building appeared to have been occupied recently, for all of the facilities were in working order as if waiting for visitors.

In reality more of a country estate than the castle that the name implies, the house was presented to Goebbels a few years ago in "grateful appreciation" from the citizens of Munchen-Gladbach, which was the Propaganda Minister's boyhood home town. It is doubtful if Goebbels ever actually lived in the Schloss for it seemed rather to have been one of the many country estates he frequented on occasion.

Loaded With Liquor

There is evidence, however, that the building was used off and on by other high-ranking Nazi civil and military officials, for all the furniture was in place, carpets were on the floors, and linen, china and glassware were about in lavish abundance. The silverware had been removed but the basement was loaded with wine and liquor and the library upstairs included a book of photographs of Nazi movie queens, who had visited the castle.

On hand to greet the guests last night was Lieut. Col. William O. Blandford, of Washington, D.C., regimental commander, who stood before a roaring fire in the upstairs living room, decorated with heavy drapes, massive mission-style furniture, tremendous overstuffed couches and ornate lamps which belonged in some New York hotel.

At a huge oak side table, white-coated enlisted men served champagne and gin in gleaming goblets monogrammed with Goebbels's initials.

Tour Of The House

When the formalities were over, Tony Miller took the guests for a quick tour of the house, pointing out the resplendent thick-carpeted bedroom where he and Blandford slept in soft, double beds in strange contrast to the usual mud and muck.

The other officers used similar, slightly less ornate rooms scattered through the house and wings.

A few of those at last night's party were: Major Albert G. Warfield, Earl Court Apartments; Major George Nevius, Baltimore.; Capt. Robert Wallis, Baltimore; Major Victor P. Gillespie, Centreville; Lieut. Col. Randy Milholland, Cumberland; Lieut. Col. John P. Cooper, Pikesville; Major George S. Paxson, Westminster; Capt. John Whittington, Exmore, Virginia; Lieut. Col. Glover S. Johns, Corpus Christi, Texas; Major Theodore A. Cross, Cleveland.

WITH 29th DIVISION IN GERMANY

OUTPOST ON ROER RIVER BANK — Sergt. Louis A. Hickman, of Crisfield, Md., at the gun; Lieut. Karl F. Knuhter, of Jeannette, Pa., beside him. This picture was taken while Germans still held opposite bank of the river, seen through break in wall. BEL-366-BS

Holbrook Bradley Photographs Action

The camera which Sunpapers' War Correspondent Holbrook Bradley carries has made a pictorial record of the Blue and Gray Division's progress from England to Germany. Some of those pictures appear on this page and others, many during the crossing to France, and during the battle of Brest, but which had been delayed, will be reproduced in a subsequent issue of The Sunday Sun. For many months Bradley recorded the 29th's doings. He was long assigned to the division during the dreary period of training in England; landed in Normandy with some of its elements shortly after D-day; described the fighting at the beachhead and the advance through Isigny to St. Lo; reported the Germans' surrender at Brest. Then, when the Maryland-Virginia-Pennsylvania division was transferred to Germany, he accomplished it. This correspondent knows hundreds of the 29th's officers and men, has mentioned the names of innumerable Marylanders and others in his dispatches. He has shared the rough life of the fighting men whose achievements he has recounted and, at times, their danger, for he was wounded by mortar fire at Vire on August 8.

GERMAN PARATROOPERS WHO DIDN'T HAVE TO JUMP — Some 29th men came across this German JU-52 wreck. Plane was carrying paratroopers when ack-ack brought it down in a crash that littered field with plane parts and dead Nazis. AHO-203-BS

BALTIMOREANS OUTSIDE HEADQUARTERS — Lieut. Lawrence Brandon, of 3 St. Johns road, and Sergt. William T. Littleton, of 3019 Overland road, of the 29th. BKI-479-BS

THEIR LAST FIGHT — In upper picture a GI of the 29th lies where he fell in the fighting for the German sports center near Julich, where the terrain made the Yank attack costly. BKI-527-BS.

Lower picture: A fallen German defender. BKI-528-BS

MORE PICTURES OF 29th
FROM BRADLEY'S CAMERA

GERMANS DUG THIS TRENCH — Men of B Company, 175th Infantry, on the alert in a silt trench on high ground above Julich. The position was taken from the Germans, now provides these Yank riflemen with protection as they scan the country ahead for targets. BKI-465-BS

These pictures made by Holbrook Bradley, Sunpapers' War Correspondent are of fighting about Broich and the important German city of Muenchen-Gladbach. The fighters appearing in them, in many instances, are men Bradley has known many months, for his close acquaintance with the division goes back to the training period in England. He crossed to Normandy with the division, has observed it in all the major actions in which it has participated and has reported its achievements in numerous dispatches.

ONE DOWN — Twenty-ninth doughboys stand guard as German medic administers first aid to one of his own men. BKI-471-BS

ALLIGATORS WERE USEFUL — Alligator above was used by 115th Infantry in crossing Roer near Broich. Town was taken by Second Battalion, commanded by Major Al Warfield. BKI-468-BS

SWAMPY — Alligator in background is coming through swampy ground near Broich during 29th's attack on that town. BKI-473-BS

HERDING SOME OF 2,000 PRISONERS — Bradley does not identify this ruined town, in which 29th men are gathering in prisoners to be sent under escort to the rear, but it may be Julich, which was severely battered. The Blue and Gray took well over 2,000 prisoners in its drive to Muenchen-Gladbach, the correspondent-photographer notes. BKI-466-BS

PRISONERS — A load of captured Germans is brought back from Broich in an Alligator. From this point they will be marched to rear. BKI-467-BS

BATTLE PICTURES OF 29th
BY HOLBROOK BRADLY

A SHERMAN POURS IT INTO JULICH'S CITADEL — Pictures made during final stages of the assault at this point. The tank has been firing and the doughboys appearing at the right are about to charge across the open ground to the wall. BKI-512-BS

GERMANS STILL HOLD OUT BEHIND THESE MASSIVE WALLS — Tanks move toward the Julich citadel, obviously no easy nut to crack, the defenders having good cover and the attackers being in full view of those behind walls. BKI-513-BS

The smoke of battle drifts over some of these pictures of the attack on Julich, Roer River town that was wrested from the Germans by the Blue and Gray Division in sharp fighting during the push that carried the Allied armies to the Rhine. They were taken by Holbrook Bradley, Sunpapers War Correspondent, the work of whose camera, which is incidental to that of his typewriter, recently has filled this page more than once. Readers of Bradley's dispatches, which have described nearly all the actions in which the 29th has been engaged, and before the unit went into action, its training in England, will perceive from these pictures that the correspondent obtains information of battlefield incidents by going with the men into the fight.

VICTORY PAID FOR WITH BLOOD — One of the 29th's wounded lies on the stretcher on jeep. Another is being placed on the stretcher on the ground. All about are the battered buildings of Julich. BKI-507-BS

AT STETTERNICH — Riflemen under command of Capt. Ben Pollard, of St. Dunstan's road, put up covering fire as a platoon attacks near-by pillbox. BKI-508-BS

IN A HURRY — The doughboy lifts his feet with reason: there is lead flying around. The puff of smoke at the right center was made by German fire. The enemy is behind the thick old wall. BKI-517-BS

MOPPING UP — The pillbox in the basement of this house has been silenced. Question is: "Did we get them all?" These wary riflemen — note weapons in firing position — are there to find the answer to that. BKI-509-BS

VENTILATED — Inside the Julich citadel doughboys run about searching for Germans, not all of whom have been killed or captured by the first unit to get to this point. Note bullet-marked wall. BKI-514-BS

IN GOOD HANDS — Fritz and his buddies pile out of this building with hands held so that there is no mistaking the completeness of their surrender. Yank rifleman gazes at wood. BKI-511-BS

CHAPTER 9

THE RHINE RIVER CROSSING

From Bradley Back to McCardell

THE BALTIMORE SUN, MONDAY, FEBRUARY 26, 1945

The accompanying article is part of a series by Mr. McCardell on the American crossing of the Saar River.

McCardell Watches 3d Army Infantry Jump Off For Crossing Of Saar

By Lee McCardell [Sunpapers War Correspondent]

With the U.S. 3d Army on the Saar, Feb. 24 [By Radio — Delayed]. "You better get some sleep, sir," the major said to the colonel. "There isn't time now," the colonel said.

It was 2130 Army time — 9.30 P.M. in Baltimore. The infantry was to jump off on its river crossing at 2300.

"You could sleep for half an hour," said the major.

"Colonel, sir," said the sergeant, "there's a bed in the room just over this, and I've got my bedroll on it if you'd like to sleep there."

The Colonel Gives In

"Aw, hell," said the colonel, looking down at his muddy combat boots, "not like this — I'm too muddy."

"You can't hurt my bedroll, sir," laughed the sergeant.

"I'll call you at 10 o'clock," said the major, "there isn't anything more you can do now. You've just got to wait. You might as well sleep that half hour."

"Well, if you'll be sure to call me."

"Don't worry, we'll call you all right," said the major.

"Okay," said the colonel.

He went out of the room and upstairs to get half an hour's sleep. He needed it badly. Every engineer in his battalion needed it badly. They'd been on the go for the last 60 hours.

Clearing Mines, Roadblocks

They'd been clearing mines and roadblocks, bridging anti-tank ditches and blown culverts and filling shell craters along their command's line of march.

Now they were ready to ferry an infantry regiment across the Saar River. The infantry had been supposed to cross early that morning, but the assault boats hadn't come up in time.

The boats were here now. There couldn't be any further delay.

Their command was one which had raced down the valley of the Moselle River to outrun the Moselle-Saar triangle after the "Siegfried switch" had been broken by the 94th Infantry Division.

It is a gorgeous valley even in this winter of its ruin and neglect. Its mellow hills, terraced with vineyards, sweep down majestically to the noble river that curls around their feet and ripples with silver in the February sunshine.

Last season's unpicked grapes have shriveled brown and dead upon their vines. The farmers' plows are rusting in the fallow fields where they were left last fall.

The abandoned villages, bombed from the air and blasted by long-range artillery, are dreary in their desolation. Everywhere, uphill and down, the Germans have been digging their interminable zigzag trenches and their endless tank ditches.

But none of this can destroy the old valley's natural beauty.

"It's lovely country, isn't it," the colonel said that afternoon. "I kept looking at it all along the way as we came through, and thinking, 'God, how I'd like to come back here some day when there isn't any fighting.'"

Tanks Tore Through Swiftly

The Germans didn't fight too hard to hold it, in spite of all their ditches and trenches — miles and miles of ditches and trenches. The American tanks tore through too quickly after the 94th had broken the switch line. The tanks sped down along the Moselle to its confluence with the Saar.

The Germans fled across both rivers, blowing bridges behind them. Our tanks turned up the Saar and charged into Saarburg to link up with other American forces moving in from the west and south.

The infantry crossed the Saar by assault boat below Saarburg early that morning. Another regiment was supposed to have crossed above Saarburg at the village of Ayl, but in the confusion of the rapid advance and engineer truck-train carrying boats for the Ayl crossing had missed the road and been lost for eight hours.

Ayl Faces Mountains

"It's a damn shame," the colonel had said. "We might have been in Trier tonight if we'd had those boats this morning."

It was late afternoon when I got into Ayl, a little village a mile west of the Saar and facing more terraced vineyards on the high, bare hillsides across the river.

Hills? Better say mountains. They're 1,500 feet high, and steep. And they were still in German hands.

It was easy to understand how the truck-train of boats had been lost. I came into Ayl the back way, along the winding, muddy country roads. I had an officer, who had been there before, as a guide. Otherwise, I'd never have been able to find my way through the maze of unmarked crossroads even by daylight.

A Few Civilians Left

Ayl was full of American troops, tanks, halftracks, trucks and jeeps when I got there. Unlike other villages through which we have passed, there were also a few civilians still in Ayl. In the kitchen of one house a woman was working an old-fashioned butter churn.

An aged man carried buckets of water from the town fountain into his stable for his two horses. But the civilians had been ordered by the American civil-affairs officers to evacuate. And in front of another house, a half-grown girl was piling suitcases and eiderdowns into an open farm wagon.

There wasn't any shooting in the town. But there were German snipers down along the river. It wasn't healthy to venture beyond the log barricade the Germans had built beyond the village on the river road leading down to Saarburg.

Snipers Fire From Graveyard

The German snipers were firing on the road from a graveyard on a hill this side of the river, just outside the village.

Other German snipers were firing from pillboxes across the river. You could also see the river, which twisted out of sight behind the nearest mountain. The meadows of Ayl through which it flowed were flat and treeless. Snipers controlled both banks of the river during the daylight.

When the lost assault boats had been found, it was decided to attempt the river crossing during the daylight under cover of a smoke screen.

A Negro chemical company with a train of smoke generators in jeep trailers had been sent down the river road to build up a smokescreen.

Two of three engineer trucks with trailers of assault boats had followed them. While the chemical company got its generators going, the engineers unloaded the boats and lined them up along the road a few hundred yards from the river bank.

Germans Open Fire

Then the snipers opened fire from the graveyard on the hill and from the pillboxes across the river. They riddled three or four of the chemical company's jeeps and plugged one generator and put it out of business. They peppered the wooden assault boats lined up along the road. The engineers and smoke men hit the ditches along the road. The snipers pinned some of them until after dark.

Shortly before dark I met four wet, muddy engineers coming up the river road. They looked as though they had been wallowing in the river. But one of them, Private Edmund J. Mansky, of 4518 Mannasota avenue, Baltimore said:

"We've been in a ditch. You can't get near the river."

"You can't raise your head," said Private Preston Collins, of 416 Eleventh street, N.E., Washington. "They've got snipers all over the place."

There wasn't any smoke then. The smoke-generator men didn't dare show themselves. One or two who had tried to stick with the generator had been shot. So the river crossing had been called off until after dark.

I walked back up through the village looking for folk from home again among the infantrymen and engineers there.

I found Sergt. Elwood Stanton, of Lynchburg, Va.; Sergt. Charles Cowan, of Glade Springs, Va., and Privates Fred Gibson, Sycamore, Va.; Roy Sprouse, Charlottesville, Va., whose wife's home is at 2137 Vine street, Baltimore; Robert Holdcraft, of 2315 Harlem avenue, Baltimore; Earl Markey, of 3148 Tildham drive, Baltimore, and Louis Gray, of 800 Taylor street, N.E., Washington.

Impatient to Cross River

The infantrymen waiting to cross the river were impatient to get on with it. Many carried, in addition to their regular combat equipment, sections of fused bangalore torpedoes with which to blow up barbed wire reported strung along the far shore of the river.

All wore winter shoepacs and said they wished the Army had thought to issue them earlier in the winter when the weather was colder.

Shoepacs are hard on arches and cumbersome things in which to walk through deep mud, which has succeeded the snow in the battle area.

Ration trucks came up at dusk with cold K's for the infantry, and at dark the soldiers were herded off the streets into the vacant houses. I went back to join the engineers in another house.

Colonel Makes Final Check

After dark the colonel went down along the street to make sure everything was all set for the crossing.

"It's got to go off tonight without any hitch," he said.

He took a couple of us along with him in his jeep. It was deathly quiet now and pretty lonely along the river. The smoke generator company's jeeps, a wire jeep and a couple of engineer trucks knocked out during the afternoon by the snipers were still sitting along the deserted road.

The moon was coming up and in the dark you could readily pick out those assault boats which would be useless. Little moonbeams came through the holes in them caused by sniper bullets. Two or three scattered rounds of enemy artillery fire burst along the road, but things did not look too tough just then.

When we got back to the house in the village, the engineers had been taken over by Capts. George Garwood, of Denver, Col., and John Israelson, of New York city.

Companies Briefed

They were briefing the two companies who were to man the assault boats. The number of boats damaged by the snipers had been checked and the trucks with the additional boats had been brought up. Everything was set up for the operations.

Then the colonel, obviously weary, went upstairs for a half-hour nap. The rest of us sat around in the little downstairs living room. The engineers had rigged up an electric light from their portable generator out in the front yard. They had also built a fire in the small German stove.

In a house across the street they had found a company kitchen with hot coffee.

The sergeant on whose bedroll the colonel was sleeping stared at the wall clocks in the living room. We drank coffee in cups borrowed from the kitchen of the departed householders and watched the hands of the clock.

Return To River

Further, to kill time, Capt. Warren S. Simonds, former University of Maryland student from Prince Georges Island, got out his penknife and took apart a small alarm clock he had been carrying in his pocket.

At 10 o'clock they called the colonel. We went back to the river with him, passing the engineers who were moving silently down the road from the village.

The new assault boats had been hauled down the road. There was no sound from the river, 200 yards away. The engineers worked quietly, talking in hushed voices.

There wasn't much to see. The smoke generator company's bullet riddled jeeps, tires flat and windshields shattered, were still leaking oil on the grease-smeared road.

Gasoline trickled slowly from a small bullet hole in the tank of a disabled engineer truck. The moon wasn't very bright.

Opposite River Bank Visible

You could just make out the far shore of the river dimly, and, stretching across the stream, which was not more than 100 yards wide here, the dark shadowy line of the wreckage of a wooden highway bridge destroyed by our fighter-bombers before the German retreat.

The infantry would cross the river at two places, here above the ruined bridge and at another point a short distance below.

The infantry came along presently, as quietly as the engineers, moving down either side of the road in single file. When they halted they dropped into the roadside ditches while the engineers organized them into boat crews, three engineers and six infantrymen to a boat, and made sure each boat crew had a bag of paddles.

A little before 11 o'clock the light American tanks back on the hill began firing red tracers across the river.

Artillery Opens Up

About 11 o'clock the American artillery opened up with a heavy covering fire, walking their bursts up and down the mountainsides opposite the river, bringing them down to the very bank on the opposite shore.

The flash and thunder of the barrage was a pretty terrifying spectacle even for the men it was designed to protect. In the midst of the barrage the order came to begin crossing.

The men picked up their heavy boats and started down the slope toward the river banks. The colonel was down along the bank seeing the first wave off.

THE BALTIMORE SUN, TUESDAY, FEBRUARY 27, 1945

The accompanying article is the second of two by Mr. McCardell on the American crossing of the Saar River.

German Gunners Catch Boats Returning From Saar Crossing

By Lee McCardell [Sunpapers War Correspondent]

With the U.S. 3d Army, Feb. 25 [By Radio — Delayed] — The colonel wore a long light trench coat. Nobody else along the river had a coat like that, so you could pick him out among the other figures moving in the darkness.

The moon had gone down under a cloud and it was good and dark now along the river. The infantry, waiting to cross the Saar in the second wave of assault boats, lay still in the ditches on either side of the road or flat on the narrow strip of ground sloping down from the road to the muddy river bank.

How It Works In Theory

Some raised their heads to watch the red tracers of the guns of the light tanks across the river, and the fiery shattering blasts of our artillery's high-explosive shells bursting like Fourth of July flower pots on the far shore. The artillery struck fire along the hills from the crest down their faces to the river's east bank. And the hills held the racket in the river valley, tossing it back and forth until the sound ceased having any meaning.

This is the standard procedure for river crossing. Your own artillery pours it on to drive enemy snipers, machine gunners and observers under over. The Germans can watch and shoot small-arms from the protection of pillboxes, but their observation and field of fire is restricted to gun embrasures and they cannot operate mortars from pillboxes.

Before they can get outside to reorganize their defenses, troops making the assault are on top of them — in theory.

First River Crossing For Many

This was the first river crossing many of the infantrymen along the road had ever made. It was the heaviest barrage the new reinforcements had ever been under. But many were not interested in watching. Who is? They kept their heads down. They did not look while the guns roared in the hills behind them and the river valley shook with fire and thunder. Clouds of smoke and dust drifted vaguely against the blacker darkness of the hill masses hidden in the night beyond.

The first wave ought to be across now. It was. You knew it when you heard the hard, sharp ripple of German burp guns, saw their tracers streaking across the river and along its far bank. Then you heard a mighty whistle and knew it was coming. You lost interest in everything but the depth of the nearest ditch as the German artillery began plastering your side of the river. You hugged the ground and prayed as you only pray when under artillery fire while the shells searched the darkness around you for that river road.

When you crawled out and looked around, there was the colonel, moving up and down and back and forth across the road, sorting out the infantry for the second wave. Then came more whistles and more dives into ditches. Maybe the colonel dived too, but you didn't see him. At least he was always out before you were and the last one in.

"C Company! C Company! Where's C Company?" he called.

He got C Company together on the slope of open ground running down toward the river.

Could Hear Men Shouting

Small-arms fire was brisk now on the other side of the river. You could hear men shouting over there in the darkness. You could not see anything but streaking tracers in the gloom.

"Where the hell are those boats?" asked Captain Israelson, pacing along the road. "They oughta be coming back by now."

There was a truck in the road with the trailer still loaded with another nest of assault boats.

"Let's unload them," said the colonel. "Get some more engineers, Israelson. Let's organize some more crews and get going."

There weren't many engineers left. Most of them were manning the boats not back yet. Israelson went up and down the ditches calling:

"Engineers? What are you, soldiers or engineers?"

The ditches were full of soldiers taking cover from the artillery. You couldn't see who they were in the darkness. You couldn't tell engineers from infantry.

"Are you an engineer?" Israelson would ask.

"Infantry," was the usual reply.

He found half a dozen in the ditches and three or four more in a big foxhole, where they had been detailed to care for engineer casualties. He got them out on the road, where the colonel supervised the unloading of the trailer.

"Heave! Heave!" yelled the colonel. "Don't drag those boats."

More German Shells

The infantry slung rifles, dumped their mortars, machine guns and ammunition boxes into assault boats, picked up the heavy boats, four men to hand grips on either side, and started down the slope toward the river bank.

In the darkness the boat paddles had been misplaced. Israelson and a couple of engineer lieutenants ran up and down the road trying to find the paddles, while more German shells came in, shrapnel whistled around their legs, tearing through the trees over their heads.

Some stragglers, separated from their outfit in the dark, came along the road asking:

"Are you in D Company? Do you know where D Company's at?"

"I'm No Hero"

Then the colonel was trying to find a missing platoon supposed to cross the river in the next wave.

I'm no hero. I hit the ditch every time a shell came in. My favorite ditch was a deep, muddy one, opposite the smoke generator company's disabled jeeps. The smoke men had rolled a lot of big 50-gallon oil drums into the ditch earlier in the day but there was still room for shelter.

The colonel's jeep driver used the same ditch for shelter. He had parked the jeep farther up the road and was waiting for the colonel, who had said he would be going back to the village within an hour. But at midnight the colonel was still loading boats. The last time I saw him, he was hurrying along the road. His jeep driver called to him from the ditch:

"Ready to go back, colonel?"

"Hell, no," said the colonel. "I've got to get these men across the river."

"Got Us Coming Back"

The jeep driver rolled back into the ditch moaning:

"He'll get me killed some day the way he runs around in hot spots."

Machine-gun fire was coming back from across the river. But evidently the infantry had landed on the far shore and was going through barbed wire. You could hear explosives that must be Bangalore torpedoes. And still no boat crews came back. Israelson could not understand it.

More German shells came in. We all hit the ditches again. We were still in them when a soldier — an engineer — came running up from the river and tumbled into the ditch. He was drenched hysterical and sobbing. He said:

"They got us coming back! We drifted down into the bridge! I've lost Joe! We've lost the boat! Jeepers! I don't know where any of them are!"

"I'll Try," He Said

"We've gotta get more boats," said Israelson calmly. "We've gotta get these people across."

He remembered there were some motor-driven stormboats back in the village. The noise of their outboard motors wouldn't make any difference at this stage. He sent a lieutenant back to the village to find the stormboats and bring them up.

When the truck with the trailer load of stormboats arrived, there was a motor for only one of them. It was just as well. Of the half dozen engineers still around only one knew anything about outboard motors, and he was not sure he could handle this one.

"I'll try," he said, unslinging his carbine and whipping off his cartridge belt.

He Didn't Move

Where was the next platoon of D Company? It was their turn to cross the river.

"They are over on the other side of the road," said a platoon sergeant.

He led the way down the slope toward the river bank. Fifteen or twenty soldiers were sprawled face downward on the ground. "Good God! Have they all been hit?" asked Israelson.

"They ain't been hit," said the sergeant fetching one with a kick on his backside, "Hey soldier, you Company D?"

"No," said the soldier without moving.

"You hurt?" asked Israelson.

"No," said the soldier, still without moving.

Soldier Is Hit

The others belonged to D Company and the sergeant rounded them up and took them back to the road to carry the stormboat down to the river and launch it.

The German shells were still coming in. By some miracle they missed the road, falling either long or short. We stuck to our ditches, the men piled two deep when the concentrations were heaviest and the dirt and stone kicked up by the shellbursts rained down on top of us.

One soldier, beyond the road, had been hit. He was crying like a child. Two aid men carried him into our ditch. He had got it in the leg. I got a litter and offered to help carry him back.

"We're infantry company aid men," the medics said. "We've got orders to stay with our company. There's a medical jeep back up the road a little way."

"How's It Going Up Ahead?"

I went back to look for the medical jeep. It had been shot up. I went back almost to the village hunting for an aid station and litter-bearers.

The muddy, watery ditch along the road was filled with infantrymen waiting to cross the river. They asked:

"How's it going up ahead?"

"Slow," I said and hurried on in the dark, feeling very much like a coward to be seen going in that direct and calling "Medic? Medic? Any medics around here?" The aid station was in a house beside the road outside the village.

I got a wheel litter there and a couple of medics and started back. On the way the colonels' jeep sped past us bound in the opposite direction. There was a man lying across the gear in the back seat and he turned out to be the one we had expected to evacuate. But we went on and found another and brought him in.

Three more engineers who had manned the boats in the first wave came back from the river drenched and shivering.

"The Jerries have got a machine-gun crossfire on the other side," they said. "We got over but couldn't get back. They shot the boats to pieces. A lotta our boys drifted down into the bridge."

The infantry on this side was still trying to cross. The artillery fire was still heavy and they hated to leave the ditches but the officers and noncoms talked them out:

"You'll be killed if you stay here. Come on — let's get moving."

At about 1.30 I went back to the village, again feeling very cowardly. When I walked into the house that the engineers had taken over, the colonel's jeep driver was sitting by the stove with his head in his hands.

Colonel Is Missing

He looked up and asked anxiously:

"Did you see the colonel?" I hadn't seen the colonel for an hour and a half. Nobody else had seen him. Captain Israelson was there talking to the major who had taken command. Israelson said he needed more boats.

He had located another truckload. He'd take them back and load them up with infantry and send them across. The boats would have to stay there and be salvaged later. Israelson said that all of his engineer crews had been scattered.

At another point, where the infantry was crossing below the bridge, the operation was going much better. At the second point Captain Garwood's company of engineers had ferried one battalion across the river and was beginning to move another. They had not had much fire. Most of it seemed to have come in on Israelson's men.

By dawn the entire regiment was across the river with the exception of its headquarters company. Most of the missing engineers had straggled in, soaked and exhausted. One group of three had been pinned down under the wreckage of the bridge by German machine-gun fire. They came in covered with ice.

The Captain Passes Out

The battalion medical officer said casualties had been comparatively light. He had been out searching the river bank and the aid station for some sign of the missing colonel without success. There was a report that the colonel had been seen on the far shore.

At about 8 o'clock Captain Garwood came in to report. He is six-footer, solidly built. He sat down on the edge of the table, closed his eyes, toppled over and crashed on the floor. They picked him up, a job for three men and laid him on a couch in the corner of the room. Without sleep for the last 72 hours, he has passed out from exhaustion. They brought him around and put him to bed.

Captain Israelson, fingering a ragged hole in his trousers over his knee, pulled up his pants leg to investigate. Israelson had been nicked by a shrapnel splinter, but had almost forgotten about it. The major told him to go to bed, too, before he also passed out from loss of sleep.

THE BALTIMORE SUN, MONDAY, MARCH 26, 1945

MARYLANDERS IN GERMANY —

In the following dispatch, Mr. Bradley mentions four Marylanders, three of them Baltimoreans.

Ships Crisscrossed Rhine As 9th Swept Across

By Holbrook Bradley [Sunpapers War Correspondent]

With U.S. 9th Army Across the Rhine, March 24 [By Radio — Delayed] — Battle-hardened doughboys of Lieut. Gen. William H. Simpson's command attacking with the British 2nd Army and Allied airborne elements have swept across the Rhine River south of Wesel and already are reporting steady progress inland against light German opposition.

Under cover of intense artillery preparation, American forces early today crossed the muddy waters of the Reich's largest river, landing from an area north of Duisburg to the industrial section bordering the communications center of Wesel, which was under storm by British Commandos and empire troops.

Others Cross Hour Later

The first waves of infantry slid their storm and assault craft into the river on the nose of 2 A.M. H-hour, and secured beachheads and were driving toward the small towns between Gotterswicherhamm and Wesel.

An hour later other elements crossing north of Duisburg were pushing east after securing the initial bridgehead with little difficulty.

By noon units were reporting advances up to 5,000 yards, with still no indication of serious opposition.

Tanks Ferried Over Rhine

More than a dozen tanks and tank destroyers already had been ferried over the Rhine, which by then was crisscrossed with a pattern of army and navy-operated landing craft moving men, equipment and supplies in the follow-up waves.

Although the warm sun and balmy breezes showed decidedly that spring had arrived, there was still the chill feeling of impending combat as we drove to the west bank of the Rhine and the assembly area.

All along the highways were convoys of vehicles carrying men, guns, bridging equipment, ammunition, assault boats and everything needed for an operation of the scale that this was to be.

Once or twice we could see the Rhine itself as the road wound near the river and then doubled back toward Wesel. Off to the left a low black cloud formation seemed foreboding until it was recognized as the burning of some oil-storage tanks on the east bank, probably set afire during the recent bombing runs.

We knew the immediate plans for the British and the American armies of the combined Allied air drop which in turn was the key for the whole operation, for Field Marshal Montgomery would have to delay the whole campaign for a week or more if necessary should the weather turn bad.

Toward the middle of the afternoon, when the ground haze seemed to threaten visibility, it looked as if the plan would be postponed but at 4.30 word came through that everything would follow the original plan.

Bombers Flatten Wesel

An hour later we watched what looked like the total destruction of Wesel as Allied fighter-bombers, medium and heavy bombers came in wave after wave to drop thousands of tons of high-explosives on the target area, from which flame and smoke billowed more than a mile into the sky.

The plan called for a British Commando raid on Wesel at 10 P.M., to be followed by a night air strike on the same area by the RAF and then infantry support from the 2d Army.

The American attacks across the Rhine were to be made south of the British sector, with 2 A.M. as H-hour, and the second wave to follow one hour later. Regardless of the success of these combined operations, the Allied airborne troops were scheduled to drop at 10 o'clock this morning.

How Job Was Planned

Other than the usual methodical cover of artillery, which scarcely varies day in and day out under normal circumstances, there was little to indicate one of the biggest operations since D-day, certainly the greatest river crossing of this war, was about to begin, so we drove to the regimental command post of the colonel.

With two visiting colonels from the 9th Air Force we were given a detailed picture of both the part the regiment would play in the crossing and those to be played by other associated elements, including the importance of the co-operation and support of the air and ground troops and the manner in which it would work.

A few hours later, at approximately, 11.30 the colonel prepared to take off for the riverfront command post, and suggested we come along, as this was the best opportunity of seeing how the operation would be carried out.

Stream Of Vehicles

Outside, on the narrow roads of Rheinberg, convoys already were rumbling up through the brilliant, clear, starlit night toward the areas where they had been assigned.

For a moment the mass of armor, assault boats, bulldozers, amphibious craft and the profusion of material overshadowed us, then we, too, were moving and were lost in the steady stream of men and vehicles.

There were heavy flashes and earth-shaking concussions to the north of us as the British artillery went into action in support of the Commandos, who were then in the process of crossing the Rhine below us.

In the bright moonlight every figure, tree and house seemed to stand out almost as if it were day.

The fact made us rather uncomfortable a few minutes later as we walked along the top of a dike only 60 yards from the river and less than 400 yards from the German positions.

Yank Batteries Open Up

Someone in the command dugout had just finished noting the time that the artillery commenced when the first American batteries opened up behind us with an ear-splitting roar that seemed almost on top of us. There seemed to be no response from the Jerry gunners, so the observers took a chance of lying on top of the dike to watch the shelling.

For the next hour until the jump-off it seemed as if every piece of artillery in the entire American Army was cracking behind us, sending steel by the thousands of tons onto the German-held ground before us.

In a few seconds the whole scene was covered with smoke that rolled over the lowlands, bluffs and river, while the phosphorus shells scattered sparks, outlining blazing houses, or scarred treelines.

Plan Carefully Worked Out

To the south, fire poured in where other troops were crossing. Each phase of the plan had been worked out on sand tables and at training ground back of the Maas River.

Overtoned against the backdrop of the continuous heavy rumble of artillery battalions was the constant plop of 60 and 80-mm. mortars firing from the field not 1,000 yards from the river's edge.

Engineers had brought fast storm boats and smaller assault boats to the back edge of the dike shortly after darkness fell. Now, as 2 o'clock approached, doughboys, packs on their backs, rifles or heavy weapons over their shoulders, filed forward in silent columns, going about the job ahead with the precision of experts, although then none knew what the next few hours would bring.

H-Hour Arrives

Suddenly as the hands of our watches pointed to H-hour, the artillery as at one command ceased, then went into action again with increased volume as the fire lifted to the rear of the target area.

At the same moment, to sharp commands issued by captains and platoon leaders, the first boats were lifted over the dike and carried down to the river's edge.

With the move of the infantry and the engineers to the Rhine, the supporting direct fire of machine guns, tanks and tank destroyers broke out along the levee, spraying the whole area under attack with a raining hail of lead and steel.

To those watching from the top of the dike it seemed almost like some fantastic Hollywood set, only an occasional incoming or shot from our own guns reminding us of the deadly seriousness of this business.

River 300 Yards Wide

The first boat could be made out halfway across the 300-yard width of the Rhine, when a green and then white flare shot up from German-held ground. This seemed a miracle after the saturation of artillery that was still going off.

The sound of a patrol clash a short while later showed some of the Krauts still held out, probably in cellars, but they certainly must have been groggy.

From the briefing beforehand we knew that Capt. Charles W. Moncrieff, of Kansas City, was leading G Company in on the left, while Capt. John M. Jacobsen, of Omaha, would hold the right flank with F Company in the initial assault.

Boats Stream Across

As the boats continued to stream across the Rhine the men of the leading units were soon lost in the smoke-filled darkness, but it was possible to follow the progress for a few hundred yards by the flash of small-arms and grenades.

The first few hours ashore, as reported back to the regimental command post by radio, told of preliminary moments of confusion brought about by outfits landing at unscheduled spots, the general difficulties of the terrain and the intensity of the battle.

But there was no sign of aimless moving about, for the unit commanders gave situation reports of steady progress toward the objectives, a group of small communities spread over a couple of miles of ground.

Nazi Artillery Silent

A couple of hours later the situation had settled down to a well defined bridgehead attack that was progressing smoothly against some enemy resistance, mainly from scattered small-arms fire and mortars.

There was little indication of Jerry artillery and no signs of the *Luftwaffe*, which so far had failed to put in an appearance anywhere along the front.

Back on the west bank, priority vehicles and pieces of equipment were assembling in marshaling spots under the direction of a beachmaster prior to being ferried across to the far shore.

Alligators had been brought in to supplement the assault boats, but there was no sign of the navy-operated LCVP's and LCM's or other landing craft.

Shortly after 5 A.M. the colonel felt the battalion already over had advanced far enough to warrant moving the regiment command post across, and as daylight came a steady stream of men and vehicles were moving to the bridgehead.

German Guns Open Up

Then, as a couple of us talked an alligator driver into giving us a lift across, there came a familiar whine and carrump of Jerry artillery as three shells crashed into a levee 50 yards from where we stood.

There were a couple of casualties when the smoke and flying debris cleared away, but down at the river's edge the doughboys were loading as if nothing had occurred, even as a couple of more rounds landed downstream from us.

It seemed probably the Jerrys had one or two guns across from us and were taking shots at random, as usual, in the hopes of hitting something.

By the time we reached the east bank the incoming mail was passing well over our heads. From the first moment that we hit the beach it was evident why the men had had no tougher time getting in.

Defenses Unprepared

The ground seemed excelled for defense, but the Krauts never had time to prepare it properly and, as a result, all opposition was from a few hastily dug ditches, firing positions or outposts. There were few mines, little or no wire.

One Yank lay face down in the mud where he had fallen, but a shell crater beside him showed he fell to artillery rather than infantry. In a trench were a couple of dead Germans, probably ordered to hold out to the last regardless of the cost — and they paid in full.

But on a stretch a couple of thousand yards by F Company, there were no other Germans and none of the usual litter and equipment found when the enemy retreats.

Prisoners File Back

The German gunners back from the river were going through the usual routine of throwing a few rounds into every village and crossroad as we moved up.

A couple of files of prisoners under guard of doughboys came down the road, but the only other signs of life were barnyard fowls wandering aimlessly through the ruined houses and a couple of gaunt pigs rooting in the shell-torn gardens.

Off to the right the burp of a German Schmeisser told that a few snipers were holding out, but the doughboys of the following waves were busy mopping up and it would only be a matter of a short time before they would be stretched out with the rest who stayed to fight.

In this sector, the 9th Army's crossing of the Rhine has gone well so far. Under difficulties of terrain and approach, riflemen and weapons in support had moved in to take their objectives in stride. As had been expected, enemy resistance turned out to be light, a fact which has meant very few casualties to date.

5,000-Yard Advance

As the infantry continued to push into Germany, by H-plus seven hours some elements had moved almost 5,000 yards. Those of us at vantage posts on the ground could watch flight after flight of cargo planes carrying in British and American paratroopers, who jumped behind the German lines to confuse the issue further.

A few Marylanders seen here today were: Tech. 5/G Carl F. Brooks, Baltimore; Pvt. Nevin Croncie, Frederick; Pvt. William T. West, Baltimore; Pvt. John Meredino, Baltimore.

From Bradley back to McCardell

THE BALTIMORE SUN, SUNDAY, APRIL 1, 1945

MARYLANDERS IN GERMANY —
In the following dispatch Mr. McCardell names four Marylanders, of whom three are Baltimoreans.

McCardell Trails Patton's Tanks In Trans-Rhine Dash

By Lee McCardell [Sunpapers War Correspondent]

With the U.S. 3d Army Beyond the Main, March 28 [By Radio — Delayed] — Artillery rolled across the Rhine River pontoon bridge, battalion after battalion. Medium artillery towed by truck. Heavy artillery towed by tractor. Howitzers, Long Toms and ack-ack batteries.

Artillery trains followed the long truck convoys loaded down with ammunition. Behind them came the armored divisions — tanks, halftracks and tank destroyers with their trains of bulldozers, treadway bridges, Bailey bridges, ordnance trucks and ambulances.

They poured into the bridgehead, which the 5th Infantry Division had established on the flat, irrigated farmland east of the river. They fanned out through the fields and small German towns, artillery guns going into position, armored columns dispersing or parking along the narrow dusty roads.

4th Armored Leads

The 4th Armored Division was the first armored outfit to get away. Its combat commands headed southwest, then turned sharply to the northeast below Darmstadt and raced toward the towns of Hanau and Aschaffenburg.

The 6th Armored Division turned north toward Frankfurt. A magnificent road, the German National Autobahn, streaks away across the flats from Darmstadt to Frankfurt. But the armor could not use the superhighway; its long, level straightaways were shooting galleries for the German artillery guarding that approach into Frankfurt.

Every time an American tank showed its turret on the super highway a German 88 or self-propelled gun set its shells literally skipping along the road's surface.

Defenses Among Best

The German ack-ack defenses of Frankfurt are reckoned among the best in the world. They include dual-purpose mobile guns, some of which were brought out along the superhighway and ranged on its long, straight stretches. No tank could stand up against all that.

To complete the obstruction of the superhighway, the Germans blew all overpasses of steel and concrete construction, so that even when the fighter-bombers chased the enemy artillerymen under cover and knocked out some of their guns, the superhighway was barricaded with rubble and debris.

But there was cover for the tanks, excellent cover. Nine thousand acres of forest, mostly pine and cedar, the Frankfurter Stadtwald, covers the flats directly south of the city. The 6th Armored took to this woods and followed its network of trails toward the suburban town of Niederrad, just south of the Main River from Frankfurt.

The Stadtwald encloses the Rhine-Main airdrome, one of the largest in Europe, equipped to handle dirigibles as well as planes. Since the war began this had been a *Luftwaffe* base. Our own air force has pretty well bombed it out of business.

The Germans set fire to the few remaining barracks and buildings concealed in the woods around the airport before the armor got there. But a few damaged planes were still sitting on the field, and the pits in the woods around the field were still stocked with gasoline and oil drums.

With the headquarters group of one armored combat command when we caught up with it in the woods near the airport was Tech. Sergt. Edward Curran, of 1302 Valley street, Baltimore. Curran, who formerly was employed by the Sunpapers business office, was acting as liaison officer for the 15th Tank Battalion.

Boy There From Bel Air

Curran said that another Marylander, a boy named Slingluff from Bel Air, was with his headquarters but we hadn't time to look him up. The armored infantry farther ahead had entered Niederrad and we took off after it.

A few German prisoners had been taken in the woods. Those we saw included a truckload of beardless boys who couldn't have been more than 15 years old. But the woods were alive with Polish, Russian and French slave laborers trucking toward the rear with their bundles and packs of personal belongings.

Niederrad had already hung its white flags and had been captured without opposition. A short time later a four-man delegation rowed across the river from another town and told Major Leon Burnham, of Salt Lake City, the military government officer of the 6th Armored, that their community was ready to surrender.

The spokesman of the group was a Communist about 35 years old. With him was a factory personnel manager, who said that he could speak for the business men of the town and who, incidentally, had been naturalized as a citizen of the United States back in 1898. He still had his papers.

The Communist spokesman said that all the German soldiers in their town had been rounded up and there would be no shooting when the Americans entered. But he had not calculated on a few German stragglers who had drifted into town later and who were blamed for the sniper fire when two American officers subsequently tried to cross the river.

This disposition of the Communist leader to take over the German communities as the American troops approach and then turn over the affairs to the military government officers has occurred in several other instances. They say they are working as Communists but have no connection with the Moscow Government.

Bridge Reported Intact

Meanwhile, an artillery liaison plane pilot had reported to Lieut. Col. Philip H. Pope, of Washington, commanding officer of an armored unit, that one of Frankfurt's nine bridges across the River Main was still intact.

A tank battalion and an armored infantry company already were farther up the river bank, reconnoitering the ruins of a blown railway bridge to determine the feasibility of putting infantry across it into Frankfurt, south of the Main, to take a look at the other bridge still standing.

We followed them through the bombed outskirts of the city. Again the German civilians turned out en masse to wave white handkerchiefs and smile at the American soldiers. When the column halted, the Germans surrounded the tanks and halftracks and tried to talk to the soldiers.

Failed To Destroy Bridge

The column was after the Wilhelmsbruecke, an arched masonry structure connecting Saar Alle on the Sachsenhausen side of the river with Bahnhofplatz in Frankfurt proper. The Germans already had made one effort to blow up the bridge but had not used an explosive charge sufficiently heavy.

Three light tanks started across the bridge. There was another explosion. Over his radio in the lead tank, Lieut. James K. Parks, of Roy, Washington, reported:

"We have just gone over a mine."

But his battalion commanding officer, Lieut. Col. Embry Legrew, of Lexington, Ky., who was watching the tanks from a filling station farther up the street, knew better and told Parks:

"Mines, hell! They are trying to blow the bridge out from under you."

Battle Is Begun

The light tanks backed off. Medium tanks and tank destroyers, which had followed them down to the bridge, began firing across the river.

Armored infantrymen dismounted from the halftracks and started down the Saar Alle, a broad park thoroughfare, toward the bridge. One company got across and the second was on its way when the Germans opened up on the bridge with one of the most intense artillery barrages I have ever seen.

Several of us caught just this side of the bridge ducked into an apartment-house basement. We stayed there for the next two hours while the Germans shelled the bridge with self-propelled guns and ack-ack batteries from the far shore. Armored infantry kept crossing the bridge, running for it in small groups every time the artillery died down.

When our small group of correspondents and photographers came out of the cellar at dusk, the bridge was still too hot for us to cross. The Germans were still pounding it with direct fire and showering it with airburst. A few blocks farther up the street we ducked into another cellar.

"And I wrote a story yesterday saying the war was over," groaned Bob Cromie, of the Chicago *Tribune*.

"Did them guys across the river read it?" asked a soldier in the cellar.

"They must have got some rations, or else they are mad at us," said another.

Shelling Continues

The Germans were shelling Saar Alle and its intersecting streets now. We stayed in our second cellar for about two hours more. Several members of our party stayed there all night. A light tank and an engineer truck parked outside in the street had been hit and set on fire, preventing them from driving their jeeps out.

Yesterday morning we had to reorganize our press party. One of our drivers had been injured and three of our jeeps damaged by shrapnel.

I'll never be able to use my helmet for a bucket again. It has a shrapnel hole in it. Fortunately I was not wearing the helmet when it was plugged.

Fire Kept Up Most Of Night

The Germans kept the bridge and its southern approaches under heavy fire for the better part of the night. Yesterday morning when the 5th Infantry Division started across the bridge, the Germans brought it under fire again, and, waiting for an opportunity to cross, we timed the shells. One came in every five seconds.

Shortly after noon they must have figured they'd discouraged us, for they stopped shooting for a few minutes. More of our infantry dashed across and we followed them. The bridge was still standing, but its deck had been beaten to rubble. We got across all right and then the German artillery started to open up again.

Few Snipers Killed

From what we saw and heard, the enemy resistance wasn't too stiff north of the Main. A few snipers had been killed. Our losses appeared to have been light. Hermann Goering Ufer, which parallels the river's northern bank, was barricaded, as were the streets leading into Bahnhofplatz.

The townsfolk said the *Wehrmacht* troops had withdrawn from the city and the resistance being put up to the American occupation was largely that of Nazi police and SS troops. The 5th Infantry Division was taking over the job of cleaning up the remaining snipers and silencing the guns firing on the bridge.

The town was badly battered from air-raids. On the day before we entered we had the rather novel experience of standing on the opposite bank of the river and listening to the wail of the city's air sirens as our fighter-bombers came in. But thousands of civilians were still living in cellars, and some said they hadn't been above ground for the last three days.

We saw only one other Baltimorean around Frankfurt. He was Private Howard C. Simpson, of 1810 North Caroline street, who is a 50-caliber machine-gunner on an armored infantry halftrack. An infantry company commanded by Lieut. John D. Kennedy, of Baltimore, was among the first troops of the 5th Division to enter Frankfurt. We didn't see him, but a brother officer said he was safe.

In one of the cellars where we "holed up" to get out of the artillery fire we made the acquaintance of Tech. 5/G John Jesse Joseph James Kyranakis, of Garden City, N.Y., a forward artillery observer who deplored the fact that there was no New York correspondent in our party to note his name. John Jesse Joseph James said he used to work for the May Company in Baltimore and on the strength of that claim we pass on his name. He, too, is okay.

CHAPTER 10
SCENES OF MASS MURDER

THE BALTIMORE SUN, SATURDAY, APRIL 7, 1945

McCardell Visits Scene Of Nazi Mass Murder

By Lee McCardell [Sunpapers War Correspondent]

With 4th Armored Division, Germany, April 6 [By Radio] — There on the blood-soaked ground before you lay the bodies of 31 miserable men. Each had a bullet hole in the back of his head. They had been shot three days ago by SS guards, you were told.

You had heard of such things in Nazi Germany. You had heard creditable witnesses describe just such scenes. But now that you were actually confronted with the horror of mass murder, you stared at the bodies and almost doubted your eyes.

"Good God!" you said aloud, "Good God!"

Piled Like Cordwood

Then you walked down around the corner of two barren, weather-beaten, wooden barrack buildings. And there in a wooden shed, piled up like so much cordwood, were the naked bodies of more dead men than you cared to count.

"Good God!" you repeated, "Good God!"

These dead, more horrible in death than any carnage you had ever seen on a battlefield, belonged to German Concentration *Lager* North S-3, on the desolate hills just north of the German Army barracks on the outskirts of the town Ohrdruf, 8 miles south of Gotha.

One Was An American

Until three days ago, when the camp commandant grew uneasy over the approach of Lieut. Gen. George S. Patton's 4th Armored Division, 2,000 prisoners, Germans, Czechs, Serbs, Yugoslavs, Russians, French and Belgians, were held there under a guard of 150 of Hitler's SS men.

One prisoner was an American soldier. He told the other prisoners he was a paratrooper. Some of the others were soldiers. Many were Jews. A few were non-Jewish prisoners. All were males. The youngest was a Jewish boy, 16 years old, who had been in the camp for four years.

The health conditions in the camp were appalling. It was being swept by a typhus epidemic. The deaths from typhus averaged about 30 per day. The prisoners had been dying at that rate for weeks.

The dead were stripped. They were numbered with a black crayon scrawl on their naked skin. They were carried down into the charnel house, that wooden shanty beside the latrine. Here they were stacked like slaughtered pigs and sprinkled with lime.

When the shanty was filled, the SS men backed up a truck and the other prisoners loaded the corpses onto a truck. The truck hauled the bodies out of the camp, to a pit in the woods 2 miles. Here the bodies were burned. The prisoners who survived say three to five thousand had been burned in the pit.

They Shot The 31

The SS guards shot the 31 whose bodies were seen today. They shot each one in the back of the head. They shot the American paratrooper where he lay in his dirty litter.

Fifty-three other prisoners still remained in camp to act as a burial detail. Their first task was to fill in the pit in the woods where the other bodies had been thrown for disposal. Some of the last bodies tossed into the pit had not been completely buried.

But the tanks of the 4th Armored were drawing closer to Ohrdruf every hour. The SS guards were eager to take off. One man in the burial detail hid under a bunk in the barracks. Another ducked off into the woods. Fourteen escaped. Some waited in hiding around the camp and town of Ohrdruf until the American tanks arrived.

Yanks Hesitate To Believe

They told the German interpreters their story. The Americans hesitated to believe it. Major John R. Scotti, of Brooklyn, N.Y., Armored Combat Command surgeon, was sent out to the concentration camp to investigate.

The dead were still there.

"I couldn't believe it even when I saw it," Major Scotti said. "I couldn't believe that I was there looking at such things."

Other prisoners who had escaped drifted back into camp. They told Major Scotti and an interpreter that the horror under their eyes was only part of the story. Other prisoners had been flogged to death and shot, so many that they couldn't remember the number. Others had disappeared in small groups from time to time.

"Ha! You Like It?"

The prisoners said that the camp had several methods of torture. On one occasion the officials had made them stand at attention continuously for 24 hours. At the end of the stretch one of them remarked:

"Ha! You like it, yes? You may stand at attention ten hours longer."

On days when small groups of prisoners were selected for the mysterious mission described by the guards as "labor in underground shelters" the commandant lined up the entire population of internees held in "protective custody" under the Nazi law.

Then he lighted a cigar, strode up and down before the assembled prisoners, puffing the cigar violently. He looked them over, and finally stopped before one group.

"Those"

He would take the cigar out of his mouth and flick ashes at the group he had selected and say:

"Those."

The prisoners in these groups were taken away. None who remained knew what happened to them. "Those" selected for "labor in underground shelters" never returned to Concentration Lager North S-3.

When first I head of the camp I put it down as another atrocity story, probably true. Today I went out to the camp with a small group of other newspaper correspondents, Col. Hayden A. Sears, of Boston, 4th Armored Division combat commander and Major Scotti.

THE BALTIMORE SUN, THURSDAY, APRIL 12, 1945

Fugitives Tell Of Slaughter Of Jews In Camp

By Lee McCardell [Sunpapers War Correspondent]

With an American Infantry Division near Erfurt, April 11 [By Radio] — It was an old story, one you have read and heard many times before. But here in the stuffy little parlor of the house in the German village where the four men told it over again, you listened with new interest. They were telling their own story, not one they had heard.

"I was four months in a German concentration camp at Auschwitz in Silesia," said a stubby little gray-haired Jew, "and 500,000 Hungarian Jews were brought in while I was there. In two months 400,000 were killed."

Astonished At Question

How did he know?

He seemed astonished at the questions.

"Have you not heard about these things in America?" he asked.

Yes, we have heard it second hand, and in general terms. How did you know 400,000 had been killed?

"They kept very careful records, the Germans at the camp," he said. "And then we saw them taken away to be killed in the gas chamber of four crematories. Every day 10,000 or 12,000."

Outside the parlor windows the April sunshine was soft and warm on the blossoming apple trees. On a high-pitched roof farther up the village street a stork stood like a rigid sentinel on one leg above his nest. The fields around the village were velvet green with winter wheat.

Tells About Ohrdruf

"At Ohrdruf," said the little Jew, "3,400 died within four months. Most of them were beaten, starved and worked to death."

Yes, you knew about Ohrdruf. You'd been there. You'd seen the bodies, or what was left of the bodies. The four men in the parlor had been prisoners at Ohrdruf. They'd been marched away with other prisoners, in groups of 100, each group guarded by four SS men when the American tanks captured the neighboring town of Gotha.

The group with which the four men in the parlor had marched away had been the last group to leave the Ohrdruf camp. In the darkness of a woods where they'd been bivouacked their first night out of camp the four escaped. They had been recaptured the next day by *Volkssturm* troops, but the officer in command had let them go.

The four fugitives lost their way, walked back into the German lines, were recaptured a second time and thrown into a cellar in the village of Neudietendorf, about 5 miles southwest of Erfurt. Here the American troops found them last night and set them free,

The Americans fed them, gave them soap with which to wash, and lent them razors with which to shave. The soldiers took them into an abandoned German house and told them to throw away the filthy rags of their prison garb and dress themselves in any decent civilian clothes they could find.

Prison Numbers Tattooed

One found a gray homespun suit and a pair of high, black leather boots. Another found a bright plaid silk necktie. But their shaved heads still marked them as prisoners. And on their right forearms each still wore his blue tattooed prison number.

The first of the four to tell his story was a little gray-haired Jew, Dr. Bela Fabian, aged 56, of Budapest, a novelist and former president of the Hungarian Independent Democratic party.

Listening to the stories of the four Jews, you couldn't help but wonder again at the complacency of the average German now when you ask him about racial persecution under Hitler's regime.

The average German says he knows nothing about it and that he is not aware of any slave laborer having been mistreated.

Suggests Lack Of Curiosity

Why did the average German suppose the slave-labor camps were enclosed by barbed wire, and with SS guards at the gates? What made him think the people were happy, or at least content, in those filthy, wretched, wooden barracks?

Did no questions ever arise in his mind? Was he completely without curiosity, without concern?

Dr. Fabian said that he was a personal friend of United States Congressman Sol Bloom, and that during a visit to the United States five years ago had lunched with President Roosevelt.

Dr. Fabian served in the last World War as a soldier in the Hungarian Army, was taken prisoner and sent to Vladivostok. Two of several novels he wrote after the war — "Six Horses and Forty Men" and "One Thousand Men Without Women" — were based on his experiences as a prisoner of war.

Fabian speaks five languages — Russian, Hungarian, French, German and English — and he apologized for his English.

He said he hadn't any opportunity to use it during the last few years. Lieut. Theodore Gutman, of Los Angeles, staff officer of an American infantry division, helped him out from time to time as interpreter.

Arrested 10 Months Ago

Three years ago the Germans ordered Fabian's Independent Democratic party dissolved. Ten months ago he was arrested on charges of being a Jew. He was sent to Auschwitz concentration camp in Silesia, through which, he says 5,000,000 Poles, Hungarian and Russian Jews have passed as prisoners.

His tattooed prison number at Auschwitz was B-12305 (later at Ohrdruf he became number 102-921). Last October 26 he was moved from Auschwitz to another prison camp at Oranienburg, near Berlin. From there he was sent to Ohrdruf.

The officer in command of the Auschwitz camp stood on a ramp where the trainloads of incoming Jews arrived at the camp and by a simple gesture of his thumb indicated those who were to be gassed and those who were to be held as slave laborers.

Lied About Age To Save Life

"We were asked out age," said Dr. Fabiam. "I lied about mine and said I was 46. I lied because I knew that anyone over the age of 50 would be sent to the gas chamber immediately.

"I was passed into the camp, but a close friend who was by my side, Stephen Farkas, Hungarian publisher, did not know about this distinction. He gave his correct age and they took him away. I never saw him again.

"Anyone who was under 50, but didn't look strong and healthy enough to work, also was sent to the gas chamber. The *Haupsturmführer* picked over the youngest ones, took his choice, made the necessary gesture with his thumb and that was the end of it.

"Of the 150 children sent to the camp, all but 50, who were kept as runners, messengers and servants, were sent to the gas chamber without questions. All young mothers who refused to leave their children were gassed. The strong and healthy young ones and the good-looking women, including mothers willing to abandon their children, were kept.

Saw 1,000 Boys Taken Away

"On one occasion I saw 1,000 Jewish boys, 14 and 15 years old, loaded onto trucks and taken to the gas chamber and crematory. They knew where they were being taken and that this was the end. Some of them began to weep like little children.

"One of the boys, the son of a Hungarian lawyer named Wienberger, stood up in his truck and made a speech, telling the others, 'Brothers, we should not cry. We are dying for the betterment of mankind.'"

Another of the four Jews in the parlor told his story. He was Desidere Kohlmann, aged 34, of Bratislava, a professional philatelist — a stamp dealer.

Wife And Son Taken

Kohlmann was arrested with his wife and their 6-year-old son. They arrived by train at Auschwitz concentration camp on September 19, 1942.

"That same night my wife and son were taken away and sent to the crematory," Kohlmann said. "There were about 1,000 Jews on the train which took us to Auschwitz. Of these, 260 men and 72 women were sent to the gas chamber as soon as they got off. I learned from the clerks in the prison office later that by the end of November, 1942, not one woman in our original party remained alive."

Another of the four Jews with whom we talked, Sam Ezratty, aged, 28, was a graduate pharmacist and medical student living in Salonika when he was arrested on May 16, 1943.

45,000 From Salonika

Ezratty was one of 45,000 Jews, mostly Spanish, constituting Salonika's Jewish community, the largest in Greece. Of these he said he did not know of more than 50 or 60 still alive. The majority he believed had been gassed as soon as they fell ill or became too sick to work. That was prison-camp routine.

The fourth man in the group was Meyer Heinz, aged 22, a Hungarian violinist who had been playing in Berlin before he was arrested. He described the reception of the Jewish internees at Auschwitz.

"The people were pulled out of the cars onto a ramp as soon as the train arrived. All their baggage and personal belongings were taken from them and placed in special enclosures where the bags were broken open and the contents distributed in bins — one for women's dresses, one for children's clothes, one for food and so forth.

Kept Glasses, Belts And Shoes

"The inmates were herded into another enclosure where they were stripped and their heads were shaved. They were also deloused so to speak, and given striped prison uniforms. The only personal belongings they were permitted to carry into the prison with them were eyeglasses, belts and shoes."

The three younger men of the group said it was remarkable that Fabian, considering his age, had survived the rigors of work at the camp at Ohrdruf, where the prisoners had been beaten, staved and worked in the underground tunnels until they died from exhaustion or became so weak from disease and malnutrition that their SS guards shot them and burned their bodies.

"I wasn't worked so hard as some of the others because I was able to speak so many languages which were useful to the guards in controlling their prisoners," Fabian said.

Criminal Superior To Guards

"A few of the prisoners with whom we worked were German criminals. The man with whom I worked was a murderer but a very superior man to the SS guards.

"It is impossible to describe the conditions under which we lived and worked. They were incredible. I have seen men, strong as steel, broken down completely within six weeks after they arrived."

Dr. Fabian said he had had no word from friends or relatives in Hungary since his arrest ten months ago. He was particularly concerned about his wife, who had remained in Budapest when he was arrested.

He implored us to try to pass on a plea to Representative Bloom to make some inquiry about his wife through Russian authorities.

THE BALTIMORE SUN, MONDAY, APRIL 30, 1945

GERMANS SEE JEWS' BURIAL – All Townsfolk Compelled To Witness Mass Funeral

By Lee McCardell [Sunpapers War Correspondent]

Neunburg, Bavaria, April 29 [By Radio] — The little men of Neunburg, who say they did not know what went on in the Nazi concentration camps, know now. So do the women and older children of Neunburg.

By an order of an American Army Corps commander they served as pallbearers today at a mass funeral of 160 Jews, who, suffering from slow starvation, had been shot and killed by the SS guards one week ago in a woods overlooking Neunburg.

Proclamation Read In German

Every man, woman and child above the age of 5 in Neunburg who was able to walk attended the funeral by military order. They stood in the cemetery with the mutilated and emaciated bodies of 160 murdered Jews lying in front of them in open coffins.

They listened to the statement, in German, read over the loud-speaker. They were told:

"You have been ordered here to look upon this indisputable, this gruesome evidence of barbarity, and to be solemnly told that the people of the world hold the Germans responsible for this horrible crime that has resulted in the death of these innocent men.

Accuses German People

"The German people, all of you, conspired to tear these wretched victims from their homes and families — from their wives, children and other dear ones in foreign lands. You conspired to transport them here to work as your slaves in your factories, your farms and your homes.

"None among you raised his voice or arm in protest.

"You were content to profit by their blood and sweat and misery."

Many of the Germans standing in the little cemetery, among the marble monuments and well-tended burial plots of their own dead, had heard the indictment before. At least they had hear it indirectly when American soldiers, aghast at the murder of the Jews in the woods above town, had asked them: "Why? Why?"

Answer Always Same

All over Germany that question is asked every day by the Americans. Almost always the answer is the same;

"I don't know anything about it. I am only a little man."

But the little men of Neunburg know about it now. The women and children know about it. And to make sure that there was no misunderstanding they were required to file past the open coffins of the 160 murdered men when they left the cemetery.

Neunburg is a country town with a normal population of about 3,000. Some 1,200 people evacuated from other parts of Germany also are living there now. The town lies in a pretty green valley dotted with lakes and surrounded by wooded hills, 60 miles east of Nuernberg.

A week ago a column of prisoners being moved eastward under SS Guard from Buchenwald and Flossenberg concentration camps halted on a road about a half mile west of Neunburg. The 160 half-famished prisoners, reduced to skin and bones, were shot and killed there.

Many others had been shot and killed along the route of the march. Their bodies were found by American troops which entered Neunburg last Monday. Later the Americans were told about a wholesale shooting west of the town. On the crest of the hill from which the road widens down into Neunburg they found the 160 bodies.

They were the bodies of Polish, Hungarian, Romanian and Yugoslavian Jews. They had been hastily buried in two pits — or rather the bodies had been dumped into two pits like so much garbage, and covered with earth.

Ordered To Remove Bodies

The Neunburg folks were ordered to open the graves and remove the bodies. The bodies were ghastly to behold but no different than those of other SS victims found at Buchenwald, Ohrdruf and other German prison camps. All must have been close to death from hunger before they were killed.

Most of them had been shot, others appeared to have been brained by clubs or rifle butts. Some had their eyes gouged out. They were dressed in the filthy rags of striped prison garb and broken wooden-soled shoes. A few were barefoot.

Dirty pots and pans from which they had been fed had been tossed into the pits with them. The ground where they had been shot down was still gory from their wounds. The empty shells of the cartridges, which had killed them, still lay among the gore.

Ordered By Corps Commander

An American Army Corps commander ordered the 160 bodies reburied decently by the townsfolk of Neunburg and directed that the entire town should attend the funeral services to be conducted by United States Army chaplains. The hour for the funeral was set at 10 o'clock this morning.

At 8 o'clock this morning every man, woman and child of Neunburg, with the exception of the toddlers and a few aged, infirm and ill adults, lined the main streets. Many of the children were under five and one mother carried a-year-old baby in her arms.

The 160 rough wooden coffins built by village carpenters, had been stacked in the fork of the crossroad just west of the town.

Strips of mourning black crepe had been attached to the white flags of surrender hanging from the upstairs windows of most of the houses in the town.

Liberated Laborers On Street

A group of about 100 liberated slave laborers and surviving stragglers of the ill-fated march from the prison camps — it was from these stragglers that the Americans got the first-hand eyewitness account of the mass shooting — were also in the street.

They marched up the hill to the pine woods where the exhumed bodies lay on the floor of the forest and held Jewish funeral rites there.

Then the male inhabitants of the village started up the hill, each group of four men carrying an empty coffin from the pile at the crossroad. They carried them in the old-fashioned way on two sticks, one fore and one aft, and two men on either side.

Women, Children Carry Some

The burgomeister, who had arranged the details, had hoped to have at least 700 men to serve as pallbearers, but there were not that many men in the village. About 50 of the coffins were carried by women and half-grown boys and girls.

They walked up the road in single file, turned off in to the pines and there the Jewish men of the group who had held the service were waiting to lift the corpses into the coffins. Some of the bodies were too long for the boxes. Their gruesome, mutilated heads and mouths gaping, hung over the ends of the coffins.

The Germans accepted the task stoically. Several of the women faltered and wept and one fainted with hysteria, but the other struggled along with set faces.

Put Pocketbooks In Coffins

Some had come up to the pine woods carrying umbrellas and pocketbooks. Now they had their hands full with the weight of the body in the coffin they carried. They tucked their pocketbooks and umbrellas in the coffins beside the dead and took to the stick.

"It's pretty tough on the women" remarked one American who watched the cortege move out of the pines.

"It was tougher on the people in the woods — the ones they are carrying out," replied another.

The bodies were heavy for the boys and girls. It took six to ten to carry a coffin. The road winding down the hill to the village was slippery and muddy and the women pallbearers worked in relays, spelling each other along the way back into town.

Column More Than Mile Long

The funeral procession stretched out for more than a mile. When the head of the column passed under the arched way of Neunburg's ancient Rathaus, the last in line were just leaving the crest of the hill, the pine woods which look down on the little town's tiled roofs and vinegar cruet church steeple.

The Neunburgers not needed as pallbearers packed the sidewalks of the village main street, looking at each body in its open coffin as it was carried past. The American soldiers watched them too. Some of the Germans carrying the coffins plainly felt humiliated but most of them bore up proudly.

Neunburg is a Catholic town. The cemetery of its small Lutheran church was not large enough to provide space for the burial of all these dead.

Three Common Graves

So three large common graves had to be dug in the Catholic cemetery at the eastern edge of the town. The bodies of about 40 other SS victims, picked up along the roads around Neunburg, already had been placed in one of these graves.

The Neunburg Catholic padre, a tall, dignified man, was among the townsfolk who watched the funeral procession. He strode along the street slowly, gravely and sadly, looking at each body as it passed but he took no part in the services at his graveyard.

They were conducted by Capt. Barnabas E. McAlarney, of Chicago, Catholic chaplain of a tank destroyer group and Capt. Dean W. Geary, Altoona, Pa., Baptist chaplain of a Negro ordnance battalion. But before the service proper, a statement, explaining the purpose of the ceremony, was read to the Germans over the loudspeaker.

Due To "Wretched Treatment"

"You have been ordered to attend this funeral today for a definite purpose," the statement began. "Look upon the mutilated, broken and bloody bodies.

"They are bodies that have been starved for food.

"They are bodies carrying the marks of cruel disease brought about by the wretched treatment they have suffered in your own land.

"They are bodies that have been so brutally beaten and violated that they are scarcely recognizable as human beings.

Committed No Crimes

"The men who lived in these bodies had committed no crimes. They were weak, helpless and indefensible. They have been slaughtered for no reason justifiable in the eyes of God or man.

"We condemn Adolf Hitler and the foul assassins by whom he has been surrounded for ordering these things done.

"May the memory of these tragic dead rest heavily upon the conscience of every German so long as each of you shall live."

Father McAlarney prayed and made the sign of the cross over the silent throng standing in the graveyard before him. He recited the Lord's Prayer and Hail Mary. Captain Geary read the Twenty-third Psalm and offered another prayer.

Survivor Makes Speech

Benjamin Kraywanowski, a Polish Jew among those who survived the unhappy march of the prisoners and whose experiences started in the infamous Nazi prison camp at Auschwitz, made a short impassioned speech in German to the people of Neunburg.

"These," he said, "were those of but one massacre. Thousands of others have been killed. Germans can no longer dismiss these horrors as propaganda."

The people in the graveyard listened without any show of emotion as far as I could see. The small children, too small to understand the Pole's speech, peeked timidly into the open coffins ringed around the cemetery, and examined the dead curiously. Far back in the cemetery, a middle-aged German, his right leg off at the knee, supported himself on two canes, glowering at the American soldiers who stood around him.

Many Turn Heads Away

When the ceremony was over the people of Neunburg lined up in single file and walked past the open coffins. Many were inclined to turn their heads away. The women and children went home; the men stayed behind to help bury the dead.

One of those who survived the march was Marcel Cadet, aged 34, an English-speaking Frenchman arrested as a political prisoner in Paris four years ago after serving in the French Army. He has been in Nazi concentration camps along the Czechoslovakian boarder.

He said many who began the march were shot by SS guards on the slightest provocation. Another said one prisoner was left for dead every ten yards of the road from Flossenberg. The original group to which Neunburg's dead belonged was estimated to have numbered 11,000, of whom only about 6,000 are known to be alive now.

Tells About March

"On the morning of April 8, we were told, we would leave Buchenwald, because the Americans were coming close," Cadet said in describing his experiences on the march.

"None of the men in our block of barracks showed any signs of happiness at leaving the camp. They had heard tales of horror about other prisoners who had been forced to evacuate their camps.

"But the SS men cleared the camp with clubs, rifles and rubber truncheons. They drove us all into the yard and I heard shooting and saw some of the men go down. We had been given only a cup of ersatz coffee and the men were weak from hunger.

"As we marched through the gates the SS men had dumped sacks of corn on the ground and each man was supposed to stuff his pockets full. But as the column approached the grain the guards speeded up the column so that it was impossible to secure food.

50 Beaten To Death

"The killing started again outside the gates of the camp. I saw 50 men beaten to death by the guards. All guards were SS troops, and there was a guard along the column about every five yards equipped with a rifle and a heavy club."

Cadet's column marched about 9½ miles to Weimar where the men were herded into trains.

"During the trek about 100 men were shot," Cadet said. "When we reached Weimar we lived in an agony of fear. Eighty-five men were crowded into each car. Each man was issued 1½ pounds of bread and 100 grams of margarine for a two-day ration. No one in the train knew the destination. On the train each man was given a slice of bread with a small piece of sausage and water. The fourth day there was a soup made of water and animal fodder."

400 Or More Die Of Hunger

"On the fifth day," said Cadet, the train arrived at Dachau. Many had died from hunger, maybe four or five hundred. In the station the SS guards separated the invalids who couldn't march or work, from the stronger of the men. We never saw the sick again.

"There were about 4,000 of us who left the station for an unknown place. We were followed closely by another column of 5,000. We started up a hill and before the head of our ranks had reached the top the shooting started again. About 100 people were killed and it became worse as we went on.

Barred From Aiding Others

"At night we slept in rain-soaked fields with the horror of the day in our minds. When my column reached the

Flossenberg camp there were about 2,000 of us left.

"During the march, if we tried to help our comrades, the SS guard would push us away and shoot our friends. The guards never aimed and sometimes had to shoot a man two or three times before he died. They seemed to do it with pleasure. They shot when a man stopped to tie his shoe laces and when another tried to pick up grass to eat.

"I saw my comrades pile as many as ten high. Some Poles were elected to follow along in the back of the column and dig hasty graves."

Remnants of the column arrived at Flossenberg April 15. Five days later the prison grapevine reported American troops approaching.

So Happy They Cried

"Everybody was so happy we cried," related Cadet. "It wasn't until later in the day that we received the news we would evacuate the camp.

"Again, with newcomers from Flossenberg making about 5,000 of us, we started off. Five minutes outside the camp the shooting started again. All the way we heard it and the men were dropping every ten yards.

"When the day was done the SS guards would come to us and ask us for razor blades, underwear and soap and then they would shoot us during the day."

American Planes Seen

On the fourth day of the march, American Cub planes were seen in the air.

"Then we saw four vehicles coming toward us, and your tanks," said Cadet. "There was one cry: 'Here come the Americans.' We were so happy to see the white stars on your cars that we wept."

The SS guards in the rear turned the automatic weapons into the weary prisoners and killed 200 persons outright in a desperate effort to effect a roadblock of human bodies. The tanks opened fire on the Germans as they ran into the woods, killing more than 100.

McCARDELL PICTURES OF A BURIAL

Pictures on this page were made by Lee McCardell, Sunpapers' War Correspondent, at Neunburg, Bavaria, April 29, to illustrate a dispatch, carried in The Sun, and reading, in part: "By an order of an American Army corps commander they (citizens) served as pallbearers today at a mass funeral of 160 Jews, who . . . had been shot and killed by the SS Guards one week ago . . . Every man, woman and child above the age of 5 attended the funeral. They stood in the cemetery with the mutilated and emaciated bodies . . . lying in front of them in open coffins . . . Over the loudspeaker they were told: 'You have been ordered here to look upon the gruesome evidence of barbarity . . . .'"

PALLBEARERS — People of Neunburg were required to file past bodies of those cruelly slain (above) ADX-726-BS and were forced to serve as pallbearers (right). Bodies had been put by SS in shallow pit. Germans were required to make coffins. ADX-727-BS

PROCESSION — Up the road to the cemetery, where there were funeral services attended by Americans as well as by all who lived in the town. The coffins had been hastily made and many were too short though few were too narrow, for the bodies of men nearly starved. Most had been killed by bullets. ABA-123-BS

MASS FUNERAL — Polish Jews, slain by German SS troopers, lie in open caskets in the town cemetery of Neunburg, where burial services were held at the direction of American Army officers. ADX-657-BS

TO GRAVE — A scene inside the churchyard at the funeral. Town ordered by American military authorities to attend funeral and provide pallbearers. ABA-118-BS

IN TOWN'S CATHOLIC CEMETERY — Listening to the funeral service. Note the children; none over 5 was excused. It was the Army's intention that no person in Neunburg should be left in doubt that Germans had committed crimes of a sort to cause horror all over the world and to justify harsh treatment of the conquered nation by the occupying authorities. ABA-107-BS

CHAPTER 11

TWO ARMIES MEET ON THE ELBE

From McCardell Back to Bradley

THE BALTIMORE SUN, SUNDAY, APRIL 15, 1945

Bradley Rides Hell On Wheels

By Holbrook Bradley [Sunpapers War Correspondent]

With the U.S. 2d Armored Division.

By now old "Hell on Wheels" may be in Berlin. But first the famed 2d Armored Division, spearheading element of General William H. Simpson's 9th Army armor, had to break out of the Rhine bridgehead. Its first 100-mile plunge, carrying it nearly to the industrial city of Bielefeld, may have been the toughest going of its race across Germany. Here's how that operation went:

The first indication that the American 9th Army had achieved an early bridgehead breakthrough came after the 2d Armored moved off from lines northeast of Dorsten. The initial German defenses amounted to some show of ground troop strength supported by an occasional emplaced dual-purpose 88 and a few tanks which strove vainly to contain the Americans.

Montgomery's Men Loose

To the north, General Montgomery's troops of the 2d British Army already had cracked the light Nazi opposition. Muenster was captured after the Churchills pushed on to seize the advantage gained with the initial breaching of the German lines.

With the northern flank supported by the British during the early stages of the attack, the 2d Armored jumped off against the enemy, who proved unable to stand even the first blows of the attack.

As the drive gained strength and momentum, it became more and more evident that Brig. Gen. Isaac D. White's tanks had made a complete breakout from the Rhine bridgehead rather than merely a strong advance.

For a few hours elements of Combat Command A, directed by Brig. Gen. J. H. Collier, of Dallas, were held up at the Dortmund-Ems Canal, where the Germans had blown a bridge serving as the only crossing in that area. The leading reconnaissance cars in advance of the main force tore down the straight roads over the flat, level country in an attempt to forestall such a move, but arrived a half hour too late.

While the engineers threw a bridge across the short stretch of water, armored elements of Combat Command A formed behind the canal ready to strike out immediately as soon as the last pontoon was in place, and then drive on east into Germany. At the same time Combat Command B was slashing its way toward Berlin along the southern flank, but early indications were that the going was a bit rougher.

The first reconnaissance cars were already across the canal when we arrived at the crossing site. Doughboys stood by ready to fill in the ruts as the vehicles rolled, for the soft banks cave easily and might have caused a further holdup if not watched. Overhead Thunderbolts working with the command crossed and recrossed each other's trails as they patrolled the skies against any action of the *Luftwaffe*, or stood on call for strafing or bombing missions against ground targets.

Invitation To Ride Accepted

A medium Sherman tank, commanded by Lieut. Philip H. Reisler, of Indianapolis, was about to move onto the bridge and, at an offer of a ride, we climbed in.

The others in the crew were Tech. 5/G John J. Delsignore, Glenn Falls, N.Y., gunner; Private A. Geindel, Hartford, Conn., driver, and Private Wallace T. Ward, Bowling Green, Fla., assistant driver.

There was little sign of action ahead as we bowled along behind a dozen vehicles, which were sending clouds of dust streaming into the warm spring evening. By 6 P.M. the canal was more than a mile behind us and there had been few signs that the Germans were going to make any attempt to stop us. Once or twice a handful of prisoners filtered back, mostly small groups of third-rate troops who made little attempt to put up a fight.

As the leading elements began to roll out over the countryside, Col. William M. Stokes, of Lynchburg, Va., task force commander, called a temporary halt to organize his group, made up of elements of reconnaissance vehicles, tanks, artillery and infantry. By now the prisoner-of-war count was well over 100 and more were filtering back all the time.

The constant dull rumble of idling tank motors reverberated through the twilight as the column waited to straighten out, and take a breathing spell before moving on. What the night's objective was had not filtered back down to the tank crews.

Almost at last light there was a momentary bit of excitement as a Jerry jet-propelled plane winged in low over the treetops, obviously reconnoitering our position, then zoomed up into the clouds chased by anti-aircraft and 50-caliber machine-gun slugs.

Moving In Moonlight

It was 10 P.M. when Combat Command A again ground into high gear and rolled off again under the brilliant light of a full moon. From the assistant driver's seat it was possible to watch mile after mile of the German countryside roll by, almost without a shot being fired. Once or twice we could hear machine-gun fire somewhere up ahead and see tracers bouncing from the group, then the tanks ground on again and a couple more prisoners filtered back.

Shortly before midnight CCA rolled up to a small village which commanders believed might be a trouble spot. To right and left of us tanks deployed through fields, stringing out in line, then advancing slowly through grain, firing on the run with both 75-mm. guns and coaxial machine guns.

In the light of the bright moon it was possible to watch the fight from what was literally a front-row seat. A few shots were sent back our way and then the first tanks were moving on through and stepping up speed again as they broke into the open. From then until dawn it was a steady drive forward, covering mile after mile of ground in what had become a spearhead thrust.

The *Luftwaffe* was out early as we rolled into the outskirts of Drensteinfurt just after 6 in the morning. A lone ME-109 slipped down through clouds, took a quick look and then, following the usual tactics, headed upstairs again as our anti-aircraft batteries went to work. Most of us wondered if that first visit would be followed by more but we didn't particularly worry, as by now Goering had his hands full attempting to spread the thin remnants of his air force over all the Allied fronts.

Using the same tactics followed during the attack of the night before, the tanks spread out through fields west of the town, the artillery pulling in behind the forward elements and reconnaissance units already probing the main avenues of approach.

First-wave tanks began slowly moving up to the edge of Drensteinfurt shortly after 7, firing as they went, carrying doughboys up to the dismount point, where the infantrymen clambered down and went on in afoot. As we ground to a halt there was a sudden, sharp report of mortars bursting in the same field and we could see that three or four riflemen had been hit ahead of us.

The medics were on their way forward to take care of the wounded when the first prisoners started climbing out of ditches at the edge of the first row of buildings and came forward with hands over heads, dazed by the heavy artillery pounding and apparently wondering how the Americans had come so far through their lines.

Buildings were burning throughout the town by now and every house visible had a white flag or some makeshift flying from a staff or window as the civilians woke to find conquerors at their doorsteps. Some came running across the fields, surrender flags in hand, others hid in cellars or stood timidly behind windows or closed doors, apparently wondering if the Yanks would treat them as their own Wehrmacht had treated the conquered from Poland to France.

The fight for Drensteinfurt was brief. Doughboys and tanks working as a team flushed Krauts from ditches, woods and buildings, the riflemen covering the ground if there was question whether all the foe had come out, then tanks moving in fast to support them. By noon the building area had been secured and a couple of hundred prisoners were on the way back to camps.

Our vehicles had made more than 60 miles since the takeoff and the drivers took time out now while fuel trucks came alongside to dump can after can of gasoline into their tanks. We backed into a yard across from which were three Kraut soldiers, two dead and one who lay dying, his brains spilled over the sidewalk. Although most of the Germans encountered had showed little desire to fight us, there were in a few instances diehards who had given their lives for the Fatherland and Nazism.

Slave Laborers Set Free

It once looked as if we'd bagged additional prisoners when four soldiers came across the fields toward us, but soon we saw that they were Allied POW's, French and Russians who had been held as slave labor by the Germans. The Frenchmen came running up to us in a wild frenzy of joy, and when they found we were Americans it was impossible to get away from their handshaking and pats on the back. One little Frenchmen, who had been given a couple of cigarettes, did a jig in the street from pure happiness that set us all to roaring. The German civilians who lined the street as our tanks pulled out seemed almost apathetic to the whole scene. Some tried to appear friendly, waving, smiling and even cheering, but for the most part they stood in shops or doorways as if they failed to comprehend what had happened or were too dull to gather the full meaning of the fact that Americans had driven so far.

Meeting More White Flags

Then the column began to roll again and the push was simply one of passing through small village after village where white flags were broken out almost as we reached them. And as the column drove on mile after mile into Germany the roads became lined with straggling groups of Frenchmen, Russians, Poles and others who apparently gathered the meaning of the advancing armor and simply walked away from Germans who had been their masters, in some cases for five years.

There were few German soldiers now. Once in a while we bumped into small groups in towns or villages, but they failed even to make a show of fighting and were herded along with those from friendly nations about to be liberated. Some Germans attempted to flee on bicycles or afoot. Crumpled bodies along the roadside told what happened to them. Shortly after 3.30 the leading tanks' CCA rolled into Ennigerloh, where the whole town turned out waving white flags, lining sidewalks as we moved through. One thing was so forced it was obvious: many aged men and even some women held youngsters in their arms, who were made to wave white flags in an appeal to the American sense of decency. Hell on Wheels hit the highroad outside the town only a couple of minutes after the first Sherman had entered its outskirts and moved on to the main line railway, where a freight train stood on the tracks, steam still up. So fast was our advance now that Germans were no longer able to blow bridges in front of us, and we coasted under this one with the speed of greased lighting to find the command forming up in fields to make plans for the forthcoming attack farther into the Reich. Artillery had pulled ahead and already was sending round after round along Hitler's Reichsautobahn, which stretched off into the distance below us.

Special Task Force Formed

Although it then was 4.45 in the afternoon, the colonel and his staff had decided to form a special task force to be under command of Major C. J. Warren, of Lancaster, Pa., and to consist of one company of tanks, a battery of 155-mm's and a company of doughboys. The objective of this force was to secure the Hitler highway to Teuto-burgerwald Pas, some 25 miles to the eastward.

The infantry had just pulled aboard when our tank took off about the middle of the force, which then was rolling downhill and up onto the *autobahn*. As we hit the wide, four-lane strip, reminiscent of Maryland's Ritchie highway, there were road signs which indicated Berlin was slightly less than 230 miles away.

From the moment we hit the highway it was apparent that the Germans were unaware that any Americans were within 50 miles. For the first time the civilians had no flags out. They stood in their tracks, eyes open wide in astonishment as we clipped along. Once an ME-109 came in behind us, apparently thinking he was following a Panzer column, but he veered off in a frenzied scramble when tanks and doughboys began to spray lead.

By 7.45 we were more than 10 miles along the highway, moving as fast as the column could do. Off to the left we passed the town of Olde, which was bypassed in our run to close the gap. As we came to an overpass a Jerry halftrack rolled by unconcernedly, then stepped into a frenzied burst of speed as we opened up. A few miles farther along two German soldiers stood watching us from a bridge overhead, then realized we were enemies and started to run. They ran too late, for the machine gun of one of the lead vehicles cut them down before they could make the edge of the bridge. Once a German staff car came down a left-hand side road, oblivious to the approaching column of American tanks. Too late the driver realized what had happened, for our driver turned the tank and our gunner sent a spray of tracers crashing through the windshield of the German vehicle, lighting up the inside of the car and sending it careening into a cement abutment.

Then, as darkness fell in a hurry, we pulled off into an assembly point on the side of the highway to form in defensive position for the night. The first tank had just pulled onto dirt when there was a loud report followed by a blinding flash. A German bazooka team had attempted to knock out the tank but was unsuccessful. A few seconds later a platoon of doughboys flushed the wood and knocked off the Krauts. CCA holed up for the night more than 100 miles east of the Rhine and 25 miles along the road to Berlin.

THE BALTIMORE SUN, TUESDAY, APRIL 17, 1945

Struggle Fierce Across Elbe

By Holbrook Bradley [Sunpapers War Correspondent]

Gutergluck, Germany, April 15 — [By Radio — Delayed] — Doughboys and tankers this afternoon battled their way into this small hamlet 4 miles east of the Elbe River against some of the toughest resistance met since the armored forces broke though the enemy Rhine defenses two weeks ago.

After more than 24 hours of action across the river, elements of the 2d Armored Division's Combat Command Roger, operating with the 329th Infantry Regiment of the 83d Division, had ground slowly forward to enlarge the bridgehead, seized initially Friday, to an area slightly more than 4 miles in depth.

Resistance At New Peak

Enemy resistance, which made its first appearance in strength in many weeks shortly after elements of the 2d Armored's infantry first established a bridgehead over the Elbe Thursday night at Magdeburg, has continued to be heavy in most sectors of the present bridgehead to the southeast where a number of SS and Hitler youth troops have been encountered.

Indications that the 9th Army has bumped into something other than the usual small, isolated pockets of resistance came early Friday morning when the German artillery first zeroed in on the Magdeburg bridge site to knock out pontoons, cause casualties and combined enemy armor and infantry then counterattacked a number of times, inflicting heavy casualties among the armored infantrymen already far ashore.

Pontoons Thrown Across

Later the same day, riflemen of the 329th Infantry, commanded by Col. E. B. Crabill, Galax, Va., succeeded in securing a bridgehead some miles to the south and by 6 o'clock Saturday morning, engineers had thrown a pontoon bridge over the river, enabling tanks, tank destroyers and other vehicles to make the crossing.

Wheeling south from a reserve position near Magdeburg, the Hell on Wheels Division's Combat Commander Roger sped to the 83d Division's area to put a reconnaissance platoon across before 11 o'clock that morning.

Three hours later, Lieut. Col. Russell W. Jenna, Macomb, Ill., commander of Combat Command Roger, had forward elements into contact with the enemy at a point near Gödnitz, a couple of miles north along the river.

4 Square Miles Taken

In the action that followed their assault crossing of the Elbe, 329th infantrymen pushed slowly but steadily forward to take more than 4 square miles of ground in the first 24 hours, despite four heavy counterattacks by Nazi infantry and armor supported by more than usual artillery fire.

A long line of supply vehicles was sending up a huge cloud of white, powdery dust as we drove to the bridge site yesterday afternoon after bucking convoys more than two hours. MP's on duty held us up momentarily while guards marched a couple dozen prisoners back to cages, then waved us on over the swirling, muddy waters of the Elbe.

Tanks and tankers, doughboys and the artillerymen marched up both sides of a dirt road to Walterneinburg, where we turned left and headed up to the east bank to catch Lieut. Co. Wilson M. Hawkins's 3d Battalion, which had made contact with the enemy an hour or so before.

Behind us there was a steady roar of artillery supporting infantry and armor, and off to the left squadrons of Thunderbolts wheeled and turned in screaming dives to strafe and bomb targets close to the front.

A couple of Yanks from the 83d asked for a lift as we wound along the dusty road and a few minutes later pointed out the bodies of more than 50 Germans who had been mowed down by our machine guns during the counterattack earlier in the day. Most of the enemy dead were SS troopers and all carried automatic weapons.

Colonel Hawkins, whose home is Pass Christina, Miss., stood in the turret of his command Sherman a short distance from a woods where other tanks of his regiment were clearing out German elements still holding out in dug-in positions. Although the opposition artillery had quieted down, there still was strong small-arms and occasional mortar fire, which was slowing the operation up considerably.

Warfare of this sort meant that doughboys attached to Combat Command Roger had to dismount and move out along the flanks to clean out the area as tanks moved slowly up behind them. Once an open spot was reached the infantry climbed back aboard and the armor ground forward to the next obstacle.

No Fight Left

There was a sudden increase in our artillery activity in the direction of the small settlement of Lubs and a few minutes afterward, four Company C tanks, commanded by Lieut. Jacob W. Piatt, Middletown, Ohio, took off to secure the next objective while armed engineers fighting as infantry followed in halftracks.

From the deck of the platoon leader's tank it is possible to look over flat fields into the town under attack, but from the first it seemed evident there was no fight left. Ten minutes later tanks had nosed their way up the main street, fanned out to cover approach roads and take four prisoners, liberate a couple hundred Serbians among the usual slave-labor group.

Bristling With Brick Roads

Almost before the tankers had settled down to guarding the town, orders came in from Combat Command Roger headquarters to withdraw a few miles, then form up a new and more closely co-ordinated defense against a possible counterattack rumored to be forming up in considerable infantry and armored strength a few miles to the east.

Jerry would have had a job breaking through had he counterattacked during the night, for the whole bridgehead area bristled with roadblocks, anti-tank positions, infantry perimeter defenses and co-ordinated artillery. The attack never materialized and early today an order came down to armor and 83d elements to prepare to attack.

Shermans In The Morning

Led by Shermans, companies of the 67th Armored Regiment rolled out across the open fields 2 or 3 miles from Güterglück on the dot of 9.45 almost under the heavy artillery preparation.

Up ahead squadrons of Thunderbolts roared down to make pass after pass at the town, spraying buildings and the ground around it with a hail of bombs that exploded with a ground-shaking carrump.

Firing as they went, medium tanks moved slowly over yard after yard of ground, stopping to concentrate on every suspicious spot, then moving on.

A couple of times a bunch of jack rabbits took off with a bounce over the fields, once a herd of deer bounded in front of the tanks and both times doughboys riding deck let loose with a barrage.

The Enemy Replies

Then, as the outskirts of the town were reached, enemy artillery shells and a hail of small-arms fire began to land about the force. Almost before the tanks ground to a halt doughboys were off and taking cover to drive out Kraut infantry evidently dug in along the perimeter of the town, from which columns of black smoke and flame billowed skyward.

The fight into Gutergluck from that point on was one of routing out stubborn SS and Hitler youth troops while at the same time sweating out the almost direct 88-millimeter fire from guns in back of the town.

Once or twice a concentration landed amid doughboys crossing the open fields, but casualties were somehow low and the line moved doggedly forward into the building line.

8 SS Men Quit

Once a single Kraut ran from a clump of bushes waving a white flag, then 20 minutes later, eight SS men came running up the road after they had surrendered to tankers and riflemen. But back in town was the sound of heavy machine-gun fire, interspersed with the familiar noise of a Burp gun and an occasional Jerry mortar.

From the few prisoners we talked to we found out that a small number of SS troops and a special "division" made up of men recruited as recently as a week ago from specialized industrial jobs were included in the town's defense.

Those troops who remained in town put up a tough fight to the bitter end, but the doughboys and tankers cleaned them out in house-to-house fighting. By late afternoon they had more than a hundred prisoners, including a good many ranging from 13 to 16 years of age.

Even though the town was completely cleared, enemy artillery, mortar men and self-propelled gun crews were sending in enough fire to make the spot anything but a healthy one.

Baltimorean Seen

Besides a Baltimorean, T/4 Earl H. Schlossberg, Jr., 627 North Payson street, the following men were seen in action: Pfc. John R. Williams, of Laurel; Pfc. John D. Maske, Mount Gilead, North Carolina; Major John T Mauldin, Atlanta, Georgia; Pfc. Raymond Shafer, Wilford, West Virginia; Capt. Milton J. Novotny, Robertsville, Alabama; Pvt. Ellsworth Evans, Squire, West Virginia; Pfc. Albert Dayton, Huntington, West Virginia; Corporal Buck P. Bradley, Huntington Park, Georgia; Sergt. Edward E. Blake, Winchester, Illinois; Pvt. Charles A. Morehouse, Elkhart, Indiana; Sergt. John A. Turner, Detroit, Michigan; Tech. Sergt. Harold V. Brown, Arnco, Georgia; Pfc. Vernon C. Sublette, Jr., Knoxville, Tennessee.

From Bradley back to McCardell

THE EVENING SUN, WEDNESDAY, APRIL 25, 1945

Yank Who Contacted Red By Radio Once A Salesman In Maryland

By Lee McCardell [Sunpapers War Correspondent]

With an armored Division at Mittweida, Germany, April 24 [Delayed] — For two days Staff Sergeant Alexander J. Balter, of Pittsburgh, a Russian-speaking communications sergeant of an armored division combat command, had been trying to establish radio contact with the approaching Russian forces. The division was waiting along the Mulde River. The Russians were known to be moving in from the east, not far away.

Balter, aged 37, squat, baldish, spectacled, was a peacetime carpet and furniture traveling salesman whose territory included Maryland and Pennsylvania. Born in Elizabeth, N.J., he learned to speak Russian fluently in Russia, where his mother, a native Russian, took him to live with his grandparents for a time after the death of his father in America.

Speaks German Also

Balter also speaks German. Last August when his division was attacking a Brittany seaport, he was sent forward as an interpreter and returned with 795 German prisoners he talked into surrendering. He wears the Bronze Star ribbon in reward for that exploit.

The headquarters to which he is attached having been set up near Mittweida. Balter took an Army Signal Corps CW-506 radio set out of his halftrack and installed it in the house where he settled down to go fishing among the wave bands for the proper Russian frequency. His set has an ordinary range of about 25 miles, up to 40 miles in wet weather.

No Replies In Two Days

He could hear Russian broadcasts and Russian field radios transmitting military orders. But for two days he received no replies to his own calls to the Russians.

"These are American forces approaching the south of Germany," he'd shout over his transmitter in Russian. "Listen! American forces! Listen! American forces! This is the voice of your American allies now at Mittweida waiting to meet you here."

Then Success

Then he'd switch off the transmitter and listen anxiously for some reply. When none came he'd try another waveband.

After two days of fruitless calling, he was beginning to lose patience yesterday morning when at 8.20 o'clock he heard a Russian voice:

"*Bravo Americanski! Bravo Americanski! Bravo Americanski! Bravo Americanski!*"

The Germans must have been listening, too, because a moment after the Russian voice came in the radio channel was jammed with a burst of German music — "*Ach du Lieber Augustine, Augustine, Augustine.*"

More than one hour passed before at 9.37 o'clock, Balter managed to hear the Russians again. This time he gave them the position of the American forces waiting to link up with them and asked for their position.

Nazis Interrupt Again

Again a German voice broke in, this time with considerable profanity about "Jew lovers" and "enemies of the Reich and Fatherland."

None of the radio reception had been very good during the forenoon, but at 1.10 P.M. the Russians came in again, this time loud and clear.

"It sounded like a whole regiment shouting greetings and cheers," Balter said, "hurrahing for the Americans."

The Russian radio operator told Balter the Russians were proceeding to the American lines, but gave no position. There was a steady flow of continuous greetings to the "American comrades" and repeated admonitions to "expect contact in the morning."

Inquires For Germans

The Russians were so jubilant they even began joking with Balter. The Russian operator said:

"Where are these Germans? They wait until they're good and hungry and then they surrender in large groups."

Everything looked good for the Russians and the Americans, the operator rattled on. A great victory was ahead. We were all good comrades together, brothers tomorrow, brothers.

"Brother Americans, we greet our American comrades. Be watchful tomorrow morning, tomorrow morning."

Given American Position

Later the Russians asked Balter for the exact location of the American front line. He gave it to them on the direction of his commanding officer, orienting the position in relation to the town of Chemnitz.

"They went off the air for a while like they were examining a map," Balter said. "Then they came on and corrected my pronunciation of Chemnitz, giving it back to me in Russian. But everything was most polite and cordial, real palsywalsy."

"God be with you, friends," the Russians said. "Greetings and health to our American allies. Tomorrow at 8 o'clock. Wait where you are. We are coming. Hold your position. We'll contact you at present location. Stay where you are."

Coming Closer, They Say

"Third Army! 3d Army!" the Russians called later in the day. "We're coming closer to you continuously now. We'll contact you soon now. We Russians are not sleeping. There's much work being done by us now."

And again a German voice chimed in angrily: "Cease your worrying Americans. You'll soon meet up with your hoodlum friends."

Then another voice came over the air in broken English. Balter said is sounded like a German speaking, but he couldn't be sure. It was a foreigner speaking English with a heavy accent.

Get-Together Anticipated

He said:

" A great Russian and American get-together is now being formed. Stay where you are. You will be contacted."

Balter told the Russians the American forces were intact and had reached their destination. The Russians replied with another outburst of "Happy greetings — blest be our friends!"

THE BALTIMORE SUN, SATURDAY, APRIL 28, 1945

McCardell At Junction Of Armies — Depicts The Momentous Scene On The Elbe And Yanks And Russians Who Took Part In It

By Lee McCardell [Sunpapers War Correspondent]

With 1st Army Troops, April 26 [By Radio — Delayed] — Two major generals, one Russian and one American, shook hands about 4 o'clock this afternoon on the east bank of the Elbe River opposite the old Saxon town of Torgau.

Their troops, fighting from the east and west across Germany, had met. The long-anticipated join up of the Eastern and Western fronts in the war against the Nazis had become a historic fact.

Lower-ranking officers and ordinary soldiers of the two armies had met yesterday on the western bank of the river. But the supposed junction did not become formal or official, whichever way you choose to put it, until the two division commanders met each other this afternoon "through the channels," as the army says.

We Are Tired

The meeting was one of the great historic scenes of the war and calls for a close report, but to those of us whose job it is to report it, and who sat on a plot of grass bordered with pansies in front of a German barracks this afternoon, waiting for the generals to arrive, it does not seem to matter much whether we describe the event or not.

Like everyone else in the war we are tired. We know that the Russians and the Americans have met. The end of the war is much closer. And I think all of us correspondents would have been much happier this afternoon if we could have just sat there on the grass until the sun went down — instead of running back to army headquarters to file dispatches like this one.

What will we remember of this great historical drama — because it was a historical drama — as the years roll by? The significance of the occasion? I doubt it. They will have been absorbed in the chronicles of time. But I think we will always remember this day's sunshine, warm and mellow on the Elbe. We will always remember the Russians as we saw them, many of us for the first time, not very different from ordinary GI's.

And we will always remember their simple, wholehearted hospitality and friendliness, things which somehow I never associated with the Russian Army.

When I look back upon this day in years to come, I shall think, first, of a river, not very wide, blue-green, and rather lazy, with the laziness that seems to belong to every river on a sunny holiday in spring.

I shall think of the deep, green meadow grass that grows lush on its eastern bank, a broad, flat bank running back to a road lined with trees.

I shall think of a liberated young Russian slave laborer, in his shirt sleeves, sitting on the western bank of that river, looking across and playing polkas on the yellow, silk-pleated accordion he holds in his lap.

The eastern bank of the river slopes steeply in a series of terraces from the riverside promenade. Behind the terraces rise the roofs of Torgau, dominated by the conically capped central tower and the crenelated battlements of Torgau's Renaissance castle.

The accordion player is not alone. All around him, sitting and standing on the terraces down to the river are other liberated Russian slave laborers. Some of the women wear black leather boots and their hair is tied up in bright yellow kerchiefs. Their suitcases, their wooden boxes and their bundles, tied up in white sheeting, lie around their feet.

Both Bridges Blown

The Russians are watching two varnished shells, that are being sculled back and forth across the river, ferrying little groups of other Russians and their belongings to the eastern shore. They are waiting their turn to cross the river.

Both bridges across the Elbe at Torgau have been blown by the Germans. The upper one was a highway bridge, the lower a railway bridge. The heavy central spans of both bridges, which look very much alike, lie in the river, broken and crumpled.

The Russian soldiers loitered along the river bank. I'll always remember them because they were slim, youthful, smiling and talkative. In American uniforms they would have passed unnoticed for average American soldiers.

And Submachine Guns

Their uniforms were grey-green, belted smocks and flaring riding breeches. They carried spoons and candles tucked in the tops of their leather boots and their wrap-around leggings.

Most of them were armed with submachine guns slung like carbines behind their shoulders.

The uniforms, were of lighter coarser wool than those of our soldiers. They were no dirtier, no cleaner. The officers wore visored garrison caps and the enlisted men — and some of the younger lieutenants — wore overseas caps on a rakish British slant.

Some carried Nazi knives and German pistols on their belts — souvenirs — just as our soldiers. They carried grenades in their belts, too, just like our men. Their own regular weapons had a worn and shiny look as if they had been handled a great deal.

"Terror" Not So Terrible

I shall remember in the years to come the officers of the Russian regimental mess, with whom we had lunch. Except for the high military collars of their tunics and their Russian regimentals, they might have been the officers of any American regiment as they sat around the table after their meal smoking, laughing and talking seriously.

And I shall never forget the hundreds of frightened German civilian refugees, whom we passed on the road fleeing toward our lines, when we crossed the narrow strip of farmland between the Mulde and the Elbe rivers on our way to meet the Russians. The "terror" of which they had been warned was upon them. The "terror' did not look so terrible to us.

And I shall remember that although I spoke no Russian and few of the Russians who I met today spoke any English, there were never any periods of strained silence, never any lack of understanding between us. They were plain people who liked us. We were plain people who liked them. We filled our glasses and smiled at each other and drank to each other's health and good luck.

Old, Unhappy War

As for the rest of today — it shall not matter as the years go by. It will be a date in the almanacs and history books. But among my own memories it will be a day when I came among strangers, who took me in and shook my hand and smiled as if they meant it, and a day of sunshine on the Elbe River when an old, unhappy war receded into the distance.

We had been waiting for the Russians for a week. Our army might have contacted them much sooner had there been no tactical considerations which halted the American advance eastward at the Mulde River.

Last Saturday night we were told that contact might be made Sunday. We left another front in southern Germany and went to the Leipzig sector.

Our army radio operators could talk with the Russians by radio. Our artillery observers could see Russian shellbursts in enemy territory a few miles ahead of our lines. But the weather was showery and the ground hazy. Aerial observers were unable to pick up any Russian columns.

The First Contact

American ground reconnaissance patrols could locate no strong forces of Germans on their front. An armored division seized three bridges intact across the Mulde River, but until yesterday afternoon the American front-line troops had no definite information that Russian forces had crossed the Elbe.

About noon yesterday a 69th Infantry Division reconnaissance patrol of twenty men, led by Albert L. Kontzebue, of Houston, Texas, met a small party of Russian soldiers near a village a few miles west of Riesa.

"There's A Bunch of Ruskies"

The Russians took them down to the Elbe where they had rigged a hand-and-rope ferry across the river and carried Kontzebue's force, including a couple of jeeps, to the east bank to see their commander.

About two hours later, Major Fred W. Craig, of Friendship, Tenn., was leading another patrol of the same American outfit into a village a little farther to the northwest when one of his men shouted:

"There's a bunch of Ruskies."

A force of Cossack infantry was riding up the road toward the village from the opposite side. The Russians galloped over to the American jeeps and dismounted. The Joes were already out of their jeeps, and for the better part of the next hour the Ruskies and the Doughs (all Russian soldiers are "Ruskies" to the American doughboys) shook each other's hands and swapped each others' cigarettes.

Mission Completed

The Cossacks insisted that Major Craig cross the Elbe with them, and they took him over on another improvised ferry to see their commander. At 3 o'clock Kontzebue radioed his regimental command post that he had "completed his mission," but late this afternoon he had not yet returned to give full details of his contact with the Russians.

"We had supper with the Russians," Major Craig said when he came back tonight. "It was an excellent meal of chicken, fresh green onions and wine, and we drank a good many toasts, bottoms up. At 1.30 this morning my hosts decided that we ought to eat again so we had another supper just as good as the first."

About 4 o'clock yesterday afternoon Lieut. William D. Robertson, of Los Angeles, Cal., and three men, one of them Pfc. Frank P. Huff, of Washington, Va., were rounding up a flock of German prisoners of war in Torgau when they sighted Russian troops across the river.

Synthetic Stars And Stripes

The Russians were firing into Torgau, still occupied by the Germans as far as they knew. With mercurochrome, a blue dye obtained from a drugstore and a white bed sheet, Robertson hurriedly designed a crude American flag and hoisted it over Torgau's ancient castle tower.

Pretty soon the Russians began coming across what was left of the blown highway bridge. Robertson crawled out on the steel girders of what was left on his side of the bridge and met the Russians on the wreckage of the span lying in the river.

"Hello," said Robertson, who speaks no Russian.

Chocolate And Schnapps

He wasn't near enough to shake hands, so he reached out and slapped the knee of the nearest Russian. They urged him to come over to their side of the river, so Robertson and Huff made the crossing. They were greeted on the far shore with a picnic tea of sardines, biscuits, chocolate, Schnapps and wine.

There was more handshaking, but not much conversation. None of the Americans spoke Russian. They just said, "Hi, there," and shook hands all around and drank toasts to the United States, Russia and the Allied forces. Robertson also traded watches with the Russian captain he met on the far shore.

About dark Robertson drove back to his regimental headquarters with four Russians, a major, a captain, a lieutenant and an enlisted man. The major carried an invitation from his division commander to the American division commander to meet at the bridge today.

Hush-Hush And Hocus-Pocus

The 69th Division, relatively new to combat and totally unpracticed in the art of public relations, didn't know how to break the news of their contact with the Russians. But after considerable hush-hush and hocus-pocus, during which this correspondent was all but bodily tossed out of regimental headquarters, they revealed the bare facts.

The four Russians who had come back with Lieutenant Robertson were whisked around to division headquarters, where they were introduced to the commanding general, Maj. Gen. E. F. Reinhardt, of Detroit, and sleepy press correspondents were called in at midnight to meet the distinguished guests.

Ride, Drink Or Fight

More toasts were drunk and each of the three Russian officers made speeches, which an interpreter translated. The Russian lieutenant Alexander Sylvako, who commanded the platoon which met Robertson at the bridge said:

"My men were so astonished and overjoyed at meeting the Americans that they didn't know what to do next. They didn't know whether to go for a ride with the Americans in their jeeps, drink vodka or fight Germans."

The informal press reception for the Russians at divisional headquarters was held in the parlor of the home formerly occupied by a German dentist. The builder of the house hadn't calculated upon events of such international importance taking place there and the parlor suffered some minor property damage due to the overcrowding.

The Inevitable Giggles

Pictures were knocked off the walls and glassware was smashed as army photographers scaled bookcases for better elevation. The Russians and their interviewers, including the inevitable female war correspondent afflicted with giggles, kept getting mixed up in the tassels of a yellow chandelier.

Young staff officers, thrilled at the thought of "making history," added a sort of college football rally tone. But the Russians took everything in their stride.

Lieutenant Sylvako and Lieutenant Robertson posed, with their arms around each other, in front of a large oil painting depicting a soldier of the 69th Division greeting the Russian soldiers, with the flags of the two nations and the large provisional insigne in the background.

It was a pure coincidence that this huge poster, the work of the division artist, happened to be at headquarters, the officers said.

The confusion in the parlor, however, was nothing compared with that prevailing in the German lines being squeezed by the Americans on the Mulde and the Russians on the Elbe. German propagandists circulated reports that the American Ambassador to Moscow has been murdered and the United States has declared war on Russia.

Fire On Reds, Not Yanks

Some German soldiers later taken prisoner said they had been told to fire on the Russians, but not on the Americans. Troops of German *Volkssturm* were ordered to disband take off their uniforms and resume civilian status to escape death from the Russians.

In the case of at least one German military hospital, later occupied by the Americans, the medical personnel was armed, even the women nurses carrying small-caliber automatics in their belts "for protection against the Russians."

Many German soldiers, palpably bewildered as to whom they were supposed to fight, threw away their arms and surrendered to the Americans. A large number marched to the rear without a guard of any sort. More than 5,000 German prisoners were taken yesterday by the 69th Infantry Division alone.

Breakfast: Cognac

Adding to the confusion were large numbers of civilians, slave laborers abandoned by their guards and long columns of liberated Allied prisoners of war. The inmates of the principal German military prison at Torgau also were set free.

At midnight last night Col. Charles S. Adams, commanding officer of the regiment whose patrols had contacted the Russians, set out for the Elbe to meet the Russian regimental commander opposite Torgau. He arrived in time for breakfast, which included cognac, vodka, champagne and wine.

At breakfast time the 1st Army war correspondents set out from behind the American lines with a military escort to make contact with the Russians. We found the roads jammed with German civilian refugees, some in wagons, some on bicycles, others on foot, all bound for the nearest Mulde River bridge.

Many who were on foot, carried children and personal belongings in baby carriages, hand wagons and two-wheeled carts. They were trying to get away from the Russians.

No Evidence Of "Terror"

German soldiers without arms were still making for the American lines. We passed one German calmly shaving by a small stream preparatory to giving himself up. Later in the day, numbers of German Army Red Cross nurses tried to get through the American lines.

A small Russian force had crossed the river into Torgau by the time we got there. The city had been shelled a little, and one small block of buildings was on fire, but we saw no evidence of Russian "terrorism."

Perhaps that's where the liberated Russian slave laborer got the instrument he was playing on the river bank. We asked no questions. After shaking hands with what seemed about 100 Russian soldiers, we made the riverside and were ferried across the Elbe in one of the racing sculls plying back and forth across the stream.

On the far shore we were met by a Russian lieutenant who spoke English. He said he had learned English in school, but had never had an opportunity to practice it before upon English-speaking subjects. He apologized for his imperfection in language. He needn't have. He spoke English very well.

He addressed each of us as "my dear," which at first sounded strange, but for all I know that may be the Russians' conversational custom among friends.

We were invited into the officers' mess for lunch, which included sardines, zweiback, brown bread, cheese and spice cake, and the Russians still had enough wine and vodka for several noontime toasts.

The Big Event

These were drunk in the mess hall of a captured German headquarters under the stern eyes of an oil painting of the late General von Hindenburg.

The Russians kept open house for the visiting Americans all day, but the big event occurred this afternoon when General Reinhardt and the members of his staff were ferried across the river by scull to be greeted by the major general commanding the 58th Division of the 1st Ukrainian Army of Marshal Konev.

The Russian general conducted General Reinhardt up the hill toward his headquarters. More toasts were drunk during the course of the late afternoon and evening. They traded insignia and "short snorters" and several other choice items in their collections.

CHAPTER 12

SURRENDER AT REIMS

From McCardell to Day

THE BALTIMORE SUN, WEDNESDAY, MAY 9, 1945

Price Day was the only staff correspondent of an individual newspaper to witness the surrender of Germany at Reims. He was offered a last-minute opportunity to cover the historic surrender for Exchange Telegraph, a British news agency, which enabled him to be present.

SUN ONLY PAPER IN WORLD WITH OWN MAN ON SCENE
Final Articles Of Capitulation Signed In Berlin, Stalin Reports

Price Day's Eyewitness Report of German Surrender

By Price Day [Sunpapers War Correspondent]

Reims, France, May 7 [By Radio — Delayed] — At 2.45 o'clock on this warm spring morning, Col. Gen. Gustav Jodl signed his name for the fourth time and carefully put down his pen. Europe's war was over.

Jodl stood up. His back was rigid, his heels in their black boots were close together. He rested the tops of his fingers on the wide, battered oak table that filled a good part of what, until tonight, was the most secret of all the secret chambers of Europe — SHAEF's War Room.

For Better Or Worse . . . Into The Victor's Hands

General Jodl said in German:

"With this signature the German people and German armed forces are for better or worse delivered into the victors' hands."

Lieut. Gen. Walter Bedell Smith, chief of staff to General Eisenhower, watched him impassively. So did four other Americans, three Russians, one French and three British officers seated at the table.

On Jodl's left a German admiral, on his right a German major stared straight ahead. Still speaking of the civilians and soldiers of his beaten nation, Jodl said:

"In this war, which has lasted more than five years, they both have achieved and suffered more than perhaps any other people in the world. In this hour I can only express the hope that the victors will treat them with generosity."

He sat down and then at once stood up again. The admiral and major stood up with him. There was no answer. There were no salutes.

His face gray with strain, but his step steady, Jodl turned and walked from the room.

He was followed by the others, the major carrying Jodl's cap with its German high command insigne. Seventeen Allied war correspondents shifted aside to let them pass.

With their going, the solemn tableau of the surrender broke up. The Allied officers spoke a few words to each other, rose from their chairs, chatted quietly for another moment and strolled from the room. Everybody was very tired.

That was how it was. That was it — the victory of all the Allies over all the German forces on land, sea and air. This was not an armistice, it was surrender, total and complete.

More than 45 hours must still go by before the peace effected tonight at General Eisenhower's headquarters in Reims' barrackslike pinkish brick Ecole Professionelle would settle over the battlefields.

But of these battlefields only a few were still the scenes of battle. Every man around the table knew that this ceremony was in large part simply the proper recognition of the accomplished fact of the defeat of Germany.

The signing of the surrender document by Smith, Jodl, Major General of Artillery Ivan Susloparov, of the Red Army; and General F. Sevez, of France, came at the waning of a long night, in the course of which it had begun to seem certain that the great event would have to wait at least until the dawn of another day.

For five and a half hours the German representatives had been conferring alone in a billet in a house on Rue Godinot near the great Cathedral of Reims.

The Americans, British, Russians and French had no word from this conference throughout the evening. Then, deciding that the acceptance seemed unlikely tonight, they all left headquarters. Many went to bed.

As midnight came and went a hush fell over Reims, except in one corner of the G-4, or supply sector, of the main building of SHAEF's command post, where the correspondents waited.

Military police guarded every corridor and gate as, indeed, they do on all nights. Perhaps tonight they watched even more carefully, and stood a bit straighter at their posts.

Light On The Foliage

Out in the darkness of the wide, graveled courtyard, enclosed by low, utilitarian brick buildings, rested jeeps, trucks and dozens of high-echelon staff cars with their red-plaqued fronts and rears studded with a milky way of stars.

A faint, warm breeze came through the open windows. Here and there an electric light shone out on the pale green foliage of the trees that ringed the courtyard. Everything was still and suspended, waiting.

At 1.58 o'clock this Monday morning, Brig. Gen. Frank A. Allen, public relations director of SHAEF and once commander of Combat Command B of the 1st Armored Division, called the correspondents together in one small room.

"I Think This Is It"

"I think something is going to happen shortly," he said, and then when the scuffling of feet ceased, he said, "Gentlemen, I think this is it. All the staff officers have been recalled."

We filed through the wide barren hallways, with their checked floors of gray and black tile, up a flight of concrete steps and into Room No. 119.

Before this room lies a short entrance way cluttered tonight with photographers' gear. On the other side of the entrance way a door opens into the room, which is in shape a fat L that for the past months has been the brain center of the Allied armies in the west.

Maps, Maps, Maps

It is a room of maps. Its walls are papered entirely from floor to ceiling with maps — of that bugaboo, the "national redoubt"; the regions of China, Burma and the Philippines; of the air operations; a mine sweepers chart of the North Sea; maps of the pockets on the Atlantic coast; of the Army's railway system, and of the airfields of the world.

Over the widest wall stretches the battle map, showing in heavy crayon the battle order of the triumphant Allied armies.

Tonight, even if the German chief of staff cared to examine these maps — in fact, he will not so much as glance at them — or to read the tabulations of casualties on the side wall, it wouldn't matter. At last, it wouldn't matter.

Edges Nicked And Scarred

The conference table, 20 feet long and 8 wide, is directly in front of the battle map. Its top is painted black and its edges are nicked and scarred. Its perimeter is crowded with plain pine chairs, except on the long side away from the map, where there are only three chairs, precisely centered.

Each chair but one has before it a thick block of ruled white paper with a new yellow pencil, with eraser, laid neatly on its top. Most of the places are marked with names printed on narrow strips of paper.

There are six unusually small white porcelain and two unusually large green brass ashtrays. There is a small microphone and a stand holding two pens. The paper, pencils and ashtrays were not used. Nor were these particular pens.

More Like A Movie Set

At the moment the room looks more like a movie set than either a war center or a place for a great conference. From all angles and elevations batteries of cameras are aimed at the most important table on earth, while the photographers are making their last-minute adjustments and scurry and climb about like monkeys.

The room blazes with a stark white light.

Air Marshal Sir J. M. Robb, chief of air staff, who walked into this light at 2.29 A. M., was the first of the conference group to enter the room, though he was preceded by one minute by Capt. Harry C. Butcher, naval aide to Gen. Dwight D. Eisenhower.

Butcher carried two pens of brown composition material with gold tops which, never used, had been carried by Eisenhower since the end of the African campaign. Another pen, a plain brown one, turned up later. Nobody knew where it came from.

Robb was followed by weathered Gen. Carl A. Spaatz, whose United States Strategic Air Forces brought victory much sooner than it would otherwise have come. At 2.34 General Smith, moving quickly, came into the room.

Like guests at a party, they found where they were to sit by looking at the place cards. Within four minutes they were standing in front of the chairs.

Looking toward the battle map, the three chairs at the left end of the table were vacant; then along the back of the table, from left to right, stood Lieutenant General Sir F. E. Morgan, deputy chief of staff, with a sandy mustache and a brown, British face; small trim Gen. Francois Sevez; big, broad Admiral Sir Harold Burrough, commander of the Allied naval forces, and General Smith, looking tired, but, as always extraordinarily self-contained and precise.

Best Of The Best

On Smith's left, behind the table was Maj. Gen. K. W. D. Strong, G-2, or intelligence officer, of SHAEF, a tall, quick man of the best type of those who have made British intelligence the best in the world.

Next to Strong loomed huge, neat, genial Maj. Gen. Ivan Susloparov. Then came Spaatz, and Robb in an RAF uniform. Slightly to the rear of Spaatz and Susloparov was First Lieut. Ivan Cherniaev, a young officer with a shaven head who interpreted for the Soviet signer.

Along the short right end of the table the chair closet to Robb was marked for Maj. Gen. H. R. Bull, assistant chief of staff of G-3 of SHAEF, who at this moment was arranging on the table two cream-colored cardboard folders.

The documents contained in the folders were three — the instrument of surrender to be signed in quadruplicate by Smith, Jodl, Susloparov and Sevez; the naval terms for the signature of Burrough and presentation to the Germans, and a similar, paper, covering the land and air forces, to be signed by Smith.

The Three Vacant Chairs

Before the second of the three chairs at the right end of the conference table stood the third Russian, Col. Ivan Zenkovitch, a big man with a shock of unruly dark hair. The chair on his left was unoccupied.

It was not on this empty place, however, nor on the three at the opposite end of the table that attention was focused. The most important things in the room at 2.38 o'clock were the three vacant chairs in the center of the table, facing the battle map.

Admiral Burrough leaned forward and tested his pencil on the pad of paper before him — the only mark made on any of the pads. General Smith glanced quickly around, then nodded toward the door.

If Bowing, Slight

At 2.39, Jodl, the new German chief of staff, and Admiral Hans George von Friedeburg, the new commander in chief of the German Navy, walked into Room 119, followed by Jodl's aide. They went straight to their chairs and all the men around the table sat down at once. If there was any bowing, it was extremely slight.

Jodl sat in the center, with Friedeburg, on his left and his aide on his right.

Friedeburg, who wore a blue uniform, held his cap in his lap; Jodl put his, with his gloves inside, top down on the table by his right arm. The aide placed his cap on the door beside him.

Two Minutes With Eisenhower

Jodl's gray-green uniform was new and of good fit, its flared trousers showing a wide red stripe down the outer seams. The scarlet and gold of his epaulets were no less brilliant than that of the British staff officer's across the table.

At 2.40 began a flurry of silent signing of names. Seventeen minutes later it would be all over. The Germans by then would have walked from Room 119 to meet the escort to take them upstairs to General Eisenhower's simple and comfortable suite and spend two minutes with the supreme commander.

Leaving him, they would stand for a while in the narrow hall talking among themselves before leaving the scene of the final act of Germany's greatest defeat.

The signing of the paper that symbolized that defeat grew directly from the earlier surrender of the German troops in the north to Field Marshal Montgomery.

After that agreement of capitulation had, on May 3, become history, the Germans made it known that they wished to discuss the question of the surrender of the whole of the German armed forces.

Eisenhower agreed. He named Reims, already rich in history, as the place of discussion, and he named May 5 as the date.

It Was A Rough Trip

Escorted by Lieutenant Colonel Viscount Bury and Major F. J. Lawrence, of Montgomery's headquarters, von Friedeburg and Col. Fritz Poleck, supply expert of the *Wehrmacht's* high command, set out.

It was a rough trip. The party left Lueneberg, the scene of the northern surrender, at 8 o'clock in the morning, flying to Vorst, where they changed planes. Bad weather forced them to land at Brussels at 11.15, followed onto the airport by Air Marshal Sir Arthur Coningham's white command ship.

At the RAF snack bar, the group lunch on the fare typical of all the RAF snack bars all over the world — Spam and ale. Von Friedeburg drank ale, which was a Brussels brew called "Kiltie Scotch," straight from the bottle.

At 1.30 in the afternoon, Miss Bobbie Alexander, of Inverness, Scotland, who is an ATS private, appeared with a staff car and drove the drowsy Friedeburg and gloomy Poleck, with their escort, toward Reims.

Friedeburg, who said he had found little time to sleep in the last ten months, immediately dozed off. Poleck, who does not speak English, showed little inclination to speak German, either.

What He Did Say

He did express displeasure at the sight of all the wrecked *Wehrmacht* transport along the roads.

The car reached SHAEF's forward command post at Reims at four minutes past 5 o'clock, and was met at the entrance to the unimposing building by British Brigadier J. Foord, assistant for SHAEF's G-2, who was wearing his customary old battle jacket displaying its single decoration — a faded African Star — and by Lieut. Col. K. A. S. Morrice, assistant secretary of the general staff.

The Allied officers and German officers exchanged salutes. Those of the Germans were not Nazi salutes. Sixteen minutes later General Strong, of SHAEF's G-2, escorted Friedeburg to the office of General Smith, where the three men conferred alone for 22 minutes.

Not Authorized

At this first interview Friedeburg was required to show his credentials and his authority to represent Grand Admiral Doenitz. He did so. His authority was not such as to authorize him to surrender.

In writing, the chief of staff gave Friedeburg General Eisenhower's terms — all German forces to remain where they were; an "undertaking" that air and water craft, both surface and undersea, were not to be allowed to scatter, and a guarantee of the execution of all the orders of the Allied commands.

When the stock German fear was expressed that if the *Wehrmacht* were not allowed to give up to the western Allies alone, many of its soldiers would be killed by the Red Army, Smith replied that SHAEF was not prepared to talk about anything other than simultaneous unconditional surrender to all the Allies.

Enemies Until Surrender

In reply to a statement on the sufferings of the German people, General Smith said that until complete surrender the German people were our enemies, but that after surrender they would be treated according to the "normal dictates of humanity."

To think this over, Friedeburg took the terms back to an office in the building where Colonel Poleck, a stack of sandwiches and a supply of whiskey awaited him.

For a time, General Strong conferred with them in a further clarification of the Supreme Commander's demands. Friedeburg, it developed, was willing to discuss full surrender if he could obtain the necessary authority from Doenitz.

By this time London, Washington and Moscow had been told of the progress of events. General Smith had also fully informed the Russian representatives waiting in the map-filled SHAEF war room for any formal meeting that might take place. As the evening wore on it became apparent that no surrender was forthcoming immediately, and the officers in the war room dispersed.

At length, Friedeburg made his decision. He was willing, he said to send a message to Doenitz.

Message To Doenitz

Dispatched in SHAEF code to the headquarters of the British 2d Army for relay from there by courier to Doenitz, this message contained the following:

1. The outline of two proposals put forward by General Smith — that Friedeburg be given full authority to negotiate the complete surrender of the German troops in all theaters, or that Doenitz should send to SHAEF his chief of high command, along with the commanders in chief of high command, along with the commanders in chief of his army, navy and air forces, with full authority to surrender.

2. The statement of Allied conditions restricting the movement of troops, aircraft and ships, and demanding compliance with all Allied orders.

3. Friedeburg's own opinion that, unless the new German Government complied at once with Eisenhower's terms, it would be charged with guilt for the continuance of hostilities.

4. A request for a prompt decision on the alternatives offered by SHAEF's chief of staff.

The matter, Friedeburg wrote was of the utmost urgency. If he were to be given the power to surrender he asked for immediate written authorization, even though the signatures of the service heads might be required later.

3 Rue Godinot

With this document sent on its way, the German emissaries were escorted to a seven-room house at the temporary quarters for officers visiting SHAEF.

With them — and to remain in the house with them at all times — were two British officers, who had escorted them from Lueneburg, and an American second lieutenant, George Reinhardt, of New York City, assigned to the Germans as an official interpreter.

The first request of Friedeburg and Poleck was for soap. After they had washed, they and their three escorts supped at 10.45 o'clock on tomato juice, pork chops and wine, mashed potatoes, the standard United States Army mixture of peas and dehydrated carrots, fruit and coffee.

"Must Be Rich"

The meal was apparently marked by little in the way of verbal exchange. The only reported spoken words was a comment by Friedeburg that the owner of the house "must be rich" since the table linen was so fine.

Actually, the entire furnishings of the house, while not opulent, were in excellent taste. On the outside the building, which sits directly on the street almost under the great cathedral of Reims, is a faded gray stucco with weathered shutters.

The rest of this Saturday evening in this French home was mildly social. The Allied officers mixed Martinis for the Germans. There were, however, no biscuits to serve with these belated cocktails, so WAC Pfc. Joyce Bennett, of New York, rather reluctantly contributed some of the contents of her most recent package from home.

As he had done at intervals throughout Saturday, Prime Minister Churchill again telephoned for news and was told of the progress of events up to that time.

While the German representatives sipped their Martinis, General Eisenhower and General Smith talked the situation over.

Their interpretation was that the outlook was favorable for surrender.

The position of SHAEF at this point was that the hostilities should be terminated at the earliest possible moment, followed, if necessary, by more formal rites of surrender.

At 12.15 on the morning of Sunday, May 6 — the day which at the time looked as if it might be the day of victory — Friedeburg and Poleck, after listening to the radio for a while, went to bed.

Guards Not Picked

They were guarded as they slept by six American military policemen in relays of three. These men were all privates (first class) and they just happened to be on duty then; they were not specially selected.

As they had requested, the German negotiators were awakened at 7 on Sunday morning and breakfasted with their escort on the same food as that served at the same meal at SHAEF's junior officers' mess. This consisted of grapefruit segments taken from a can, fried eggs and bacon, toast and coffee.

In contrast to the day before with its chill air, lowering skies and intermittent dull rain, Sunday was warmer. Patches of sun and shadow slid over the bright green fields, forests and villages of this section of France.

And Picture Magazines

For the two Germans there was little to do but wait. After breakfast they asked for "picture magazines." Private First Class Bennett supplied these, as well as Sunday's *Stars and Stripes*, which told of the surrender of a German Army group to Gen. Jacob L. Devers Allied 6th Army Group in the south.

While SHAEF personnel from the Air Chief Marshal and General of the Army to lance corporals and a marine buck private went about their errands through the air of expectancy that filled the barnlike halls of headquarters buildings, the Germans who had caused the excitement read and listened to the radio.

Chicken And Wine

At 1 o'clock they lunched on fruit cocktail, fried chicken, wine, mashed potatoes, American corn, peaches and coffee. Then they resumed their waiting.

Meanwhile, in the north, the events that were to bring their wait to an end were under way. The message had reached Doenitz. He conferred with his commanders. They made up their minds.

By midafternoon, Jodl, with his aide, Major G. S. Wilhelm Oxenius, was at Montgomery's headquarters. A short time later, under escort of Maj. Gen. Frederick Guingard, Montgomery's chief of staff, they were in a C-47 transport plane en route to Reims.

The task of Friedeburg was almost finished. His advance mission, which had affected him so greatly that after his first talk with General Smith he asked hopelessly for "washer," had done its work.

Foord Waiting Again

At eight minutes after 5 o'clock on Sunday afternoon the wheels of Jodl's plane touched the bright greensward of the Reims airport. Again Brigadier Foord, in the same neat but almost threadbare battledress, was waiting. He and Jodl exchanged military salutes.

That Jodl did not offer the Nazi salute was apparently affectation. A member of the Nazi party and long close associate of Hitler, he was wearing when he got off the plane and wore throughout his mission the golden Nazi Ritterkreuz.

This time he carried with him credentials from a leader other than Hitler — a short statement by Doenitz in Flensburg declaring that Jodl was empowered to sign terms.

Passes Prisoners

As he was driven toward the SHAEF command post, the German chief of staff passed bunches of German prisoners marching under a light guard down the streets of Reims on the way to their barracks after the day's work. He was not acknowledged by any of these, but it is quite likely, though this cannot be said from direct knowledge, that a few United States Negro troops saluted his car as it went by.

Staff cars in Reims always get salutes. There is no telling who might be in them.

At 5.20 o'clock the car carrying Jodl turned under the low rounded arch that leads into the headquarters courtyard. He was taken to a room where he was to meet Friedeburg and Poleck.

They arrived after their long day of rest at 5.45.

Friedeburg was heard to exclaim cryptically, "Aha," as the door closed on the trio. It opened again in a few minutes, when Friedeburg came out to ask for coffee and a map of Europe. Through the half-opened door, Jodl was perceived marching up and down the room.

"At A Low Hum"

At 6.15, General Strong called for Jodl and Friedeburg and took them to General Smith's office, where they were still closeted at 7.15 when Harry Butcher, having put his ear to the door, came downstairs to report to the correspondents:

"They're proceeding at a low hum."

The 40 minutes between 7.30 and 8.10 saw a good deal of activity. During that time the following happened:

Smith and Strong returned to the former's office. Susloparov went to the rooms set aside for the Soviet representatives, where he was joined by Zenkovitch. The Germans left Smith's office. The Russians went into a conference — this was at 7.46 — with Smith and Strong. At 7.53 they sent out for coffee. Four minutes later Strong came out to report that a delay of at least three hours seemed likely.

"It Isn't All Easy"

Strong then went into the room where the Germans were waiting, stayed a short time, and then came out. This flurry of consultation was followed by a lull of an hour, during which the correspondent in the G-4 waiting room could contemplate a chart of the *Luftwaffe's* activities on May 5. On that day one German plane was sighted. It was destroyed.

Shortly after 8.15, Harry Butcher reported again:

"They're still talking about their recess, but you'd better stand by in case they don't take it. There are a lot of things not settled. It isn't all easy."

Some Hope Left

It was clear that the Germans were playing for time, but what the purpose of this game might be, we could not guess. We knew the Allies were willing to discuss only one thing — unconditional surrender to all the Allies. We knew that the Germans had no choice but to accept.

It was 9.15 when Jodl and Friedeburg came out of the office in which they had been talking and returned to, the house on Rue Godinot. This meant that another message was on its way to Flensburg. The communications were good. Some hope still remained of a break tonight.

And Then —

But the hope waned gradually toward midnight, and swiftly thereafter. When all chance seemed gone, the drowsy atmosphere of the headquarters tightened again, new staff cars came into the courtyard and the soft spring air itself crackled once more with the great events in progress.

Then, in what seemed no more time than is needed for the drawing of a breath, the Allied officers had arrived, the Germans had come, all were seated at the big ugly table, Jodl signed his name, once, twice, a third time, and a fourth time; then, carefully, neatly, he put down the pen.

THE  SUN

FINAL

Weather Forecast
Sunny, cool today; fair, with warmer temperature tonight; warmer tomorrow. Yesterday's temperatures: Maximum, 69; minimum, 58; mean, 64......Page 23

Vol. 216—No. 147—F | MORNING, 35,580 EVENING, 192,680 | PAID CIRCULATION APRIL 360,940 | SUNDAY 275,260 | BALTIMORE, WEDNESDAY, MAY 9, 1945 | Entered as second-class matter at Baltimore Post Office | Zone 3 | 24 Pages | 3 Cents

Final Articles Of Capitulation Signed In Berlin, Stalin Reports

Price Day's Eyewitness Report Of German Surrender

SUN ONLY PAPER IN WORLD WITH OWN MAN ON SCENE

Price Day was the only staff correspondent of an individual newspaper to witness the surrender of Germany at Reims. He was offered a last-minute opportunity to cover the historic surrender for Exchange Telegraph, a British news agency, which enabled him to be present.

By PRICE DAY
(Sunpapers War Correspondent)

Reims, France, May 7 [By Radio—Delayed]—At 2.45 o'clock on this warm spring morning, Col. Gen. Gustav Jodl signed his name for the fourth time and carefully put down his pen. Europe's long war was over.

Jodl stood up. His back was rigid, his heels in their black boots were close together. He rested the tips of his fingers on the wide, battered oak table that filled a good part of what, until tonight, was the most secret of all the secret chambers of Europe—SHAEF's War Room.

For Better Or Worse ... Into The Victors' Hands

General Jodl said in German:

"With this signature the German people and German armed forces are for better or worse delivered into the victors' hands."

Lieut. Gen. Walter Bedell Smith, chief of staff to General Eisenhower, watched him impassively. So did four other Americans, three Russians, one French and three British officers seated at the table.

On Jodl's left a German admiral, on his right a German major stared straight ahead. Still speaking of the civilians and soldiers of his beaten nation, Jodl said:

"In this war, which has lasted more than five years, they both have achieved and suffered more than perhaps any other people in the world. In this hour I can only express the hope that the victors will treat them with generosity."

He sat down and then at once stood up again. The admiral and major stood up with him. There was no answer. There were no salutes.

His face gray with strain, but his step steady, Jodl turned and walked from the room.

He was followed by the others, the major carrying Jodl's cap with its German high command insignia. Seventeen Allied war correspondents sidled aside to let them pass.

With their going, the solemn tableau of the surrender broke up. The Allied officers spoke a few words to each other, rose from their (Continued on Page 8, Column 1)

THE SURRENDER CONFERENCE—This picture was taken at Reims, France, on May 7 during the German surrender to the Big Four Allies. Seated left to right around the table, the conferees are: (for Germany's Maj. Gen. Wilhelm Oxenius, Col. Gen.

Gustav Jodl, Admiral Hans G. von Friedeburg; (for the Allies) Lieut. Gen. Sir F. E. Morgan, Gen. Francois Sevez (France), Admiral H. M. Burrough, Lieut. Gen. Walter B. Smith, Lieut. Gen. Ivan Susloparov (Russia), Lieut. Gen. Carl A. Spaatz (Signal Corps).

other people in the world. In this hour I can only express the hope that the victors will treat them with generosity.

He sat down and then at once stood up again. The admiral and major stood up with him. There was no answer. There were no salutes.

His face gray with strain, but his step steady, Jodl turned and walked from the room.

He was followed by the others, the major carrying Jodl's cap with its German high command insignia. Seventeen Allied war correspondents sidled aside to let them pass.

With their going, the solemn tableau of the surrender broke up. The Allied officers spoke a few words to each other, rose from their

chairs, chatted quietly for another moment and strolled from the room. Everybody was very tired.

That was how it was. That was the victory of all the Allies over all the German forces on land, sea and air. This was not an armistice, it was surrender, total and complete.

More than 48 hours many still go by before the peace effected tonight at General Eisenhower's headquarters in Reims' barracks-like pinkish brick Ecole Professionelle would settle over the battlefields.

But of these battlefields only a few were still the scenes of battle. Every man around the table knew that this ceremony was in large (Continued on Page 6, Column 1)

VICTORY ANNOUNCEMENT IS MADE IN 3 CAPITALS; EUROPE'S GUNS SILENCED

Russians Capture Dresden And Olmuetz, Tito Frees Zagreb, Czechs Raise Flag In Prague In Final Battles Of War

London, Wednesday, May 9 (AP)—The Paris radio broadcast an unconfirmed report today that German holdout garrisons in the French Channel ports of Lorient and La Rochelle had surrendered and that French troops have entered both cities.

London, Wednesday, May 9 [Reuter]—Prague radio announced this morning that the Germans reopened fire on the capital at 1.50 A.M.

Paris, Wednesday, May 9 (AP)—Germany bowed today to the most crushing defeat ever inflicted upon a nation, her surrender proclaimed to the world by the United States, Britain and Russia.

The Moscow radio, in behalf of Premier Stalin, announced that the German armed might on the Eastern front, announced the unconditional surrender to the Russian people at 1.10 A.M. today, 10 hours and 10 minutes after President Truman and Prime Minister Churchill proclaimed V-E day.

Reports Final Signing Of Articles

The announcement said the final articles of capitulation were signed yesterday in Berlin.

Field Marshal Wilhelm Keitel, chief of the German high command, signed the articles in the presence of Marshal Gregory K. Zhukov, assistant commander of the Red armies; Air Chief Marshal Sir Arthur Tedder, deputy supreme commander in the west; Gen. Carl A. Spaatz, chief of the United States Strategic Air Forces in Europe, and Lieut. Gen. Jean de Lattre de Tassigny, commander of the French 1st Army.

For Germany it was a crowning ignominity—Keitel, whose armies all but mastered Europe, forced to sign in the ashes of Germany's first city the surrender articles which stripped the Reich of its last vestige of military strength.

Guns Silenced At Minute Past Midnight

The guns of Europe, which through five years, eight months and seven days of unexampled war inflicted possibly 40,000,000 casualties, fell silent at one minute past midnight today (6.01 P.M. Tuesday, E.W.T.).

Actually, guns on the Western front were stilled yesterday to prevent further bloodshed as the Allied world celebrated V-E day eleven months and two days after General Eisenhower's armies stormed into France.

The Red Army's battle against the Germans apparently went on until the official deadline.

Dresden Captured In Final Victory

The Russians yesterday captured the Saxon capital of Dresden and won final-hour victories in southern Germany, Austria and Czechoslovakia, while Czechoslovak Partisans hoisted the flag of the republic over liberated Prague.

Meanwhile, the German commander of the Dodecanese Islands in the Aegean Sea, General Wagener, surrendered about 30,000 troops under his command gave up their arms. There was no word from Crete—the only remaining Nazi outpost in the Mediterranean.

Another last-minute victory was won by Marshal Tito's Yugoslav Army of National Liberation which freed the Croatian city of Zagreb, last of the puppet capitals.

Some Prague Looting Continues

"Cease fire" was ordered in Prague, in flames from Nazi destruction, at 7.25 P.M., although a few Nazi fanatics continued to loot and fire the Czechoslovak capital. Late broadcasts from the city said that some German troops—who now become outlaws outside the scope of international law—were shelling Prague's hospitals and had set fire to historic Hradcany Castle, for centuries the symbol of Czechoslovak national life.

In successive orders of the day, following by four, then seven hours, the victory proclamations of President Truman and Prime Minister Churchill, Marshal Stalin announced the capture of Dresden; the fall of the Czechoslovak city of Olmuetz (Olomouc); and the seizure of four strongholds in Czechoslovakia and Austria between Prague and Vienna.

Soviet Forces Surge Into Bohemia

The Soviet operational war bulletin also announced that Soviet forces had surged into the Province of Bohemia from Saxony and had captured Most (Bruex), 43 miles northwest of Prague.

Dresden, ninth largest city of the Reich and the last great German city in Nazi hands, fell to Marshall Ivan S. Konev's 1st Ukrainian Army.

It was south of Dresden that Konev's troops crossed the high Ore Mountains and broke into Bohemia to take the towns of Most, Duchov (Dux) and Telpice-Sanov (Teplitz-Schoenau).

At the same time, Konev's troops also surged into four towns near the Sudeten border following the collapse of the lower Silesian capital of Breslau.

Soviet troops of Gen. Andrei I. Yeremenko's 4th (Continued on Page 2, Column 1)

OKINAWA'S V-E DAY: AGONY AND DEATH

"What Are They Going To Do, Forget Us?" One Yank Asks

The following dispatch, by Gordon Cobbledick, former sports writer and now war correspondent for the Cleveland Plain Dealer, tells of Okinawa on V-E day.

Okinawa, May 8 (AP—Via Navy Radio)—We stood in the rain this morning and heard the news from San Francisco, only half believing. There had been so many false reports. But this seemed to be the McCoy.

"Confirmed by General Eisenhower's headquarters," the voice was saying. "Prime Minister Churchill proclaimed May 8 as V-E day."

Artillery thundered and the planes roared low overhead and we couldn't hear all that the voice was saying.

"President Truman announced—the Canadian Government at Ottawa—another tired announcement — American news agencies—"

Ambulances Skid And Bounce

So this was V-E day. It was V-E day in the United States and Great Britain and Russia, but on Okinawa the ambulances skidded through the gluey red mud and bounced over rutted rocky coral roads.

Smiled Sheepishly And Died

When he tumbled backward the rifle clattered on the rocks. The boy looked up and smiled sheepishly and said, "I hurt my arm when I fell," and the blood gushed from his mouth and ran into a quick torrent over the stubble of beard on his young face and he was dead.

It was V-E day at home but on Okinawa men shivered in fox holes half filled with water and waited for the command to move forward across the little green valley that was ridged from both sides by machine-gun fire.

It was V-E day, but on Okinawa a very young Marine cried like a frightened child and his voice rose. "I can't stand it any more. Oh Jesus, I can't stand it." A grizzled sergeant watched him for a minute, half in compassion, half in contempt, and then called: "Corporal.
(Continued on Page 6, Column 5)

Londoners Observe V-E Day With Genteel Sort Of Gaiety

By THOMAS M. O'NEILL
[London Bureau of The Sun]

London, May 8 [By Cable]—A pretty girl in a uniform, a ludicrous paper hat perched on her service cap, stepped up briskly to St. James's Palace, smartly rang the bell beside the gate, and stepped back a pace until the door was opened.

Then she bowed until her hat fell off and said: "Regards to good King James."

It didn't make sense. Neither did most of the myriad other things that happened today in London.

Freedom And Ersatz Ice Cream

A city that had passed through trial by terror found itself free today to do as it pleased. What it pleased was generally a genteel sort of gaiety. Millions put on peculiar headgear, slung ridiculous slogans around their necks and bought Ersatz ice cream.

They walked the streets of London in the quiet joy of knowing that the stroll would bring an air-raid siren, that nothing would drop from the skies to mar the pleasure of a beautiful British day. London was itself today for the first time since Munich.

'Stop Me And Buy One'

A soldier wearing a mug of beer had taken off his blouse and tied the sleeves around his waist to resemble an apron. He walked along the streets shouting, "Stop me and buy one."

It didn't make sense, but this was a day when it won hearty applause.

London, biggest city in the world, can always provide the biggest crowds. It outdid itself today. London itself was just a crowd, packed shoulder to shoulder over hundreds of square miles.

This reporter, long inured to the biggest crowds that America can produce, could think only of a political convention with enough delegates to fill the State of Connecticut from border to border. It was everybody was glad to see it.

With Picnic Luncheons

The demonstrative Briton, given a two-day holiday with pay to celebrate the event, rejoiced in his own unpremeditated way.

Millions came from the suburbs with picnic luncheons. Gay people, since the restaurants were closed and those who had to work also starved and tried hard to the unbelievably green lawns of St. James's Park, assuredly the world's most beautiful park, and the atmosphere was in the exact heart of the metropolis.

Other millions set out to walk or to bicycle through the city's streets.

The Cigar Waver

No estimate can have any validity, but a well-intentioned guess set the no fewer than 10,000,000 people crowded into the middle of London to express their satisfaction that the years of toil and trouble had been marked by triumph.

The densest part of the crowd gathered where it had gathered almost every time before and the Houses of Parliament to see the Prime Minister go there to tell the (Continued on Page 4, Column 5)

TRUMAN V-E TALK WARNING TO JAPS

President Says Fighting Job Is Only Half Done

Churchill announces that Germany remains "unsubdued"......Page 3

By DEWEY L. FLEMING

Washington, May 8—This day of victory in Europe was a day of warning to Japan.

President Truman made it so in official utterances which put precise emphasis upon the job that lies ahead than upon "the task which now happily is done."

"Our victory is but half won," he said in his radio address to the world.

And in his formal proclamation of victory he declared:

"The power of our peoples to defend themselves against all enemies will be proved in the Pacific war as it has been proved in Europe."

Blows Will Not Cease

"Our blows will not cease until the Japanese military and naval forces lay down their arms in unconditional surrender."

In an aside to newspaper men to whom he read his speech and proclamation just before he went on the air, the Executive said that "our war is only in Europe. Down here in Bavaria it is a pre- (Continued on Page 5, Column 2)

11 Nazi Planes Land In Sweden

Stockholm, May 8 (AP)—Eleven German planes made forced landings, crash landed or were shot down today in southern Sweden. Swedish press reports said. They were believed to have come from Norway mainly.

How Long After The Shooting Stops Does A War Really End?

By LEE McCARDELL
[Sunpapers War Correspondent]

With U.S. 3d Army, May 8 [By—was—"At last—Thank God I'm Radio]—The end of the war is an still alive and I can go home." anti-climax. The silent war ceased at Or Maryland And Rosebush 6 o'clock yesterday morning. Unofficially, it ended days, but it ended in different times for different soldiers. It ended when the Germans in front of them gave up.

Here with the 3d Army, on the last of the fighting fronts, we watched the war peter out for the last ten days. The end was not less welcome when it did come. But we were expecting it, waiting for it. Now that it's here, most of the soldiers accept it quietly.

There has been no signs of wild rejoicing. There has been no sudden silence after a steady and continuous roar of guns. The sound of gunfire died away gradually days ago.

The Artificial End

I am writing this at 8 o'clock on the morning of Tuesday, May 8. The war ended more than 24 hours ago. But I have been told that I will not be permitted to file this dispatch until midnight tonight.

That is the hour at which the official announcement of the end of the war will be made—the artificial and anticipated end.

So this, I suppose, is sort of that last day of the war in Europe. Down here in Bavaria it is a gorgeous day. After a long spell of cold, rainy weather, the sky is cloud blue. The sun is bright and the air is warm.

Up And Down The Sidewalks

The window at which I write this looks out on the street of a German town, a narrow street leading into an old cathedral square. Opposite my window are the bomb-shattered windows of a German drugstore. They are still boarded up. And there is no traffic in the street except for occasional American Army vehicles.

German civilians and a German policeman walk up and down the sidewalks. The women carry market bags and the men carry brief cases. I don't know whether or not they know that the war has ended. I rather suspect they think that it has. But there is no change in their manner or in their attitude since yesterday.

At this particular moment—or rather as it struck this morning—Baltimore time—I imagine the people of Baltimore will be walking through Mulberry street, past Baltimore's Cathedral, in much the same manner these people walk past theirs—except that the shop windows of Mulberry street will be whole, and the people of Baltimore will not be a defeated people.

When I awoke this morning at 6.30, the first morning I have awakened to know that the war was actually over, I was conscious only of a great relief, but it was only a moment to realize why. And my next thought, naturally enough, was the thoughts of many others.

And I thought of Maryland, with its summer morning across it gently, and of a letter which arrived last night from home, a letter in which someone I love very much had written:

"I leaned out of our front window this morning. The rosebushes are filled with buds. Do you really think you'll be home in time to smell them?"

There were German voices in the street before my open bedroom window. One woman was talking very loudly, and another was saying: "Yaw. Yaw. Yaw." And then the sound of people walking by and the sound of a passing army truck, rattle of a passing army truck.

One Of The Lucky Ones

Sunshine streamed through my window, and I was keenly conscious of the fact that I was one of the lucky ones; one of the lucky who could think about going home. There were others, not so lucky, who would never go back.

They were the dead whose graves belonged to the sandy wastes of North Africa, the olive groves of Italy, the hedgerows of Normandy and the hills of the Ardennes. Men who, in some higher mathematical calculations of the infinity, were killed in battle in order that we, the lucky ones, might survive.

For the last few months, I think, most American soldiers have been fighting a cautious war. There were so many signs of the approaching end. No one wanted to be killed at the end. No one wanted to be the last to die. If you break into any German town and you see, even at this late stage in the war, they'll swear that they have never been Nazis. To listen to them, you'd think there were no Nazis in all Germany.

If They Had Known

I think perhaps if the Germans had known as much of the hopelessness of their military situation as we knew, they'd have given up long ago. But their communications were in such turmoil at the end of their last retreat that few of them knew where to go or what they knew that the war has ended. I rather suspect they think that they had no complete picture of what was happening.

As German resistance collapsed, one after another murdered in cold blood increasing numbers and our troops were halted, apparently for no concept that they had reached pre-determined phase lines, and became a matter of only days, then only hours.

Rumors

We correspondents with the 3d Army had some idea of what was coming when we told that negotiations for mass surrender were under way. Correspondents with other armies in the field had felt the pressure of events building up to the climax. It couldn't last much longer on the Silesian end.

We never knew, when we left headquarters to go into the field this morning, the actual hour of (Continued on Page 5, Column 1)

---

49 Men Die Off Maine Coast When Naval Craft Blows Up

Cape Elizabeth, Maine, May 8 (AP)—Forty-nine men died in the frigid waters of the Atlantic Ocean only 3 miles offshore after a terrific explosion split their navy Eagle boat amidships in New England's first naval disaster of the war.

Only thirteen of the crew of the Patrol Ship PE-56 survived the mysterious blast that came April 23 during a noon lull in target-practice maneuvers.

Many of the men were below decks when the explosion came and few had time to grab life jackets as stunned and bewildered they struggled topside through debris-cluttered passageways.

Many of those who got over the side before the explosion vanished perished in the frigid water where numbed hands no longer could retain their hold on boxes and oil drums and shoring that floated in the wreckage.

Those who survived suffered from internal injuries, cuts, shock and immersion and they had many conflicting theories of what caused the blast that sent the vessel to the bottom in but a few minutes.

Some believed they saw a submarine lurking near by and one was positive that it was not an accidental explosion.

Conflicting Theories

The PE-56 had been engaged in target maneuvers with aircraft from the Brunswick Naval Air Station off the entrance to Portland harbor.

Lieut. (j.g.) John P. Scagnelli, 25, New York, was the only one of the ship's six officers among the survivors.

Scagnelli had just turned into his bunk for a nap after chow "when there was a terrible explosion."

"I was thrown just as if someone (Continued on Page 4, Column 1)

thought the explosion sounded like that created by a depth charge or mine.

The boilers of the vessel had been overhauled ten days previously and were described as in good condition.

Within 17 minutes service craft had picked up the survivors, but of the 49 men who were lost only two bodies were recovered. The other 47 were listed on navy records as "missing" and are presumed to be dead.

A rescue destroyer dropped depth charges where survivors reported seeing a submarine but it was the Eagle craft's grave that was marked by two huge oil slicks in her bubbling up and was an Eagle debris-filled area.

One Officer Saved

Got some men turned into bunk for a nap after chow

CHAPTER 13

PIER 51 ON THE HUDSON

THE EVENING SUN, TUESDAY, JANUARY 5, 1946

First Combat Team of 29th Div. To Go Overseas Comes Full Circle

By Lee McCardell [Evening Sun Staff Correspondent]

New York, Jan. 4, First elements of the 29th Infantry Division to return to the United States from Europe as organizations today are at Camp Kilmer, N. J., having their records checked prior to breaking up into smaller groups which, during the next 36 hours, will move to various separation centers where officers and men will be discharged from the Army.

It has been a long, long time — almost five years — since a handful of former National Guard officers who went overseas with the division and returned last night aboard the transport LeJeune entered US Federal service. Practically all of the old enlisted personnel which survived combat came home months ago.

Beginning Of End

Last night's homecoming was a joyous affair for those aboard the LeJeune. They had been at sea since Christmas Day. It was a great occasion for Maj. Gen. Charles H. Gerhardt, who commanded the division in combat, and for half a dozen members of his staff with whom he met the LeJeune at the entrance of New York harbor and saw her safely berthed about 6 P.M. at Pier 51, on the Hudson River.

It was the beginning of the end of the 29th Division as a World War II combat outfit. The division had come full circle. Two organizations which last night came ashore, the 116th Infantry Regiment and the 111th Field Artillery Battalion, comprised the first combat team of the division to go overseas on September 26, 1942.

From Camp Kilmer, the division's staging area in September, 1942, this combat team had followed almost identically the same route by which it was returning. Troop trains had carried the soldiers from Kilmer to a ferry slip on the Jersey side of the Hudson. Ferry boats had carried them across the river to a pier at which the Queen Mary was waiting for them.

Destination Unknown

In the warm, damp darkness of a late September night they had gone aboard the Mary. The pier was dimly lighted. They had filed up a gangplank, one by one, as their names were checked from long typed passenger lists by embarkation officers hunched over a high wood table illuminated by a gooseneck.

The soldiers weren't sure where they were going. The pier entrance was guarded by police and no one in West street, outside the pier, knew the Queen Mary was loading troops. The dimout was going into effect in New York. The skyscrapers were dark. The lights on the Statue of Liberty had been turned off.

Sleep On Decks

The Mary was crowded. Many soldiers slept on her broad promenade decks, which had been boarded up and fitted with bunks. The food — British food — was badly prepared and badly served as far as enlisted men were concerned. One of several temporary messes had been set up in the liner's swimming poll. Many soldiers subsisted through the entire voyage on candy and cakes purchased at an army PX aboard ship.

The Mary made the crossing alone, without escort. Her zig-zag course took her far south, almost to the Azores. Turning north, through the Irish Sea, she ran down and cut in half the British cruiser Curacao. Soldiers crowded her decks when that happened. They watched the two halves of the cruiser sink. The Mary didn't stop. She kept going, putting in at Gourock, Scotland.

"I only hope I got a round-trip ticket," was a common saying among the soldiers when they went ashore.

22,000 Casualties

Many didn't. Hundreds were killed when the combat team which had crossed on the Mary made the D-day assault on Omaha Beach, June 6, 1944. Many more were killed during the year of fighting which followed in France and Germany. All told, the 29th Division suffered about 22,000 casualties in killed and wounded. More than 4,600 of its officers and men were decorated for gallantry in action.

At 8.15 last Christmas morning the combat team which had led the division overseas boarded the LeJeune at Bremerhaven. The 110th Field Artillery, part of the 29th Division headquarters and a number of other smaller units not attached to the 29th also went aboard. But of these, not more than possibly a dozen officers had crossed with the combat team and an advance detachment of division headquarters aboard the Queen Mary in September, 1942.

Most Are Virginians

Most of these officers were Virginians — Valley of Virginia men, officers of the 116th Infantry, an old Virginia National Guard outfit which traces its history back proudly through the famous Stonewall Brigade of the Civil War to the Colonial days of the province of Virginia.

Lieut. Col. Harold Cassell, of Roanoke, came back as the regiment's commanding officer. Lieut. Col. Fred McManaway, of Roanoke; Lieut. Col. Lawrence F. Meeks, of Roanoke, and Major Asbury Jackson, of Winchester, came back as battalion commanders. Four other officers of the original regiment returned aboard the LeJeune. They were Major Carroll B. Smith, of Charlottesville; Capts. John L. Flora, Charles H. Kidd and George W. Boyd, all of Roanoke.

Beans For Breakfast

But none of their old enlisted men were with them. Of the original 111th Field Artillery, there were neither officers nor men. The whole combat team was filled up with men from the 69th, the 95th and half a dozen other divisions.

There was more space than on the Mary. The food for the enlisted men was much better, although they complained of beans for breakfast. Almost every night there was a movie show. On New Year's Eve the transport ran into a storm with a 70-mile wind that rolled breakers over her bow. Passengers stuck to their bunks. There was no New Year's celebration.

General Gerhardt, meanwhile, had returned to the United States by plane. With him came Col. William J. Witte, of Baltimore, his chief of staff; Lieut. Col. Stanley Phillips, of Washington; Lieut. Col. Lucien Laborde, of Marksville, La.; Major Robert Minor, of Columbia, Ohio, and Lieut. William Pinson, of Greenwood, S.C.

Go Down On Yacht

General Gerhardt, Colonel Witte and Lieut. Col. Phillips were joined in New York by their wives. The entire party went down the bay on small craft late yesterday afternoon to meet the LeJeune. They met her just outside the Narrows.

There was no mistaking her. Draped over her lifeboats and life-rafts on her starboard side were two huge banners, one bearing the blue and gray insignia of the 29th and the other the crest of the 116th Infantry. Her decks were covered with troops who, when the small yacht bearing General Gerhardt drew closer, recognized the division commander and yelled:

"Yeh! Uncle Charley!"

For the three officers' wives aboard the yacht there was another cheer, and the inevitable individual greeting: "Hi Babe!"

Women Introduced

In response to yells from the transport, "Who are the women?" Colonel Witte introduced each lady by megaphone.

An army tug, with a band and two girl singers, pulled alongside the LeJeune, still making her way through the Narrows. They played and sang "Sentimental Journey" and "Roll Out the Barrel." Soldiers crowded the rails of the transport, many with their feet hanging over the side, to listen and roar applause.

Among the officers on an upper deck, the General and his staff picked out those they knew one by one — Lieut. Col. Harold (Father Mike) Donovan, of Baltimore, division chaplain; Lieut. Col. Jimmie Hayes, formerly of Baltimore, now a New Yorker; Major Moe Becnel, of Ama, La., one of the most popular of the younger officers of the old division.

Lights Come On

It was almost dark when the LeJeune passed the tip of Manhattan and started up the North River. The lights were just coming on at Bedloe Island. But they could see the Statue of Liberty in the dusk. It was a murky day. And all the windows of the skyscrapers of lower Manhattan were lighted up with gold.

A Negro orchestra from Camp Shanks was on Pier 51 to play the transport in. General Gerhardt, who had come ahead, was waiting to go aboard as soon as the gangplank should be secure. Pretty Mrs. Nancy Witte, the colonel's lady, standing on the end of the pier and listening to the soldiers yell as the tugs pushed the transport into the slip, said she wanted to cry.

Then a small welcoming party pushed up the gangplank behind the General. Three were men in civilian clothes. Lieut. Col. Jimmy Hayes yelped when he saw them — the clothes. One man had a velvet collar on his overcoat. The colonel wanted to feel that with his hand. Then he and Major Becnel dug deep in a valpack in their stateroom and came up with a bottle of cognac.

Captain Kissed, Too

Mrs. Witte appeared in the stateroom door, Jimmy kissed her. And Capt. Moe Horwitz, of Fargo, N.D., another of the few old division officers coming home, asked Colonel Witte:

"Colonel, could I kiss your wife, too?"

And the colonel said "Sure." So Moe kissed her.

Moe had a dog, a boxer pup, named Major Domo, from Copenhagen. And there was a German shepherd in the stateroom, Caesar, belonging to Colonel Witte. Caesar formerly pulled an ammunition cart in the German army.

Others Show Up

Other Maryland officers showed up: Capt. William Gniecko, of Denton; Lieut. Malcolm Baer, of Frederick; Lieut. William Millhouse, of Hagerstown. By this time the troops were disembarking. And leading an advance detachment of division headquarters was Chief Warrant Officer Alexander Sabo, of Johnston, Pa., who went overseas with the original 29th. But the old-timers were few. Major Moe Becnel, now division AG, said the division had had a turnover of close to 50,000 men.

Down the gangplank they went, barracks bags over their shoulder, calling out their first name in response as their last was called aloud by a man checking the passenger lists at the foot of the gangplank. This was the night of September 26, 1942 in reverse. There were the embarkation officers, standing hunched over the passenger lists on their high desk, illuminated by the gooseneck. But this time the soldiers were coming home, not going away.

Baltimore Men Listed

Among Baltimoreans coming off the transports were: Pfc. Irvin Beigel, 521 North East avenue; S/S Kurtz Byrb, 1449 West North avenue; T/S George Shepter, 3702 Cold Spring lane; Corporal Charles Milstein, 1617 North Appleton street; T/5 William J. Rubenstein, 1225 Riverside avenue; PFC. William S. Fletcher, 417 Folsum street.

Other Marylanders included: Tech. 4/G Ulysses Demond, of North East; Pfc. John O'Neal, of Mount Savage; Pfc. Charles W. Jones, of Cardin; Pfc. William W. McLaughlin, of Cambridge; Tech. 3/G Richard H. Ackley, of Westminster; Pfc. Frederick Redman, of Lutherville; Tech. 5/G Arthur Brockmeyer, of Fullerton; Pfc. James Lynch, of Berlin.

Women workers of the American Red Cross were waiting on the pier to distribute milk, coffee, doughnuts. Each disembarking unit dropped its barracks bags and halted long enough to be served. Then they moved on, to the end of the pier, and aboard the waiting ferry boats that shuttled them across the Hudson River — 4,600 men when the last ferry pulled away at 1 o'clock this morning.

With grateful acknowledgement to the staff and
pages of The Baltimore Sun, The Evening Sun and The Sunday Sun.

THE BOOK STAFF

Article and Photography Researcher: Zachary J. Dixon

Arranged By: Zachary J. Dixon

Newsroom Editor: David Rosenthal

Copy Editor: John McIntyre

Book and Cover Design: Marsha Miller

Project Manager: Zachary J. Dixon

CPSIA information can be obtained at www.ICGtesting.com
Printed in the USA
BVOW06s0345110614

355898BV00002B/2/P